ROUTLEDGE LIBRARY EDITIONS: THE FRENCH REVOLUTION

Volume 5

FRANCE ON THE EVE OF REVOLUTION

FRANCE ON THE EVE OF REVOLUTION
Britsh Travellers' Observations 1763–1788

JOHN LOUGH

LONDON AND NEW YORK

First published in 1987 by Croom Helm Ltd

This edition first published in 2016
by Routledge
2 Park Square, Milton Park, Abingdon, Oxon OX14 4RN

and by Routledge
711 Third Avenue, New York, NY 10017

Routledge is an imprint of the Taylor & Francis Group, an informa business

© 1987 John Lough

All rights reserved. No part of this book may be reprinted or reproduced or utilised in any form or by any electronic, mechanical, or other means, now known or hereafter invented, including photocopying and recording, or in any information storage or retrieval system, without permission in writing from the publishers.

Trademark notice: Product or corporate names may be trademarks or registered trademarks, and are used only for identification and explanation without intent to infringe.

British Library Cataloguing in Publication Data
A catalogue record for this book is available from the British Library

ISBN: 978-1-138-66567-5 (Set)
ISBN: 978-1-315-54584-4 (Set) (ebk)
ISBN: 978-1-138-68100-2 (Volume 5) (hbk)
ISBN: 978-1-138-68105-7 (Volume 5) (pbk)
ISBN: 978-1-315-56420-3 (Volume 5) (ebk)

Publisher's Note
The publisher has gone to great lengths to ensure the quality of this reprint but points out that some imperfections in the original copies may be apparent.

Disclaimer
The publisher has made every effort to trace copyright holders and would welcome correspondence from those they have been unable to trace.

FRANCE ON THE EVE OF REVOLUTION
British Travellers' Observations
1763 – 1788

John Lough

CROOM HELM
London & Sydney

© John Lough 1987
Croom Helm Ltd, Provident House, Burrell Row,
Beckenham, Kent BR3 1AT
Croom Helm Australia Pty Ltd, Suite 4, 6th Floor,
64–76 Kippax Street, Surry Hills, NSW 2010, Australia

British Library Cataloguing in Publication Data
Lough, John
　France on the eve of Revolution: British
　travellers' observations 1763–1788.
　1. France — Description and travels 1600–1799
　I. Title
　914.4′0434　　　　DC25
　ISBN 0–7099–4157–9

Photocomposition by Pat and Anne Murphy,
Highcliffe-on-Sea, Dorset
Printed and bound in Great Britain by Mackays of Chatham Ltd, Kent

Contents

Preface	vi
A Note on French Money in this Period	viii
Sources and Abbreviated Titles	ix
Map of France	xv
Introduction	1

Part I. ECONOMIC AND SOCIAL CONDITIONS

1.	The Land and the Peasants	31
2.	The Towns, Trade and Industry	72
3.	The Privileged Orders	146
4.	Justice	188
5.	Popular Amusements	211

Part II. THE COLLAPSE OF ABSOLUTE MONARCHY

6.	The Last Years of Louis XV	231
7.	Louis XVI and Marie Antoinette	262

Conclusion		304
Appendix A	Notes on Travellers Whose Writings Have Been Quoted	308
Appendix B	Notes on Other Accounts of Travels in France	318
	Index	320

Preface

This book is more limited in scope than its predecessor, *France Observed in the Seventeenth Century by British Travellers* (Oriel Press, 1985). It deals only with the twenty-five years between the end of the Seven Years War and the collapse of absolute monarchy in 1788. Even for this much shorter period the sources drawn upon are half as numerous again as for all the years between the end of the Wars of Religion and the death of Louis XIV. As changes came slowly in Ancien Régime France, to include the whole period from 1715 to 1789 would not only have required a much longer book, but would also have meant repeating a good deal of what is covered by the earlier work. No account of how people travelled has been given; although with better roads they sometimes went slightly faster, until the coming of the railways there were no fundamental changes. They continued to make many of their journeys by water, down the Saône from Chalon to Lyons and then down the Rhône to Avignon, or else between Béziers and Toulouse on the Canal du Midi and then sometimes down the Garonne to Bordeaux.

Again, British travellers' contacts with French writers and scientists were so much more numerous in this period that they furnished too much material for a mere chapter; a separate account of them will appear in due course in *Studies on Voltaire and the Eighteenth Century*. A chapter giving an account of such a large number of travellers and of when and where they travelled would have taken up too much space; this information is furnished more concisely in an appendix. A second appendix provides a list of other sources, published and unpublished, which, although they have not been used here, may be of interest to scholars with rather different aims.

Preface

As in the earlier book, by France is understood, not the country within its present frontiers, but France as it existed in the period concerned. Lorraine, formally annexed in 1766, is included, but not Savoy and Nice, which were not added until 1860; in our period French territory ended at Pont-de-Beauvoisin and Antibes. Avignon and the Comtat Venaissin, which remained papal territory until 1791, have also been omitted, although use has been made of an interesting comparison between conditions there and in Ancien Régime France.

A fair proportion of the sources drawn on here are to be found in works available in most university libraries or obtainable through Inter-Library Loan, but a great many of the books published at the time are now rare and libraries are reluctant to lend them or even to own up to having them in stock. They have sometimes to be read in distant places like the manuscripts dispersed in archives and libraries. A good deal of time and travel is required before this scattered material can be put between the covers of a book.

I have recently had the good fortune to come across a younger colleague in the same university — Dr Jeremy Black of the Department of Modern History — while he was working on his *The British and the Grand Tour* (Croom Helm, 1985). I have profited greatly from our exchange of information about sources and our discussions of the problems encountered in dealing with travellers' accounts. As in the past I have profited from the resources available in the university libraries of Durham and Newcastle upon Tyne; I also owe a considerable debt to three local institutions — the Chapter Library, Durham, Ushaw College Library, Durham, and the Library of the Literary and Philosophical Society of Newcastle upon Tyne.

A Note on French Money in this Period

After various manipulations of the coinage by Louis XIV, and the upset caused by Law's System, its value was fixed by a decree of 1726 and, apart from a minor technical change in 1785, it remained unchanged until the Revolution. The basic money of account was the *livre*. 3 *livres* = 1 *écu*. 24 *livres* = 1 *louis*. The livre was divided into *sous* and *deniers*. 1 *livre* = 20 *sous*. 1 *sou* = 12 *deniers* or 4 *liards*. Travellers who changed English money in France generally received a *louis* for each guinea.

Sources and Abbreviated Titles

Anonymous

[Philip Playstowe?], *The Gentleman's Guide in his Tour through France, Wrote by an Officer in the Royal Navy*, Bristol, n.d.   *The Gentleman's Guide*

The Gentleman's Guide in his Tour through France, 10th edition, with additions and corrections, London, 1788.   *The Gentleman's Guide* (1788)

A Journal of a Tour to Italy made in the Company of the Earl of Exeter & Dr Patoune, Sept. 13th 1763 (Nottingham University Library, Me 244/2a).   Nottingham University Library, Me 244/2a

Notes made in a journey into France, chiefly relating to picturesk circumstances of the country (British Library, Add. MS. 12130).   BL, Add. MS. 12130

Remarks on the character and manners of the French, in a series of letters, written during a residence of twelve months in Paris and its environs, London, 1769, 2 vols.   *Remarks on the character and manners of the French*

Sketch of a Trip to Paris in 1788 (*Gentleman's Magazine*, 1797–8).   *Gentleman's Magazine*

A Tour, Sentimental and Descriptive, through the United Provinces, Austrian Netherlands, and France, interspersed with Parisian and other anecdotes with some observations on the Howardian System, London, 1788, 2 vols.   *A Tour, Sentimental and Descriptive*

Travel Diary (West Sussex Record Office, Add. MSS. 7236–7).   W. Sussex RO, Add. MSS. 7236–7

Travels into France and Italy, in a series of letters to a lady, London, 1771, 2 vols.   *Travels into France and Italy*

ix

Sources

List of authors

[Andrews, John.] *An Account of the Character and Manners of the French, with occasional Observations on the English*, London, 1770, 2 vols. (Revised version published London, 1785 under title *A Comparative View of the French and English Nations in their manners, politics and literature*, under the author's name.) — *An Account of the Character and Manners of the French*

Andrews, John. *Letters to a Young Gentleman on his setting out for France*, London, 1784. — *Letters to a Young Gentleman*

Armstrong, John. ('Lancelot Temple'). *A Short Ramble through some Parts of France and Italy*, London, 1771. — *A Short Ramble*

Ayscough, George L. *Letters from an Officer in the Guards to a friend in England, containing some accounts of France and Italy*, London, 1778. — *Letters from an Officer in the Guards*

Bennet, William, Bishop of Cloyne. *Travel Diary* (Bodleian, MS. Eng. Misc. f.54) — Bodleian, MS. Eng. Misc. f.54

Bentley, Thomas. *Journal of a Visit to Paris 1776*, ed. P. France, Brighton, 1977. — *Journal of a Visit to Paris*

Berry, Mary, *Extracts of the Journals and Correspondence from the year 1783 to 1852*, ed. Lady T. Lewis, London, 1865, 3 vols. — *Journals and Correspondence*

Blaikie, Thomas. *Diary of a Scotch Gardener at the French Court at the end of the Eighteenth Century*, ed. F. Birrell, London, 1931. — *Diary of a Scotch Gardener*

Boswell, James. *The Boswell Private Papers, Isham Collection*. Vol. 7. *The Journal 1765–1768. Corsica, Italy, France, England, Scotland*, n.p., 1930. — *Boswell Private Papers*, Vol. 7

Burney, Charles. *Music, men and manners in France and Italy*, ed. H. E. Poole, London, 1974. — *Music, men and manners*

R.W.C., 'Letters from France, 1788–1789', ed. J. Lough (*Durham University Journal*, December 1961, pp. 1–12.) — *Letters from France, 1788–1789*

[Cage, ? .] *Diary of a Tour in the South of France, 1784–5* (Bodleian, MS. Eng. Misc. f.55). — Bodleian, MS. Eng. Misc. f.55

Cayley, Cornelius. *A Tour through Holland, Flanders and part of France 1772*, Leeds, 1777. — *A Tour*

Coke, Lady Mary. *Letters and Journals*, ed. J. A. Home, Edinburgh, 1889–96, 4 vols. — *Letters and Journals*

Cole, Rev. William. *A Journal of my journey to Paris in the Year 1765*, ed. F. G. Stokes, London, 1931. — *Journal*

Cradock, Mrs Anna Francesca. *Journal inédit*, traduit de l'anglais par Mme O. Delphin Balleyguier, Paris, 1896. — *Journal*

Cradock, Joseph. *Literary and Miscellaneous Memoirs*, London, 1828, 4 vols. — *Memoirs*

Ellis, Henry. *Letters to William Knox* (Historical Manuscripts Commission 55, Various Collections, vi.) — HMC, 55.vi

Essex, James. *Journal of a Tour through Part of Flanders and France in August, 1773*, ed. W. E. Fawcett, Cambridge, 1888. — *Journal of a Tour*

Garden, Francis (Lord Gardenstone). *Travelling Memorandums made in a tour upon the Continent of Europe in the years 1786, 87 and 88*, Edinburgh, 1791–5, 3 vols. — *Travelling Memorandums*

Garmston, Richard. *A Journal of Travels through France, Switzerland and Mont Blanc in Chamony* (British Library, Add. MS. 30271). — BL, Add. MS. 30271

Garrick, David. *Journal describing his visit to France and Italy in 1763*, ed. G. W. Stone, New York, 1939. — *Journal*

——. *The Letters*, ed. D. M. Little and G. H. Kehol, London, 1963. — *Letters*

Gibbon, Edward. *Letters*, ed. J. E. Norton, London, 1956, 3 vols. — *Letters*

——. *Memoirs of my life*, ed. G. A. Bonnard, London, 1966. — *Memoirs*

Herbert, Lord George (11th Earl of Pembroke). *Diary* in *The Pembroke Papers (1734–1780). Letters and Diaries of Henry, 10th Earl of Pembroke, and his Circle*, London, 1942. — *Pembroke Papers*

Hobhouse, Sir Benjamin, Bart. *Remarks on several parts of France, Italy, &c. in the years 1783, 1784, and 1785*. Bath, 1796. — *Remarks*

Hume, David. *Letters*, ed. J. Y. T. Greig. Oxford, 1932, 2 vols. — *Letters*

——. *New Letters*, ed. R. Klibansky and E. C. Mosner, Oxford, 1954. — *New Letters*

[Jardine, Lt.-Col. Alexander.] *Letters from Barbary, France, Spain, Portugal, etc.*, 2nd edition, London, 1790. — *Letters from Barbary, France, etc.*

Jervis, John, 1st Earl of St Vincent. *Journal of Tour of France* (British Library, Add. MS. 31192). — BL, Add. MS. 31192

xi

Sources

Jesse, J. H. *George Selwyn and his Contemporaries*, 2nd edition, London, 1882, 4 vols. — *George Selwyn and his Contemporaries*

Johnson, Samuel. *French Journal* in *The French Journals of Mrs Thrale and Dr Johnson*, ed. M. Tyson and H. Guppy, Manchester, 1932. — *French Journal*

Knight, Ellis Cornelia. *Autobiography*, London, 1861, 2 vols. — *Autobiography*

Knight, Lady Philippa. *Letters from France and Italy 1776–1795*, ed. Lady Elliott-Drake, London, 1905. — *Letters from France and Italy*

Latham, Mrs (?). *Journal of a Tour of France with Lord and Lady Clive*. (Somerset Record Office DD/SH/67/19C/2480). — Somerset RO DD/SH/67/19C/2480

Leinster, Emily, Duchess of. *Correspondence*, ed. B. Fitzgerald, Dublin, 1949–52, 2 vols. — *Correspondence*

Mrs Montagu, 'Queen of the Blues'. Her Letters and Friendships from 1762 to 1800, ed. R. Blunt, London, 1923, 2 vols. — *Mrs Montagu*, ed. R. Blunt

Moore, John. *A View of Society and Manners in France, Switzerland and Germany*, London, 1779, 2 vols. — *A View of Society and Manners*

Muirhead, Lockhart. *Journals of Travels in parts of the late Austrian Low Countries, France etc. in 1787 and 1789*, London, 1803. — *Journals of Travels*

Parminter, Jane. *Extracts from a Devonshire Lady's Notes of Travel in France in the Eighteenth Century*, ed. C. J. Reichel (*Reports and Transactions of the Devonshire Association for the Advancement of Science, Literature and Art*, vol. XXXIV, 1902). — *Notes of Travel*

[Peckham, Harry.] *A Tour through Holland, Dutch Brabant, the Austrian Netherlands and Parts of France*, London, 1772. — *A Tour*

Pennant, Thomas. *Tour on the Continent 1765*, ed. G. de Beer, London, 1948. — *Tour on the Continent*

Pennington, Rev. Thomas. *Continental Excursions, or Tours into France, Switzerland and Germany in 1782, 1787 and 1789*, London, 1809, 2 vols. — *Continental Excursions*

Percy, Elizabeth, Duchess of Northumberland. *Diaries of a Duchess*, ed. J. Greig, London, 1926. — *Diaries of a Duchess*

Piozzi, Mrs (formerly Thrale). *French Journal* in *The French Journals of Mrs Thrale and Dr Johnson*, ed. M. Tyson and H. Guppy, Manchester, 1932. — *French Journal*

Sources

——. *Observations and Reflections made in the course of a Journey through France, Italy and Germany*, London, 1789, 2 vols.　　*Observations and Reflections*

Pulteney, Daniel. *Letters to the Duke of Rutland* (Historical Manuscripts Commission, 24, iii Rutland).　　HMC 24, iii Rutland

Rigby, Edward. *Letters from France etc. in 1789*, ed. Lady Eastlake, London, 1880.　　*Letters from France*

Roget, S. R. (ed.). *Travel in the two last Centuries by three generations*, London, 1921.　　*Travel in the two last Centuries*

Romilly, Sir Samuel. 'Extract of a letter containing an account of Bicêtre, taken from the French' (*The Repository*, 1788, 2 vols., vol. II).　　*The Repository*, vol. II

——. *Memoirs*, London, 1841, 3 vols.　　*Memoirs*

Rutt, J. T. *The Life and Correspondence of Joseph Priestley*, London, 1831, 2 vols.　　*Life of Priestley*

St John, James. *Letters from France to a Gentleman in the South of Ireland, written in 1787*, Dublin, 1788, 2 vols.　　*Letters from France*

Sinclair, Sir John. *Correspondence*, London, 1832, 2 vols.　　*Correspondence*

Smith, Adam. *An Inquiry into the Nature and Causes of the Wealth of Nations*, eds. R. H. Campbell, A. S. Skinner, and W. B. Todd, Oxford, 1976.　　*Wealth of Nations*

Smith, Sir James Edward. *A Sketch of a Tour on the Continent in the years 1786 and 1787*, London, 1793, 3 vols.　　*Sketch of a Tour*

Smollett, Tobias. *Travels through France and Italy*, ed. F. Felsenstein, Oxford, 1979.　　*Travels through France and Italy*

Spencer, Lady Harriet. *Travel Diary*, in *Lady Bessborough and her Family Circle*, ed. Earl of Bessborough, London, 1940.　　*Lady Bessborough and her Family Circle*

Stanhope, Walter, *Letters* (West Yorkshire Archive Service, Bradford, Sp St 6/1/115).　　West Yorkshire Archive Service, Sp St 6/1/115

Sterne, Laurence. *Letters*, ed. L. P. Curtis, Oxford, 1935.　　*Letters*

Swinburne, Henry. *Journey from Bayonne to Marseilles* in *Travels through Spain in the years 1775 and 1776*, 2nd edition, London, 1787, 2 vols.　　*Journey from Bayonne to Marseilles*

——. *The Courts of Europe at the close of the last century*, ed. C. White, London, 1841, 2 vols.　　*The Courts of Europe*

Swinburne, Mrs Martha. *Political Extracts from Mrs. Swinburne's letters from Paris in 1788 and 1789*, British Library, Add. MS. 33121.　　BL, Add. MS. 33121

Sources

Thicknesse, Philip. *Observations on the customs and manners of the French nation, in a series of letters in which that nation is vindicated from the misrepresentations of some late writers*, London, 1766. — *Observations*

———. *Useful hints to those who make the tour of France in letters written from that country*, 2nd edition, London, 1770. — *Useful hints*

———. *A Year's Journey through France and part of Spain*, 2nd edition, London, 1778, 2 vols. — *A Year's Journey*

Townsend, Rev. Joseph. *A Journey through Spain in the years 1786 and 1787, and remarks in passing through a part of France*, London, 1791, 3 vols. — *A Journey through a part of France*

[Villiers, John Charles, 3rd Earl of Clarendon.] *A Tour through part of France, containing a description of Paris, Cherbourg and Ermenonville*, London, 1789. — *A Tour*

Walker, Adam. *Ideas suggested on the spot in a late excursion through Flanders, Germany, France, and Italy*, London, 1790. — *Ideas suggested on the spot*

———. *A sketch of the police, religion, arts and agriculture of France, made in an excursion to Paris in 1785* in *Remarks made in a tour from London to the Lakes of Westmorland and Cumberland in 1792*, London, 1792. — *A sketch*

Walpole, Horace. *Correspondence*, ed. W. S. Lewis *et al.*, London, 1937–83, 48 vols. — *Correspondence*

———. *Memoirs of the Reign of King George the Third*, London, 1847, 4 vols. — *Memoirs*

Wharton, Rev. Robert. 'An Englishman's Impressions of France in 1775', ed. G. E. Rodmell (*Durham University Journal*, March 1967). — *An Englishman's Impressions*

Wilkes, John. *Letter* in R. A. Davenport, *New Elegant Extracts*, Part X, Chiswick, 1827. — *New Elegant Extracts, Part X*

Wraxall, Sir Nathaniel William. *A Tour through the Western, Southern, and Interior Provinces of France*, London, 1784. — *A Tour*

Young, Arthur. *Travels during the years 1787, 1788 and 1789; undertaken more particularly with a view to ascertaining the cultivation, wealth, resources, and national prosperity of the kingdom of France*, 2nd edition, London and Bury St Edmunds, 1794, 2 vols. — *Travels in France*

Map of France showing the principal places visited by British travellers 1763–1788

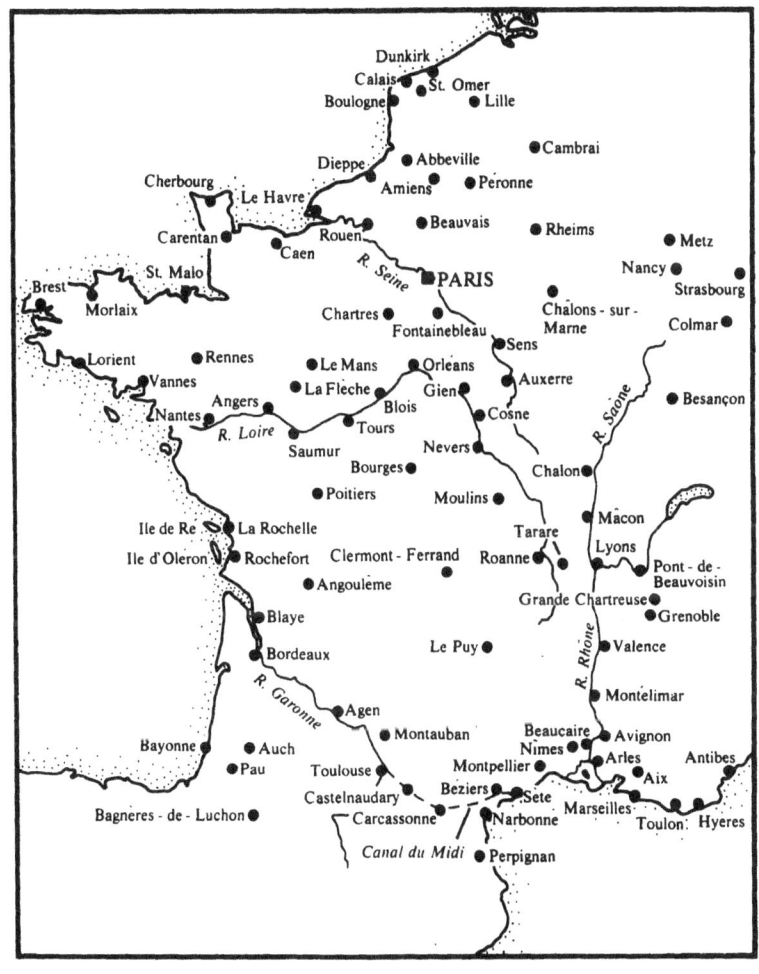

Introduction

Out of the quarter of a century covered by this book, five years, from 1778 to 1783, saw Britain and France involved in the War of American Independence. The modern reader tends to imagine that, while this war was in progress, no British citizens travelled to or from France. However, in the eighteenth century a state of war between the two countries did not completely rule out such journeys. Long before the Seven Years War was brought to an end by the signing of the Treaty of Paris in February 1763, Sterne had crossed the Channel. On 31 January 1762 he wrote to Garrick from Paris: 'I have been a fortnight in this metropolis . . . The Baron d'Holbach has offered any security for the inoffensiveness of my behaviour in France — 'tis more, you rogue! than you will do.' In the same letter he speaks of 'fifteen or sixteen English of distinction who are now here.' In May he informed his archbishop: 'The D[uke] of Choiseul has treated me with great indulgence as to my stay in France, & has this moment sent me Passports for my Family to join me.'[1] Naturally the formal ending of the state of war led to a great rush to France in which Gibbon, among many others, took part. Two years later Walpole attributed the fact that the country between Calais and Amiens was 'wonderfully enriched since I saw it four-and-twenty years ago' to 'the crumbs that fall from the chaises of the swarms of English that visit Paris'.[2]

Hostilities between Britain and France in the American War of Independence did not completely put an end to travel to Paris or other parts of the country. In 1779 Mme Du Deffand wrote to George Selwyn:

Voilà, Monsieur, votre passeport! c'est Madame de Cambis qui à pris les soins qu'il falloit pour le faire expédier. Vous auriez pu vous en passer, le ministre[3] a dit que les Anglais pouvaient arriver, sèjourner et partir, sans crainte d'éprouver aucune difficulté; cependant je suis bien aise que vous en ayez un: on ne sait pas quels évènemens peuvent arriver, et quels changemens ils pourraient produire; hâtez vous de faire usage de ce passeport. Je me fais un extrême plaisir de vous revoir.[4]

From Selwyn's correspondence we learn that he did visit Paris in that year, that the Rev Dr Warner was there during at least part of the war and that the Dowager Countess of Carlisle was travelling around the South of France.

In 1780 Swinburne crossed France on his way to Italy; he took the boat to Ostend and travelled via Lille, Paris and Lyons to Turin.[5] In March 1782 Pennington arrived in France via Ostend and travelled through Lille and Amiens to Paris and returned by Ostend. At Lille he noted: 'There are always many English in this city in time of peace, but not many at present.' He stayed some time at Amiens where he took French lessons, and there he wrote: 'I meet with no incivilities, though at their desire I talk politics every day at the Caffé Militaire with the officers.'[6]

However, the most surprising story is that of the travels of Lord Herbert across France in 1780 on his return from his mammoth Grand Tour which began in 1775 with a stay at Strasbourg. In the interval he had visited Holland, Germany, Hungary, Austria, Poland, Russia, Sweden, Denmark and Italy. Before he set out on his travels he had been made an ensign in the British army so that he could wear a uniform when he was presented in the different courts he visited. In 1779 he had been promoted to the rank of captain without, of course, ever having seen any military service. When he arrived in Lyons from Italy, he was faced with a problem: 'Not being able to wear my Uniform in an Enemy's Country, I was obliged to take into serious consideration my dress which after much reflection, I settled should be mourning, as the cheapest and most convenient in travelling.' Even so, he met with some embarrassment on the boat from Lyons down the Rhône valley:

We were about eighteen passengers, two of which were Women, five Swiss Officers going to join their Corps in Corsica, among whom was Mons. de Muralt, whom I had known at Strasbourg. I was rather sorry to meet an acquaintance, as I find it very disagreeable and inconvenient at all times to be known for a Milord Anglois, and more disagreeable now to be known for a Britton, however I desired him not to call me Milord; for an Anglois, I was allready blown. Some few of the Passengers have dropped off during the Day, and many of them have been plaguing their own Souls and mine to know what I am, and as I had as much as possible disguised my military appearance, I was in hopes of nobody's discovering me to be of that trade, but still the Officers are firmly perswaded I am, in either the Land or Sea Service. Three parts of the Day, the whole Body supposed me a Sea Officer in the French Service, and I took care to answer their questions so as neither to diswade them nor perswade them of the truth of their supposition.

At Marseilles he fell in with a Swiss officer whom he invited to dinner; but after declining the invitation because of a previous engagement, 'he returned however in ¼ of an hour, telling me some of his Brother Officers had told him, it would be proper that I should call on the Commandant Mr de Mirand to ask his leave to make a few days Stay at Marseilles'. Just as Lord Herbert had changed in order to make this call, back came the Swiss officer '& said that he had been to the Commandant who was sorry he was just going into the Country & could not see me, that he was infinitely obliged to me for the attention I had paid, etc. etc.' The following day he dined with Swiss officers in the fortress: 'I felt very odd in being in a French Fortress and seeing a fresh guard mount, but found also a great deal of hearty wellcome from my honest Swiss. They soon found out I was of their trade.' The next day he was back again at dinner in the fortress.

After his pleasant experiences at Marseilles Lord Herbert was quite disgusted with the very different reception he met with when he arrived in Bordeaux:

After Dinner I dressed and as a proper & civil thing, called on Mr de Fumel the Commandant as I did at Marseilles and elsewhere, and was surprized to be very differently received, particularly as Skiner[7] had mentioned him as so civil a man. He began by asking me for my Passport which I had by the merest chance in my pocket. He asked for it two or three times before I gave it to him, as I had never yet been asked for it by a Native of any Quality or Denomination. He read it and having seen my name, said, Milord, ceci est fort beau et fort bien, mais moyennant que la Cour n'ait donné des ordres contraires, upon which I told him I had not heard of any & that several People of consequence to whom I had Letters told [me] I might equally come to Bourdeaux as to Marseilles. In short he told me his orders were not to permit any Seigneur Anglois de séjourner more than 24 hours, so that I thought he was going to be after sending me off from the Town, which I did not much relish; I then raised a fresh Battery against him & thundered out the names of de Guines, the Archbishop of Toulouse, Mons. de Cambis, etc. etc., at him with some success, for he told me I was le Maitre to stay two or three days, if I thought proper. Upon this I took my leave, much discontented with my visit.[8]

All this is somewhat disconcerting to a modern reader. The return of peace in 1783 brought, of course, a large influx of British travellers which lasted for some time even after 1789.

As we see from such snippets of French as travellers like Lord Herbert inserted in their accounts of France, their command of the language did not rival that acquired by Gibbon during his youthful exile in Lausanne. Some of them are quite modest about their knowledge of French. Thicknesse, for instance, appends to a text which he had given in French: 'The above letter being hastily copied, you are desired to correct the errors, as I am not ashamed to own I am but a very indifferent Frenchman.'[9] In the seventeenth century travellers whose French was weak or non-existent frequently had recourse to the international language, Latin, but in our period this seems to have happened only rarely. Apparently Johnson would not risk speaking French when he came to France. Mrs Thrale records that at Rouen 'we picked up an Abbé who conversed in Latin with Mr Johnson, who had hitherto been unlucky in not finding Company he could talk to', and Johnson himself says of his visit to the literary journalist, Fréron: 'He spoke Latin very scantily, but seemed to understand me.'[10]

In these last decades of the Ancien Régime even a competent knowledge of French was not sufficient to ensure a smooth journey round the kingdom and useful contacts with any of its inhabitants encountered on one's way. Our travellers provide ample evidence of the lack of linguistic unity which was brought home to the Convention in 1794 in a famous report by Abbé Grégoire. Illiteracy and semi-illiteracy were widespread. In 1788, after noting that English was to be found on shop signs in Calais and Boulogne and even further on the road to Paris, one of our travellers observes:

> It is remarkable that the inscriptions over the doors of the tradesmen in the whole kingdom, not excepting Paris and Versailles, are most wretchedly spelt. It has been well observed by a late satirical writer, that ignorance is there engraved in letters of gold. In this respect the learning of the common people in England appears to great advantage, as few of their inscriptions, except perhaps in the meanest villages, exhibit such glaring blunders as *au*, or even *o*, for *eau*, *autel* and *othel* for *hotel*.[11]

These remarks were made, not by a first-time visitor to France, but by a man who claims to have spent a good part of his youth there.

What is more, the French language was not even spoken except by a small minority over large areas of the kingdom, either in the outlying regions where completely foreign tongues were spoken or in large areas south of the Loire in which various dialects of the *langue d'oc* were the native language of the inhabitants.

When on her return journey Mrs Thrale travelled from Lille to Dunkirk, she noted: 'What has taken most of my Attention on this day's Journey is the new Phenomenon of Flemish Words written under the Signs, & the Peasants when one speaks French to 'em not understanding a Word one says.'[12] When he visited French Flanders, Young found the language barrier was a serious obstacle to his inquiries: 'The difficulties, however, of gaining intelligence increased every step, for not one farmer in twenty speaks French.' He was faced with a similar problem in Alsace: 'In Savern, I found myself to all appearance truly in Germany; for two days past much tendency to a change, but here not one person in an hundred has a word of French.' Of his journey from St Brieuc to Guingamp in Brittany, he writes: 'Pass Chateaulandrin, and enter Bas Bretagne. One recognizes at once another people, meeting numbers who have not more French than *Je ne sais pas ce que vous dites*, or *Je n'entend rien*.'[13] Several of our travellers ventured as far as the Pyrenees and came up against Basque. 'The common language of the country', wrote Muirhead at Barèges, 'is a dialect of the biscayan, which sounds harsh in the ear of a stranger',[14] while Swinburne, who was an early climber in the Pyrenees, also mentions the linguistic change which he encountered there.[15] Even at Bayonne, Wraxall wrote, 'they speak a jargon called the Basque, which has scarce any affinity either with the French, Spanish, or even the Gascon dialect'.[16] At the eastern end of the Pyrenees Catalan was encountered. At Perpignan Thicknesse notes: 'The barbarous language of this province, is very convenient, as they understand French, and can make themselves understood through a great part of Spain',[17] while Young, returning from his trip into Catalonia, declared: 'Roussillon is in fact a part of Spain; the inhabitants are Spaniards in language and in customs; but they are under a French government.'[18]

Besides Catalan, our travellers encountered south of the Loire various forms of another Romance language, *langue d'oc*, otherwise known as *Occitan*. In discussing the languages spoken at Nice — *patois* along with French and Italian — Smollett gives a reasonably accurate account of the derivation of *Occitan* from Latin, pointing out that this language, 'with some variation, extends over all Provence, Languedoc, and Gascony'.[19] Muirhead first encountered linguistic problems when travelling down the Rhône valley on his way to Avignon: 'Slept at Le Palud, a village, where the patois is so prevalent that it was with difficulty we could understand or be understood.'[20] In roughly the same region, on his way from Le Puy to Montélimar, Young had a narrow escape when his mare backed his chaise over a precipice. 'A blessed country for a broken limb', he exclaims, 'confinement for six weeks or two months at the *Cheval Blanc*, at Aubenas, an inn that would have been purgatory itself to one of my hogs: alone, without relation, friend or servant, and not one person in sixty that speaks French.'[21]

At Aix Lord Gardenstone noted: 'The language of the common people in this country begins to have some mixture of Italian, and they often use the termination of *o* — as *jouro, prominado, voituro*, &c.' At Marseilles he gave a somewhat bizarre account of the *Occitan* spoken there, though he does note that the educated minority spoke French: 'Their common language now is either a Celtic jargon, called Patois, or a mixture of French and Italian; but the better sort speak French properly.'[22] Wraxall comments just as oddly on the language spoken there by the ordinary people: 'Their language, so famous in ancient romance, is a corrupt

Italian, more intelligible to a Neapolitan than to a Parisian.'[23] When Hobhouse's party got lost in the country between Marseilles and Arles, they found that neither one member's command of French nor a servant's Italian could secure admission to a miserable lodging: 'At last we met with a person who interpreted our wants in *Patois*, a mixture both of French and Italian, spoken by the common people in these parts; to him we were indebted for a reception.'[24]

When they moved further west, our travellers found other forms of *Occitan*. At Montpellier Smollett speaks scornfully of the Dr Fizes whom he consulted and whom he depicts as a ridiculous figure since, among other oddities, he 'affects to speak the *Patois*, which is a corruption of the old *Provencial* tongue, spoken by the vulgar in Languedoc and Provence'.[25] At nearby Pézenas Muirhead noted: 'The common people speak a jargon, which, to the ear of a stranger, sounds like that of Provence — a dialect, no doubt, of the old Romans, now a prey to daily corruption, and which may soon be obliterated in modern French.'[26] Further west, in Toulouse, R. W. C. observed once again social differences in the use of language: 'The French Language (except by the best sort of people) is most insufferably spoken, the lower class making use altogether of the Patois which is very soft and agreeable to the ear, but so different from the French that there are many persons here who do not understand it.'[27]

In other respects too Ancien Régime France was far from being a unified country. The chaos of weights and measures was notorious and is eloquently described in a couple of pages of Young's *Travels*:

> In France, the infinite perplexity of the measures exceeds all comprehension. They differ not only in every province, but in every district, and almost in every town; and these tormenting variations are found equally in the denominations and contents of the measures of land and corn. To these sources of confusion, is added the general ignorance of the peasantry, who know nothing of the Paris arpent, or the Paris septier, the most commonly received measure of the kingdom. For the knowledge of a French farmer is limited absolutely to his farm and market; he never looks into a newspaper or a magazine, where the difference of the measures of the kingdom would probably strike his attention, many times in his life. And if he were rather better instructed, yet, as

there are two national measures of land, they would occasion a confusion of which we can form no judgment: the arpent de Paris, and the arpent de France, are both legal and common measures; notwithstanding which, they are of very different contents; and, what is strange to say, are sometimes confounded by French writers on agriculture.

While in England such terms as 'bushel' and 'acre' were used all over the country which 'encouraged proportioning the contents to the common standards', Young points out that 'in France, they have no common denomination: if you travel seventy miles from Paris, in some directions, you hear no more of the septier, or the arpent: you find the *mine* of land, even within thirty miles of the capital, — and a little farther, you will be bewildered with *franchars* of corn, and *mancos* of land.' Young writes with some bitterness: 'The reader will be ready to credit me in assuring him, that the labour, perplexity, and vexation, which the present chapter has given me, both in travelling, and in writing, has much exceeded any thing I could have conceived before I went abroad.'[28]

If there was no uniform system of weights and measures, neither was there any uniformity in the laws of France. Most of the southern half of the kingdom was under Roman law (*droit écrit*), while the rest of the country was under customary law (*droit coutumier*), which varied not only from province to province, but even from district to district. This state of affairs was rarely commented on by our travellers. One of those who did so points out very reasonably that 'a knowledge of those customs requires a long residence in the nation, and much study, at the same time is useless to a stranger'. He does, however, correctly describe this lack of uniformity in the laws and the opposition to change which meant that it had to await the Revolution and Napoleon: 'Add to the general laws, each province has its peculiar customs and privileges, by which the inhabitants are to be judged with regard to inheritance, and many other affairs . . . The great variety of these customs produces so many inconveniences, it has been proposed to make a general code for the kingdom. The attachment of each province to its peculiar usages, has hitherto, and I believe ever will prevent the scheme taking place.'[29]

Especially for the last 100 years or so France had been a highly centralised country in which the central government was, as

Jardine noted, omnipresent:

> Here government, or the king, is already supposed and expected to do every thing that concerns the public or any part of it. Such things as with us are done by townships or counties, by individuals or subscriptions, as roads, canals, sea-ports, piers, storing up provisions, regulating prices; even stage-coaches, it seems, cannot be tolerably established but by his Majesty becoming proprietor. In other countries trade supports the state; in this the state must support trade: every trifling thing here requires the hand of government.[30]

The agent of the central government in every province or *généralité*, the *Intendant*, appears in our travellers' accounts chiefly in his social role. During the meetings of the provincial estates of Languedoc at Montpellier he and the governor kept open house not only for the deputies, but also for others. Naturally British visitors took advantage of this free entertainment, as Lady Knight explains in a letter:

> The Governor, the Intendant, the Treasurers of France and of the Estates, and the First President, gave us suppers alternately all the time. We had generally about two hundred persons of the best fashion every evening. About eighty sat down to the grand table, others took refreshments in different apartments. The suppers were of two courses. The second course was interspersed with ornaments of temples, rocks and hills, with cottages and cattle. The desserts were an assemblage of beautiful sweets, ices in all forms and shapes.[31]

At another meeting of the Estates at Montpellier the Dowager Countess of Carlisle enjoyed similar hospitality. After saying that she was 'well and cheerfully lodged', she goes on: 'I also like my society extremely, and especially the *Intendant*'s house, which is open on the most agreeable footing three times a week. I am sure you would be charmed with *Madame l'Intendante*; she is so sensible and well-bred, and lives on such terms of harmony with her numerous family.' Her relations with the *Intendant* of the province are referred to in a letter written a few months later to George Selwyn, inquiring whether he was coming to Paris:

> If you go there, I shall beg a favour of you, which is to bring

me over a small parcel, which I am very unlucky to have failed in already and I must write to inquire after it. It is some flannel for *le Comte de Saint-Priest*, the Intendant of Montpelier, to whom I was much obliged for many civilities; and he has set his heart on having this flannel which I know was bought, and sent, as I thought, by Sir John Lambert.[32]

All this, it should be noted, was in 1780 when Britain and France were at war.

In contrast with these agreeable social relations we find a furious diatribe by Young against the abuse of power by the *Intendants*, particularly in the matter of taxation. It should be borne in mind that what follows only applies to the *pays d'élections*, those provinces which did not have estates of their own to levy the taxes to be paid to the Treasury.

> The abuses attending the levy of taxes were heavy and universal. The kingdom was parcelled into generalities with an intendant at the head of each, into whose hands the whole power of the Crown was delegated for every thing except the military authority; but particularly for all affairs of finance. The generalities were subdivided into elections, at the head of which was a *sub-delegué*, appointed by the intendant. The rolls of the *taille, capitation, vingtiemes*, and other taxes, were distributed among districts, parishes, and individuals, at the pleasure of the intendant, who could exempt, change, add, or diminish at pleasure. Such an enormous power, constantly acting, and from which no man was free, must, in the nature of things, degenerate in many cases into absolute tyranny. It must be obvious, that the friends, acquaintances, and dependents of the intendant, and of all his sub-delegués, and the friends of these friends, to a long chain of dependence, might be favoured in taxation at the expence of their miserable neighbours; and that noblemen, in favour at court, to whose protection the intendant himself would naturally look up, could find little difficulty in throwing much of the weight of their taxes on others, without a similar support. Instances, and even gross ones, have been reported to me in many parts of the kingdom, that made me shudder at the oppression to which numbers must have been condemned, by the undue favours granted to such crooked influence.[33]

Though somewhat highly coloured, this passage obviously reflects complaints which Young had picked up in the course of his travels.

By the second half of the eighteenth century only a small number of French provinces still possessed their estates; where they had existed in the sixteenth century the government had often caused their demise simply by failing to summon their members. Their functions, where they continued to meet, consisted in agreeing to the amount of the *don gratuit* and other taxes to be paid to the Treasury (they were allowed to assess and levy the taxes involved) and to concern themselves with such public works for the province as roads and canals. Their powers, as we shall see, had been severely limited by the development of absolutism.

Some small provinces in the region of the Pyrenees had managed to keep their estates. During his stay at Tarbes, Swinburne describes the Estates of Bigorre, and later he gives a brief account of those of Béarn.[34]

Most provincial estates met either once a year or every two years, but those of Burgundy only every three. Wharton, who was in Dijon in May 1775, gives a brief account of the opening of the Estates at which the Prince de Condé, the governor of the province, was the King's representative: 'The Procureur General opened the Assembly. Then the Premier President spoke, then the Prince, who was much applauded, then the Bishop of Autun who spoke with much more freedom than I should have Expected, on the Present Disturbances & received deservedly very great Applause. The Assembly then broke up, and the Bishop in going out was again Applauded.'[35] In describing his tour of Provence, Swinburne gives a clear account of the rather peculiar situation which obtained in that province:

> We passed through Lambesc . . . ; here the committee of the States of Provence is held: the states themselves have not been called together since the year 1639; but to supply their place with great convenience to government the king issues out a commission annually to the archbishop of Aix, two bishops, two gentlemen, the consuls of Aix, and thirty-five deputies of districts, ordering them to assemble under the direction of the military commandant, and the intendant of the province. In this meeting are settled the free gifts to the king, and all extraordinary impositions; the method of imposing and collecting the taxes is regulated by the number of families in each district.[36]

Introduction

Two large provinces — Brittany and Languedoc — still had their Estates. Meetings of those of Brittany, which the central government often found it difficult to manage and which were to prove particularly obstreporous in the crisis year 1788,[37] are unfortunately nowhere described by our travellers. Breton cities were much less frequented by them than Montpellier, where the Estates of Languedoc met. Their meetings gave rise to some quite interesting accounts. The *Gentleman's Guide*, which delivers a blistering attack on the town's reputation as a health resort, does concede that the place livened up when the Estates met: 'The town has nothing curious to induce a stranger to stay longer in it than three or four days, except he arrives there about Christmas; at which time, it is very gay, as all the nobility of Languedoc meet there at that time, to settle the affairs of the Province, though it is not the capital, but esteemed nearly the centre.'[38] Swinburne agrees with this view: The states of Languedoc assemble here every winter, and during the meeting Montpellier is a place of great gaiety.' After giving an account of the composition of the Estates, he summarises their functions thus: 'Their business is to grant money to the king, to parcel out the contributions, to inspect the accounts of preceding years, and to watch over the privileges of the province.'[39]

Sterne, who was in Montpellier during the winter of 1763–4, was obviously not impressed either by the Estates or the entertainments which accompanied them. In February 1764 he wrote: 'The states of Languedoc are met — 'tis a fine raree-show, with the usual accompanyments of fiddles, bears, and puppet-shows. — I believe I shall step into my post-chaise with more alacrity to fly from these sights, than a Frenchman would to fly to them . . . My wife chooses to go to Montauban, rather than to stay here.'[40]

Fortunately the eleven-year-old Lady Harriet Spencer who was present with her mother and elder sister at the opening of the Estates in December 1772 and at the final session, took more interest in the proceedings and described them in her diary.[41] Lady Knight and her daughter were in Montpellier five years later in November 1777, when the Estates met. As well as partaking of the free entertainments offered on such occasions, they also did their duty by attending the opening session. Of the two accounts the daughter's is much the fuller and more interesting:

We were present at the opening of the Assembly of the States on the 27th. It was held in a great hall in the Hôtel de Ville.

Introduction

At the upper end was a throne, under a canopy of crimson velvet. Long benches were ranged on each side, and parallel rows in front below, with a table covered with green cloth. The galleries and the rest of the hall were filled with spectators. First entered the Archbishop of Narbonne, at the head of the clergy; the bishops in their violet robes, covered with fine lace; and the 'grands vicaires' representing the prelates who were absent, in black cassocks. They took their places on the right hand of the throne, which was occupied by the Comte de Périgord as soon as he came in, followed by the barons and by the gentlemen who acted as representatives of the absent nobles. The count and barons were robed in black velvet mantles lined with gold stuff, hats with long feathers hanging over them, and their hair dressed with two queues. The barons took their places on the left, and below sat the 'tiers état', consisting of deputies from the towns. The 'greffiers' and lawyers were at the table. On the left hand of the count, and above the barons, sat the intendant of the province, M. de St. Priest, and two treasurers of France, in black, with black caps, surmounted by a tuft. A greffier having read the commission which the Count de Périgord, as commandant of the province, had received from the king to hold the states, the count made a speech, complimenting the intendant, the barons, and the bishops, and particularly the Archbishop of Narbonne, whom he characterised as 'a prelate who supported the interests of the people at court without flattery, and the interests of the court with the people without ostentation'.

At this point Cornelia Knight gives a long account of the speech delivered by the archbishop; this will be discussed later in the section on the clergy.[42] She then continues:

At the close of this speech, which had a very good effect, the governor, the intendant, and the treasurers, as commissaries for the king, left the Assembly, and were accompanied to the door by the archbishop and bishops, who then returned to their seats, the archbishop occupying the throne. The hour of the next meeting having been fixed, mass was said by the archbishop's almoner, and served by his grace's footmen in livery. The prelates, the intendant, the treasurers, and barons afterwards dined with the governor in their robes, with their hats on, which, however, they took off while they stood to drink the health of the king, the queen, and the royal family. We went to see this ceremony, which was called 'le Dîner du Roi'.

She and her mother rounded off the day by being received by the commandant and having supper at Madame l'Intendante's.

They went back for another session of the Estates:

> On the 2nd of December the Assembly met, that the king's commissaries might ask for the 'don gratuit' from the province. The demand was made by the intendant, in what struck me as being a very authoritative style. The Archbishop of Narbonne replied in a manner equally pathetic and spirited. He lamented that, at a season dedicated to joy and festivity, the misfortunes of the province should cast a cloud over the public cheerfulness. He remarked, that after a long and severe winter the distress of the inhabitants had not been mitigated by a genial spring and summer, in the happiest country as to situation that could be imagined, inhabited by a people endowed with the most industrious activity, and enjoying a climate which drew so many illustrious strangers from less favoured lands. He pointed out in the most lively colours the losses sustained by the province from the frosts, which had destroyed nearly all the vines, and from the failure of the most promising harvest. Nor could the unhappy hope for any alleviation of their distress while subjected to such heavy imposts. It was dreadful, he said, to find, after fifteen years of peace, that the taxes were still the same as in time of war, though it was right to expect that they should be taken off. The province was, therefore, in no state to give any further testimony of duty than what they had already afforded.[43]

The archbishop's task was obviously to ensure that, whatever he might say about the disasters which had befallen the province, the amount demanded from the Estates for the *don gratuit* and other taxes was forthcoming.

There was again no uniform system of direct or indirect taxation, a point which particularly struck Adam Smith, whose lengthy stay in France in the 1760s was no doubt responsible for the observations on this subject which are to be found in the *Wealth of Nations*. He distinguishes correctly between the *taille réelle*, assessed in the *pays d'états* on the amount of land held, and the *taille personnelle*, assessed in the *pays d'élections* on estimated income. He writes first of the *taille réelle*:

> The taille in the provinces of Languedoc, Provence, Dauphiné, and Brittany; in the generality of Montauban, and in the elections of Agen and Condom, as well as in some other districts of France, [is a tax] upon lands held in property of an ignoble tenure. In other countries the tax was laid upon the supposed profits of all those who held in farm or lease lands belonging to other people, whatever might be the tenure by which the proprietor held them; and in this case the taille was said to be personal. In the greater part of those provinces of France, which are called the Countries of Elections, the taille is of this kind.

Though the difference between these two forms of *taille* was not perhaps as great as he implies (there were abuses too in the *pays d'états*), there were, as he maintains, greater disadvantages in the *taille personnelle*:

> The real taille, as it is imposed only upon a part of the lands of the country, is necessarily an unequal, but it is not always an arbitrary tax, though it is upon some occasions. The personal taille, as it is intended to be proportioned to the profits of a certain class of people which can only be guessed at, is necessarily both arbitrary and unequal.[44]

The practical consequences of these two different forms of the *taille*, the principal direct tax, will be examined in the next chapter.[45] Two other direct taxes, the *capitation* and the *vingtième*, both introduced during the wars at the end of the reign of Louis XIV and later brought in again in a different form, were levied in a different fashion in the *pays d'élections* and the *pays d'états* as the latter were allowed to compound for a fixed sum.

There were similar differences in the way in which the indirect taxes were raised. These were mainly four: the *gabelle* (salt tax), the duty on tobacco, the *aides* (excise duties) and the *traites* (customs duties). The last were levied not only at the frontiers, but also on goods passing from one part of the country to another.

Introduction

Adam Smith has a well-informed passage on the almost endless variations in the methods by which these taxes were raised:

> In France, the different revenue laws which take place in the different provinces, require a multitude of revenue officers to surround not only the frontiers of the kingdom, but those of almost each particular province, in order either to prevent the importation of certain goods, or to subject it to the payment of certain duties, to the no small interruption of the interior commerce of the country. Some provinces are allowed to compound for the gabelle or salt-tax. Others are exempted from it altogether. Some provinces are exempted from the exclusive sale of tobacco, which the farmers general enjoy through the greater part of the kingdom. The aides which correspond to the excise in England, are very different in different provinces. Some provinces are exempted from them, and pay a composition or equivalent. In those in which they take place and are in farm, there are many local duties which do not extend beyond a particular town or district.

He gives most space to an account of the extraordinary system of internal customs barriers:

> The Traites, which correspond to our customs, divide the kingdom into three great parts; first, the provinces subject to the tarif of 1664, which are called the provinces of the five great farms, and under which are Picardy, Normandy, and the greater part of the interior provinces of the kingdom; secondly, the provinces subject to the tarif of 1667, which are called the provinces reckoned foreign, and under which are comprehended the greater part of the frontier provinces; and, thirdly, those provinces which are said to be treated as foreign, or which, because they are allowed a free commerce with foreign countries, are in their commerce with the rest of France subjected to the same duties as other foreign countries. These are Alsace, the three bishopricks of Metz, Toul and Verdun, and the three cities of Dunkirk, Bayonne, and Marseilles. Both in the provinces of the five great farms . . . and in those which are said to be reckoned foreign, there are many local duties which do not extend beyond a particular town or district. There are some such even in the provinces which are said to be treated as foreign, particularly in the

city of Marseilles. It is unnecessary to observe how much, both the restraints upon the interior commerce of the country, and the number of the revenue officers must be multiplied, in order to guard the frontiers of these different provinces and districts, which are subject to such different systems of taxation.[46]

No doubt on his numerous journeys inside France Adam Smith had to suffer the same vexations and delays as other British travellers when he encountered these internal customs barriers, although unfortunately he did not leave behind, either in letters or in a travel diary, any details about the two and a half years which he spent in France. However, others provide abundant information on this point. One change noted by an English traveller who had known France before the Revolution when he returned to Paris in 1801, was this: 'You are not now plagued, as formerly, by custom-house officers on the frontiers of *every* department, My Baggage being once searched at Calais, experienced no other visit.'[47] There were, of course, ways of reducing the amount of inconvenience caused by these frequent searches inside the country. Thicknesse explains that on these occasions 'a twenty-four *sols* piece, and on assuring the officer that you are a gentleman, and not a merchant, will carry you through without delay'.[48]

Cole found that his determination not to grease the palm of customs officials with a fairly modest bribe could lead to much inconvenience and exasperation. After paying up once on leaving Calais on his way to St Omer, he was in no mood to fork out a second time:

> Near La Rècousse is a Toll Gate, where the King has some officers to search all Passengers for Contraband Goods: as I knew they only wanted to squeeze something out of me under a Pretence of looking into my Portmanteaus for run Goods, and would have been contented to let me pass had I given them a Livre, yet I was so provoked with their Impertinence, (having paid a Livre or two in coming out of the Gates of Calais for the same Affair), that I told them I would give them nothing, but that they were at Liberty to search my Valise; accordingly they set about it, & I had like to have suffered for my Refusal: for the first Thing they lit upon in opening my Servant's Portmanteau were a Pair of new Boots which he had never put on his Legs: these they presently seized, as

pretending no new Goods were suffered to come into the Kingdom without paying Duty: but I, resolutely telling them that they might take them at their Peril, as they were the only Boots he had to make use of, after some Altercation, & no Bribe, went off much to their Dissatisfaction.[49]

Even Smollett, who was not the most accommodating of men and who speaks of 'those vermin who examine the baggage of travellers in different parts of the kingdom', consented to use bribery. On his arrival in Lyons he wrote: 'From Paris our baggage (though not plombé) was not once examined till we arrived in this city, at the gate of which we were questioned by one of the searchers, who, being tipped with half a crown, allowed us to proceed without further enquiry.'[50]

British travellers who chose to take the longer route through Flanders to Paris met with a good deal of trouble at Péronne, which had been the original frontier town, as Burney explains:

At present its only garrison is custom house officers; for at the entrance into this town all travellers and even the inhabitants, are visited and very narrowly searched, and this to prevent the bringing into France the productions of Flanders, which are subject to a very high duty: such as the laces of Valenciennes, Lille, Dunkirk, cambricks of St. Quinten, Arras, Douay and above all Cambray whence this beautiful manufacture had its name . . . Tobacco, too and snuff are seizable at the gates of Peronne, as they are ⅔ cheaper without than within them.[51]

When confronted with such rigorous searches, Blaikie found it 'extraordinary, countrys under the Same government to be so differantly administrated'.[52]

Travellers could encounter a fair amount of inconvenience on this route from Calais to Paris. After describing a strict customs examination at Calais, Lady Mary Coke writes: 'I lay at Peronne in a terrible dirty Inn, & had again the pleasure of having all the boxes of the inside of my Coach search'd . . . I forgot to tell you my Coach was search'd again at St Quentin.'[53] Even here, however, a bribe could on occasion expedite matters as Peckham makes clear: 'Peronne . . . is called one of the keys of the kingdom; our baggage would have undergone a severe scrutiny at the Douane or Custom-House, if we had not taken off the edge of the officer's vigilance with a six livre piece.'[54]

Our travellers' troubles were not over when they arrived in Paris. Although all the customs formalities had been observed on the way, Smollett and his party had a disagreeable experience when they got there: 'Although our portmanteaus were sealed with lead, and we were provided with a passe-avant from the douane, our coach was searched at the gate of Paris by which we entered, and the women were obliged to get out, and stand in the open street, till this operation was performed.'[55] Cole too was somewhat disgruntled by his reception: 'We got in to Paris about 7 o'Clock in the Evening, & were set down at the Custom House or *Bureau de Roi*, where my Portmanteaus were again rummaged over & searched.'[56] Yet although Garrick and his wife had carelessly mislaid the form given them by the customs at Calais, they got off lightly in Paris: 'We met with so much politeness from the Officers through the Kindness of a Monsr. D'Agencourt the Director of the Custom house who seeing our distress took pity on us, & made this disagreeable Circumstance as little troublesome to us as it possibly could be at the End of a Journey.'[57]

Travellers met with customs barriers at all sorts of places. After Smollett's encounter with customs officers at Lyons, he met them again at Pont St Esprit in the Rhône valley: 'Here we entered Languedoc, and were stopped to have our baggage examined, but the searcher, being tipped with a three-livre piece, allowed it to pass.'[58] When travelling by *coche d'eau* down the Rhône from Lyons, Lord Herbert noted: 'We were obliged to stop at Vienne, for the Custom Officers to visit the boat, during which Muralt and I runn about the Town.'[59] On entering Franche-Comté from the north, 'we were accosted', writes Muirhead, 'by one of those nuisances, a petty buralist, who affected extreme impatience to search out trunks. A twelve sol piece corrupted his sense of duty to his king and country, and spared us the trouble of detention.'[60] Young too encountered them when leaving Brittany: 'Glorious view of the Loire from a village, the last of Bretagne, where is a great barrier across the road and custom-houses, to search every thing coming from hence.'[61] For travellers these customs posts represented a minor inconvenience, especially as we are told again and again that trouble could easily be avoided by offering a modest bribe; but the delays and expense incurred in the transport of goods must, as Adam Smith pointed out, have had serious consequences for the internal trade of the country.

Introduction

A curious point made by Young and quite a number of other travellers was the small amount of circulation between the different parts of France. Their comments relate for the most part to the movement of persons rather than that of goods. It is true that in 1785 Mary Berry describes the road from Aix to Marseilles as 'abominable', adding: 'The narrow wheels of the loaded charrettes of this country would spoil the best road in a short time, and the more so from the heavy weights being placed upon two instead of upon four wheels.' She also writes: 'In the environs of Marseilles ... the road was filled with carriages, and all betokens a commercial town and a large population.'[62] Twenty years earlier, Pennant, on his way from Péronne to Paris, noted some movement of goods, even on a Sunday, between Roye and Pont Ste Maxence: 'Set out early in the morning; and tho Sunday met more waggons and carts than I had done all the road before. Many were drawn by mules, which became now a common beast of carriage.'[63] In May 1780 the Dowager Countess of Carlisle wrote from Montpellier that, after exceptionally heavy rains, the roads were so bad that she was compelled to delay her departure: 'The roads are still horrible between this place and Lyons, but I hope a month will do a great deal towards their amendment ... As the traffic here is very great, their carts cut the roads to pieces.'[64] In 1787 even Young was struck by the greatly increased circulation caused by the fair at Beaucaire,[65] and two years later Rigby too found the road from Nîmes 'crowded with people' going there. Earlier, in writing of his journey from Calais to Lille, he describes the roads as 'full of people, carriages, carts, waggons, etc. etc.'[66]

Yet the balance of opinion leans heavily towards the other view. Before examining our travellers' impressions of the state of affairs in the Paris region, we may first look at what they have to say of the provinces at some distance from the capital. 'Not a single carriage, horse or foot traveller did I yesterday meet from Calais to St Omer', wrote Burney in 1770.[67] Two years later Peckham found the journey from Chantilly to Calais somewhat depressing, partly because there were 'no carriages on the road, no appearance of traffic'.[68] If Mary Berry found the approach to Marseilles full of carriages, Muirhead declares that the road from Aix, 'considering that it lay between two distinguished cities, was little frequented'; it is true that this was in September 1789.[69]

Most of Young's observations in his travel diary on what he saw (or rather failed to see) on provincial roads concern the south of France. Of the last part of his journey from Montauban to

Toulouse he writes: 'Pass St Jorry; a noble road . . . It is a desert to the very gates of Toulouse; meet not more persons than if it were 100 miles from any town.' The road from Perpignan to Narbonne was splendid, but out of all proportion to what was needed for the traffic on it: 'In 36 miles, I have met one cabriolet, half a dozen carts, and some old women with asses.' He was disgusted when, in the burning heat, he tried vainly to hire a carriage either at Carcassonne or Mirepoix:

> Riding fatigued me, and I enquired for a carriage of some sort to carry me, while these great heats should continue; I had done the same at Carcassonne; but nothing like a cabriolet of any sort was to be had. When it is recollected that that place is one of the most considerable manufacturing towns in France, containing 15,000 people, and that Mirepoix is far from being a mean place, and yet not a voiture of any kind to be had, how will an Englishman bless himself for the universal conveniences that are spread through his own country, in which I believe there is not a town of 1500 people in the kingdom where post chaises and able horses are not to be had at a moment's warning? What a contrast!

A bad inn which he encountered at St Girons in the Pyrenees gives rise to a long passage in which he complains about the extravagantly expensive roads and bridges which he had encountered in Languedoc, quite beyond what was needed by the number of travellers which was too small to give rise, as in England, to decent inns even in small places. On a nine-day journey from Bagnères-de-Luchon to Bayonne and Auch he once again encountered amazingly few travellers: 'In the 270 miles, from Bagneres de Luchon to Auch . . . I have not met with one country equipage, nor any thing like a gentleman riding to see a neighbour. Scarcely a gentleman at all.'[70]

So far as the approaches to Paris are concerned, throughout the whole of our period our travellers all agree about the astonishingly small amount of traffic to be seen on the roads leading to and from the capital. They make the inevitable comparison with London which was, of course, a great sea port and commercial centre with a population which represented a much higher proportion of that of the whole kingdom than was the case with Paris in relation to the rest of France. Even so, those travellers who comment on the contrast were struck by the relatively deserted roads which they

Introduction

found when going into and out of Paris. In 1765 Pennant wrote of the last stage of his journey from Calais: 'Lay at a wretched inn at Ecouen within fifteen miles only of Paris, yet the best in the place; no appearance of wealth, nor neatness as in the Environs of London, scarce any people on horse, and only a few single horse chairs or hired chaises. The same effect was continued even to the gates of Paris; having met only one Gentleman's coach.'[71] A visit to the royal palace at Choisy-le-Roi drew this comment from Mrs Thrale: 'The Prospect from the Windows is delightful — & the Seine at Choisy would be very like the Thames at Greenwich, if it had any Boats or Ships upon it — but sure never were Rivers so bare of Vessels, or Roads so barren of Carriages, as in France; One may travel 20 Miles by land or Water and meet absolutely no one.'[72] By coincidence seven years later a visit to the same place produced a similar reaction from Pennington: 'The road is pleasant and good, and near the Seine, but remarkably dull, and so little frequented, that at two miles from the city, you might fancy yourself to be a hundred miles from it; and the quantity of game running about the fields, helps not a little to strengthen this thought, as that is a thing not very common in the environs of a great city.' To this he adds a footnote: 'In this point, there is an essential difference between London and Paris.'[73] In 1788 another traveller wrote of his journey from Calais to the capital: 'In the vicinity of Amiens the bustle of a great manufacturing town is remarkable. Here too we saw a few private carriages, of which the whole road from Calais had afforded only one, at Flixecourt. From Amiens we saw none until we came to St. Denis.'[74] Even Rigby was surprised at the emptiness of the road near Paris: 'Though in the course of our journey from Calais we went seldom more than one hundred yards without seeing some people, yet when we approached Paris we did not observe the crowds which fill the roads in the vicinity of London.'[75]

These observations — all unpublished when Young composed his *Travels in France* — certainly confirm what he has repeatedly to say about the comparative scarcity of movement on the roads into and out of Paris. As he got near to it in a post-chaise in May 1787, he tells us, 'the last ten miles I was eagerly on the watch for that throng of carriages which near London impede the traveller. I watched in vain; for the road, quite to the gates, is, on comparison, a perfect desert. So many roads join here, that I suppose this must be accidental.' Yet when three days later he left Paris for Orleans on his way to the Pyrenees, he found that his first impression was confirmed:

> The road to Orleans is one of the greatest that leads from Paris; I expected, therefore, to have my former impression of the little traffic near that city removed; but on the contrary, it was confirmed; it is a desert compared with those around London. In ten miles we met with not one stage or diligence; only two messageries, and very few chaises; not a tenth of what would have been met had we been leaving London at the same hour. Knowing how great, rich, and important a city Paris is, this circumstance perplexes me much.

He found the same thing when he returned to Paris from Fontainebleau three months later: 'Enter Paris once more, with the same observation I made before, that there is not one tenth of the motion on the roads around it that there is around London', and when he returned a few weeks later from Liancourt via Beauvais and Pontoise, he was again struck by the small number of travellers on the roads leading into Paris.[76]

It would be possible to fill several chapters with the varied impressions of French inns recorded by our travellers. In considering them one has to remember that France covers a much larger area than Great Britain, though this was to some extent counterbalanced by the fact that in our period its population was at least twice that of England, Wales and Scotland combined. Travellers, Young included, found good, even excellent inns, particularly, though by no means exclusively, in the larger cities. They also encountered some horrors, mainly in out of the way places, but not only there; they were met with even on the post-roads. One of Young's worst experiences was in Brittany, at Guingamp on the road to the great naval port of Brest. 'This villainous hole, that calls itself the *grand maison*, is the best inn at a post town on the great road to Brest, at which marshals of France, dukes, peers, countesses, and so forth, must now and then, by the accidents to which long journeys are subject, have found themselves. What are we to think of a country that has made, in the eighteenth century, no better provision for its travellers?'[77] Smollett makes the same point in discussing the disadvantages of posting in France. He begins by complaining of 'the insolence and imposition' of both post-masters and postillions, and continues:

> Another great inconvenience which attends posting in

Introduction

France, is that if you are retarded by any accident, you cannot in many parts of the kingdom find a lodging, without perhaps travelling two or three posts farther than you would choose to go, to the prejudice of your health, and even the hazard of your life, whereas, on any part of the post-road in England, you will meet with tolerable accommodation at every stage.[78]

Like Young, Smollett must have been aware that France was a much larger country than Britain. Yet, given its much larger population (too large according to Young), they deduced from the number of miserably inadequate inns that the circulation of persons inside the country was surprisingly small.

In his travels in the provinces, made in 1789 in the critical period between the end of June and the middle of September, first eastwards to Strasbourg, then by a meandering route to Marseilles, and finally to the Italian frontier, Young was astounded that at such a time when the sudden freedom of the press had vastly increased the number of newpapers, in so many towns through which he passed there were none to be found. Metz, Strasbourg and Marseilles, it is true, satisfied his appetite for news, but when he was only a few miles out of Paris, he was already lamenting that he was going to be cut off from the momentous events taking place there, in particular through 'the detestable circumstance of having no newspapers, with a press much freer than the English'. At Château-Thierry, some sixty miles from Paris, where he arrived on 4 July, he exploded: 'I arrived there by five o'clock, and wished, in a period so interesting to France, and indeed to all Europe, to see a newspaper. I asked for a coffee-house, not one in the town. Here are two parishes, and some thousands of inhabitants, and not a newspaper to be seen by a traveller, even in a moment when all ought to be anxiety. What stupidity, poverty, and want of circulation!'[79] He was better pleased with what he found at Metz and Strasbourg, both of which had *cabinets littéraires*, but all the way to Besançon which he reached on 27 July, he could find no useful newspapers:

From Strasbourg hither, I have not been able to see a newspaper. Here I asked for the *Cabinet Literaire*? None. The gazettes. At the coffee-house. Very easily replied, but not so easily found. Nothing but the *Gazette de France*;[80] for which, at this period, a man of common sense would not give one *sol*. To four other coffee-houses; at some no paper at all, not even the *Mercure*; at the *Café Militaire*, the *Courier de l'Europe*, a fortnight old; and well dressed people are now talking of the news of two or three weeks past, and plainly by their discourse know nothing of what is passing. The whole town of Besançon has not been able to afford me a sight of the *Journal de Paris*, nor of any paper that gives a detail of the transactions of the states; yet it is the capital of a province, large as half a dozen English counties, and containing 25,000 souls; — and, strange to say, the post coming in but three times a week.

Four days later, at Dijon, he fared only slightly better: 'I went to search coffee-houses; but will it be credited, that I could find but one in this capital of Burgundy where I could read a newspaper? — At a poor little one in the square, I read a paper, after waiting an hour to get it.' A week later at Moulins, 'the capital of a great province, the seat of an Intendant', he again exploded: 'To read the papers I went to the coffee house of Madame Bourgeau, the best in the town, where I found near twenty tables set for company, but, as to a newspaper, I might as well have demanded an elephant.' At Le Puy, on 17 August, he noted wearily: 'Many coffee-houses, even considerable ones, but not a single newspaper to be found in any.' It was only when he reached Marseilles, on 5 September, that he could once again express satisfaction, as he was able to declare that it was 'absolutely exempt from the reproaches I have so often cast on others for want of newspapers. I breakfasted at the *Café d'Acajon* amidst many.'[81]

No doubt in the summer of 1789, at a critical moment in French history, this absence of newspapers was particularly noticeable, especially as the breakdown of the old press laws had produced an enormous increase in their number. It cannot be said that this is a topic which is prominent in accounts of journeys made before 1789. However, in 1785 Cradock, who, on his travels round France, was always keen on keeping up with the news, recorded on his arrival at La Rochelle: 'As soon as ever I had procured some refreshment, I went out to hunt for a Courier de l'Europe, or some public Gazette; for since I had left Bourdeaux . . . , in point of news, "the famine had been sore in the land".'[82]

Our travellers leave us with the impression of France as a country which, though highly centralised thanks to the system of

Intendants established in the previous century, was still far from being unified. In addition to the obstacles presented by great distances and the slowness of travel before the coming of the railways, on top of the illiteracy of the majority of its inhabitants was a national language which was neither spoken nor understood by vast numbers. There was no national system of weights and measures, no code of civil law applying to the whole country, no uniform system of administration, with the country divided into *pays d'élections* and *pays d'états*, and endless differences in the way in which both direct and indirect taxes were raised. Inside this large country circulation both of persons and of news seemed to British eyes remarkably poor.

Notes

1. *Letters*, pp. 151–2, 164.
2. *Correspondence*, vol. 39, p. 8.
3. The Comte de Vergennes.
4. *George Selwyn and his Contemporaries*, vol. III, pp. 387–8.
5. *The Courts of Europe*, vol. I, pp. 297–304.
6. *Continental Excursions*, vol. I, pp. 20, 68.
7. 'Waited upon Mr. Skinner, the banker' (Cradock, *Memoirs*, vol. II, p. 225).
8. *Pembroke Papers*, pp. 432, 437–8, 441, 442, 458.
9. *Useful Hints*, p. 86.
10. *French Journals*, pp. 82, 173.
11. *Gentleman's Magazine*, 1797, p. 637.
12. *French Journal*, p. 160.
13. *Travels in France*, vol. I, pp. 321, 153, 99.
14. *Journals of Travels*, p. 308.
15. *Journey from Bayonne to Marseilles*, p. 285.
16. *A Tour*, p. 100.
17. *A Year's Journey*, vol. I, p. 349.
18. *Travels in France*, vol. I, p. 43.
19. *Travels through France and Italy*, pp. 180–2.
20. *Journals of Travels*, p. 189.
21. *Travels in France*, vol. I, p. 182.
22. *Travelling Memorandums*, vol. I, pp. 92, 104n.
23. *A Tour*, p. 131.
24. *Remarks*, pp. 56–7.
25. *Travels through France and Italy*, p. 90.
26. *Journals of Travels*, p. 258.
27. *Letters from France*, p. 8.
28. *Travels in France*, vol. I, pp. 315–16.
29. *Travels into France and Italy*, vol. I, pp. 34–5.
30. *Letters from Barbary, France, etc.*, vol. I, pp. 201–2.

Introduction

31. *Letters from France and Italy*, p. 40. See also Cornelia Knight, *Autobiography*, p. 43.
32. *George Selwyn and his Contemporaries*, vol. IV, pp. 313, 340.
33. *Travels in France*, vol. I, p. 598.
34. *Journey from Bayonne to Marseilles*, pp. 292-3, 335-6.
35. *An Englishman's Impressions*, pp. 90-1.
36. *Journey from Bayonne to Marseilles*, p. 453.
37. See below, pp. 290-3.
38. *Gentleman's Guide*, p. 74.
39. *Journey from Bayonne to Marseilles*, p. 382.
40. *Letters*, p. 210.
41. *Lady Bessborough and her Family Circle*, pp. 23-4.
42. See below, pp. 156-8.
43. *Autobiography*, pp. 35-6, 39-40.
44. *Wealth of Nations*, vol. II, p. 854.
45. See below, pp. 55-7.
46. *Wealth of Nations*, vol. II, pp. 900-1.
47. Francis William Blagden, *Paris as it was and as it is*, London, 1803, 2 vols., vol. I, p. 12.
48. *A Year's Journey*, vol. ii, p. 268.
49. *Journal*, pp. 8-9.
50. *Travels through France and Italy*, pp. 43, 71.
51. *Music, men and manners*, p. 7.
52. *Diary of a Scotch Gardener*, vol. III, p. 190.
53. *Letters and Journals*, vol. III, pp. 448-9.
54. *A Tour*, p. 130.
55. *Travels through France and Italy*, p. 43.
56. *Journal*, p. 32.
57. *Journal*, p. 6.
58. *Travels through France and Italy*, pp. 78-9.
59. *Pembroke Papers*, p. 439.
60. *Journals of Travels*, pp. 81-2.
61. *Travels in France*, vol. i, p. 105.
62. *Journals and Correspondence*, vol. I, p. 144.
63. *Tour on the Continent*, p. 6.
64. *George Selwyn and his Contemporaries*, vol. IV, pp. 322-3.
65. See below, pp. 116-18.
66. *Letters from France*, pp. 130, 11.
67. *Music, men and manners*, p. 3.
68. *A Tour*, p. 217.
69. *Journals of Travels*, p. 354.
70. *Travels in France*, vol. I, pp. 21, 45, 53-4, 58.
71. *Tour on the Continent*, p. 8.
72. *French Journal*, p. 118.
73. *Continental Excursions*, vol. I, pp. 155-6.
74. *Gentleman's Magazine*, 1797, p. 637.
75. *Letters from France*, p. 19.
76. *Travels in France*, vol. I, pp. 6, 11, 70, 75.
77. *Travels in France*, vol. I, p. 99.
78. *Travels through France and Italy*, p. 342.

79. *Travels in France*, vol. I, pp. 140, 145.
80. The official government newspaper.
81. *Travels in France*, vol. I, pp. 160–1, 163–4, 170, 179, 192.
82. *Memoirs*, vol. II, p. 246.

Part One
Economic and Social Conditions

1
The Land and the Peasants

Although on the eve of the Revolution and indeed for long afterwards France was predominantly an agricultural country, the great majority of our travellers, particularly in their diaries and letters, have relatively little to say about what was happening on the land. Occasionally they make interesting short observations about things seen while travelling through the countryside, but it is clear that some of their remarks are superficial and often exaggerated. Although the more interesting of their observations will be made use of in this chapter, it must inevitably be based to a considerable extent on the writings of Arthur Young, a man well known for his very detailed and often pungent comments on French agriculture.

Between May 1787 and January 1790 Young made three separate journeys across France, working in short trips to Spain and Italy while he was abroad; he certainly saw very much more of France than any other traveller of the time who has left behind an account of his journeys. His *Travels in France*, best consulted in the fuller second edition of 1794, consists of the famous travel diary and his observations on the French Revolution, together with the much longer, but much less read thirty-two chapters which cover French trade and industry besides conditions on the land. Young is notorious for his sharp criticisms of these conditions; yet, as we shall see, if one gets beyond the travel diary, one finds that he was very favourably impressed with at least some aspects of French agriculture.

Although our travellers were convinced of the superiority of British agriculture over French in most respects, they did concede that in its vineyards France had an asset which had no equivalent on the British side of the Channel. In 1786 the Scottish judge, Lord Gardenstone, wrote: 'The French have this evident advantage over us in Britain, that they can profit by *our* example in the culture of grass and grain, and in improvements by inclosures and planting; whereas we can derive no advantage by *their* skill and experience in the management of vines.'[1]

The same point is made very forcefully by Young. He was struck by the high prices which vineyards commanded even though many were 'in some of the poorest soils in the kingdom, as sands, sharp gravels, and lands so stoney as to be inapplicable to the plough'. Thanks to the climate the produce of vineyards was amazingly large: 'There is no part of Europe in which a crop of wheat, of such value, is not exceedingly large, and much beyond the average.' Vineyards offered employment to vast numbers of people, not only in tending the vines, but also in making casks and obtaining the necessary wood from the forests. Above all, they gave rise 'to one of the greatest trades of export that is to be seen in Europe' as well as supplying the home market 'with a beverage, the effect of their own industry, and the result of their own labour'. And all this was obtained from France's 'sands, gravels, declivities and rocks', from 'those lands which her less fortunate neighbours are forced to cover with copse or rabbits'.[2] That this form of agriculture had one serious disadvantage — an excessive division of the land leading to much peasant poverty — is also stressed by Young, as we shall see later.

Flanders was one region of France which, as it often lay on the route British travellers followed from Calais to Paris, repeatedly earned high praise for its prosperous and technically advanced agriculture. It is true that Jardine found French Flanders decidedly inferior to the part of the region which lay in the Austrian Netherlands, where 'agriculture is still kept up to perhaps a more useful degree of perfection than even in England itself'. He goes on:

> Even in French Flanders, though the same kind of soil with the Austrian, waste and fallow lands, weeds and negligence, begin to be seen, and as we advance into France, many other sad changes for the worse we are doomed to experience. We gradually lose the noble spacious farmhouses with great barns like churches, in exchange for wretched half-ruined hovels;

we leave the comfortable neat Flemish dresses, for French rags, dirty, woollen night-caps, wooden shoes, and every sort of misery.[3]

However, this was definitely a minority view among British travellers.

Thus in describing what she saw on her way from Béthune to Lille in July 1767, Lady Mary Coke wrote: 'This country at this time of the year, from the very great richness of the Soil, and the amazing crops of all sort of grain, is a very fine sight.'[4] When Priestley accompanied Lord Shelburne on a continental tour in 1774, he was not at all impressed by the state of French agriculture around Calais; 'but', he continues in a letter to his patron's six-year-old son,

> everything wore a much better aspect as we advanced farther into the country; and yesterday, in which we travelled from St Omers to Lille, we saw every where the finest cultivation possible, and the harvest nearly got in. It seemed to be much superior to the generality of English husbandry . . .
>
> All the way we have come, we were surprised at the prodigious quantity of tall, fine beans, which are all standing, and especially with the plantations of tobacco and poppies, which are not cultivated in England. The tobacco was very green, and looked exceedingly beautiful; the poppies were all reaped and formed into sheaves or ricks. We could not imagine of what use so much poppy seed could be, but upon inquiry we were informed that they get a great deal of oil from them, and that the many windmills we saw in that neighbourhood were all employed to press that oil, which is used for lamps.[5]

In June 1785 William Bennet, Bishop of Cloyne, travelled through French Flanders with a companion who was always anxious about finding somewhere for the next meal. Hence the jocular tone of the opening sentence of his praise of the agriculture of the region:

> The fertility of French Flanders indeed is such that all idea of starving disappears at the sight of it. The whole Country is covered with the most wonderful Crops of every kind of grain, that we know, and many that we do not, and we are

forced to make exclamations every moment of wonder and delight. We see it indeed to great advantage as it is now in its full beauty, the harvest just calling for the sickle, but not a field yet touched.[6]

Perhaps the best-known eulogy of the agriculture of Flanders is that penned by Edward Rigby, who combined the practice of medicine with that of farming. Of his journey from Calais to Lille he wrote in July 1789:

> The most striking character of the country through which we passed yesterday is its astonishing fertility. We went through an extent of seventy miles, and I will venture to say there was not a single acre but was in a state of the highest cultivation. The crops are great beyond any conception I could have had of them — thousands and tens of thousands of acres of wheat superior to any which can be produced in England; oats extraordinarily large. There is also an immense quantity of beans, a good deal of flax, some tobacco, and woad, (*Isatis tinctoria*). We were told at Calais of the scarcity of corn, but there is no appearance of it here.[7]

Young too was naturally enthusiastic about the agriculture of Flanders, 'this celebrated province, which, among the French themselves, has the reputation of being the best cultivated in the kingdom'. He contrasts its agriculture with that of 'the open fields, which have travelled with me more or less, all the way from Orleans':

> After Valenciennes, the country is inclosed; here also is a line of division in another respect. The farms in the open country are generally large; but in the rich deep low vale of Flanders, they are all small, and much in the hands of little proprietors. A fourth distinction also is in the husbandry; from Orleans, nearly to Valenciennes, the course is every where similar, — 1, fallow; 2, wheat; 3, spring corn. But in Flanders the land is cropped every year . . . Wheat is not here the only dependence; flax and cole-seed excel it: and beans, carrots, turnips, and a variety of products, receive the farmer's attention sufficiently to cover the whole country with cultivation every year.[8]

Elsewhere he writes in praise of the agriculture of Flanders and part of Artois: 'Crops are in constant succession, without a fallow being known: — the superiority of the husbandry between Valenciennes and Lille may be easily conceived, from this common course: — 1, wheat, and after it turnips the same year; 2, oats; 3, clover; 4, wheat; 5, hemp; 6, wheat; 7, flax; 8, coleseed; 9, wheat; 10, beans; 11, wheat.'[9]

Flanders was by no means the only region of France whose agriculture aroused Young's approval, even his admiration; it merely came first on his list:

> ... We cannot but admit, that France is in possession of a soil, and even of a husbandry, that is to be ranked very high amongst the best in Europe. Flanders, part of Artois, the rich plain of Alsace, the banks of the Garonne, and a considerable part of Quercy, are cultivated more like gardens than farms. Perhaps they are too much like gardens, from the smallness of properties ... The rapid succession of crops, the harvest of one being but the signal of sowing immediately for a second, can scarcely be carried to greater perfection; and this in a point, perhaps of all others the most essential to good husbandry, when such crops are so justly distributed, as we generally find them in such provinces; cleaning and ameliorating ones being made the preparation for such as foul and exhaust. These are provinces, which even an English farmer might visit with advantage.[10]

Elsewhere, after mentioning the great advantages which France derived from its vineyards and the cultivation of maize, he continues: 'Olives, silk, and lucerne are not to be forgotten, nor should we omit mentioning the fine pastures of Normandy, and every article of culture in the rich acquisitions of Flanders, Alsace, and part of Artois, as well as on the banks of the Garonne. In all this extent, and it is not small, France possesses a husbandry equal to our own.'[11]

Praise of some of these regions, particularly of Alsace and the valley of the Garonne, is also to be found in the writings of other travellers. When Priestley re-entered France through Alsace on his continental tour, he wrote:

> The cultivation of all the tract of country through which we travelled along the Rhine is excellent, especially about

Manheim, and in Alsace is most excellent, resembling a rich garden. This look is much favoured by the variety of crops, and the division of fields, being often distinguished by rows of vines. All our varieties of corn, turkey wheat, canary seed, hemp, pumpkins, kidney beans, vines, turnips, potatoes, tobacco, and many other things, all intermixed in long and narrow fields, makes a new and curious spectacle to an Englishman. The roads, and also many of the fields, are planted with fruit trees, especially the walnut trees, the fruit of which is used for making oil.[12]

In his journey Young describes the road from Saverne to Strasbourg as being 'through one of the richest scenes of soil and cultivation to be met with in France, and exceeded by Flanders, only'. Once again he found, as in Flanders, a plain 'clouded with crops in endless and quick succession'. Later he points out that 'in this flat vale of rich land the fields are never fallowed; the crops substituted, and preparatory to wheat, &c. are potatoes, poppies for oil, pease, maiz, vetches, clover, beans, hemp, tobacco, and cabbages'. He repeats that Alsace is inferior to Flanders in its agriculture, giving as one reason that 'there is not an equal number of great towns to yield equal quantity of manure'.[13]

The fertility of the valley of the Garonne drew comments from various travellers besides Young. Lord Herbert on his journey from Marmande to Bordeaux speaks of 'travelling over the finest and richest & most fruitfull Country I have yet seen',[14] while even on the other side of Toulouse, coming from Castelnaudary, Bennet wrote: 'The soil was now totally alterd to a fine brown mould, so rich that the Farmer when he has cut his wheat in June, sows another crop of Maize or Indian Corn, which he reaps the beginning of October. It is now ripe, and ready for the sickle.'[15] Even in December the unidentified 'R.W.C.' found the journey along the Garonne from Bordeaux to Toulouse extremely agreeable:

You coast along the Banks of the Garonne, which is to your right, and on your left the whole face of the country wears a most joyous appearance, lofty hills, clothed with Evergreens such as Olives, Fig Trees &c which are most delightfully interspersed with Country seats, cornfields and Vineyards . . . When about half way from Toulouse, a most sensible alteration was to be observed in the atmosphere and in

Cultivation. Here the Noon was warm, mild and grateful, the young wheat was already shooting up, and the Sun made all smile around. My Portugueze friend and myself, locked arm in arm, would often quit our vehicle and, with my servant following, loiter behind the Messagerie (for that was the name of our Vehicle), listening to the chearful songs of the Peasants, who were busied on the sides of the hills lopping off last year's sprouts from the vines.[16]

Although slightly more technical, Young's comments on this region are equally enthusiastic; he describes it as 'one of the most fertile vales in Europe; the hills covered with the most productive vineyards to be met with perhaps in the world; the towns frequent and opulent; the whole country an incessant village, and all gilt and invigorated by a genial sun. He who has not viewed this animated scenery has not seen the finest thing in France. Flanders, with all its fertility of soil, has the foggy climate of the N[orth] and yields a *coup d'oeil* every where flat and *sombre*, nor are her productions, flax excepted, of equal value.'[17]

Rare indeed were the travellers who ventured into Auvergne. Of the few who did so, Wraxall wrote only of Clermont-Ferrand and missed the extremely fertile region of the Limagne, much praised by Young. Yet though he speaks of its 'extraordinary fertility' and mentions that the land 'never reposes in a fallow', he was much less impressed by its agriculture: 'Cultivation is so ill understood here, and I saw such execrable ploughing, that I am clear that the products of common crops are not by half, certainly by one-third, equal to what they ought to be, except in cases of meadow, hemp grounds, gardens, or orchards, in all which the management is excellent, and the produce adequate to the soil and culture.'[18]

Young also felt great admiration for the agriculture of parts of Normandy. He visited 'the rich pasturages, or grazing lands, of the Pays d'Auge, of which the valley of Corbon is the most famous, and classes with the finest in the world'. He maintains that 'in the vicinity of Bernay, there is some of the finest arable land to be seen in the world'. If he was highly critical of the cultivation of the province's arable land, 'nothing too great', he declares, 'can be said of the rich pasturages which are applied to fattening bullocks to the highest advantage, except in the article of the breed of the sheep that are found among the cattle. They ought to be large, and bearing long combing wool; except this point, their herbages, as they call them, are very well managed, and no want of capital appearing among them.'[19]

Although he had a poor opinion of French sheep, Young was often impressed by the fine cattle he saw, even if he declared that, taking the country as a whole, 'there is not, perhaps, a tenth of what there ought to be'. In the province of Marche he noted: 'In coming to Paris, we have met a great many droves of these oxen, to the amount, I guess, of from twelve to fifteen hundred, and they were, with few exceptions, very fat; and considering the season, May, the most difficult of the year, they were fatter than oxen are commonly seen in England, in the spring. I handled many scores of them, and found them an excellent breed, and very well fattened.' In Normandy he found the finest cattle. Thus at Pont-Audemer he noted: 'Very many fine grass inclosures, of a better countenance than any I have seen in France, without watering; grazed by good Norman cows, larger than our Alderneys, but of the same breed.' At Pont-l'Évêque, in the Pays d'Auge, he observed that this region was 'all grazed by fattening oxen: the system is nearly that of many of our English counties. In March or April, the graziers go to the fairs of Poitou and buy the oxen lean at about 240 liv. . . . At Michaelmas they are fat; and sent to the fair at Poissy, that is Paris: such as are bought in at 240 liv. lean, are sold fat at 350 to 400 liv.'[20]

French mutton Young held to be inferior to English, but although this was also true of beef in smaller towns, in many parts of France it was 'exceedingly good and well fattened; better is not to be found any where than at Paris; and I have remarked, elsewhere, the great numbers of fine oxen fattened in Limosin in winter, and in Normandy in summer, for the Paris market. I think, therefore, that the beef of England, and of the great cities in France, may very fairly be compared.'[21]

One crop which greatly impressed those travellers who explored the southern part of the country was maize. In 1763 Smollett describes how 'in passing through the Maconnois, we saw a great many fields of Indian corn, which grows to the height of six or seven feet: it is made into flour for the use of the common people, and goes by the name of *Turkey wheat*.'[22] 'This noble plant' is how Young describes maize. Elsewhere he writes:

> Perhaps it is the most important plant that can be introduced into the agriculture of any country whose climate will suit it. It is a more sure crop than wheat; its product, in the food of

man, is so considerable, that the populousness of a country is necessarily very different without, or with this article of culture; it is, at the same time, a rich meadow for a considerable part of the summer, the leaves being stripped regularly for oxen, affording a succulent, and most fattening food, which accounts for the high order of all cattle in the south of France, in Spain, and in Italy, in situations which seem to deny all common meadows.[23]

On his travels in the South Young was impressed by the attention given to irrigation. Of the journey from Avignon to L'Isle-sur-la-Sorgue he wrote: 'There can hardly be met with a richer, or better cultivated tract of sixteen miles; the irrigation is superb.' In the chapter which he devoted to the subject he writes:

In some parts of France, particularly in the southern provinces, this branch of rural economy is very well understood, and largely practised; but the most capital exertions are very much confined; I met with them only in Provence and the western mountainous parts of Languedoc. In the former, canals are cut, at the expence of the province, for conducting water many miles, in order to irrigate barren tracks of land; in England we have no idea of such a thing.[24]

Young was not much impressed with the attempts at the improvement of waste land which he encountered in France. He mentions the royal *déclaration* of 13 August 1766 which offered exemption from the *taille, capitation* and tithes on land abandoned for at least forty years which was brought under cultivation. He thought this was 'in the right spirit' and he quotes the figure of 950,000 *arpents* improved which was given by Necker for the period 1766–84. Yet he remains very sceptical about its long-term results: 'There can be bo doubt but the greater part of these are long since abandoned again to nature.' He even goes so far as to say: 'I never met with a single person in France who had half an idea of improving waste land.'

He was particularly scornful of the attempt at improvements made by some Englishmen which he found abandoned to the north of Nantes:

In the *landes*, which, strange to say, extend to within three miles of Nantes, there was an improvement attempted some years ago: four good houses of stone and slate were built, and a few acres run to wretched grass, which have been tilled, but all savage, and become almost as rough as the rest: a few of the banks have been planted . . . I inquired how the *improvement* had been effected: pare and burn; wheat; rye; oats!!! Thus it is for ever: the same methods, the same failures, the same folly, the same madness. When will men be wise enough to know, that good grass must be had, if corn is the object?

After taking immense pains to track down the estate, near Le Flèche, of the late Marquis de Turbilly, the author of the famous *Mémoire sur les défrichemens* (1760), he remarks rather coldly of the improvements which had been attempted on large areas of waste land that 'they make a much better figure in the *Memoire sur les défrichemens* than at Tourbilly'. On his way from Valogne to Cherbourg he inspected the improvements made in an area of derelict forest. Though he allowed that the enterprise had some merit, he strongly criticised the principles on which it was based:

The first business in the improvement, was to grub up the wood; then to pare and burn; and manure with lime; . . . as soon as it was cleared, it was fallowed the first year for wheat. Such infatuation is scarcely credible! A man in commencing his operations in the midst of 3000 acres of rough ground, and an immense pasturage for cattle and sheep, begins with wheat; the same follies prevail every where: we have seen just the same course pursued in England, and prescribed by writers. Such people think cattle and sheep of no importance at the beginning of these improvements.

Even the farm which he twice visited near Paris — that of a man whom he describes as 'a very intelligent cultivator' and 'the only practical farmer in the Society of Agriculture' — failed to impress him as, although he had given up fallows, he 'sows white corn twice, thrice, and even four times in succession'.[25]

There are scattered references to occasional good features of French agriculture in the writings of those travellers who had no special interest in the subject, but taken as a whole their comments, like those of Young, tend to be critical. Thus the Scottish gardener, Thomas Blaikie (his spelling is somewhat eccentric), wrote scornfully of the agriculture he encountered near Argentan:

> Although the country hereabouts is all enclosed and the soil seems good by reason of some exceeding large trees yet the culture is rediculous; in above half of there inclosures there is nothing but Broom at a prodigeous height, some I saw at least near 10 feet high. I inquired at the Steward what was the reason of there cultivating there land in that maner but he told one that it would not do otherwise, that they genersly took three crops of corn of there land and then let it run to Broom for 4 or 5 years to refresh as he caled it the ground; he told me the land in that country did not produce enough for the inhabitants; this is not surprizing after seeing there maner of culture although the soil is many places where the roads and water had hollowed out whilst from 4 or 5 feet deep of a fine light hasel loam.[26]

While, like many of our travellers (indeed like Young himself in a good part of his travel journal), Villiers was more intent on describing landscapes than making notes on agriculture, on his journey from Cherbourg to Caen he was not impressed by what he observed in the country through which he passed: 'It does not bear those marks of cultivation which I expected to have found. There is very little pasture ground and, where there is any, the herbage is thin and coarse. The fields seem to be badly cultivated, and are covered over with hillocks, and such-like rude asperities as an English farmer would be ashamed of.'[27]

The few livestock which Cole saw on his journey from Cambrai to Paris seemed to him very poor: 'Hardly a Cow to be seen for Miles, & when you do see them, they are poor starved Creatures, about half the Size of our own.'[28] Jardine offers much more detailed criticisms of French agriculture:

> Except in the wine countries, we met with little else but corn-husbandry; no proportional number of cattle, nor a grass farm to be seen, though these are probably the life and soul of agriculture. In the proper number of animals to labour, to manure, and to feed upon the land, probably consists the main spring and force of agriculture, which improves with population . . .
> The few cattle they have throughout most parts of France

are too generally but miserable carrion. The horses, the cows, the sheep, all seem of a poor degenerate race, and all of the same kind — no variety and cross-breeds of them, as in England.

Although he does allow of some exceptions, French agriculture seemed to him in a backward state:

> The corn countries of France are mostly, I think, what we should call a light soil, not much strong clay, or rich mould, not what we would esteem a fine country. Though there is, perhaps, less waste land than in England, I do not think that their soil in general is so far superior to ours than some imagine . . . We must, however, except some parts of Normandy, Burgundy, and generally the land on their great rivers, especially in the Loire, which is beautifully wooded, a rich and productive soil, and well peopled . . .
>
> The scarcity of cattle, or pasture land, and of the cultivation of grasses every where, sufficiently show their deficiency in husbandry; unacquainted with the advantages of a change of crops, and of a sufficient stock of cattle, of converting arable to pasture, and the reverse; I believe that the same crops of eternal corn, with perpetual plowings, must not only impoverish but pulverise the soil, increase its natural dry and light quality, and render it unfit for grass or meadow, without more expence, labour, and skill, than the proprietors could furnish.[29]

This was certainly a long catalogue of failings only slightly redeemed.

On the journey from Calais to Paris Mrs Piozzi noted: 'The cattle . . . are miserably poor and lean; but where there is no grass, we can scarcely expect them to be fat; they must not feed on wheat, I suppose, and cannot digest tobacco.'[30] French sheep generally created an unfavourable impression. At Boulogne Smollett observed that since the harvest had been ruined by heavy rains, all that was left was the depressing sight of 'a few flocks of meagre sheep that crop the stubble'.[31] Although Priestley greatly admired the agriculture of French Flanders, Lord Shelburne and he were evidently much entertained by the pigs they saw there. He wrote to his patron's son: 'At Bethune we were amused as we went through the market with the sight of a number of the slenderest and leanest pigs we had ever seen. They might almost have been taken for greyhounds.'[32] Another point, made most fully by Lord Gardenstone, was how poorly equipped French farms were compared with those on the other side of the Channel. He speaks of the lack of 'the proper utensils of husbandry, waggons, carts, ploughs, harrows, harness, rollers, &c. &c.' and adds: 'The useful arts are certainly brought to a perfection in Britain yet unattained on the continent' and suggests that some young men, trained by Crichton of Edinburgh, would make a fortune if they set up in other European countries.[33] Peckham observes that 'for want of money to purchase wagons' small peasants 'are obliged to carry both their corn and their hay on the backs of their cattle; and it is with much ingenuity they will load a horse till you can see only its head and feet'.[34]

In the second part of his *Travels in France* Young deals more systematically and in much greater detail with those aspects of French agriculture of which he was critical. He condemns the common practice of leaving the land fallow one year in three:

> When we see some of the finest, deepest, and most fertile loams that are to be met with in the world, such as those between Bernay and Elbeuf, and parts of the Pays de Caux, in Normandy, and the neighbourhood of Me[a]ux, in the Isle of France, destined to the common barbarous course of 1, fallow; 2, wheat; 3, spring corn; and the produce of this spring corn beneath contempt; the whole exertion and produce being seen in a crop of wheat, we must be convinced, that, agriculture, in such a kingdom, is on the same footing as in the tenth century.

He offers a comparison between the products of this system over an eleven-year period and those of a typical English rotation which would add to wheat and barley or oats a variety of other crops:

> The Englishman, in eleven years, gets three bushels more of wheat than the Frenchman. He gets three crops of barley, tares, or beans, which produce nearly twice as many bushels per acre, as the three French crops of spring corn produce. And he farther gets, at the same time, three crops of turnips and two of clover, the turnips worth 40s. the acre, and the clover 60s. that is 12 l. for both. What an enormous superiority! More wheat; almost double of the spring corn;

and above 20s. per acre per annum in turnips and clover. But farther; the Englishman's land, by means of the manure arising from the consumption of the turnips and clover, is in a constant state of improvement, while the Frenchman's farm is stationary.

He condemns even more severely the practice of leaving the land fallow one year in two. In poor provinces such as Sologne, Bourbonnais and Nivernais, he declares, 'but one feature is found . . . ; 1, fallow; 2, rye . . . It is not produce and success that should make them in love with fallows; for the farmers are as poor as their crops; the common produce is four times the seed, and they have often less.'[35]

It was not only the compulsory nature of the rotation of crops imposed on the peasants in the open field system to which Young objected; as a strong advocate of enclosures, he denounced what he called the 'detestable common rights'[36] such as the *vaine pâture* and the *droit de parcours* which prevented the peasant from enclosing his land, and the existence of large amounts of common land which he regarded as ripe for enclosure. That many poor peasants eked out an existence mainly because of the possibility of grazing some livestock on the commons and making use of other communal rights made no impression on Young since he argued that the English agricultural labourer who seldom possessed either land or cattle was much better off.

He was, of course, fully aware that even in those regions where the open field system prevailed there were pockets of enclosures and that they were the norm over a great part of the kingdom. Yet, he argued, this did not make for an improved agriculture:

> The marvellous folly is, that in nine-tenths of all the inclosures of France, the system of management is precisely the same as in the open fields; that is to say, fallows as regularly prevail, and consequently the cattle and sheep of a farm are nothing in comparison of what they ought to be . . . Sologne is inclosed, yet it is the most miserable province in France, of the same rank with Bretagne itself. The Bourbonnois, and great part of the Nevernois are inclosed; yet the course pursued is, 1, fallow; 2, rye, and 1, fallow, 2, rye, 3, left to weeds and broom — and all these on soils, as Bretagne, Sologne and the Bourbonnois, highly improveable, and capable of the best Norfolk husbandry. With such miserable systems, of what good are inclosures?[37]

He was particularly shocked by the backward state of agriculture in such areas of Central France as Sologne, Nivernais and Bourbonnais. On his first journey he was struck by what he saw of 'the miserable province of Sologne, which the French writers call the *triste* Sologne'. Yet he later observed of its soil:

If we can judge by the size and growth of every sort of wood, it has sufficient principles of fertility for the production of any crop, well adapted to the nature of its surface. In every hole, and in every ditch there is stagnant water; so that in a dry sandy country one of the first improvements would be a partial draining, which is an extraordinary circumstance. I have rarely seen a country more susceptible of improvement of the most obvious nature; nor any better adapted to the Norfolk husbandry of 1, turnips; 2, barley; 3, clover; 4, wheat.

As he regarded the land in Bourbonnais as highly improvable, he was strongly tempted to buy an estate there. 'The whole agriculture of it', he declares 'should be subservient to sheep; and the course of crops so arranged, as to keep, by means of turnips and durable cultivated grasses, as large flocks as possible . . .' This would produce corn 'and very different from the beggarly rye at present in these provinces'.[38]

Young was disgusted with the large quantities of waste land which he encountered in various parts of France such as Maine and Anjou. In his travel diary he describes his journey from La Flèche to the estate of the late Marquis de Turbilly 'across a range of such ling wastes as the Marquis speaks of in his memoir. They appear boundless here; and I was told I could travel many — many days and see nothing else.' The next day on his journey from La Flèche to Le Mans he crossed 'a quantity of moors' and was assured at one point on the way 'that they are here 60 leagues in circumference, with no great interruptions'. But it was Brittany which most horrified him from his first entry into the province. On his way from Dol to the ancestral home of the Chateaubriands at Combourg 'the country has a savage aspect; husbandry not much further advanced, at least in skill, than among the Hurons, which appears incredible amidst inclosures'. Though he made an exception for the region round St Pol-de-Léon on the northern coast, he was appalled by the amount of waste land. He found to his amazement that it reached 'within three miles of the great commercial city of Nantes'. 'Three-fourths of all Bretagne waste', he writes; '... the whole forms a picture of misery hardly to be equalled in the whole kingdom, in point of a contemptible culture'. And yet the province had many advantages:

> It was to me an astonishing spectacle, to see such a wretched state of agriculture in a province like Bretagne, which I knew enjoyed some of the most valuable privileges in the kingdom; which possessed one of the greatest linen fabrics in Europe; and which was surrounded in every part by the sea, and abounded with ports and commerce. But Flanders itself would, if cropped like Bretagne, become poor and contemptible.[39]

The neglected state of these provinces where improvements would at least double their produce seemed to Young a scandal.

Although he is sometimes regarded as a systematic denigrator of everything to do with French agriculture, we have already seen that some of the cattle which he saw on his journeys greatly impressed him. In the chapter on cattle he praises the way in which they are managed in quite a number of provinces: 'From the preceding notes it appears, that in Normandy, the Bas Poitou, Limousin, Quercy, and Guienne, the importance of cattle is pretty well understood; in some districts very well; and that in the pasturage part of Normandy, the quantity is well proportioned to the richness of the country.' However, he was extremely critical of what he had seen over the greater part of the kingdom, for he goes on:

> In all the rest of the kingdom, which forms the greater part of it, there is nothing that attracts notice. There would, in eighteen-twentieths of it, be scarcely any cattle at all, were it not for the practice of ploughing with them . . .
>
> On an average of the kingdom, there is not, perhaps, a tenth of what there ought to be: and of this any one must be convinced, who reflects, that the courses of crops throughout the kingdom are calculated for corn only; generally bread corn; and that no attention whatever is paid to the equally important object of supporting great herds of cattle, for raising manure, by introducing the culture of plants that make cattle the preparation for corn, instead of those barren fallows which are a disgrace to the kingdom. This system of

interweaving the crops which support the cattle, among those of corn, is the pillar of English husbandry, without which our agriculture would be as miserable and unproductive as that of France.[40]

Young was not impressed with the sheep and pigs which he saw in France. No doubt one must not take as typical the wretched animals which he saw in a small town between Verdun and Metz: 'Leave Mars-la-Tour at four in the morning: the village herdsman was sounding his horn; and it was droll to see every door vomiting out its hogs or sheep, and some a few goats, the flock collecting as it advances. Very poor sheep, and the pigs with mathematical backs, large segments of small circles. They must have abundance of commons here, but, if I may judge by the report of the animals' carcases, dreadfully overstocked.' He was none the less highly critical of the place occupied by sheep in French agriculture — the poor breeds, bad management, their very small numbers and the consequent necessity for importing large quantities of wool. He sums up on the subject in his usual forthright manner:

> The management of sheep, throughout the kingdom, is the most abominable that can be conceived. It appears, by the notes, that in winter they are, according to our ideas, universally starved; that is, fed upon straw; for as to a provision of green winter food, cultivated purposely for them, of which no good farmer in England is ever destitute, there is not such a practice in France, from one end of the kingdom to the other. The consequences of this, are these poor fleeces, a bad quality of wool, and one sheep kept where there might be an hundred. Hence also the necessity of an immence import of every kind of wool; and, what is still much worse, such a deficiency of sheep in eighteen-twentieths of the kingdom, that every article of husbandry suffers; and meat is so much dearer than bread, that it cannot be purchased by the poor.

Young returns to the topic in the chapter on French trade where he points out that her exports of woollen goods did not equal her imports of the raw material: 'Considering the climate, soil, and population of the kingdom, this state of her woollen trade certainly indicates a most gross neglect. For want of having improved the breed of her sheep, her wools are very bad, and she is obliged to import, at a heavy expence, other wools, some of which are by no means good, — and thus her manufactures are under a heavy disadvantage, on account of the low state of agriculture.'[41]

Young was astonished at the small amount of capital that the French peasant, even a fairly prosperous one, had at his disposal:

> The pastures of Normandy, and the arable lands of Flanders, and part of Artois, are well stocked; but there is a great deficiency in every other part of the kingdom, even in the best provinces. The quantity of sheep and cattle is every where trifling, in comparison with what it ought to be. The implements of husbandry are contrived for cheapness, not for duration and effect; and such stacks of hay in store, as are found all over England, are rarely seen in France. Improvements invested in the land, by marling, draining, &c., which, on farms in England, amount to large sums of money, are inconsiderable even in the best parts of France.

If the capital invested in the land by the tenant was inadequate, so was the landlord's share: 'The investments, which in England fall back upon the landlord, such as all sorts of conveniences in building, fencing, gates, stiles, posts, rails &c., which he must provide or repair for a new tenant, are done in England at an expence unknown in the greatest part of France.' Although he makes an exception for the large and substantial buildings to be found in a few provinces, especially in the north of the country, he estimates that at least twice as much was spent in England as in France on 'building, inclosing, marling, claying, draining, laying to meadow, and other *permanent* improvements'.

Although on his travels Young did see some agricultural implements which he admired, in general he found them much inferior to those in use in England and clearly attributed part of their deficiencies to the small amount of money spent on them: 'Upon the implements in general, I may observe, that they will in all countries be proportioned to the wealth of the farmers. There is nothing in the kingdom comparable to those which we see in every part of England, where the implements of husbandry are carried to a perfection of which one sees nothing in any other country which I have viewed.'[42]

It is not always easy to determine the standpoint from which some of our travellers judged the considerable amount of poverty which undoubtedly existed in the French countryside on the eve of the Revolution. Occasionally one has the feeling that they somehow imagined that poverty on the land was unknown in the England of their day and that there was no such thing as a Poor Law. Certainly there are moments when one feels that an excessively gloomy picture of life on the land is produced by their often brief and superficial comments on what they observed.

Generalisations about the lot of the peasants are found alongside comments on what travellers actually observed in particular regions of the country. To the first category belong the observations of Jervis, who was critical of other sections of French society, but had a soft spot for the peasants in their downtrodden state: 'This useful and laborious body of people, which forms the bulk of the Nation, is held in the most Abject subjection. They are Naturally a harmless, cheerfull and courteous people whom nothing but the extreeme necessity of Hunger can induce to offend the Law. Both Men and Women are remarkably industrious and cheerfull even under oppression.'[43] Jardine's remarks on this subject are rather mournful: 'Their own countries are mostly large, naked, melancholy plains, without trees, fences or divisions, and thinly inhabited by a poor, weak and sickly race too often in rags and wooden shoes; thus the labouring and most useful part of the nation is considered and treated with rigour and contempt'; or again, 'On examining the country, and seeing how the people live, — bread almost their only food, and not always good, nor plenty: so small a share of the fruits of their own labour for themselves, and that share not very secure: though often apparently contented and happy, we must doubt the reality of their happiness.'[44]

Thicknesse certainly appears to view the poverty which he saw in the French countryside as if in England prosperity was universal: 'The poverty of the peasants takes much away from the beauties the yet delightful country would otherwise afford, could we meet, as we do in most parts of England, with tight, little cottages, inhabited by clean, decent-appearing men, women, and children; but amongst the peasants in France, no such poor are to be seen, no such houses are to be found. Dirt, extreme poverty, ignorance, and boldness, without any sense of shame, universally prevails.'[45]

With these generalisations we may compare some first impressions of travellers on their way from Calais. Thus Burney wrote of the journey from St Omer to Béthune: 'The country much the same as yesterday, but better the further one is off from Calais . . .

But whether the country is rich or otherwise, there is always an appearance of great poverty and wretchedness in the inhabitants; more, indeed, from their garb, than countenance, though they have not quite that gaiety there which is to be met with in other parts of France. The Flamands were always a heavy people.'[46] Entering France from the east on his way through Dunkirk and Gravelines to Calais, Cayley was struck by the amount of poverty which he saw: 'As we passed through some villages, I observed the peasants seemed poor indeed: several little boys and girls barefooted and ragged running along the chaise side and begging hard for some small money. The villages in Holland and Flanders have a much more pleasing appearance of plenty than here.'[47] Yet the same experience was seen in a different light by Essex when he made the same journey in the opposite direction: 'We had on one side the Sea which afforded a pleasing prospect, on the other we saw many prity villages, in those we passed through we were much troubled with the children of the Cottagers who ran after us begging for Alms but though they were poor they appeared much cleaner more healthy and better cloathed than the people of that Class do in England.'[48] This is a most unusual concession for one of our travellers to make.

Although on the journey through St Omer and Péronne to Paris in 1763, Garrick declared that he had formed a more favourable opinion of the countryside than on his visit in 1751, he observed that 'the appearance of Poverty among the lower sort was very great'.[49] Proceeding in the opposite direction, from Chantilly to Calais, Peckham noted the absence of traffic and 'but now and then a straggling village swarming with beggars; a dreary prospect indeed, where every object betrayed the strongest symptoms of poverty and distress'.[50]

Of a journey in a much less frequented region, from Cherbourg south to Coutances, Wraxall was pleased with the varied landscape, but once again we find in him a traveller taking a somewhat rosy view of conditions in the English countryside: 'There is notwithstanding an apparent penury in the dwellings of the people. The hand of oppression is visible in their dress, their hovels, and their whole appearance. I saw none of those neat and pretty peasants so common in our most secluded villages.'[51] Jervis, after declaring that the villages he encountered between Paris and Lyons, were 'a Chaos of dung & dirt', goes on: 'Most of their Peasants make a most wretched appearance, & we scarce observ'd one among the lower Class of an healthy, manly figure, unless in the Army, among the Perruquiers or Laquays.'[52] On the other side of France, in travelling from Souillac to Uzerche, a woman in Lord Clive's party touring France in 1768 wrote: 'It is surprising to me that this Garden of France is not better inhabited, for except Brives, a tolerable town . . . , the Towns & villages in this part of the province are miserable, and the people bear the strongest marks of poverty and wretchedness.'[53]

Despite the attractions of Provence for British tourists, the lack of fertility in most of the land inevitably led to much peasant poverty: as Lord Gardenstone put it, 'we observed the symptoms of corresponding poverty among the peasants; meagre and pallid looks of men and women; two asses in each of the scratching ploughs; and sheep kept from starving by shaking down the autumnal leaves of those trees.'[54] A similar picture of Provençal poverty is presented even more forcefully by *The Gentleman's Guide*: 'You will no doubt be astonish'd at the dirt and poverty that prevails in this garden of France, as it is term'd, only (as I apprehend) because oranges and lemons grow there, and almost in as great perfection as in the West-Indies; the people, by their rags and meagre yellow look, shew, very conspicuously, the misery that reigns amongst them, proceeding more from the barrenness of the country (which is mostly rocks and pebbles) than their own indolence, though a person who did not make enquiries, would think their distresses partly owing to that.'[55] Smollett extends this gloomy picture to the whole of the southern half of the country when he writes: 'The peasants on the South of France are poorly clad, and look as if they were half starved, diminutive, swarthy, and meagre.'[56]

It is obvious that such generalisations, whether they concern the French peasantry as a whole or their condition in particular regions, do not take one very far. However, once again Young does allow the reader to form a reasonably clear picture of the very wide range of wealth and poverty to be found on the land. He makes it clear that there were well-to-do peasants, though they formed a very small minority. In his classification of the different types of land tenure he lists 'hiring at money rent, as in England',[57] and elsewhere he speaks of 'large farms let at a money-rent in the north of France',[58] of which the farm he twice visited at Dugny near Paris was an example. He relates how while he was staying at Liancourt, he was invited by the Duke to attend a dinner of the provincial assembly of Clermont:

> Three considerable farmers, renters, not proprietors of land, were members, and present. I watched their carriage narrowly, to see their behaviour in the presence of a great lord of the first rank, considerable property and high in royal favour; and it was with pleasure that I found them behaving with becoming ease and freedom, and though modest, and without anything like flippancy, yet without any obsequiousness offensive to English ideas. They stated their opinions freely, and adhered to them with becoming confidence.[59]

Again, on visiting the Pays d'Auge, he observed that 'these Norman graziers are generally rich'[60] — once more an example of how a small minority of those on the land were far removed from the class of poverty-stricken peasants whose existence is remarked upon in so many travellers' accounts. However, he also noted that, as leases were short, there was little incentive for tenants to carry out improvements: 'Leases are generally for nine years; and a tenantry fixed in confidence upon estates is rarely found'; or, as he puts it more strikingly in his travel journal, 'a peasant does not think of rendering his pig comfortable, if his own happiness hangs by the thread of a nine years lease'.[61]

A great deal of the land of France was in the hands of the clergy, nobility and middle classes, but none the less the peasants owned a considerable share. Yet as they greatly outnumbered all other landowners, the individual holding was often small, indeed almost insignificant. Although Young was hostile to small farms, he was quite enraptured with those which he found near Pau:

> A succession of many were well built, tight, and COMFORTABLE farming cottages, built of stone, and covered with tiles; each having its little garden, inclosed by clipt thorn hedges, with plenty of peach and other fruit-trees, some fine oaks scattered in the hedges, and young trees nursed up with so much care, that nothing but the fostering attention of the owner could effect anything like it. To every little house belongs a farm, perfectly well inclosed, with grass borders mown and neatly kept around the corn fields, with gates to pass from one inclosure to another. The men are all dressed with red caps, like the highlanders of Scotland. There are some parts of England (where small yeoman still remain) that

resemble this country of Bearne; but we have very little that is equal to what I have seen in this ride of twelve miles from Pau to Moneng. It is all in the hands of little proprietors, without the farms being so small as to occasion a vicious and miserable population. An air of neatness, warmth, and comfort breathes over the whole. It is visible in their new built houses and stables; in their little gardens; in their hedges; in the courts before their doors; even in the coops for their poultry, and the sties for their hogs.[62]

In his general survey of French agriculture he does concede that as small proprietors were to be found in a number of the most fertile regions of France, some of these were relatively prosperous:

The small properties of the peasants are found every where, to a degree we have no idea of in England; they are found in every part of the kingdom, even in those provinces where other tenures prevail; but in Quercy, Languedoc, the whole district of the Pyrenees, Bearn, Gascoign, part of Guienne, Alsace, Flanders, and Loraine, they abound to a greater degree than common. In Flanders, Alsace, on the Garonne, and Bearn, I found many in comfortable circumstances, such as might rather be called small farmers than cottagers, and in Bas Bretagne, many are reputed rich, but in general they are poor and miserable, much arising from the minute division of their little farms among all the children. In Loraine, and the part of Champagne that joins it, they are quite wretched. I have, more than once, seen division carried to such excess, that a single fruit tree, standing in about ten perch of ground, has constituted a farm, and the local position of a family decided by the possession.

While willing to admit that the possession of a small landed property gave rise to the most unremitting industry, he repeatedly criticises the excessive division of the soil which he found in many provinces:

Forty or fifty acres in property are not incapable of good husbandry; but when divided, twenty acres *must* be ill cultivated; again divided, they become farms of ten acres, of five, of two, and even one; and I have seen some of half, and even a quarter of a rood, with a family as much attached to it, as if it were an hundred acres. The population flowing from this division is, in some cases, great, but it is the multiplication of wretchedness. Couples marry and procreate on the *idea*, not the *reality*, of a maintenance; they increase beyond the demand of towns and manufactures; and the consequence is, distress, and numbers dying of diseases, arising from insufficient nourishment. Hence, therefore, small properties, much divided, prove the greatest source of misery that can be conceived.

Again and again Young denounces the poverty and poor husbandry produced by what he regarded as an excessive division of the land:

... I would prohibit the division of small farms, which is as mischievous to cultivation, as it is sure to be distressing to the people ... Go to districts where the properties are minutely divided, and you will find (at least I have done it universally), great distress, and even misery, and probably very bad agriculture. Go to others, where such subdivision has not taken place, and you will find a better cultivation, and infinitely less misery; and if you would see a district, with as little distress in it as is consistent with the political system of the old government of France, you must assuredly go where there are no little properties at all. You must visit the great farms in Beauce, Picardy, part of Normandy, and Artois, and there you will find no more population than what is regularly employed and regularly paid; and if in such districts you should, contrary to this rule, meet with much distress, it is twenty to one but that it is in a parish which has some commons that tempt the poor people to have some cattle — to have property — and in consequence misery.

Such peasants, Young argues, would be better off as landless labourers; he points to the example of England where one finds 'a set of peasants well cloathed, well nourished, tolerably drunken from superfluity, well lodged and at their ease; and yet amongst them, not one in a thousand has either land or cattle'.[63]

Another section of the peasantry among which Young found a great deal of poverty was the *métayers* (sharecroppers) who, being unable to pay a money rent, received from their landlords both the land and the stock necessary for it, and in return gave them a share of the crop, generally one half. His verdict on *métayage* is harsh. He saw no merit whatsoever in what, passing through Sologne on his first journey in France, he describes as 'a miserable system, that perpetuates poverty'. Two years later, in Bourbonnais, he was assured by a nobleman 'that estates were rather given away than sold: that the *metayers* were so miserably poor, it was impossible for them to cultivate well'. Later he stresses (not without some exaggeration) how widespread the system was in France and also offers a detailed account of some of the varied forms which it assumed:

> This is the tenure under which, perhaps, seven-eighths of the lands of France are held; it pervades almost every part of Sologne, Berry, La Marche, Limosin, Anjou, Bourbonnois, Nevernois, Auvergne, &c. and is found in Bretagne, Maine, Provence, and all the southern counties, &c. In Champagne there are many at *tier franc*, which is a third of the produce, but in general it is half. The landlord commonly finds half the cattle and half the seed; and the metayer labour, implements, and taxes; but in some districts the landlord bears a share of these. In Berry some are at half, some one-third, some one-fourth produce. In Rousillon the landlord pays half the taxes; and in Guienne, from Auch to Fleuran, many landlords pay all. Near Aiguillon, on the Garonne, the metayers furnish half the cattle . . .

Young's repeated denunciations of *métayage* are perhaps best summed up in a passage in which, after stressing how much the landlord loses by the system, he goes on: 'In this most miserable of all the modes of letting land, after running the hazard of such losses, fatal in many instances, the defrauded landlord receives a contemptible rent; — the farmer is in the lowest state of poverty; — the land is miserably cultivated; and the nation suffers as severely as the parties themselves.'[64]

What made worse the lot of the poorer peasants and, with those that were better off, blocked the road to agricultural improvements, was the heavy burden of direct taxation. The *taille*, the principal direct tax, was theoretically less heavy in the so-called *pays d'états*, where it was levied by the provincial estates and where it was *réelle*, i.e. levied on the amount of land held, in contrast to the system in the greater part of the country where it was *personnelle*, i.e. levied on estimated income. In *The Wealth of Nations*

The Land and the Peasants

Adam Smith has some critical observations to offer on the French system of direct taxation, especially as it affected the peasants. He stresses particularly the bad effects which it had on agriculture in the provinces where the *taille* was *personnelle*:

> ... The farmer is commonly assessed in proportion to the stock which he appears to employ in cultivation. He is, upon this account, frequently afraid to have a good team of horses or oxen, but endeavours to cultivate with the meanest and most wretched instruments of husbandry that he can. Such is his distrust in the justice of his assessors, that he counterfeits poverty, and wishes to appear scarce able to pay anything, for fear of being obliged to pay too much ... The publick, the farmer, the landlord, all suffer more or less by this degraded cultivation.

He also points out that the main burden of the *capitation* fell on the peasants, on 'those subject to the taille, who are assessed to the capitation at so much of what they pay to that other tax'.[65]

On his travels round France Young too heard many complaints of the injustices in the levying of the *taille*, even in those provinces which had estates. The splendid roads which he encountered in Languedoc were paid for by '*tailles*, and, in making the assessment, lands held by a noble tenure are so much eased, and others by a base one so burthened, that 120 arpents in this neighbourhood, held by the former, pay 90 livres, and 400 possessed by a plebeian right, which ought proportionally to pay 300 liv. is, instead of that, assessed at 1400 livres'.[66] It was, however, against the arbitrary manner in which the *taille personnelle* and the *capitation* were levied over the greater part of the country that he directed his main fire in his chapter on the Revolution. He denounces the enormous power wielded in these matters by the *Intendant* 'who could exempt, change, add, or diminish at pleasure'.[67] In any case, he asks, 'what must have been the state of the poor people paying heavy taxes, from which the nobility and clergy were exempted? A cruel aggravation of their misery, to see those who could afford to pay, exempted because able!' While condemning the excesses and cruelties which took place on the land in 1789, Young asks whether the oppression under which the peasants had suffered was not to blame for them. 'Who gives us the awards of the Intendant and his sub-delegues', he asks among other pointed questions, 'which took off the taxes of a man of fashion, and laid them with accumulated weight, on the poor, who were so unfortunate as to be his neighbours?'

He saw in heavy taxation the main obstacle to France developing at least a prosperous minority among its peasants: 'That the tenantry should generally be poor, will not be thought strange, when the taxes laid upon them are considered; their tailles and capitation are heavy in themselves; and the weight being increased by being laid arbitrarily, prosperity and good management are little more than signals for a higher assessment. Under such a system, a wealthy tenantry, on arable land, can hardly arise.' 'A rich man', he writes elsewhere, 'will affect poverty to escape the arbitrary rise of a tax, which professes to be in proportion to his power of bearing it: hence poor cattle, poor implements, and poor dung-hills, even on the farms of men who could afford the best.'[68]

Another burden on the peasants, the *corvée* — forced labour on the roads for so many days in the year — leads Adam Smith to contrast the very different ways in which the same business was handled in Britain and France:

> Under the local or provincial administration of the justices of the peace in Great Britain, the six days labour which the country people are obliged to give to the reparation of the highways, is not always perhaps very judiciously applied, but it is scarce ever exacted with any circumstance of cruelty or oppression. In France, under the administration of the intendants, the application is not always more judicious, and the execution is frequently the most cruel and oppressive. Such Corvées, as they are called, make one of the principal instruments of tyranny by which those officers chastise any parish or *communeauté* which has had the misfortune to fall under their displeasure.[69]

The *corvée* is also vigorously denounced by Walpole, who describes it as 'the quintessence of cruel and ostentatious despotism'. He was indignant when he received a copy of the proceedings of the Paris *Parlement* early in 1776 and read the speech of the *avocat général* opposing Turgot's plan to replace it by a tax payable by all landowners:

> He tells the King, that the intended tax on the proprietors of land will affect the property not only of the rich, but of the poor. I should be glad to know what is the property of the

poor? Have the poor landed estates? Are those who have landed estates the poor? Are the poor who will suffer by the tax, the wretched labourers who are dragged from their famishing families to work on the roads?[70]

Young too was highly critical of this institution. On his first French journey he was struck by the fine roads between Boulogne and Montreuil, 'which', he declares, 'would fill me with admiration, if I had known nothing of the abominable *corvées* that make me commiserate the oppressed farmers, from whose extorted labour this magnificence has been wrung'. In his chapter on the Revolution he declares that the *corvées* 'were annually the ruin of many hundreds of farmers' and that 'more than 300 were reduced to beggary in filling up one lane in Loraine'. He also denounces the militia, another burden which fell on the peasants alone, giving characteristically as his reason that the exemption of married men 'occasioned in some degree that mischievous population, which brought beings into the world in order for little else but to be starved'. He delivers too a fierce tirade against the salt tax (*gabelle*) which, as we have seen,[71] varied enormously from one part of the country to another. 'All families, and persons liable to the *taille*, in the provinces of *Grandes Gabelles*', declares Young, are 'inrolled, and their consumption of salt for the *pot* and *salière* (that is the daily consumption, exclusive of salting meat, &c. &c.) estimated at 7 lb. a head per annum, which quantity they are forced to buy whether they want it or not, under the pain of various fines according to the case.' He also attacks the savage punishments inflicted on men, women and children for smuggling salt.[72]

On the whole tithes — bitterly attacked before the Revolution and rapidly abolished when it came — attracted relatively little attention from our travellers. Young actually praises the French clergy for their moderation since, unlike their English counterparts, they did not take as much as a tenth of the produce:

> In regard to the oppressions of the clergy, as to tythes, I must do that body a justice, to which a claim cannot be laid in England. Though the ecclesiastical tenth was levied in France more severely than usual in Italy, yet was it never exacted with such horrid greediness as is at present the disgrace of England. When taken in kind, no such thing was ever known in any part of France, where I made inquiries, as a tenth; it was always a twelfth, or a thirteenth, or even a twentieth of

The Land and the Peasants

the produce. And in no part of the kingdom did a new article of culture pay any thing; thus turnips, cabbages, clover, chicorée, potatoes, &c. paid nothing. In many parts, meadows were exempted. Silk worms nothing. Olives in some places paid — in more they did not. Cows nothing. Lambs from the 12th to the 21st. Wool nothing. — Such mildness, in the levy of this odious tax, is absolutely unknown in England.

None the less Young was fully aware that in the French context tithes were an additional burden to the peasant. 'But mild as it was', he continues, 'the burthen to people groaning under so many other oppressions, united to render their position so bad that no change could be for the worse.'[73]

On the subject of feudal dues — a great source of grievance to the peasants and one which was gradually to be removed by the Revolution — our travellers as a body have remarkably little to say. They seldom get beyond such vague observations as Smollett's remarks about the peasants around Boulogne: 'The peasants are often rendered desperate and savage, by the misery they suffer from the oppression and tyranny of their landlords',[74] or Peckham's list of the burdens they had to bear which includes the item: 'Add to this, that the *seignior* or lord (for all lands are held by vassalage) exacts *ad arbitrium* from his tenant.'[75]

In his chapter on the Revolution (by this time he had read many of the *cahiers*) Young admits that he had only recently come to grasp the enormous variety and weight of feudal dues:

In passing through many of the French provinces, I was struck with the various and heavy complaints of the farmers and little proprietors of the feudal grievances, with the weight of which their industry was burthened; but I could not then conceive the multiplicity of the shackles which kept them poor and depressed. I understood it better afterwards, from the conversation and complaints of some grand seigneurs, as the revolution advanced; and I then learned, that the principal rental of many estates consisted in services and feudal tenures; by the baneful influence of which the industry of the people was almost exterminated.

As well as giving a long list of these feudal dues, he also offers a passage, derived from the *cahiers*, on the abuses of the manorial courts:

59

They speak of the dispensation of justice in the manorial courts, as comprising every species of despotism; the districts indeterminate — appeals endless — irreconcilable to liberty and prosperity — and irrevocably proscribed in the opinion of the public — augmenting litigations — favouring every species of chicane — ruining the parties — not only by enormous expences on the most petty objects, but by a dreadful loss of time. The judges commonly ignorant pretenders, who hold their courts in *cabarets*, and are absolutely dependent on the seigneurs.

On his travels he only notes one clear example of the payment of feudal dues, in this case for a tiny holding in Lorraine; a woman he met there complained that 'her husband had but a morsel of land, one cow, and a poor little horse, yet they had a *franchar* (42 lb.) of wheat, and three chickens, to pay as a quit-rent to one Seigneur; and four *franchar* of oats, one chicken and 1 s. to pay to another, beside very heavy tailles and other taxes.' He mentions another encounter, this time in Berry, but seems at first a little uncertain as to this peasant's real position: 'At Vatan, I conversed with a farmer, who, for thirty sesterées of arable, and six of meadow, pays 600 liv. and eighteen septiers of corn, each twelve boiseau, that now sells at 25s. He has two oxen, six horses, eight cows, and 700 sheep. His whole rent, therefore, is about 37 l. which, for such a stock, appears ridiculous: but it seems to be a feudal rent to the seigneur, the property of the land being in the man.' The curious thing is that even Young was far from clear about the whole matter since, in dealing with the occupation of the land of France, he lists under two separate headings what he calls 'the small properties of the tenants' and 'feudal tenures'.[76]

The nobility's monopoly of its favourite sport of hunting — the hated *droit de chasse* — did not attract the attention of our travellers as much as the system of *capitaineries* which gave all the hunting rights over a whole district to various princes of the blood. This led to a large-scale ravaging of the crops all around, and any infringement of this monopoly could lead to the galleys. This provoked Young's sarcastic comment on passing by the Duc d'Orleans's ancestral seat at Villers-Cotterêts: 'The crop of this country, therefore, is princes of the blood; that is to say, hares, pheasants, deer, boars!' Earlier, on his way to Paris, he had encountered the more famous *capitainerie* of the Prince de Condé at Chantilly; this, he was told, 'is above 100 miles in circumference. That is to say, all the inhabitants for that extent are pestered with game, without permission to destroy it, in order to give one man diversion.'[77] This *capitainerie* drew the attention of various other travellers as it was on their route to and from Paris. In August 1788 Villiers wrote:

> On approaching Chantilly, we met with continued woods . . . The scenery around now began to grow new and enchanting: game of different kinds flocked about in the utmost plenty; partridges were running before us on the road, as numerous and as tame as sparrows in England; pheasants at every step were as plenty as our turkeys, and stood unmoved, and staring at us as we drove by; whilst hares, deers, and rabbits, skipped about us in numbers. The happy retreat and sanctuary which this spot affords them, contributes to their increase, and renders them so tame; — as no one dares destroy them, under pain of perpetual condemnation to the gallies. A punishment so severe, for a crime so trivial, operates as a total prevention.[78]

Writing of his stay in Marseilles and of the galley slaves whom he saw there, Armstrong ('Lancelot Temple') deplores the fact that 'many of these poor Creatures have lost their Liberty, and are condemned to a life of nasty misery and ignominy for small Offences; such as the inexpiable Crime of having murdered a *royal* Hare or Partridge, or a most *noble* Pheasant'.[79]

In eighteenth-century England the wearing of wooden shoes in France was generally taken to be a sign of the poverty of all the inhabitants. These matters were, of course, relative, as Adam Smith, who knew his France well, points out:

> Custom . . . has rendered leather shoes a necessary of life in England. The poorest creditable person of either sex would be ashamed to appear in publick without them. In Scotland, custom has rendered them a necessary of life to the lowest order of men; but not to the same order of women, who may, without any discredit, walk about bare-footed. In France, they are necessaries neither to men nor to women; the lowest rank of both sexes appearing there publickly, without any discredit, sometimes in wooden shoes, and sometimes bare-footed.[80]

Sabots are frequently mentioned in the various travellers' accounts. Walker, for instance, describing the inhabitants to be met on his journey from La Charité to Fontainebleau, writes: 'The people . . . are coarsely cloathed; and men and women wear wooden shoes, which is a piece of birch or beech wood hollowed into the shape of a foot: it feels very hard to the foot, though children wear them as soon as they can walk.'[81] Peckham was even less attracted by them. 'The peasants . . . , poor devils, have no stockings, and wear large wooden shoes, lined sometimes with a piece of sheepskin to prevent galling, but that is a piece of luxury you seldom meet with.'[82] An anonymous traveller rejects the connection generally made between poverty and wooden shoes, though he can scarcely be right to state that they were unknown in the southern half of the country. Returning northwards from the Mediterranean coast he wrote: 'At Roanne we find ourselves again completely in the land of wooden shoes for [in] the southern provinces no such thing is seen. They seem to be no proof of poverty or misery. Normandy is esteemed the richest province of France. Nowhere do the peasantry wear a more comfortable appearance & these wooden shoes are universal among them.'[83]

Men without any kind of footwear were occasionally encountered, but with women this happened much more frequently. After crossing the Dordogne, Young noted: 'All the country girls and women are without shoes or stockings; and the ploughmen at their work have neither sabots nor feet to the stockings.'[84] On first landing at Calais Rigby was struck by the appearance of some of the women: 'Those of the lower class seem uncommonly strong and muscular; their legs are quite naked, with neither shoe nor stocking; and those who have shoes and stockings have petticoats no less short, but they are used to it and do not blush.'[85]

Numerous travellers, male as well as female, were shocked by the miserable lives led by women of the poorer section of the peasantry. Entering France from Germany and passing through Champagne, Lady Mary Coke wrote: 'The women seem to do the Men's business in almost all the Countrys I have passed through. 'Tis them that reap the corn, look after the Vines, & some I have seen following the plow, all which imployments seem more properly to belong to the Men.'[86]

There is plenty of evidence that many peasant women rapidly lost their youthful air. Commenting on women at work in the fields in the South of France, the author of *Travels into France and Italy* declares: 'I have seen women of eighteen look like women of fifty in England.'[87] In the same area Muirhead wrote: 'The women work much in the fields, and not a few of them without stockings or shoes, or even covering upon the head to screen them from the sun. Hence so many prematurely brown and withered complexions among the female peasantry.'[88] Speaking of the inhabitants of French Flanders, a region with which he was greatly impressed, Rigby found 'the women of the lower class . . . strong and well made', noting that 'they seem to do a great deal of labour, especially in the country. They carry great burdens, and seem to be employed to go to market with the produce of the fields and gardens on their heads.' Rather surprisingly, Rigby does not share the common reaction among travellers to this state of affairs. 'An Englishwoman', he continues, 'would, perhaps, think this hard, but the cottagers in England are certainly not so well off; I am sure they do not look so happy.'[89] Young has a number of passages on the hard lot of many countrywomen; for instance, his comment on his journey from Morlaix to Brest: 'The women seemed from their persons and features to be harder worked than horses.' The most telling is perhaps the one which concludes his account of a chance meeting with a poor peasant woman in Lorraine on 12 July 1789:

> This woman, at no great distance, might have been taken for sixty or seventy, her figure was so bent, and her face so furrowed and hardened by labour, — but she said she was only twenty-eight. An Englishman, who has not travelled, cannot imagine the figure made by infinitely the greater part of the countrywomen in France; it speaks, at the first sight, hard and severe labour: I am inclined to think, that they work harder than the men, and this, united with the more miserable labour of bringing a new race of slaves into the world, destroys all symmetry of person and every feminine appearance.[90]

The housing, particularly of the poorer section of the peasants, arouses some contradictory judgements. Up in the mountains, on his way from Lyons to Grenoble, Pennant noted: 'In these parts the houses are made of mud plaistered over with lime, but all looked neat, — far superior to most of ours in the distant parts of England.'[91] Less flattering accounts of peasant housing are not hard to come by. Near Remiremont, in Lorraine, Romilly's sister, Catherine Roget, was not impressed with the local variety:

The houses in this part of the country are covered with small square pieces of wood instead of tiles, and have no chimneys, the smoke either passing through a door or window. About a mile from here we had a proof of the inconvenience of this kind of thing. A whole hamlet consisting of eleven houses which, though they were built of stone, and some of them stood a distance from the others, were all burnt down from one of them catching fire.[92]

Much worse was the housing which Muirhead found among the peasants in the Vosges: 'Their huts, adjected to eminences, or, sunk in the earth, are damp and comfortless. A thin partition separates the cattle from the family, and the dung is heaped up before the door.'[93] On his travels round France Young did occasionally find good cottages such as those of the prosperous smallholders of Béarn and again between Souillac and Cahors, though the latter, if 'exceedingly well built, of stone and slate or tiles', had no glass in the windows. He even has high praise for the building methods which he found used in the country between Carentan and Coutances: 'They build in this country the best mud houses and barns I ever saw, excellent habitations, even of three stories, and all of mud, with considerable barns and other offices.'[94]

Yet Young also encountered examples of bad rural housing. On his return to France from Italy through Pont-de-Beauvoisin at the end of 1789, he greatly admired the scenery, but not the houses 'which, instead of being well built, and white as in Italy, are ugly thatched mud cabins, without chimneys, the smoke issuing at a hole in the roof, or at the windows. Glass seems unknown.' Between Toulouse and Montauban he encountered 'cottages without glass, and some with no other light than what enters at the door' and near Vannes in Brittany 'many cabins almost as bad as the worst Irish, a hole in the corner by way of chimney, and no windows'.[95]

The diet of the mass of the rural population was monotonous and often clearly inadequate to maintain health. 'A Frenchman, at an average', wrote Smollett, 'eats three times the quantity of bread that satisfies a native of England, and indeed it is undoubtedly the staff of his life.'[96] An entry in Young's travel journal brings out vividly the enormous place which this item of food played in the life of the peasants. At a little country town near Bayonne he noted:

Fair day, and the place crouded with farmers; I saw the soup prepared for what we should call the farmer's ordinary; there was a mountain of sliced bread, the colour of which was not inviting; ample provision of cabbage, grease, and water, and about as much meat for some scores of people as half a dozen English farmers would have eaten, and grumbled at their host for short commons.[97]

The crucial importance of bread is underlined by *The Gentleman's Guide* which praises the *arrêt du conseil* of 1731 which made it difficult to convert corn land into a vineyard:

> They have an excellent law in France, which turns out to the public good, but particularly to the industrious poor, and middling sort of house-keepers; as it keeps bread in general one third cheaper than it is in England: a farmer cannot plant any piece of ground with vines, (except it is his garden) without having tried it three years following in different sorts of grain; if he then finds (after all his endeavours) that the produce will not pay his rent, he is to appear before the intendant or a magistrate, and make his affidavit, that he has tried all ways and means to make it fertile, and that it will not answer; in consequence of which, he has free permission to turn it into a vineyard: was not this law in force, (as they profit considerably more by their wines) a great scarcity of grain would ensue, and consequently the poor (as bread is the greatest part of their diet) must be driven to great difficulties.[98]

This point is underlined repeatedly by Young both in his travel journal and in the more technical parts of *Travels in France*. According to him, in France 'the division of property has unhappily nursed up a population, which she cannot feed', with the result that distress is caused by 'the least failure in the crops; such a deficiency, as in England passes almost without notice, in France is attended with dreadful calamities'. He returns to this point in the chapter on population where he argues that France would be better off if she had five or six million inhabitants fewer. That a traveller should 'see at every turn most unequivocal signs of distress' is not surprising in view of 'the price of labour, and of provisions, and the misery into which a small rise in the price of wheat throws the lower classes; a misery, that is sure to increase itself by the alarm it excites, lest subsistence should be wanted'.[99]

Wheat was rarely consumed by the poorer peasants, but if its price rose, that of such cheaper cereals as rye and buckwheat rose even more sharply. Young found both these cereals cultivated in the poorer regions of France. He noted the use made of buckwheat in various parts of the country — in Sologne, where 'poor labourers make bread of buck-wheat, but very poor'; near Limoges where 'they eat buck-wheat made in thin cakes without leaven'; and near Bagnères-de-Luchon, where the poor 'live upon buck-wheat, either made into bread or boiled in milk'.[100] He was scornful of the French addiction to growing rye: 'The quantity of rye, in every part of France, even in the richest provinces, is probably one of the grossest absurdities in the agriculture of Europe; wheat is almost every where stained with it, to use the farmer's language. Yet throughout that whole kingdom, there is hardly any soil to be found bad enough to demand rye.'[101] In the parts of the country in which the climate allowed maize to be grown, it too provided food for humans as well as livestock. Young, a great admirer of maize, declared that 'a country, whose soil and climate admit the course of 1, maiz; 2, wheat; is under a cultivation that, perhaps yields the most food for man and beast, that is possible to be drawn from the land.'

In comparing conditions in England and France, Young points out that while bread was very much dearer in England, the French price was often for bread made with inferior grains:

> Bread in England may be reckoned at 1 3/4d a pound, but we must not, therefore, conclude, that it is near double the French price; for the materials are not the same. In England, it is generally made of wheat, and the poor, in many parts of the kingdom, eat the whitest and best, but in France, the bread, minuted in the preceding notes, is often of rye or other grains; so that the price is not double for the *same* bread; though there is cent. per cent. variation in the price of the bread consumed by the poor of the two countries. Bread being so much cheaper in France, in comparison of meat, than it is in England, occasions that great consumption of bread in France, in preference to meat, which the French poor rarely eat.

That the diet of the poorer classes before 1789 was largely vegetarian seems well established, but one cannot help finding somewhat excessive what follows: 'The consumption of cheese in England, by the poor, is immense. In France they eat none at at all.'[102] This was surely something which must have varied from region to region. Of the peasants whom he met in the Vosges near Plombières, Muirhead wrote: 'The peasants subsist chiefly on the produce of the dairy, and a coarse sort of bread of barley and oats, seldom tasting butcher meat or wine.'[103]

The spread of the potato in France seems to have been very patchy; consequently it gives rise to contradictory reports from our travellers. Blaikie, on a journey from Caen to Le Havre, noted: 'Inquired after some potatoes for planting, but did not find any; this seems little known in France.'[104] Nearly a decade later Lord Gardenstone, while travelling down the Saône valley to Lyons, commented on the absence of potatoes, though he was 'persuaded they might have great and useful crops of them in their light grounds'. Yet six days later, on his way down the Rhône valley, he noted: 'I have seen, in the course of this day's journey, several fields of potatoes.'[105] In the following year, in Lorraine, Muirhead observed that there the prejudice against the potato was giving ground: 'Some attention has even been bestowed upon the culture of the potato: for experience, the safest of all instructors, will conquer at last the combined influence of vulgar and learned prejudice.'[106] On this last point, Young's observations overlap with those of Muirhead since he writes that the potato was much more cultivated 'in Loraine and Franche Comte, than in any other parts of the kingdom with which I am acquainted'. On the other hand, when passing through the eastern part of Brittany, he noted: 'No potatoes in the country, as the people will not touch them', and he maintains that his notes show that 'it is in very few of the French provinces where this useful root is commonly found'.[107]

There were regions in France in which chestnuts formed the principal part of the peasants' diet. On his way south to Limoges, Young was tremendously impressed with the chestnut trees: 'They are spread over all the fields, and yield the food of the poor.'[108]

The growth in population had led to an increase in the number of landless or nearly landless peasants who were compelled to seek work as day labourers. Their wages and those of the members of their family were low. Young devotes a good deal of attention to this subject. He gives up several pages to notes on the rates paid in different parts of the country. Unfortunately he does not make it clear which of these were agricultural wages, and one cannot make much of such generalisations as 'Average earnings of men throughout the kingdom 19s.; mason and carpenter 30s.' or 'country labour being 76 per cent. cheaper in France than in England'. He does draw attention to the rise in prices which had taken place in recent decades and to the failure of wages to keep up with them. 'The most remarkable circumstances attending this *apparent* prosperity', he declares, 'is the still miserable state of the labouring poor; it is rather a matter of surprize, that the price of labour has not risen equally with other things; this must probably be attributed to the too great populousness of the kingdom . . . There is probably too great a competition for employment.' A great deal of the blame for this state of affairs Young laid on 'the multiplication of small properties'. For him the solution was simple: 'The system of great farms regularly employing, and well paying a numerous peasantry by day labour, is infinitely more advantageous to the nation and to the poor themselves.'[109]

As with other aspects of French life on the eve of the Revolution, what our travellers tell us about the land and the peasants has undoubted gaps. Even so, their first-hand observations of so many regions of France do help to bring to life conditions on the land in their almost endless variety in a large country with very different soils, altitudes and climates. Inevitably, since poverty strikes one more than a modest prosperity, the picture which collectively our travellers offer is probably rather too sombre. Although poverty was widespread in the countryside on the eve of 1789, there was also some degree of comfort or even real prosperity for a minority. In his chapter 'Of some Circumstances concerning the Poor', even Young writes of one favoured region: 'Guienne. — Leyrac. — They are in this rich country on the Garonne very much at their ease, make four meals a day, eat meat and drink wine.'[110] Yet this was obviously an exception worth noting.

In his account of Avignon and the Combat Venaissin, a papal enclave in French territory until 1791, Swinburne decides that on balance reunion with Ancien Régime France would be extremely disadvantageous for what he calls 'the cultivators of this delicious plain':

> Must they not receive a swarm of devouring locusts, an army of tax-gatherers and monopolisers? Must not their taxes be prodigiously augmented, their salt, their tobacco, raised to such a price as to exclude the poorer class of citizens from a

The Land and the Peasants

daily enjoyment of them? Must they not submit to the peremptory sway of intendants, subdelegates, military governors, and a long train of oppressive ministers, insteady of the drowsy, but mild administration of their present masters, who want the power, if not the will, of raising more than the stipulated contributions? . . . The first necessaries, and many of the superfluities of life, are cheap here; impositions are few and light; the husbandman is not dragged from his plough to garrison unwholesome fortresses, or pine in the cold and wet, to guard a coast against invaders: no districts are here reserved for the diversion of their sovereign, nor are their harvests devoured before their eyes by myriads of useless animals, which it is a capital offence to destroy, or even to molest.[111]

In these lines many of the grievances of the peasants in 1789 are vividly expressed.

Notes

1. *Travelling Memorandums*, vol. I, p. 54.
2. *Travels in France*, vol. II, pp. 21-3.
3. *Letters from Barbary, France, etc.*, vol. I, pp. 217, 219.
4. *Letters and Journals*, vol. II, p. 50.
5. Rutt, *Life of Priestley*, vol. I, p. 238.
6. Bodleian, MS. Eng. Misc. f. 54, f. 8.
7. *Letters from France*, p. 10.
8. *Travels in France*, vol. I, pp. 321-4.
9. Ibid., vol. I, p. 359.
10. Ibid., vol. I, p. 364.
11. Ibid., vol. I, p. 357.
12. Rutt, *Life of Priestley*, vol. I, p. 248.
13. *Travels in France*, vol. I, pp. 154, 331, 360.
14. *Pembroke Papers*, p. 457.
15. Bodleian, MS. Eng. Misc. f. 54, f. 159.
16. *Letters from France, 1788-1789*, p. 6.
17. *Travels in France*, vol. I, p. 330.
18. Ibid., vol. I, pp. 331-2.
19. Ibid., vol. I, pp. 325-7.
20. Ibid., vol. II, pp. 52, 42, 48.
21. Ibid., vol. I, p. 441.
22. *Travels through France and Italy*, p. 70.
23. *Travels in France*, vol. II, p. 70; vol. I, p. 363.
24. Ibid., vol. I, pp. 188, 381.
25. Ibid., vol. II, pp. 97n, 91-2; vol. I, p. 109; vol. II, p. 90; vol. I, pp. 85, 126.

26. *Diary of a Scotch Gardener*, pp. 145–6.
27. *A Tour*, p. 43.
28. *Journal*, p. 45.
29. *Letters from Barbary, France, etc.*, pp. 203–4, 215–16.
30. *Observations and Reflections*, p. 7.
31. *Travels through France and Italy*, p. 30.
32. Rutt, *Life of Priestley*, vol. I, p. 238.
33. *Travelling Memorandums*, vol. II, p. 58.
34. *A Tour*, p. 226.
35. *Travels in France*, vol. I, pp. 359, 357, 370–1.
36. Ibid., p. 360.
37. Ibid., p. 398.
38. Ibid., pp. 12, 370–1.
39. Ibid., pp. 107, 109, 97, 103, 334–5, 365.
40. Ibid., vol. II, pp. 52–3.
41. Ibid., vol. I, pp. 148, 430, 503.
42. Ibid., pp. 434–5; vol. II, pp. 132–3.
43. BL, Add. MS. 31192, ff. 40–1.
44. *Letters from Barbary, France, etc.*, vol. I, pp. 204, 431.
45. *Useful Hints*, pp. 179–80.
46. *Music, man and manners*, p. 4.
47. *A Tour*, pp. 85–6.
48. *Journal of a Tour*, p. 6.
49. *Journal*, p. 4.
50. *A Tour*, p. 217.
51. *A Tour*, p. 11.
52. BL, Add. MS., 31192, f. 16.
53. Somerset RO DD/SH/67/19C/2489, p. 27.
54. *Travelling Memorandums*, vol. I, p. 77.
55. *The Gentleman's Guide*, pp. 56–7.
56. *Travels through France and Italy*, p. 75.
57. *Travels in France*, vol. I, p. 402.
58. Ibid., p. 624.
59. Ibid., p. 72.
60. Ibid., vol. II, p. 49.
61. Ibid., vol. I, pp. 394, 56.
62. Ibid., p. 56.
63. Ibid., pp. 402, 412–13, 484.
64. Ibid., pp. 12, 170, 403, 405.
65. *Wealth of Nations*, pp. 856–7, 869.
66. *Travels in France*, vol. I, p. 45.
67. See above, p. 10.
68. *Travels in France*, vol. I, pp. 598, 604, 355, 405.
69. *Wealth of Nations*, vol. II, p. 731.
70. *Correspondence*, vol. 28, p. 226; vol. 41, p. 346.
71. See above, pp. 16–17.
72. *Travels in France*, vol. I, pp. 5, 598–600.
73. Ibid., p. 602.
74. *Travels through France and Italy*, p. 25.
75. *A Tour*, p. 225.

76. *Travels in France*, vol. I, pp. 602, 600-1, 148, 349-50, 402.
77. Ibid., pp. 85, 8.
78. *A Tour*, pp. 204-5.
79. *A Short Ramble*, pp. 204-5.
80. *Wealth of Nations*, vol. II, p. 870.
81. *Ideas suggested on the spot*, p. 426.
82. *A Tour*, p. 225.
83. BL, Add. MS. 12130, p. 177.
84. *Travels in France*, vol. I, p. 18.
85. *Letters from France*, p. 6.
86. *Letters and Journals*, vol. II, p. 112.
87. *Travels into France and Italy*, vol. II, p. 25.
88. *Journals of Travels*, p. 338.
89. *Letters from France*, p. 12.
90. *Travels in France*, vol. I, pp. 450, 148.
91. *Tour on the Continent*, p. 49.
92. *Travel in the two last Centuries*, p. 40.
93. *Journals of Travels*, p. 77.
94. *Travels in France*, vol. I, pp. 56, 18, 96-7.
95. Ibid., vol. I, pp. 273, 450.
96. *Travels through France and Italy*, p. 329.
97. *Travels in France*, vol. I, pp. 56-7.
98. *The Gentleman's Guide*, pp. 82-3.
99. *Travels in France*, vol. I, pp. 414, 482.
100. Ibid., pp. 448-9.
101. Ibid., p. 373.
102. Ibid., pp. 363, 442-3.
103. *Journals of Travels*, pp. 76-7.
104. *Diary of a Scotch Gardener*, p. 115.
105. *Travelling Memorandums*, vol. I, pp. 50, 70.
106. *Journals of Travels*, p. 67.
107. *Travels in France*, vol. I, pp. 369, 450; vol. II, p. 78.
108. Ibid., p. 14.
109. Ibid., pp. 446-7, 454, 417.
110. Ibid., p. 449.
111. *Journey from Bayonne to Marseilles*, pp. 439-40.

2
The Towns, Trade and Industry

One feature of French towns, particularly those on France's vulnerable north-eastern frontier, which continued to strike British travellers was that they were fortified, provided with strong walls and with gates which, as one of them found at Cambrai, were 'always shut at a very early hour, after which there [was] neither ingress nor egress'.[1] The fortified towns in this region were something quite new to Priestley, writing from Lille in 1774:

> I was very much struck with the appearance of Calais, as it was the first fortified town I had ever seen, being surrounded with a deep ditch and strong walls, built in such a manner as to make it very difficult to be taken by an enemy. St. Omers, Aire, Bethune, and Lisle, which we have seen since, are all fortified in the same manner; and they have all spacious market places, where the inhabitants may be assembled, and where the soldiers can parade.[2]

The closing of the gates could cause inconvenience to travellers. Mrs Thrale and her party, in travelling northwards from Noyon on their return journey, had to 'set out in the Morning . . . for Cambray before it was Light' in order to arrive before the gates were shut.[3] Travellers sometimes found that, if they were too late, they had to make do with very poor accommodation outside the town. Burney met with this experience at the very beginning of his 1770 journey in France, when he travelled from Calais to St Omer: 'On arriving at the gates of the town, I found them shut, and was forced to put up at a miserable house in the suburbs, where I could get nothing to eat after my sea sickness and total depletion, but stinking maquerel; a sallad with stinking oil; and an omelet made of stinking eggs. No meat of any kind or sort could be found. The room and bed were of a piece with the supper.'[4]

It is true that Cole found that a mixture of lies and tips could sometimes secure admission to a fortified town when the gates were already shut. After approaching Montreuil from the south in a state of extreme anxiety about the miserable lodging he would have to put up with as he was certain to arrive too late, he found that the postillion, on being ordered to drive him up to the first drawbridge,

> of his own accord set up such a yell as I had never heard before, which he repeated two or 3 Times before any Answer was made to him: at last a Centinel from the Parapet Wall at a Distance from the first Intrenchment appeared, & demanded, who was there, & what was wanted; when the Postilion answered, that an English Nobleman was at the Gates & beg'd it as a Favour to be admitted into the Town; to which the Centinel replied, That he would go to the Commandant & try to get the keys.

Cole was indignant at such lies being told on his behalf and insisted on telling the postillion the truth: 'I am no Nobleman, or any Person of Quality, or Fashion, but only a plain common English Gentleman.' The postillion pointed out to him that not long before two merchants whom he had brought to Montreuil were naïve enough to declare their profession and were refused entry by the commandant. Eventually, after distributing half a guinea to the soldiers at the gates and to the sentinal, Cole was let into the town where he found 'a good Fire & a good Supper, to refresh myself after so much Uneasiness'.[5]

Paris, the great magnet for nearly all our travellers, had lost its fortifications, but began to acquire in 1784 a new wall. This was the 'mur des fermiers généraux' which was intended to make more difficult the evasion of duties on goods brought into the capital. It was, naturally, extremely unpopular, as is reflected in the strong comments of the Irishman, St John, in 1787:

> At present the farmers-general are building a great wall all round the city. This wall is on the outside of the *Boulevards* and deprives the Parisians of enjoying a prospect of the country. The uncleanliness of the lower class of people in Paris, the

narrowness and filthiness of the streets, and the great height of the houses, are more than sufficient to render the air in several parts of Paris and its environs, abominably foetid and highly putrid; but this new great wall must increase the corruption of the air, by obstructing every breeze from the country, and actually occasion the death of thousands of feeble and asthmatic persons. The Parisians call this wall *le mur de captivité*, the wall of captivity; but a free-born Briton must look with contempt and scorn on almost a million of people, who tamely suffer themselves to be robbed of the right of human nature, of the right to breathe fresh air, and be shut up like birds in a cage.[6]

These last observations were a trifle premature; the wall added to the unpopularity of the *Fermiers généraux* for which they were to pay with their lives in the Revolution.

In Paris as it was before the reconstruction by Haussmann, British travellers were struck by the narrowness of the streets in relation to the height of the houses as well as by their dirtiness; it would be tedious to recite passages in which one after another makes the point pungently made by St John. Again and again they also echo the complaints of French writers of the time about the danger to pedestrians presented by these narrow streets without pavements. 'All the genteel English who go to Paris', wrote *The Gentleman's Guide*, 'keep a carriage; indeed the narrowness and filth of the streets, with the number of carriages driving, and of people crouding through them, render walking very dangerous and disagreeable.'[7] Moore enters into rather more detail on the subject. London, he claims, is well lit at night and has pavements,

> whereas Paris is poorly and partially lighted; and except on the Pont Neuf and the Pont Royal, and the keys between them, is not provided with little walks on the sides of the streets for the accommodation and safety of foot-passengers. They must therefore grope their way as they best can, and skulk behind pillars, or run into shops, to avoid being crushed by the coaches, which are driven as near the wall as the coachman pleases; dispersing the people on foot at their approach, like chaff before the wind.[8]

Walker criticises 'the furious driving of the coaches', adding: 'The poor foot-passengers here are as little regarded by those who ride as if they were cattle; so that from this, and the narrowness of the streets people are very frequently run over.'[9] Recounting a stay in Paris in the autumn of 1787, J. E. Smith writes: 'I have actually seen a poor old man run over by a gentleman's carriage with the most wanton carelessness on the part of the coachman. Not being able to restrain the indignation natural to an Englishman, "Why", said I, "is not the carriage stopped, and the fellow secured?" A shrug and a stare were the only answer. "Was it not the fault of the coachman?" "Assurement. *C'est la voiture de quelque seigneur.*"' To this Smith adds what is obviously a later comment: 'No one who has not been in France can imagine how far the aristocratic influence extended. The liveried slaves of a person of the least rank or figure, might behave with any degree of insolence to the most respected tradesman, nor were blows even to be always resented.'[10]

British travellers who made their way through the streets of Paris either on foot or in a carriage saw many unfamiliar sights. In her journal Mrs Thrale describes street scenes which seemed strange to a Londoner:

> The Streets of Paris are very entertaining to drive through; I had a long Prance over them this Morning — Coxcombs, Religious Habits, Wenches with Umbrellas, Workers with Muffs, fine Fellows cover'd with Lace, & Old Men with Woollen Wigs make a Contrast & Variety inconceivable to a Londoner, who thinks all Monks & Nuns are shut up in Convents — & have no Idea of a Sawyer working thro' a Block of Marble with his Muff and Snuff Box lying by him & his Dog to guard them.[11]

Another thing which struck one of our travellers was the sight of coffee being sold in the streets: 'Our breakfast consisted of *caffé au lait*, milk-coffee. It is the common breakfast of the Parisians: even the labourer makes it his morning meal. Women carry it in the streets in large tin vessels, and sell it two sous a dish or bason.'[12]

In addition to visiting the famous buildings of the capital (most of those frequented by tourists today were already *in situ*), travellers also went round the shops. These they continued to find as disappointing in comparison with those of London as earlier travellers had done. 'The shops here at Paris', wrote Mrs Thrale, 'are particularly mean & the Tradespeople surly & disagreeable; a Mercer will not shew you above half a Dozen Silks & those he will not cut, — they run in Pieces for Gowns & you are obliged to buy all or none.'[13] Mrs Montagu also speaks of 'the miserable air of the shops'.[14] Cole is more brutal in his comments, comparing Paris shops very unfavourably with those of London:

> The shops at Paris are the poorest gloomy Dungeons you can possibly conceive, however rich their Contents may be: as the Brillancy [sic] & Shew of ours in London make one of its chief Beauties & Ornaments, so the dead Gloom of the City of Paris is nothing beholden to the Tradesmen in shewing their Goods to the best Advantage: you here & there see a Shew-Glass about the Size & Appearance of what a ragged Jew carries before him, by the Help of a Cord thrown over his Shoulders.[15]

Such a diatribe cannot, of course, be taken literally; Cole seems to have been determined to admire nothing on his trip to Paris.

What annoyed travellers in their dealings with Paris shopkeepers, was their habit of asking very high prices for their goods and then having to be beaten down by haggling. Pennington points out that plans of Paris and its environs could be bought on the quays, but adds a warning: 'The sellers moderately ask six livres for them, and take three; and in general, at Paris, you must not venture to give, at most, above half what you are asked, for any thing that you have need to buy.'[16] In a section entitled 'Rules for an Englishman laying out his money in Paris' the *Gentleman's Guide* offers this advice about dealings with shopkeepers:

> He will never go to buy any thing, even of the most trifling nature, in which they will not attempt to cheat him; in casual expences, particularly buying trinkets, and such trifles, which one is often led into, I would, by all means, advise, never to give more than one third of what is asked, in which case, you will pay a little more than the thing is worth.[17]

Smollett was scandalised by this practice:

> ... The most reputable shopkeepers and tradesmen of Paris think it no disgrace to practise the most shameful imposition. I myself know an instance of one of the most creditable table

merchands in this capital, who demanded six francs an ell for some lutestring, laying his hand upon his breast at the same time, and declaring *en conscience*, that it had cost him within three sols of the money. Yet, in less than three minutes, he sold it for four and a half, and when the buyer upbraided him with his former declaration, he shrugged up his shoulders, saying, *il faut marchander*. I don't mention this as a particular instance. The same mean disingenuity is universal all over France, as I have been informed by several persons of veracity.[18]

At Lyons, for instance, Mary Berry found the same practice in the shops: 'For everything they demand an exorbitant price, and even with the least dishonest you must haggle during an hour for the smallest purchase.'[19]

The luxury industries in and around the capital attracted numerous British travellers. The tapestries at the Gobelins factory continued to draw many of them, as in the previous century. A more recent foundation, the *manufacture royale de porcelaine* at Sèvres, acquired by the Crown in 1760, also drew visitors, including Thomas Bentley, Josiah Wedgewood's partner, who visited Paris in 1776:

This manufactory was begun and is supported at the expense of the King in a very magnificent building about 5 miles from Paris, on the left hand side of the road to Versailles. I have been through the magazines and several of the workshops, and find a great many fine things and a great many people employed: about 1 dozen carvers or modellers and near 100 painters, and other workmen of course in proportion. The workshops are very commodious and well fitted up, and there are several fine appartments left for his Majesty when he chooses to visit the manufactory.[20]

There follow another couple of pages describing the various kinds of porcelain made at Sèvres and the methods employed in its production.

Seeing mirrors manufactured at the famous factory in the Rue St Antoine continued to attract a great many tourists who were filled with admiration at what they saw. Pennant noted fairly briefly: 'Went to the Manufacture de Glace, Rue St. Antoine: some hundreds of men employed. They make only looking glasses, some of which were three yards long and two foot four inches broad, valued at 3800 livres each; this is under the royal protection.'[21] Jervis is equally brief, but he too was clearly impressed with what he saw: 'Finish'd with the Manufacture of Glass which we saw in all the process of polishing and quicksilvering. It appears to be the most flourishing of any of the Mechanick arts we have seen.'[22]

The most detailed account of such a visit is to be found in the rather scrappy journal left by Samuel Johnson where it furnishes one of the longest entries. His description of the processes involved in the manufacture of the mirror deserves to be quoted:

> We went to see the looking glasses wrought. They come from Normandy[23] in cast plates, perhaps the third of an Inch thick. At Paris they are ground upon a marble table, by rubbing one plate on another with grit between them. The various sands, of which there are said to be five, I could not learn. The handle by which the upper Glass is moved has the form of a wheel, which may be moved in all directions. The plates are sent up with their surfaces ground, but not polished, and so continue till they are bespoken, lest time should spoil the surface, as we were told. Those that are to be polished are laid on a table covered with several thick cloaths, hard strained that the resistance may be equal, they are then rubbed with a hand rubber held down hard by a contrivance which I did not well understand. The powder which is used last seemed to me to be iron dissolved in aqua fortis. They called it, as Baretti said, Mar de l'eau forte, which he thought was dregs. They mentioned vitriol and saltpetre. The cannon ball swam in the quicksilver. To silver them. A leaf of beaten tin is laid, and rubbed with quicksilver to which it unites. Then more quicksilver is poured upon it, which by its mutual attraction rises very high. Then a paper is laid at the nearest end of the plate, over which the glass is slided till it lies upon the plate, having driven much of the quicksilver before it. It is then I think pressed upon cloaths, and then set sloping to drop the superfluous mercury. The slope is daily heightened towards a perpendicular.[24]

Jardine, who was struck by the success attained, despite the obstacles presented by the government, in various branches of French industry, particularly silk and certain kinds of woollen goods, was particularly impressed by this factory:

> The manufactory of mirrors likewise, so well known here, is a noble and profitable work, and well conducted. Eight hundred people are employed in one building. You may attempt it in England, but cannot, I fear, succeed near so well as here; for there will not be near the same demand. The superior luxury and riches of this great country, — the fashion and taste of the people for that ornament, — their having the start in the methods of working, and in the markets of Europe, are causes quite sufficient for holding their great superiority over all competitors in this branch.[25]

A similar recognition of French superiority in this industry is shown by Rigby, who visited the factory on 9 July 1789: 'We went to the manufactory of plate glass, which is a most extensive business. We saw plates of a very large size, and the application with tin the same as in England, but being on a larger scale, it seems to be done with more accuracy.'[26]

By the accident of Johnson coming to Paris with a wealthy London brewer and his wife, we learn something about a very different industry:

> We then went to Sansterre, a brewer. He brews with about as much malt as Mr. T., and sells his beer at the same price though he pays no duty for malt, and little more than half as much for beer. Beer is sold retail at 6p a bottle. He brews 4000 barrels a year There are seventeen brewers in Paris of whom none is supposed to brew more than he — reckoning them at 3000 each they make 51000 a year. They make their malt, for malting is here no trade.[27]

It is tempting to conclude with the editors of Johnson's journal that the Santerre he visited was the Santerre who was to play a prominent role in the Revolution and to command the troops present at the execution of Louis XVI. Although he set up as a brewer in 1772, three years before Johnson came to Paris, it is more than possible that the establishment in question was his father's brewery.

In the 1780s the Paris water works established by the Périer brothers were a novelty which attracted British tourists, especially perhaps because of the use made of steam engines. Mrs Cradock describes a visit which she and her husband made to le Gros-Caillous, then a village outside Paris, near which 'on a installé une pompe à feu que l'on fait manoeuvrer par la vapeur et à l'aide de tuyaux qui transportent ainsi l'eau dans plusieurs quartiers de Paris'. Shortly afterwards they made an excursion to Chaillot to see

> une pompe à feu qui sert à faire monter par des tuyaux l'eau de Seine jusque sur une haute colline à peu pres à un mille de Paris où elle est reçue dans quatre grands réservoirs de 12 pieds de profondeur, intérieurement en pierre blanche. Au bout de chaque réservoir, une écluse de fer permet à l'eau de s'écouler, de façon à en dégager de la saleté et de la boue qu'on enlève toutes les semaines. L'eau arrive ainsi claire et propre dans les conduits qui la distribuent dans différents quartiers de Paris et dans les maisons des boulevards.[28]

In the following year Walker describes how he met with a surprise on his wanderings round Paris on catching sight of one of the steam engines at work:

> Arriving at the Bottom of the Thuilleries, I saw a black, thick smoke issue from a chimney, so unlike that of Paris! — and alas! so like that of London — that I was drawn to the phenomenon; when, to my great surprise, I found a huge Steam-Engine, on Bolton and Watt's construction, to raise water from the Seine, and diffuse it over the City. Another is constructing in the same building; and so much has the value of this undertaking increased, that the original shares, which were about twenty-five pounds sterling, are now risen to one hundred and twenty pounds.

However, he was far from impressed with the quality of the water supplied by this machine, as he recorded after a second visit: 'We have visited a second time the Steam-Engine supplying Paris with water, . . . and stand astonished at its Situation, which is at the very lowest part of the River, — where all the Filth of the Town must have got duly mixed, to be sent back again for the refreshment and nutrition of the place! The mystery (so unlike the Police of the Town) confounds me.'[29] A few months later an anonymous traveller who obviously knew Boulton noted: 'Went with Lord Mountmorris to see the pomp a feu or Steam engine at Chaillot pres la grille de la conference. It is the invention of Mr Bolton who is now at Paris and the King of France has given him 2000£ as a recompence. Went to call upon Mr Bolton but he was not at home.'[30]

After his first entry on the steam engine, Walker has an interesting passage on the number of Englishmen who had been encouraged to set up various industries in the Paris region with the support of royal subsidies:

> Indeed Money seems by no means wanting for all useful purposes here; and the munificence of the King in the encouragement of ingenuity in Manufactures exceeds all belief! — He has given seventy thousand pounds sterling to two Manchester Adventurers to fix up a Cotton Spinning Machine at Passy. — The Queen has taken a Manufactory of Parker's Cut-Glass under her auspices; and two or three Renegade-Journeymen of that ingenious Artist, are making fortunes. — Mr S—, a friend of mine, has a pension from the King, for a small Manufactory of Lenses and Optical Mirrours. This man came here without anything but ingenuity and integrity, about eight years ago, and this day has entertained us with such a Dinner — sweetmeats, ices, fruit, rich wines and cordials — as I have scarce seen at the first Nobleman's table in England.[31]

Another traveller also refers to the cotton factory mentioned above:

> Since the dissolution of Arkwright's patent, the manufacturing of Manchester cottons has ceased to be a mystery — an establishment for the latter purpose has been some time since formed in the neighbourhood of Paris, under the immediate patronage of the King — a part of the palace of the Muet [la Muette] in the Bois de Boulogne (an ancient royal palace) has been assigned for this purpose, under the direction of a Lancashire manufacturer.[32]

We shall meet with many examples of Englishmen engaged in industrial undertakings in other parts of France.

Most of the larger towns in the provinces, except those in the heart of the country, were frequented by a considerable number of our travellers. Among northern towns Lille was often visited, not only by those who entered France from the Austrian Netherlands, but also by some who preferred to the more direct route from Calais to Paris the journey via St Omer, Lille and Péronne. Lille was seen as the capital of French Flanders and an extremely important fortified town as well as being, in Rigby's words, 'the residence of many genteel families'.[33] Priestley among other travellers was amused by the strange sight of 'dogs drawing little carts with very considerable loads'.[34] Young shared his amusement: 'Meet many small carts in the town, drawn each by a dog: I was told by the owner of one, what appears to me incredible, that his dog would draw 700lb. half a league.' However, travellers also noted the considerable amount of industry carried on in and around the town. Young's first impression as he approached it was that it was 'surrounded by more windmills for expressing the oil of cole seed, than I have seen anywhere else I suppose in the world'. Later he goes into much more detail:

> This is one of the most manufacturing, commercial, and industrious towns in France; there is a *manufacture royale* of fine cloths made of Spanish wool. Three callico printers houses, but not upon a very great scale. Their greatest trade is that of camblets, which employs many hands; they are made of the long combing wool of Holland, Germany, Flanders, and what they can get from England, this being the fabric which uses more English wool than any other in France. They have a cotton fabric of stuffs for linings, &c. another of blankets; also one of silk stuffs, which the proprietor refused to let me see . . .[35]

Another town in Northern France which attracted a good deal of attention was Rouen, partly because the crossing from Brighthelmstone to Dieppe was now becoming fashionable. The theatre and various public buildings, starting with the cathedral, were an attraction to tourists, though they were repelled by the rest of the town with its narrow streets and dilapidated houses. 'The inhabitants, computed to amount to 72,500 souls', according to *The Gentleman's Guide*, 'are extremely industrious and carry on a great trade. In the article of printed linens only, the sale is computed from twenty to twenty-five thousand pounds sterling per week. The quantity sold at the hall in a year amounts to thirty-five millions of livres. The cotton manufacture, introduced by Mr. Holker, is likewise very considerable.'[36]

This John Holker was a Jacobite from Lancashire who took refuge in France after 1745 and set up a famous cotton mill in Rouen. When Walker and his companions arrived from Dieppe in 1785, this was one of the places they went to see:

> In the morning we visited Mr H—'s Manufactory, where twelve hundred people are employed. This man was in the Rebellion of 1745, and fled to France, where he established the Cotton and Velvet trade of Manchester, and seems to fabricate it better, but not with the sleight or taste. — We saw the manufactory in all its stages, and it is certainly becoming hostile to Manchester, though they undersell the French at present; but the fabric is better.[37]

In 1788 Young was thrice in Rouen. His first impressions were scarcely favourable; he speaks of 'this great ugly, stinking, close, and ill built town, which is full of nothing but dirt and industry'. Later he greatly enjoyed the view from a hill overlooking the town — 'the finest view of a town I have ever seen; the whole city, with all its churches and convents, and its cathedral proudly rising in the midst, fills the vale'. In his account of the state of French industry Rouen has the following entry:

> The Manchester of France. One of the most commercial and manufacturing towns of the kingdom. They say, that at present the velours and *cotton toiles* are the most flourishing. The fabrics spread over all the country; they admit the velverets of England to be much cheaper, but assert their *pasmentiers* of silk and cotton mixed, to be cheaper than any similar fabric in England; they have also some woollens, but none fine or deserving particular notice. Asserted here that spinning cotton employs 50,000 persons in Normandy.[38]

The important place occupied by Normandy in the textile industries for which Rouen was the commercial centre will be examined later.[39]

The choice of French towns for a stay of some length made by British travellers in this period seems decidedly odd today. British tourists who happen to pass through Lyons or Marseilles or Toulouse may well decide to spend a night or two there to have a look round; they would never dream of spending weeks or even months there. In the eighteenth century a city like Lyons not only attracted a large number of British travellers, but some of them made fairly lengthy stays there. Lyons was, of course, on their way to the south of France or to Italy as well as to Geneva and Switzerland, but it was clearly more than a convenient stopping-place on the way. Indeed, on his return from a tour of the South of France which had taken him and his family (complete with a monkey dressed as a postillion!) into Spain, Thicknesse maintained that a British traveller would be well advised not to go any further south than Lyons:

> I will tell you truely my sentiment with respect to the south of France, which is, that Lyons is quite southward enough for an Englishman, who will, if he goes further, have many wants that cannot be supplied. After quitting Lyons, he will find neither good butter, milk nor cream. At Lyons, every thing, which one can wish for, is in perfection; it is indeed a rich, noble, and plentiful town, abounding with every thing that is good, and more finery than even in Paris itself. They have a good theatre, and some tolerable actors . . . Their dancers, male and female, are excellent indeed.

He spent at least a month on what he describes as 'my second visit to this great and flourishing city',[40] while Jervis stayed there for most of the winter of 1772-3.

Moore is also enthusiastic: 'After Paris, Lyons is the most magnificent town in France, enlivened by industry, enriched by commerce, and by its situation, in the middle of a fertile country, and at the confluence of the Saone and the Rhone. The numbers of inhabitants are estimated at 200,000. The theatre is accounted the finest in France, and all the luxuries of Paris are to be found at Lyons, though not in equal perfection.'[41] Although Muirhead was also impressed by the city's admirable position for trade and its pleasant surroundings, he goes on: 'Very different is the complexion of the town itself. The streets are mostly sombre, ill paved, narrow, and dirty — many of the houses are dimly lighted by oiled paper, are unequal in height, though none of them low, and all blackened with smoke. Several families reside in the same tenement, and even the most wealthy seldom occupy an entire house.'[42]

The luxury industries for which Lyons was famous attracted a good deal of attention. In 1765 Pennant visited a manufacturer of gold and silver lace: 'He showed me the process of making the gold and silver thread for the lace manufacture; the plates or leaves of gold to guild the silver weighed 12 grains, they were twelve French inches deep, seven broad; eight ounces of silver and two ounces of gold laid on it, when drawn out would form a thread 90 leagues long.' Later he watched the making of velvet:

> Visited the velvet manufactures. Saw a piece of velvet, ground white, flowers a pea green, designed for the dress of an abbess 30 l. a yard; 10000 threads are arranged with wonderful art to weave a piece of velvet. The thread for the lace is formed by twisting the beaten or rather drawn gold round a yellow thread in a pretty machine. Ingots of silver are drawn thro' holes of different sizes till it arrives at the size of a hair to produce the silver threads.[43]

When in Lyons in 1784 with her father and sister, Mary Berry made some interesting notes on the processes involved and on the conditions under which the men and women carried out their work:

> Went in the morning to several manufacturers, to silk mills, and to see cut velvet wove — the most complicated of all the looms. A weaver working assiduously from 5 in the morning to 9 at night cannot make above half a yard and a quarter a day of a stuff for which they are paid by the mercers eight livres a yard. A weaver of brocade gold-stuff, working the same number of hours, cannot make above half a yard, and the payment uncertain. All these weavers, lodged up in the fourth and fifth stories of dirty stinking houses, surprised me by the propriety and civility of their manner, and their readiness to satisfy all our questions.

The next day their investigations continued:

> In the morning at different manufacturers. To a weaver of gold-lace. Of a lace about two inches broad, a person working well can make about two yards and a half a day, for which they are paid eight or ten louis a yard by the merchant who gives them the gold to work. To a great manufacturer of gauze. There are two horses up in the fifth story of the houses,

turning silk mills, which wind I know not how many bobbins at once. The women who watch these, to arrange them, and take up the threads that break, are there from 5 in the morning till nine at night for twelve sous.[44]

Mrs Piozzi, who frequented the wealthy merchants of the city, saw things from a rather different angle; she describes the magnificent velvets that she saw:

> Nothing I ever saw at London or Paris can compare with the beauty of these velvets, or with the art necessary to produce such an effect, while the wrong side is smooth, not struck through. The hangings for the Empress of Russia's bedchamber are wonderfully executed; the design elegant, the colouring brilliant: A screen too for the Grand Signor is finely finished here; he would, I trust, have been contented with magnificence in the choice of his furniture, but Mr. Pernon has added taste to it, and contrived in appearance to sink an urn or vase of crimson velvet in a back ground of gold tissue with surprising ingenuity.[45]

Young gives a good deal of precise information about the silk industry in France as well as at Lyons in a short space:

> The import of raw silk into all France one million of 1b. of 16 oz. The crop of all France the same, but not so good by ½ of the price. The price of good silk 25 to 30 liv. The fabric here 3/4 of all the kingdom, and its exports in manufactured goods the weight of one million of pounds. There are 12,000 looms, each employing five persons, or 60,000 who earn on a average 25s. a day. The men earn by wrought silks 45 to 50s.; but on plain ones 30s. Of the fabric here 2/3 of the value is raw silk, and 1/3 labour. Throughout the kingdom in the hemp and flax fabrics 2/3 labour and 1/3 raw material. In the last 20 years the manufacture here has augmented very little.

In fact, when Young visited Lyons at the end of December 1789, he found the silk industry there suffering from a slump which had begun in 1786. 'Twenty thousand people', he declares, 'are fed by charity, and consequently very ill fed.'[46]

Marseilles was another city which attracted more British travellers than it does today, sometimes even for quite long stays.

'I am inclined to consider it', wrote Wraxall in 1775, 'as one of the most eligible places of winter residence in the world, and far superior, where health is not an object of attention, to Nice or Montpellier.'[47] Yet some people *did* regard it as a health resort. Mrs Cradock tells us that she went to spend the winter at Marseilles for the sake of her health;[48] she and her husband stayed there from the beginning of December 1784 to the middle of the following March. Nor did they lack the company of members of the British aristocracy such as the Duke and Duchess of Argyll and Lady Derby. Lord Gardenstone stayed only just over a fortnight as he intended to spend part of the winter of Hyères, but he noted the arrival of his 'worthy friend Lord D—f—s and his amiable family'.[49] Marseilles was definitely a place which must be seen and explored, if only for a shorter period, by a great traveller like the Duchess of Northumberland, who wrote of it: 'The Bay on which it is situated is a very fine One, & the City itself is large well built opulent & populous but the stink is insufferable.'[50]

Even Smollett, though he found the place expensive, was full of praise for it:

> I was much pleased with Marseilles, which is indeed a noble city, large, populous, and flourishing. The streets, of what is called the new town, are open, airy, and spacious; the houses well built, and even magnificent. The harbour is an oval basin, surrounded on every side either by the buildings or the land, so that the shipping lies perfectly secure, and here is generally an incredible number of vessels. On the city side, there is a semi-circular quay of free-stone, which extends thirteen hundred paces; and the space between this and the houses that front it, is commonly filled with a surprising croud of people.[51]

Although Thicknesse too found living dear there, he speaks of it as 'a noble city, crouded with men of all nations, walking in the streets in the proper habits of their country'. Yet characteristically, a few pages later he declares that except for 'its fine harbour, and favourable situation for trade, it has little else to recommend it, but riot, mob, and confusion'.[52] Other travellers had similar mixed feelings. Mary Berry, for instance, spent nearly two months there at the beginning of 1785:

> The street which leads from the port to the cours, and the

cours itself, are almost as thronged with people as the streets of London. The cours is the public walk in summer, the port is that of winter; there are always so many vessels, that one can see scarcely anything else on one side, and houses on the other; and as this is the place where all the trade of the town is carried on, the pavement is too narrow to move at ease — it is a perpetual mob, and very unpleasant for those who go there only to walk.[53]

Evidently she was not as taken with the crowds there as Wraxall had been. He was in Marseilles in January 1776: 'The port itself forms a delightful walk at this season of the year, as it is open to the southern sun, and crowded with vast numbers of people, not only of all the European nations, but of Turks, Greeks, and natives of the coast of Barbary.'[54]

Several of our travellers were not content with offering an account of the tourist attractions of Marseilles, but devoted some attention to its industries and especially to its importance as a great commercial centre. Lord Gardenstone, for instance, writes: 'The trade of Marseilles may be said to be universal, and their manufactures are very considerable. They do not rival Lyons in the fine and magnificent fabrics of silk, sattin, and velvets, but they manufacture the same kind of stuffs from coarser and cheaper materials, which had a more general demand and vent in the various circles of commerce, especially at Martinico, and in the Levant . . . Besides those mentioned, they have great manufactures of sugar, glass, porcelaine, oil, coral, &c.' He also describes a visit to a soap factory which employed between 800 and 1000 men. He gives an interesting account of discussions which he had about the relative merits of English and French products:

> I fortunately became acquainted, and conversed with some of the first-rate merchants. They allow that the English excel in some articles, particularly in the manufactures of steel and leather; but they pretend to have the advantage of others, and they specify their printed cottons and soap. They say they can undersell the English in many articles for the American market; but that the capital advantage of the English hitherto lies in being able to sell on longer credits.[55]

Swinburne, who spent a month in Marseilles with his family in 1776, gives an informative account of the immense trade carried on in this great Mediterranean port:

> The commerce of Marseilles is divided into a multiplicity of branches; a variety of commodities are fabricated here, or brought from the other ports and inland provinces of France to be exported, and numerous articles of traffic are landed here in order to be dispersed in this and other kingdoms. It is presumed that one year with another business is transacted upon this exchange for near fifteen millions sterling. The exports to the Levant amount annually to thirty-one millions of livres; the imports from thence are valued at fifty. Those from the West Indies and Cayenne are calculated at seventeen millions of exports, and twenty-one of imports. About three millions and a half are employed in the East-India trade, six in the corn trade, and about twenty-nine in that with Spain and the rest of Europe. Four millions worth of salt cod and train oil comes from North America; oils from Sicily, &c. to the amount of fourteen millions, exported again in soap to nearly the same value; as also various manufactures to the amount of two millions and an half. Add to this circulation the dealings in insurances and profits upon bullion, and you will have a rough, but comprehensive sketch of the commerce of Marseilles.[56]

When Sterne arrived in France in January 1762, long before the Seven Years War was over, after spending six months in Paris, he travelled via Lyons and Montpellier to a favourite haunt of eighteenth-century British travellers — Toulouse. He took a house, was joined by his wife and daughter, and remained there for the best part of a year.[57] When Adam Smith gave up his chair in Glasgow to act as tutor to the 3rd Duke of Buccleuch, he took his charge through Paris and straight on to Toulouse which they made their base for over a year before returning via Geneva to the capital for a longer stay. Cornelia Knight spent a year there with her mother in 1776–7. 'We . . . were well lodged', she writes, 'and had no want of society. At that time many of the first families of the province went rarely to Paris. They had large and handsome houses at Toulouse, where they spent the winter, as they spent the summer on their estates.'[58] The anonymous R.W.C., who arrived in Toulouse at the end of December 1788, gives some account of the English society to be found there:

There are a great number of genteel English now at Toulouse residents, so that I may say I have chose a happy moment for my visit: Lady Charlotte Fitzgerald is now here, and shortly to be married to Col. Strutt. The family of a Mr. Richardson who is settled here, is a great acquisition to all strangers, as they in a manner keep open house, and the cordial welcome to be found there always entices one to repeat one's visit. There is also a most lovely Hibernian here with her aunt, a Miss Rochford, who makes terrible havoc among the hearts of the young Frenchmen, who make love, cut capers, are au desespoir and eat a good dinner all in a breath.[59]

One strong inducement to spend long periods in Toulouse was its cheapness. This was obviously one of its attractions for Lady Philippa Knight, the widow of an admiral, who had no pension and ended her days in Italy. The cost of living in other southern towns was much higher, as Sterne explains in a letter from Montpellier:

> I had purposed to spend the winter months with my family at Aix, or Marseilles. We have been there, and found objections to both — to Marseilles especially from the dearness of Living & House rent, which last was so enormous, I could not take the most miserable Appartments under 9 or 10 Guineas a month — every thing else in proportion — so we return'd directly here — where things are moderate enough — tho' a third dearer than at Toulouse, where the cheapness and plenty of every thing is astonishing.[60]

Although an important administrative centre — it had an *Intendant* as well as its *Parlement* — Toulouse was not a considerable commercial or industrial city. According to *The Gentleman's Guide*, 'This amazing indolence can be attributed to no other cause than the boundless ambition of the merchants, who all aspire to have a seat in the council; which, once obtained, they and their children are then ennobled, and consequently lay aside trade and industry.'[61] In Young's chapter on manufactures, Toulouse rates only a short entry: 'Has a woollen and a silk fabric; in the first are worked light stuffs, and has about 80 looms, which are in the town; in the other stockings, stuffs, damasks, and other fabrics, worked in flowers; about 80 looms also.'[62]

On their way from Marseilles to Toulouse many travellers

visited Montpellier, the town in the south of France most favoured in the past by British travellers, particularly those in search of health. It had a famous medical faculty and its Mediterranean climate was regarded as excellent. Sterne spent the winter of 1763 – 4 there with his wife and daughter,[63] and Lord Clive and his party divided three months between Montpellier and Pézenas in 1768.[64] However, the fashion was now changing in favour of places such as Nice (then outside France) further along the Mediterranean coast. Smollett's famous account of his experiences in Montpellier, particularly with Professor Fizes of its medical faculty, can scarcely have provided good publicity.[65] Whatever the reason, it is clear that Montpellier became much less popular with British travellers in these years, even though, as Cornelia Knight, who stayed there with her mother in 1777, wrote decades later in her autobiography, 'its situation remains the same, its air is as good as ever, and the same medicinal virtues reside in its waters'.[66] *The Gentleman's Guide* was far from sharing this view:

This town has long been famous for (what I, and many of my countrymen, sadly experienced it does not in the least degree possess) a salabrious air, and the skill of its physicians. I pass'd six months there, at a very considerable expence, on promise of having my health perfectly established; when, to my great concern, after having gone through all the various operations, I found, in the end, my health much impair'd ... I declare upon my honour I have known it rain almost three months without intermission; and at intervals such thick stinking foggs, as nothing but the banks of Newfoundland would equal; and several times (for two or three days on a stretch) the sky so heavily loaded, that I have neither been able to see sun, moon, or star; and the streets quite wet with the humidity of the air. In summer it is so insufferably hot, that till the cool of the evening there is no stirring out.[67]

Such a write-up can scarcely have encouraged other British travellers to continue to frequent Montpellier.

Much more important industrially was Nîmes, which was situated on the route of many travellers between the Rhône valley and Montpellier. A number of those who were attracted there by its Roman antiquities and by the proximity of the Pont du Gard also made notes on its textile industries, particularly that of silk. Mary Berry's observations on the town are fairly brief: 'All the streets are small, dirty, and not paved; but it looks lively, well-peopled, and busy. There is a great manufactory here of silk stockings and cotton stuffs, and shops well furnished of all kinds.'[68] Lord Gardenstone, who visited Nîmes two years later, in 1786, goes into more detail; he also notes an interruption to the town's prosperity:

> Nismes has increased prodigiously of late years in manufactures, and consequently in population. They reckon sixty or seventy; I have reason to believe there are fifty thousand inhabitants.
>
> A silk stocking manufacture is their capital branch, in which they are generally allowed to excel, both for quality and cheapness. They have also a considerable cotton manufactory. I bought some cotton handerchiefs, on which fine pieces of mosaic work are very well stamped. They have several thousand stocking frames, but many of them are at present unemployed, which they attribute to a late ordinance of the king of Spain, prohibiting the importation of silk manufactures from France.[69]

Young, who visited Nîmes in the following year, was impressed with the town's industrial importance:

> This is one of the most considerable manufacturing places in France; they make a great variety of stuffs, in silk, cotton, and thread, but the first is the great manufacture; these are said to maintain from 10 to 15,000 hands; for the intelligence varied between those numbers. Silk stockings are said to employ 2000; handkerchiefs are a considerable article, printed linens, &c.; in the last there are workmen that earn 7 or 800 liv. a year.[70]

To the west of Montpellier, on their way to Toulouse, travellers passed through Carcassonne, whose prosperity rested on its flourishing woollen industry. Swinburne attributes its success to the efforts of Colbert, a century earlier, to see 'a constant and lucrative mart for French cloths opened in the Ottoman empire'. 'The manufacturers of Carcassonne', he continues, 'have been acquiring fresh vigour every year since his administration: the trade that other nations used to carry on with the Turks has sunk in the same proportion . . . I am assured that these looms now send out annually cloths worth fourteen millions, and furnish the home trade with cloths to the amount of two million more.'[71] Some ten years later Young too passed through this town and made fairly detailed notes on the manufacture of the famous *Londrins* which were exported to the Levant:

> Londrins the great fabric here also;[72] the master manufacturers give the materials to the weavers, who are paid by the piece, and thus the manufacture spreads into the country both spinning and weaving; they are made of Roussillon and Narbonne wool, which goes by the name of Spanish, 46 inches wide, the l'aune 8 pans. They have also established a small fabric of fine cloths, which they term à façon de Louviers, at 10 liv. an auln, but not comparable to the original.
>
> I should here observe, that these Londrins, of which at all these towns I took patterns, are a very light, beautiful, well dyed, bright cloth, that have had, and deservedly, from quality and price the greatest success in the Levant. I saw the wool they are made of, and should not have known it from a good specimen from the South Downs of Sussex.[73]

Muirhead too made some notes on this industry in 1789 in the course of which he states that 'a single house employs from 700 to 800 workmen', but otherwise adds nothing of interest; indeed he cribs the last sentence in the quotation from Swinburne.[74]

Going down the Garonne from Toulouse, a considerable number of travellers arrived at the great port of Bordeaux. *The Gentleman's Guide* writes thus of it:

> This town is large, populous, and extremely commercial. The harbour (or rather that side of the river on which the town is built) forms a half moon, and receives ships of the greatest burthen, as the tide flows full and rises twenty-four feet high; the merchant houses (which range along the quay near two miles and a half in length) are all built of hewn stone, exactly uniform; and most of them ornamented with sculpture and balconies: in the center there is a large square, one side of which is form'd by a magnificent change, with an equestrian statue of the present king.[75]

Jervis, who spent ten days in Bordeaux in 1773, maintains that because of the toll exacted by the British Navy during the Seven Years War France would have preferred to abandon her trade with the West Indies and confine her efforts to the Mediterranean. Yet, he continues,

> after all I have said of their indifference, and despondence, touching their West India Trade, my Readers will be surpriz'd to learn, that 2210 Sail of Stout ships upon an Average of 300 Tons each, are employ'd in that very Trade from Bordeaux alone which rais'd its head immediately after the Peace, notwithstanding the havock the English cruisers had made, owing to the English insuring their Ships. Insomuch that after a years Peace, they employed more and better ships in this Trade than before the War.[76]

A somewhat odd state of affairs . . .

The Duchess of Northumberland, who visited Bordeaux in the following year, definitely preferred it to Marseilles:

> I drove all about the City & Quays . . . Trade seems to flourish much here & all the people appear to be busy & employ'd in all kind of maritime & commercial works as twisting Cables, mending Sails, &c. The military stores here of all kinds is surprizing; none astonish'd me so much as the number of pitch Kettles of which I was persuaded I saw several hundred thousand collected together in a large open Place.

With her eye for picturesque detail she continues:

> The Quay is 3 Miles long & the Shops upon it are kept by all Nations as appears by the inscriptions upon them which are promiscuously in French, English, Italian, Dutch & German. There is also a vast quantity of Blacks of both Sexes, some of whom are vast Beaux & tye a bag to their Wool & powder it. Upon the whole I think Bordeaux much preferable to Marseilles, it is much sweeter, people seem busier & it appears to be more populous, all the promenades which are very numerous, are crowded every evening with well dress'd People. The public Garden is chiefly walk'd in of a morning. The peoples Complexions here are fully Mulatto and even a dark shade of that . . . The opposite shore from the Quay is extremely

beautiful and affords a most lovely Prospect. Warlike Stores such as Artillery Cables &c are in vast profusion everywhere.[77]

Lord Herbert appears to have been most struck with the new theatre which was completed in time for his arrival in 1780. He speaks rather critically of it — 'It is in a great stile, but I think not the thing' — though he reports that it 'is said to have cost the Town 3 Millions'.[78] When Young arrived there in 1787, he was much impressed with the new theatre — 'by far the most magnificent in France' — and he penned a famous passage on the prosperity of this great port on the eve of the Revolution at a time when it was ahead of its rival, Marseilles, though after its vicissitudes during the Revolutionary and Napoleonic Wars it was never to regain its old importance:

> Much as I had read and heard of the commerce, wealth, and magnificence of this city, they greatly surpassed my expectations. Paris did not answer at all, for it is not to be compared to London; but you must not name Liverpool in comparison with Bourdeaux . . . The *place royale*, with the statue of Louis XV in the middle, is a fine opening, and the buildings which form it regular and handsome. But the quarter of the *chapeau rouge* is truly magnificent, consisting of noble houses, built, like the rest of the city, of white hewn stone . . . The new houses, that are building in all quarters of the town, mark, too clearly to be misunderstood, the prosperity of the place. The skirts are everywhere composed of new streets with still newer ones marked out, and partly built.

He was also struck with the wealth of the merchants:

> The mode of living that takes place here among merchants is highly luxurious. Their houses and establishments are on expensive scales. Great entertainments, and many served on plate: high play is a much worse thing; — and the scandalous chronicle speaks of merchants keeping the dancing and singing girls of the theatre at salaries which ought to import no good to their credit.

Elsewhere he adds:

All the world knows that an immense commerce is carried on at this city; every part of it exhibits to the traveller's eye unequivocal proofs that it is great; the ships that lye in the river are always too numerous to count easily; I guess there are at present between 3 and 400, besides small craft and barges . . . Here are every sign of a great and flourishing trade; crowds of men all employed, busy, and active, and the river much wider than the Thames at London, animated with much commercial motion, will leave no one in doubt . . . Shipbuilding is a considerable article of their trade; they have built sixty ships here in one year . . . The export of wine alone is reckoned to amount to 8,000[79] tons, besides which brandy must be an immense article.[80]

As relatively few British travellers ventured into Brittany, there are few accounts of the other great Atlantic port at Nantes. Wraxall, who deliberately chose to visit parts of France which were not frequented by the average traveller, made his way in 1775 across this neglected province via St Malo and Rennes and was much impressed with what he found at Nantes:

Nantes is a noble city, and its situation is equally advantageous and agreeable, being built on the easy declivity of a hill descending on every side to the river. The Loire itself may almost vie with the Thames . . . The great quay is more than a mile in length; the buildings very superb, and chiefly erected since the late peace of 1763. As its commerce is annually increasing, the city is consequently in a state of continual improvement, and advance in beauty.[81]

Young was even more enthusiastic when he arrived there in 1788; he was particularly struck with the contrast between the wealth and luxury that he found, after all the poverty and backwardness that he had encountered on his journey through Brittany. He went to the newly-built theatre — 'twice as large as Drury Lane, and twice as magnificent':

Mon Dieu! cried I to myself, do all the wastes, the deserts, the heath, ling, furz, broom, and bog, that I have passed for 300 miles, lead to this spectacle! What a miracle, that all this splendour and wealth of the cities in France should be so unconnected with the country! There are no gentle transitions

The Towns, Trade and Industry

from ease to comfort, from comfort to wealth; you pass at once from beggary to profusion — from misery in mud cabins to Mademoiselle Saint-Huberti in splendid spectacles at 500 livres a night (21£.17s.6d.).

'The town', he adds, 'has that sign of prosperity of new buildings, which never deceives. The quarter of the *comedie* is magnificent, all the streets at right angles and of white stone.' Later he enters into a fair amount of detail about the trade of the port:

The accounts I received here of the trade of the place, made the number of ships in the sugar trade 120, which import to the amount of about 32 millions; 20 are in the slave trade; these are by far the greatest articles of their commerce; they have an export of corn, which is considerable from the provinces washed by the Loire, and are not without minoteries, but vastly inferior to those of the Garonne. Wines and brandy are great articles, and manufactures even from Switzerland, particularly printed linens and cottons, in imitation of Indian, which the Swiss make cheaper than the French fabrics of the same kind, yet they are brought quite across France. They export some of the linens of Bretagne, but not at all compared with S. Maloes, which has been much longer established in that business.

To this Young adds two further points: first, that as with other French ports its trade with Britain's former American colonies was negligible, and that in general its trade was not as great as before the War of American Independence, partly owing to the fact that the French government had recently allowed the Americans to trade with its West Indian colonies 'by which means the navigation of much sugar was lost to France, and foreign fabrics introduced by the same channel'.[82]

Although the author of *A Tour, sentimental and descriptive*, published in 1788, declares that 'Packets are now established between Havre and Southampton' and did himself return to England by that route, this port was not often visited in our period.[83] However, Young, who followed routes very different from those of the average tourist, did go there and was greatly impressed with its prosperity. This was, of course, largely owing to its position on the estuary of the Seine, which made it the port for Rouen and, beyond it, Paris: 'Enquiries are not necessary to find out the prosperity of this town; it is nothing equivocal: fuller of motion, life, and activity, than any place I have been at in France . . . The harbour's mouth is narrow and formed by a mole, but it enlarges into two oblong basons of greater breadth; these are full of ships, to the number of some hundreds, and the quays around are thronged with business, all hurry, bustle, and animation.' Of the trade carried on by this port he writes later:

> There is not only an immense commerce carried on here, but it is on a rapid increase; there is no doubt its being the fourth town in France for trade. The harbour is a forest of masts . . . They have some very large merchantmen in the Guinea trade of 500 or 600 tons but by far their greatest commerce is to the West-India Sugar Islands . . . Situation must of necessity give them a great coasting trade, for as ships of burthen cannot go up to Rouen, this place is the emporium for that town, for Paris, and all the navigation of the Seine, which is very great.[84]

The account which our travellers offer of the principal ports of the country bears ample testimony to the flourishing condition of France's foreign trade on the eve of the Revolution. As we have seen, trade inside the country, on the other hand, met many obstacles in the shape of internal customs barriers.[85] There are occasional complaints from British travellers about French backwardness in the mechanical arts which contribute to the comforts of everyday life. 'Every thing', Smollett declares, 'shews a deficiency in the mechanic arts. There is not a door, nor a window, that shuts close. The hinges, locks, and latches are of iron, coarsely made, and ill contrived. The very chimnies are built so open, that they admit both rain and sun, and all of them smoke intolerably.'[86] Peckham develops further his complaints about such deficiencies:

> Can you believe that this all sufficient people, who look on the rest of Europe with contempt, are in most of the mechanic arts at least a century behind the *savage* English, as they affect to term us? In their tapestry, looking-glasses, and coach varnish, they are confessedly our superiors, but their carriages are more clumsy than our dung-carts; their inns inferior to an English ale-house; their floors, both above and below, of brick

or a kind of plaster, without carpets; their joists unceiled, the windows without pullies, drawn up to a certain height, where they catch a hook which prevents their falling; the tables consist of three or four planks nailed together, and the houses are totally destitute of every kind of elegance, I had almost said convenience. I do not mean to include the houses of the opulent great, as money will purchase the elegant superfluities of every country. But in this situation you will find the inns and the houses of the gentry and tradesmen.[87]

While some exceptions are made, these are very severe strictures on what certain of our travellers regarded as signs of French backwardness.

Although Young's primary interest was in agriculture, he also provides valuable information about the state of French industry in the period 1787–9. When he visited Beauvais in 1787, he inspected the tapestry works, and after declaring that 'this is one of the manufacturing towns of France that seems the most brisk and active in business', he goes on to describe the other textile industries there:

> I viewed the callico printing-house of Messrs. Garnierdans and Co. which is upon such a scale as to employ 600 hands constantly; there is no difference between this fabric and similar ones in England, and all the patterns I saw were very common, seeming not to aim so much at elegance or nicety of execution, as at the dispatch of a large undertaking, yet Paris is their principal demand; they print a great quantity of Indian callicoes; their madder comes from Alsace. There are three other manufactures in the town, and all four employ about 1800 hands; but the chief fabric is the woollen, which employs 7 or 8000 hands in the town and the adjacent country. They make, under various denominations, coarse stuffs for the cloathing of the country people, for mens jackets and womens petticoats, &c. a truly useful and important fabric, which works only French wool, and in general that of the country. There are also stocking engines at work.[88]

He had earlier visited at Abbeville the famous cloth factory set up in 1675 by the Dutchman, Van Robais, with Colbert's encouragement. As he points out, this had seen better days (it was close to 1805): 'They say that 1500 hands are employed, of which 250 are weavers; but they have experienced a great declension since the establishment of the fabric at Louviers, in Normandie.'[89]

Young was particularly enthusiastic, both in his travel journal and in his chapter on industry, about the cloths produced at Louviers, which he visited in 1788:

> Monsieur Decretot's fabrics of fine cloths in this place, are, I believe, the first in the world; I know none in England, nor any where else, that can be compared with them; the beauty and the great variety of his productions remind me more of the fertility of Mr. Wedgewood's inventions, than any other fabric I have seen in france. Mons. Decretot brings out something new for every year, and even for every season.
>
> The common cloths of this place are well known; but Mons. D. has now made some of the finest and most beautiful cloth that has ever yet been seen, of the pure undyed Peruvian or Vigonia wool, if it may be so called, for it is not produced by a sheep; this rises to the vast price of 110 liv. the auln, 3/4ths wide; the raw wool is 19 liv. 10s. the lb. or thrice as dear as the very finest Spanish: other fabrics he has made of the wool of the chamois from Persia. The finest cloth he makes of common wool, unmixed, is of Spanish, at 6 liv. 4s. the lb. and the price 33 liv. the auln, 3/4ths broad. *Rayé en soie marbre* 5/8th broad, 32 liv. *Castorine rayé en soie*, same price and breadth. Of all these curious fabrics, as well as the wools they are made of, he very obligingly gave me specimens.

Of the same owner's cotton mill he has less to say: 'View the cotton mill here, which is the most considerable to be found in France. They spin to the length of 40,000 aulns per lb. machinery in this mill saves in labour in the proportion of three hands doing the work of eight.'[90]

Another Norman town famous for its textiles which Young visited was Elbeuf:

> The fabrics here are chiefly cloths, and by far the greater part are of Spanish wool, a small proportion of that of Roussillon and Berri . . . It is spun in the country for twelve leagues around; the price of spinning is from 10 to 13s. the lb. average 11s. for which they spin the fine Spanish to the length of 825 aulns of Paris; a good spinner will do a pound in a day,

but that is beyond the medium; a very few however demand two days. The carder has 6 to 8s. a lb. Mons. Grande has some jennies, by which a woman spins the work of eight.[91]

On the doorstep of Rouen, for Young 'the Manchester of France', he visited a factory at Darnétal:

> The chief fabrics here are cloths, a façon d'Elboeuf, espagnolettes, flanelles, ratteens. Of these the principal are the espagnolettes of 3/4th breadth; and price 5 liv. 10s. to 9 liv. 10s. for mens waistcoats, ladies habits, &c. The wool is in general from Spain and Berri, but not the Spanish of the first quality; the Berri is as good, or better than the Spanish for this fabric. The spinners are paid 14 to 16s. the lb. for which they spin it to the length of 600 aulns. Carding is 2s. the lb. and no other than carding wool is used here. The weaver is also paid by the pound, at 15s. therefore the weaving and spinning is nearly the same price; many of all these hands are in the country. The master manufacturers here assert, that their fabrics are as good and as cheap as similar ones in England, but they sell none thither.[92]

In his journeys round France, Young came across many examples of the factory system, but he preferred domestic industry. Instead of large factories he would rather see 'the more diffusive and by much the more useful signs of industry and employment, which spread into every quarter of a city, raise entire streets of little comfortable houses, convert poor villages into little towns, and dirty cottages into neat habitations'.[93] At Châteauroux he found that a large cloth factory which employed 500 people as well as 1,500 to 1,800 spinners in the neighbourhood had gone bankrupt. Now there were in the town 'about 80 private weavers' and he maintains that 'these private fabrics, which do not depend on any great establishment, are vastly preferable to concentrating the branches in one great inclosure'.[94] The silk industry for which Tours had once been famous had greatly declined. 'There is', he writes, 'a large building called the *Manufacture Royale*, in which many workmen were once employed, but none at present, as it is found more advantageous to give the silk to the workmen, in order for their weaving it in their own houses.'[95]

In his notes on French manufactures Young gives numerous examples of the way in which industry spread from the towns into the countryside. At Montauban, for instance, he found that there was a *manufacture royale* for woollen goods, 'but in general the spinning and weaving are carried on both in the town and country, not only on account of the master manufacturers, but also by private weavers, who make and carry their stuffs to market undressed'.[96] At Beauvais he found that the woollen industry employed '7 or 8000 hands in the town and the adjacent country' and that at Rheims there were '10,000 persons in the town and country about it, supported by the manufactures'.[97]

The spread of industry into the country enabled many poorer peasants to eke out some sort of a living by supplementing what they could earn by working their own or other people's land. Women and children were, of course, an essential part of this peasant workforce. At Caussade, near Montauban, Young noted: 'This country is full of peasant proprietors of land, who all abound very much with domestic manufactures; they work their wool into common cloths and camblets, and all the women and girls spin wool and hemp, of which they make linen.'[98] Writing of the woollen industry at Bédarieux in Languedoc he adds: 'The villages in the mountains are all employed in this manufacture', while of the same industry at Carcassonne he noted: 'The master manufacturers give the materials to the weavers, who are paid by the piece, and thus the manufacture spreads into the country both spinning and weaving.'[99] At the other end of the country, at Elbeuf, the wool, he writes, 'is spun in the country for twelve leagues around'.[100]

An anonymous army officer who visited Rouen in 1787 and took walks into the surrounding country, observed women and children at work in the villages for the local linen industry. He did not find many signs of prosperity in either of the two villages which he passed through. Of the second he writes:

> The villages in the valleys [round Rouen] appeard to be full of industry & manufactures, the fields all round being covered with linnens of various collours, some twisted round the avenues of trees which are every where to be found in France. Every rivulet turned two or three Mills. I had the curiosity to look into many of their chaumieres or huts to see if so much industry rendered them easy in their circumstances; every woman and child appeared to have employ & to be very dilligent — but their huts were the picture of misery & famine.

On the other hand, in describing the first village which he had visited, he decided that the inhabitants 'appear more happy or less miserable here than in the other parts of France which I have seen'.[101]

Young was strongly opposed to industry 'spreading into the country and turning what ought to be farmers into manufacturers':

> The greatest fabrics in France are the cottons and woollens of Normandie, the woollens of Picardy and Champagne, the linens of Bretagne, and the silks and hardware of the Lyonois. Now, if manufactures be the true encouragement of agriculture, the vicinity of those great fabrics ought to be the best cultivated districts in the kingdom. I have visited all those manufactures, and remarked the attendant culture, which is unexceptionably so execrable, that one would be much more inclined to think there was something pestiferous to agriculture in the neighbourhood of a manufacture, than to look up to it as a mean of encouragement.

He then takes the reader on a tour of these provinces and denounces in strong language the neglect of the land wherever industry spreads into the country.[102]

In the textile industry as in other manufacturing processes the role played by English expatriates was considerable, as we have already seen with the Holker cotton factory in Rouen. On his return journey in 1765 Smollett stopped at Sens where he 'visited a manufacture of that stuff we call Manchester velvet, which is here made and dyed to great perfection, under the direction of English workmen, who have been seduced from their own country'.[103] The cotton mill which Young visited at Louviers was 'conducted by four Englishmen, from some of Mr. Arkwright's mills', while nearby he found 'a great fabric of copper-plates, for bottoming the king's ships; the whole an English colony'.[104] Much further south, in Brive-la-Gaillarde, he met with another enterprise set up by two expatriates:

> They have also a cotton mill and fabric which is but in its infancy, has only one combing machine, and three double ones for spinning; they say that this machine, with the assistance of 15 people, does the work of 80; this undertaking has been established and is carried on by Messrs. Mills and

Clarke, the former an Englishman from Canterbury, the latter from Ireland, both induced by encouragements to settle in France.[105]

As with new industries established in the Paris region, English entrepreneurs and workmen could often receive government subsidies to encourage them to bring with them their more advanced technology.

The curing of leather also brought English workmen into France, as Young found at Pont-Audemer in Normandy: 'Wait on Mons. Martin, director of the *manufacture royale* of leather. I saw eight or ten Englishmen that are employed here (there are 40 in all),' At least one of these was dissatisfied with his lot. Young 'conversed with one from Yorkshire, who told me he had been deceived into coming; for though they are well paid, yet they find things very dear, instead of very cheap, as they had been given to understand'.[106]

It is clear that many British workmen must have been dissatisfied with their lot, as was the one the Cradocks met at a glassworks at Sèvres:

> Deux des principaux employés nous pilotèrent. A peine étions-nous entrés dans la manufacture qu'un des chefs d'atelier, que je reconnus aussitôt pour un compatriote, s'avanfa vers nous, et voyant que nous étions Anglais, commença à parler d'une façon offensante de tous les Français, particulièrement de ses collègues. S'animant peu à peu, il arriva à un tel point d'irritation qu'il se mit à jurer contre ceux qui nous accompagnaient. Ceux-ci, sans prononcer un mot, se retirèrent l'un après l'autre. Après leur départ, il s'excusa de son mieux vis-à-vis de nous, et nous dit que sa colère venait surtout de la manière dont on le traitait à la manufacture. Nous découvrîmes que cet homme était un habile ouvrier anglais, auquel on avait persuadé, par l'appât d'une forte récompense, de venir en France at d'y dévoiler quelques secrets de son métier; mais, lorsqu'on sut que, d'après les lois anglaises, ce traître ne pourrait rentrer dans sa patrie, non seulement on ne lui tint compte d'aucune promesse, mais on abusa même de son talent et de son travail.[107]

The best-known English immgrant, William Wilkinson, the

younger brother of the famous ironmaster, John, had begun to set up in 1777, at the invitation of the French government, an iron foundry for the making and boring of cannon on the island of Indret near Nantes. Cradock records how he and his wife visited the works eight years later and also mentions his contacts with William Wilkinson:

> Sailed on the Loire to the Island D'Indret. The iron-foundry there is said to be the largest in France. We had a letter of introduction to see it, from Mr. Wilkinson, formerly of Colebrook Dale, and now frequently at our hotel at Nantes.
>
> We met with every civility; but from the account of one of the proprietors, I soon began to suspect that our English acquaintance was, in reality, the head of the concern, and on our return he spoke openly, how much he wished to be withdrawn from thence to a station in his native country. That information I conveyed to my friend Mr. Fector, of Dover, and he kindly referred all particulars to Mr. Pitt, who soon afterwards caused him to be removed, greatly to his advantage.[108]

Cradock does not enlarge on this last remark to explain when and under what circumstances William Wilkinson returned to England.

Young, who visited the island in 1788, offers somewhat more technical detail in his account of the foundry and mentions that a steam engine was now in use:

> Messrs. Epivent had the goodness to attend me in a water expedition, to view the establishment of Mr Wilkinson, for boring cannon, in an island in the Loire below Nantes. Until that well-known English manufacturer arrived, the French knew nothing of the art of casting cannon solid, and then boring them. Mr Wilkinson's machinery, for boring four cannons, is now at work, moved by tide wheels; but they have erected a steam engine, with a new apparatus for boring seven more; M. de la Motte, who has the direction of the whole, shewed us also a model of this engine, about six feet long, five high, and four or five broad; which he worked for us, by making a small fire under the boiler that is not bigger than a large tea-kettle; one of the best machines for a travelling philosopher that I have seen.

Later he adds this further detail: 'The coals cost here 34 liv. the 2000 lb. they come by the river from the neighbourhood, and they calculate that the new steam-engine, now erected, will consume 100 liv. a day.'[109]

Although Young emphasises the part taken by William Wilkinson in the establishment of this foundry, in reality an important role was played by Ignace de Wendel, a scion of a famous Lorraine family of industrialists. Both men were also associated in the foundation of a more important undertaking, extended in the nineteenth century by the Schneider family — the famous *fonderie royale* at Montcenis, near Le Creusot. Here in 1785 they installed the most modern plant on the English pattern: a foundry using not wood, but coke, made from the coal of nearby mines, with steam engines, forges and a horse-drawn railway. Young gives two accounts of this famous foundry. The first is in his travel journal for 3 August 1789:

> It is the seat of one Mons. *Weelkainsong*'s establishment for casting and boring cannon: I have already described one near Nantes. The French say, that this active Englishman is brother-in-law of Dr. Priestley, and therefore a friend of mankind; and that he taught them to bore cannon, in order to give liberty to America. The establishment is very considerable; there are from 500 to 600 men employed, besides colliers; five steam engines are erected for giving the blasts, and for boring, and a new one building. I conversed with an Englishman who works in the glass-house, in the crystal branch; there were once many, but only two are left at present: he complained of the country, saying there was nothing good in it but wine and brandy; of which things I question not but he makes a sufficient use.[110]

The entry for Montcenis, in the chapter on industry, supplies a few additional details:

> These are amongst the greatest iron works in France, and owe their present magnitude entirely to Mons. de Calonne;[111] they were established by Mr. Wilkinson from England, in the same expedition into France, in which he fixed those on the Loire near Nantes. The iron mine is three miles off, but those of coal on the spot. They cast and bore cannon on the greatest scale, having five steam engines at work, and a sixth building:

they have iron roads for the waggons, make coak of coal, a l'Anglois, &c. &c. Here is also a pretty considerable crystal glass work, in which two Englishmen are still left. There is no navigation, as necessary as coals or iron; but the Charolais canal is within two leagues, and they hope it will come here.[112]

Here we see clearly the new forces of the Industrial Revolution at work in France on the eve of the Revolution. Yet such advanced economic developments were rare before 1789, and the foundries established at Indret and Le Creusot proved a failure.

In his chapter on industry Young enters into a considerable amount of detail about what he observed in this line — often on quite a small scale — over the length and breadth of France. One other of his descriptions of what he observed in this field must be quoted — that of the famous glass works at St Gobain which still exist. He visited them on his way from Soissons to St Quentin in 1787:

The fabric of plate glass here is by far the greatest and most celebrated in Europe; the inclosure is great, and the buildings are on a vast scale; 1800 men are employed on the works and in the provision, &c. of wood. I was so fortunate as to arrive about half an hour before they began to run; there is a vast furnace in the center of the building containing the pots of melted *metal*, and on each side of it a row of ovens with small furnaces for casting. An immense table of cast copper, as I judge by my eye (for I did not care to measure any thing), twelve feet long and eight broad, by five inches thick, stands at the mouth of the annealing oven heated by a furnace on each side of it. When every thing is ready for running the glass, a comis enters, the doors are bolted, and silence is proclaimed by one of the men striking an iron bar on the ground; if any person speaks but a word after this, he is fined heavily. The furnace, in which is the melted glass, is then opened, and the pots of 18 inches diameter are drawn out; two men, receiving it upon a sort of barrow, wheel it to the table above-mentioned, where an iron crank suspended from a windlass is fixed, and hoisting the metal, is emptied onto the table. A great copper roller is pushed over it, moving on two strips or bars of iron or copper, the thickness of which determines that of the intended plate glass, for the pot discharging its contents between them, and the roller brought gradually over it, which flattens by its great weight the metal to the thickness of those bars; the glass is then pushed forward from the table into the oven heated to receive it for annealing, or cooling gradually, to prevent cracking. The dexterity, coolness, freedom from confusion, with which every thing is done, was very pleasing.

The grinding house is great; the whole of that operation is performed by hand. The motive for establishing this manufacture here, in a situation by no means convenient for navigation, though the distance is not great, was that alone of the plenty of wood. It is in the middle of a great forest belonging to the Duke of Orleans, hired by the company that carried on the manufacture. All the fuel employed is beech wood, to which circumstance they attribute the superiority of the French glass to that of England.[113]

The importance of wood as a fuel for industry in France before the Revolution is here underlined.

The growing shortage of wood and consequently its high price were noted by various travellers as they journeyed around France. Writing in Rouen in February 1787, an army officer complained: 'Wood is a most extravagant article both here and at Paris — Here for one piece of stick about 2 feet long and 6 inches in Diameter and split in halves you must pay 12 sols or 6 pence English — We burnt yesterday and kept a moderate fire 22 of them which cost 5s 6d english, and at Paris I burnt in one week a Demi voit[114] de bois, cost 15 Livres.'[115] One of the things which struck an English clergyman a year later about the Seine at Paris was the spectacle of large quantities of wood floating downstream to the capital: 'The river is crowded with barges, ferry boats and rafts of fire-wood. The latter are committed to the current, and sometimes float more than 100 miles. A race of muddy Tritons wade through half the width of the river, and carry on their backs, by piece-meal, the dripping wood.' He obviously picked up complaints about the high price of wood: 'In the year 1783, there was suddenly an unaccountable scarcity of fuel in Paris. The consequent distress may be easily conceived. From that time the price has risen considerably, and coals are still confined to the use of manufactures.'[116]

Writing in February of the following year in Vienne in the

Rhône valley, Muirhead relates how his French companion simply helped himself when refused wood to heat their rooms: 'As the waiter peremptorily refused us fire for the bedrooms, alleging there was no timber in the house, and Monsieur de S— strongly suspected her veracity, he slyly purloined some faggots and bellows into the bargain.' Muirhead connects this incident with the general shortage and high price of wood:

> Yet fuel has become rare in Dauphiny, owing to the intricacy and absurdity of the forest laws, which, precisely in proportion to their intricacy and absurdity, have contributed to the general licence. Where communities have a right of cutting, each individual has snatched what lay first in his way, regardless of the wants of futurity; and no tribunal has been found hardy enough to enforce regulations which prescribe to landholders the complicated details of managing their forests, under the most grievous penalties. A proprietor, who thins his forests at his pleasure, is liable to have the whole confiscated, and to a fine of 3000 livres; repetition of the act subjects him to banishment, and the burning of his own trees, to death! Nor is this the only province in France, where want of timber begins to be seriously felt. As the woods diminish, and population and manufactures increase, recourse must be had, however reluctantly, to coal, of which large magazines remain yet unopened.[117]

Writing from Lille, from a region which even then did not lack coal mines, Priestley drew the extraordinary deduction: 'Their fireplaces are much unlike ours, but pretty enough, and they are all made for the burning of wood, as the country produces no coal.'[118] Thicknesse has more useful comments on this subject when he is relating his travels in this part of France:

> In the town of Aire, I saw a great quantity of coals, in a brickmaker's yard, which the man informed me, came from Condé and Valenciennes. It is generally believed in England, that there are no coals in France, but the truth is, there are great plenty in many parts of France, as well on the south, as north side of the kingdom, but the French consider them as very obnoxious, and even dangerous to burn, and French servants often object to live with English families at Calais, Dunkirk, Lisle, &c. because they burn the *Charbon de terre*.[119]

If Muirhead and Thicknesse exaggerate the reserves of coal in France, they mention the prejudice against both its domestic and industrial use. 'Pit-coal', the former writes, 'is now pretty generally used in Lyons. The smell is sensibly offensive to a stranger — and I am convinced that continental people do not affect delicacy when, on their arrival in London, they give it a place in their list of grievances.' He found that coke was also used in Lyons, both industrially and domestically: 'In the neighbourhood of Lyons are furnaces or kilns, in which coal-dust is reduced to coke (*charbon désouffré*). In this state it is used not only as charcoal in the manufactures, but frequently as fuel in private families.' When he reached Marseilles, he discovered the surprising fact that coal could be imported more cheaply by sea from the north-east of England than when brought by land from mines in the neighbourhood: 'The soaperies consume no inconsiderable quantity of coal. That of Newcastle is preferred, being of a superior quality, and *cheaper* than coal carried landways, though only fifteen miles distant.'[120]

Young devoted a good deal of attention to the use of wood and coal, both in his account of French industries and in a short chapter devoted to the subject. He refused to accept the view, generally held in France as increasing shortages sent up the price, that wood was too dear. His conclusion to his survey of the use of coal is, as usual, forthright:

> The want of vigour in working the coal-mines in France, is to be attributed to two causes; 1, the price of wood has not risen sufficiently to force this branch of industry; and, 2, the want of capital, which affects every thing in that kingdom, prevents exertions being made with the necessary animation. But these evils will correct themselves; the general rise in the price of wood, which, so far from being an evil, as it is universally thought in France, is only a proof of national improvement, will by degrees force the consumption of coals; and when these are in the necessary demand, they will be produced in greater quantities.[121]

On his travels round the country he found that coal was being mined in a considerable number of places. At Montcenis it was available on the spot and at St Étienne it was 'almost for nothing'. The coal used in the sugar refineries of Orleans came from near Moulins. Other mines in the southern half of the country were at

Givors, which supplied nearby Lyons, as well as Marseilles, which also drew coal from Provence. In northern France there were mines near Nantes, Saumur and Angers as well as in the Cotentin peninsula. Young offers slightly more detail about the mines at Valenciennes; he was informed that 'they are 700 feet deep; the coal is drawn up by four horses; they have four steam engines'.[122] Presumably this is a reference to the famous mines owned by the Compagnie d'Anzin near Valenciennes, which in 1789 employed 4,000 workers. Another traveller who passed through Valenciennes also noted the presence of coal nearby and he has some interesting comments on the steel industry to which it gave rise:

> Wood is almost universally used throughout France for fuel, but in the neighbourhood of the place coal is found, which they call *charbon du terre*. They have also some considerable works, which, upon inquiry, I found were steel ones; the French are daily gaining ground in the art of tempering this metal, and giving it that lustre and polish which has been carried to such perfection in this country.[123]

Much of the coal produced in France was of poor quality. Swinburne, a modest landowner in the Durham coalfield, noted that some of the boats going down the Loire from Roanne were loaded with 'a bad kind of coal'.[124] 'The coals of the Cotentin', Young was told at Cherbourg, 'are not half so good as what is brought from England.' At Cherbourg he found English coal used in the glassworks despite its extraordinary price which was swollen by import duties:

> In the manufacture of blown plate glass, a great quantity of Newcastle coal is burnt; 13 keel, or 103 chaldrons, cost, all English charges included, about 7500 liv.; the French duty 3600 liv.; and port charges, &c. make it in all about 11,000 liv. which being near 5 l. a chaldron, seems an enormous price, at which to buy fuel for a manufacture.

At Dunkirk seaborne English coal could compete successfully with the local product: 'There is a canal to the coal pits at Valenciennes, but the distance too great, and locks too numerous and expensive to rival the import from England.' Here, he found, coals 'are burnt in every house in the town, and are one-third cheaper than wood'.[125] At Rouen Young met a mining engineer who 'asserts the consumption of English coals, in the generality of Rouen, to be two millions a year. The price is . . . about 80 liv. a ton.' At Nantes he was told that 'one barrique of English [coal] is worth two' of French.[126] While Pont-à-Mousson drew its coal from Saarbrücken, Young too noted the presence of Engish coal at Marseilles.

Yet the demand for coal, either for domestic or industrial use, remained small. At Limoges, he noted, 'I was here assured, that a vein of coal has been found at the depth only of 12 yards, which is 17 feet thick; but it is no where used, either in houses or in manufactures; the iron forges are all worked with charcoal. If this is fact, what a want of capital it proves!' At Valenciennes, which did not lack collieries, he noted: 'Wood is burnt here at the inns, and all the better private houses, but the poor burn coal.' At Montcenis where a mine supplied the newly established *fonderie royale*, he wrote: 'It is remarkable, that at the inn here, and at every house, except those of the common workman, wood is burnt; which shews the absurd prejudices of the French, in spite of price.'[127]

The peace treaty of 1783 stipulated that England and France should appoint commissioners to negotiate new commercial arrangements between the two countries and that these should be completed within two years of 1 January 1784. However, the Foreign Office dragged its feet, and negotiations were not even opened until the spring of 1786. By the beginning of 1785 the French government lost patience at this delay and began to issue *arrêts du conseil* clearly aimed at damaging British trade in order to bring pressure on the government. One of these prohibited the import of a great variety of goods such as saddlery, woollens, hosiery, hardware and most articles of polished steel, while another banned the entry of cottons, muslins, gauzes and linens. The actual effect achieved by these measures is described in an interesting letter by Daniel Pulteney, an MP, on his return from a journey through French Flanders to Brussels. He also mentions the havoc caused in Dunkirk and other smuggling towns by Pitt's Commutation Act of the previous year which, in order to strike a blow at the enormous trade in contraband goods, had increased the tax on windows and drastically reduced the customs duty on tea, one of the most profitable goods for smugglers. Writing from London on 5 October 1785, he describes some recent experiences at Lille:

There is at present, both in France and Flanders, so great a passion for English manufactures that no *arrêt* can prevent their sale; and I was told by a banker at Lille, who was changing me a bill at the rate of twenty-five livres for 1 l. sterling, an exchange of ten per cent. advantage, that Dunkerque and the smuggling towns had been entirely ruined by Pitt's Commutation Bill, and that it would be difficult to find 100 guineas of English money in all Flanders, whereas, during the period of smuggling, 200,000 were melted down there annually; and that, as Dunkerque is a free port, the best prospect the citizens had now, under the French king's *arrêt*, was to smuggle *against* their own country. I saw myself, on the great square at Lille, a curious proof of the efficacy of an *arrêt*. The King had forbidden, under a great penalty, affixing over any warehouse Magazin Anglois, to avoid which I saw at Lille, over the greatest warehouse in the place, the following inscription verbatim: 'Magazin François', — lower in capital letters, and in English, 'where are likewise sold goods of all other nations'.[128]

In the following year, however, a commercial treaty which removed all prohibitions on the import of English goods into France and reduced many tariff barriers in both countries, was successfully negotiated in Paris by William Eden. It came into force in May 1787. The Eden Treaty was extremely unpopular with French industrialists as France was flooded with the manufactured goods of a more economically advanced country. It is true that Young, who in 1787 and 1788 made many inquiries about the effects, real or feared, of the treaty, found that opinion in Bordeaux in a great wine-exporting region was much more favourable: 'Here it is considered as a wise measure, that tends equally to the benefit of both countries.' He goes into some detail about how the treaty was working out in that part of France:

> The intercourse between this port and England has been increased a great deal since the treaty. Warehouses of English goods are opened. The article which has hitherto sold the best and quickest, is the Staffordshire potteries; the quantities of these which have been sold is very great: but the hardware sent hitherto has been found so dear, that it could not be sold in competition with French and German, except in a very few articles. Of sadlery there are several shops opened that have

sold largely. Beer has been tried, but would not do . . . Wine has increased in export to England, but not so much as was expected; before the treaty it was 8000 tonneaux a year, and is now not risen to 12,000 . . . Brandy has also increased.[129]

Manufacturers, particularly in the textile industries, were extremely hostile to the treaty. At Abbeville, for instance, Young noted in 1787: 'They expressed great apprehensions that it would prove extremely detrimental to their manufactures . . . They said that, . . . there were intelligent persons in their town, who had been in England, and who were clearly of opinion, that the similar English fabrics were some cheaper and others better, which, aided by fashion in France, would give them a great advantage.'[130] At Amiens Young reports: 'I conversed with several masters, who united entirely with those of Abbeville in condemning the treaty of commerce', and he later adds: 'They are well convinced that they cannot in any one instance, as they assert, stand the competition of English goods.' In his notes on French industry Young gives under Amiens an example of the difficulties it faced: 'I examined their cotton stockings carefully, and found that 4 or 5 livres was the price of such as were equal to those which I had brought from England, and which cost at London 2s. 6d. This difference is surprizing, and proves, if any thing can, the vast superiority of our cotton fabrics.'[131] He found the same gloom at Beauvais:

> The opinion universal among the manufacturers here is, that the English fabrics are so superior in cheapness, from the wise policy of the encouragement, that those of Beauvais, should they come in competition, must sink; so much of the fabrics here as are for the consumption of the lower people might perhaps stand it, but not any others; and they think the most mischievous war would not have been so injurious to France as this most pernicious treaty.[132]

Young was quite taken aback by the violence of anti-British feeling when he arrived in Lille in November 1787. Shortly before, Prussia, with British support, had sent an army into the United Provinces to restore the power of the Stadtholder, thus destroying the influence of France which had supported the opposition party. Young noted in his travel journal:

> The cry here for a war with England amazed me. Every one

I talked with said, it was beyond a doubt the English had called the Prussian army into Holland; and that the motives in France for a war were numerous and manifest. It is easy enough to discover, that the origin of all this violence is the commercial treaty, which is execrated here, as the most fatal stroke to their manufactures they ever experienced.

Elsewhere he adds that the manufacturers there wanted a war 'as the only means of escaping that ideal ruin, which they are all sure must flow from the influx of English fabrics to rival their own'.[133]

When Young returned to France in 1788, he found that even a great port like Nantes shared this hostility to the Eden Treaty: 'In conversation here on this treaty with some very respectable commercial gentlemen, they were loud against it; insisted that France sent no fabrics whatever to England in consequence of it; not to the amount of a single sol; some goes, and the same went before the treaty; and that England has not imported more wines or brandy than usual, or at least to a very small amount.'[134] At Rouen he met with the same hostile reaction: 'The quantity of merchandize of all sorts that has been imported here from England since the treaty, is very considerable, especially Staffordshire hardware, and cotton fabrics, and several English houses have been established. They consider the treaty here as highly detrimental to all the manufactures of Normandie.'[135] While in this province, Young had an opportunity of seeing some of these imports from England at the famous fair held at Guibray, and there he actually met a Frenchman who was prepared to take a long-term view of the Eden Treaty:

> I found the quantity of English goods considerable, hard and queen's ware; cloths and cottons. A dozen of common plain plates, 3 livres and 4 livres for a French imitation, but much worse: I asked the man (a Frenchman) if the treaty of commerce would not be very injurious with such a difference — *C'est précisément le contraire, Mons. — quelque mauvaise que soit cette imitation, on n'a encore rien fait d'aussi bien en France; l'année prochaine on fera mieux — nous perfectionnerons — et enfin nous l'emporterons sur vous.* — I believe he is a very good politician, and that, without competition, it is not possible to perfect any fabric. A dozen with blue or green edges; English, 5 livres 5 sous.[136]

Young's view of the treaty was obviously shared by an anonymous English clergyman who had spent much of his youth in France and who returned there in October 1788:

> The manufactures of Amiens, established by Colbert, are very flourishing. The treaty of commerce with England considerably injured those fabricks on its first operation. At present they revive, and have acquired additional vigour from what seemed calculated to oppress them. For, in order to maintain a concurrence with English manufactures, they have lately been brought to a degree of perfection before unknown.[137]

Another traveller picked up in Paris an optimistic view of the long-term advantages which the treaty would bring to France: 'The brief idea formed of it by the most intelligent in Paris was, that for the first four or five years the balance would be with England, and ever after with France — that the superiority of France would arise from advantages, local and fixed, as its soil and climate — that England's present superiority was adventitious, and liable to fluctuation.'[138] How the treaty would have worked out if there had been no Revolution it would be idle to speculate; but when the war between the two countries at last came to an end in 1815, France was economically backward compared with Britain.

When Young quotes the official statistics for Anglo-French trade, he has to concede that in 1788 the balance of trade in manufactured goods was definitely in favour of England, though he argues that the amount was 'very far short of the French ideas, and must, in the nature of things, lessen'. Finding in England's favour a 'balance of eight [millions] in direct objects of agriculture, as corn and meat' leads him to make a sarcastic remark about French agriculture: 'If a people will manage their agriculture in such a preposterous manner, as not to be able to feed themselves, they should esteem themselves highly obliged to any neighbour that will do it for them.'[139]

The Norman fair at Guibray was eclipsed by the more famous one held at Beaucaire near the foot of the Rhône valley, or, as Young put it, 'At this fair of Guibray, merchandize is sold, they say, to the amount of six millions (£262,500) but at that of Beaucaire to ten.'[140] The Dowager Countess of Carlisle describes what she saw there in a letter of July 1779. She perhaps enjoyed most the open-air dancing in the moonlight with the officers of a regiment stationed there and the 'women of fashion' of Beaucaire and Tarascon, but she goes into some detail about the fair itself:

> The fair is just over. The addition of an hundred thousand people every day has not a little added to the heat, or rather suffocation, but it afforded me a most agreeable spectacle for the time, and I am very glad to have seen it. The Rhone covered with vessels; the bridge with passengers; the vast meadow filled with booths, in the manner of the race-ground at York; and the inns crowded with merchants and merchandize, was very entertaining, although it was impossible, after seven in the morning, to bear the streets. The kind of things the fair produced were not such as you could have approved of for Lady Carlisle. The only thing I liked was a set of ornamented perfumed baskets for a toilet, which were indeed very pretty, but which it would have been impossible for me to have got over. The fair, indeed, seems more calculated for merchants than for idle travellers; no *bijouterie*, no *argenterie*; no nick-nacks, or china. For about thirty shillings, however, one can buy a very pretty silk dress, with the trimmings to it; muslins are also every cheap; painted silks beautiful; and scents, *pommades*, and liqueurs, very cheap.[141]

In 1787 the fair continued to attract people from far and wide. Although Young did not go to it, on his way from Montpellier to Nîmes he noted: 'The fair of Beaucaire fills the whole country with business and motion; meet many carts loaded; and nine diligences going or coming.' The next day at Nîmes he wrote of his hotel:

> The house was almost as much a fair from morning to night as Beaucaire itself could be. I dined and supped at the table d'hote; . . . we sat down from twenty to forty at every meal, most motley companies of French, Italians, Spaniards, and Germans, with a Greek and [an] Armenian; and I was informed, that there is hardly a nation in Europe or Asia that has not merchants at this great fair, chiefly for raw silk, of which many millions in value are sold in four days: all the other commodities of the world are to be found there.

Again, in returning on the following day to Nîmes after visiting the Pont du Gard, he was intrigued to meet 'many merchants returning from the fair; each with a child's drum tied to his clock-bag'.⁴² The fair was still held and still drew the crowds in the summer of 1789 despite all the turmoil, including the *Grande Peur*. On 28 July Rigby and his companions found the road from Nîmes

> crowded with people going to a fair at Beaucaire, about twenty miles off. Here we had another specimen of the populousness of this country. The streets were full of people, every house was a shop, and a long quay was crowded with booths full of different kinds of merchandise. Besides these there were a number of vessels in the Rhone, lying alongside the quay, full of articles for sale, and no less crowded with people, access being had to them by boards laid from one to the other. I observed many articles in cast iron.¹⁴³

This relic of earlier trading methods survived well into the next century. It slowly faded out after the coming of the railways.

A number of our travellers remark on the extremes of wealth and poverty which they encountered in French towns and cities. In the 1760s Thicknesse found the contrast between the lot of rich and poor more striking than in England: 'The climate, the wine, the fruit, and the ease and good breeding of the first people in France, are indeed very powerful arguments in favour of the country; but, on the other hand, the dirt and poverty of the numerous poor (and they are very numerous) renders it very inferior to England in this respect.' If there were less poverty, he goes on, 'France would be the most delightful country in the world, either to pass through, or to reside in; but the extreme poverty of the poor, and the poor day-labourers in particular, renders their villages, nay, even their great towns, very filthy.'¹⁴⁴ A decade later Jardine found that French towns lacked a sufficient number of people in between the extremes of riches and poverty: 'The whole seems divided only into two classes, the extremes of society, or the few rich and the many very poor, with too few of those middle ranks which form the best bonds of society, and the strength of the nation.'¹⁴⁵

The same point is made with particular reference to housing by Villiers, who was in France in August 1788; he contrasts 'the grandeur and magnificence of the public buildings' with the mean streets nearby: 'Whilst in one place we find edifices and statues, rivalling the arts of the world, adjoining is a miserable street, narrow, dirty, and unpaved; — houses unadorned, ill-built, and dreary; and inhabitants poor and miserable.' He even goes on to declare: 'The towns are neither pleasant, cleanly, nor well built, as are ours in England, where every part displays elegance, convenience, and propriety; where every one adorns his little habitation with the shew of neatness, and of beauty; — and where the whole place appears (to use the expression of a French gentleman, who was the other day describing Bath) *un palais continuel*.'[146] One imagines that even eighteenth-century Bath had its slums.

Of the poverty she observed in the towns through which she passed between Paris and Lyons, Mrs Piozzi writes:

Every town that should adorn these lovely plains, however, exhibits, upon a nearer approach, misery; the more mortifying, as it is less expected by a spectator, who requires at least some days experience to convince him that the squallid scenes of wretchedness and dirt in which he is obliged to pass the night, will prove more than equivalent to the pleasures he has enjoyed in the day-time, derived from an appearance of elegance and wealth.

She even prefaces her account of a visit to the Duc d'Orléans's picture gallery in the Palais Royal with some observations on the widespread deformity among the poorer classes: 'Among the objects one would certainly avoid seeing if it were possible, is the deformity of the poor. — Such various modes of warping the human figure could hardly be observed in England by a surgeon in high practice, as meet me about this country incessantly. — I have seen them in the galleries and outer-courts even of the palace itself, and am glad to turn my eyes for relief to the Duke of Orleans's pictures: a glorious collection.'[147]

Adam Smith simply states it as a fact that 'the wages of labour are lower in France than in England' without supplying any data to support this view.[148] Young collected a good deal of material on the subject of wages, though it is set out rather confusingly in two separate places: first, in the section 'Labour' of the chapter entitled 'Of the Price of Provisions, Labour, &c.', and second, in the chapter on industry in the section 'Earnings of Manufacturers'. The first set of data does not distinguish between wages in agriculture and those in urban occupations; the second would seem to concern mainly urban occupations though, as we have seen, a considerable amount of manufacturing was carried on in the country. Indeed among Young's figures in this second list those for La

Marche relate to 'women and girls employed in keeping cattle, spin wool and hemp'.

His conclusion to this second set of figures is: 'Average earnings of all the fabrics, of the men 26s. — Of the women 15s. — Of the spinners 9s. — These earnings are, without any doubt, much under those of similar manufactures in England; where I should apprehend the men earn, upon an average 20d. a-day or 40s.; women 9d. or 18s. and spinners I have shewn (Annals of Agriculture, vol. ix.) to earn 6 1/4d. or 12½s.' What he calls 'the vast superiority of English manufactures, taken in the gross, to those of France', despite the higher cost of labour,

> shews clearly, that it is not the nominal cheapness of labour that favours manufactures, which flourish most where labour is nominally the dearest — perhaps they flourish, on this account, since labour is generally *in reality* the cheapest, where it is *nominally* the dearest; the quality of the work, the skill and dexterity of performance, come largely into the account; and these must, on an average, depend very much on the state of ease in which the workman lives. If he be well nourished and cloathed, and his constitution kept in a state of vigour and activity, he will perform his work incomparably better than a man whose poverty allows but a scanty nourishment. There is doubtless great luxury amongst the manufacturing poor in England; there is little amongst those of France.[149]

Even if one cannot help smiling at the words 'great luxury', there is no doubt that Young's observations led him to the clear conclusion that the wages of industrial workers were lower in France than in the England of his day. What is more, he had earlier pointed out that in recent decades there had been a steep rise in prices and that wages had not kept up with them.[150]

The hours worked in industry were often appallingly long. Mary Berry found male weavers in Lyons working from 5 a.m. to 9 p.m. and women watching over silk mills doing the same day's work.[151] In his survey of French industry Young suddenly observes: 'It is to be noted, that a day's work in all fabrics means 15 or 16 hours (except the time taken for meals).'[152] Jervis paints a sorry picture of the lot of what he calls 'Inferior Classes in a Servile State' (to them too he attributes a love of dissipation which he finds universal in France):

Under this head we comprehend Journeymen, Prentices, Garcons Peruquiers & Servants &c. These, allowing for the Contrast, may be considered in point of Folly, expence, & dissipation, as humble imitators of the first Class. They will work and live like Slaves, 4 or 5 days in a Week in order to support the expence of a Tawdry Suite and a Mistress — which they are seldom without; at a Guinguette on a Fete where they plunge into every scene of dissoluteness. These people by the poorness of their diet, bad Air, and filth of their Apartments, are subject to putrid fevers, and every decease incident to such extremes, are by their prodigality for the most part destitute of every resource when ill, except publick Hospitals and then perish in numbers, being sometimes croud'd four in a bed with different deceases.[153]

On their journeys British travellers found plenty of evidence of the serious problem presented by *mendicité* in Ancien Régime France. Pennant does make it clear that elsewhere he had met plenty of beggars when he pens this somewhat improbable sentence: 'The City of Lyons was the only place in France where there were no beggars.'[154] Although beggars were sometimes encountered even in the depths of the country, many more were seen in towns. On his arrival in Amiens the anonymous author of *Travels into France and Italy*, published in 1771, noted: 'Here are, as I am informed, three thousand poor in the streets, and thirty thousand upon the bishop's list, more than a third of the inhabitants.'[155]

This was mere hearsay. Peckham writes from first-hand experience:

The police of France, so much admired by travellers, is in many instances wonderfully deficient: the whole kingdom swarms with beggars, an evidence of poverty, as well as defect in the laws. The observation was confirmed at every inn I came to, by crowds of wretches, whose whole appearance spoke of their misery. I have often passed from the inn door to my chaise through a file of twenty or thirty of them; even the churches are infested with them, and I have seen many a devotee in the midst of her devotions interrupted by their importunity.[156]

Thicknesse has quite a lot to say on the subject. He suggests, for instance, that on the journey from Paris to Calais travellers would be well advised to send on ahead a servant on horseback to ensure that fresh horses were ready at each post. He adds: 'You will also be relieved from the importunity of common beggars, which is not the least inconvenience in this country, where they are in greater numbers, and more troublesome, than in England.' He adopts, it must be said, a brutal attitude in the matter when he writes: 'After all (next to our own laws) the laws of France are the best of any country in Europe. They keep the poor very poor, and they are very wise in so doing: the industrious poor do not want; and if poor do not want, I do not pity their poverty. I should rejoice to see the poor in England kept in the same medium.'[157]

Today British tourists continue to visit some of the same places in Paris as their predecessors 200 years ago; one thinks of Notre Dame, the Sainte Chapelle, the Louvre and the Tuileries gardens. Unlike their predecessors, they do not head for those institutions established to cope with the sick, foundlings, prostitutes and criminals. In our period the Hôpital des Enfants Trouvés, for instance, was a great draw for both men and women travellers. In describing his stay in Rome Smollett suddenly reverts to his visit to this hospital:

> I believe the moderns retain more of the customs of the antient Romans, than is generally imagined. When I first saw the infants at the *enfants trouvés* in Paris, so swathed with bandages, that the very sight of them made my eyes water, I little dreamed, that the prescription of the antients could be pleaded for this custom, equally shocking and absurd: but in the Capitol at Rome, I met with the antique statue of a child swaddled exactly in the same manner; rolled up like an Ægyptian mummy from the feet.[158]

Pennant's account of this hospital was less critical, but more detailed:

> Visited l'Hospital des Enfans Trouvés, taken care of by the Nuns, les Filles de Charité; very neatly kept. Near 6000 admitted annually. During the few minutes I was there five were brought in. Their names &ca are kept in a little linnen purse and pinned to their Caps that their parents may know them if inclined to take them. In the Gate are two holes where those children are placed whose parents would be concealed. Sometimes 30 have been put in a night.[159]

A seaman like Jervis included a visit to this hospital in his programme of sightseeing in Paris; he compares it very favourably with the similar foundation in London: 'The elegant neatness we found the Children in here, and the attention paid to them, is not to be described, and reflects disgrace on that similar Establishment in our own Country, so shamefully mismanag'd.'[160] In October 1775 Johnson accompanied Mrs Thrale there as part of their sightseeing. His account of it is rather brief: 'We saw the boarding school, the Enfans trouvés. A room with about 86 children in cradles, as sweet as a parlour. They lose a third; take in to perhaps more than seven [years old], put them in trades, pin to them the papers sent with them. Want nurses. Saw their chapel.'[161] Mrs Thrale's account of their visit is both longer and more critical:

> The next Flight was to their Foundling Hospital, which is boasted as a boundless Charity; & indeed the Woman said they had already taken in Five Thousand two hundred Children since last January; the Place was wonderfully clean, cleaner than any I have seen in France, and the poor Infants at least die peaceably cleanly and in Bed — I saw whole Rows of swathed Babies pining away to perfect Skeletons, & expiring in very neat Cribs with each a Bottle hung on its Neck filled with some Milk Mess, which if they can suck they may live, & if they cannot they must die. The very young ones, I have a Notion, seldom get through — those who are not put in till 8 or 9 Months old seem to do well enough.[162]

In the following year Mrs Montagu visited the hospital along with Lady Hillsborough and with an *abbé* as a guide:

> We were surprised to find ourselves carried into a very long room perfectly sweet and clean (no common thing at Paris) in the middle of which were arranged two rows of a sort of white basket covered with linen. Women in a religious habit on a sudden snatched off the whole linen which covered the baskets, and behold in each lay a little infant, none above 7 or 8 days old; if some had not cried I should have taken them for dolls. After keeping them at most 8 days they are sent to be nursed in the country. I suppose there were near 200 infants in their little beds. The parents may reclaim them when they please. I believe the custom prevents some murders and other evils, but the number of children sent thither increases so

much every year that I fear in time few of the poor will educate their infants, which will be a great evil. The domestic ties and charities will be dissolved and lost, and I believe few would make good citizens or good men. The house where the children are received is admirably conducted, but God knows how the poor babes are treated at the Peasants habitations and places to which they are sent. The numbers received last year were 6505.[163]

The Hôtel-Dieu in Paris drew many of our travellers, and not only the doctors among them. Pennant provides a certain amount of detail about what he saw there in 1765:

After being at chapel at Lord Hertford's, visited the Hotel Dieu. The sick are kept in vast wards in which there are three rows of beds: in several were four or five persons yet they seemed tolerably clean; numbers at this time 3800. It is an ordinary building near Notre Dame. The sick are attended by the Nuns of St Austin; two were sitting at the door with some reliques before them; among others was a leg of one of the Innocents.[164]

At about the same period Thicknesse was much more outspoken in his criticisms:

The Hotel Dieu is an hospital largely endowed, and which receives, without any questions asked, every object that is presented. A noble charity, and worthy of the name it bears, were it well regulated. But alas! it is no uncommon thing to see four, five, six, nay sometimes eight sick persons in one bed, heads and tails, ill of different disorders, some dying, some actually dead. Last winter a gentleman informed me that he heard one of the patients there complain bitterly of the cold, and particularly of that which he felt from the dead corpse which lay next to him in the bed![165]

The Gentleman's Guide is almost equally critical, though it does end by conceding that this highly unsatisfactory state of affairs 'is now in some degree remedied': 'God's Hospital is the oldest in Paris; and receives all sorts of people, whether natives or foreigners: it is shamefully crowded, as I have seen three, and four in a bed, and perhaps each labouring under a different disorder.'[166]

A number of travellers who visited this hospital between 1785 and 1789 continue to offer depressing accounts of conditions there. Walker describes it as

> an Hospital situated on two sides of a branch of the Seine, and which exceeds in dimensions and number of patients any (as I might hope to all) of those we have in all the Hospitals of London! 5000! — It seems an assemblage of all human miseries! The sight is as humiliating as an access to the grave! in all its stages!!! — In one bed, at top and bottom, you may see two and three wretches in all the stages of approach to death! — Art arranges itself against the attacks of death in vain! scores are taken out victims to that tyrant every day! yet the rooms are high — the ventilators, on good construction continually in action: — cleanliness, medicine, advice of the best kind, and a police to be admired, stand also as a phalanx, and have *some* effect.[167]

Townsend, who went there in the following year, gives much lower figures for the number of sick people, and although he mentions hopes of improvements, he was obviously unfavourably impressed by what he saw:

> I visited the Hotel Dieu, where the sick are in number two thousand five hundred and seventy-four, beside five hundred and seventy-one officers or attendants. In all, they make three thousand one hundred forty-five persons to be lodged and fed. I observed four in a bed, but they have had six or seven, and among these the dying with the dead. The sick, though so miserably provided for, cost the public thirty sols, that is, fifteen pence each per day. They have one ward in the winter, containing about four hundred persons, set apart for those who pretend disease. The practice of stowing so many miserable creatures in one bed is to be abolished.

This prospect of changes for the better he attributes to the influence of Mme Necker who in the hospital which she founded in 1778 and which still bears her name, 'has provided each patient with a separate bed, with the best attendance, and with every thing which can administer to his comfort', and all this for little more than half of what it cost for each patient at the Hôtel-Dieu.[168]

In the following year St John, a doctor (he devotes a good deal of space to criticising the medical treatment offered in French hospitals), visited the Hôtel-Dieu, but he does not seem to have found any signs of improvement:

> Such an hospital, in such a situation, must corrupt the air, and be an eternal source of pestilential diseases. There are frequently four thousand patients together in the hospital, and yet there are only twenty-one chambers great and small, and only one thousand four hundred beds, to contain such a multitude of sick, who are crowded to the number of four, five, and even six, into the same bed . . . The corrupt air and effluvia in some parts of the hospital are more loathsome and abominable than can be conceived. It is amazing, that there are men of constitutions sufficiently vigorous, to recover in such a place of vermin, filth, and horror.[169]

Rigby, another doctor and one who tended to think highly of the way they ordered things in France, describes the hospital which he visited in July 1789, as 'very dirty and crowded, containing 8,000 patients', although he does add: 'The best ward is for stone patients.'[170]

In 1656 the government under Mazarin had set up the Hôpital Général, largely to deal with the problem of *mendicité*. This was responsible for the administration of a number of institutions, including the Hôpital des Enfants Trouvés, and two multipurpose establishments — the Salpêtrière and Bicêtre — which a number of British tourists went out of their way to visit. Pennant gives a long account of what he saw at the Salpêtrière:

> Went to the Hospital de Salpetriere, a little way out of Paris, a sort of workhouse for girls and women, of which there are in the house 7500. I saw 400 at work in one room: 500 in another. They embroider, make lace and shirts, and weave coarse linen, also cloth; all which is sold for the benefit of the hospital. In one room were 200 beds. In the day time one is run on castors under the other. The hospital for the sick is large, neat and well kept. Near it is a good apothecary's shop and laboratory. In another room were 200 little beds for young children of three, four or five years old; this place being the receptacle of the foundlings or Enfans Trouvés when they become of that age. It is also an Asylum to such poor families whoe head is dead, or has deserted them; in

short, it is the asylum of the miserable, tho' each is obliged to work to support the whole. They are clothed in a coarse grey woollen cloth that looks as if it was knit. The kitchen is large; in one part are six vast cauldrons that contain above a tun each. This is for boiling their Bouille or Soupe. One of their dishes was stewed prunes, another rice; there were also abundance of salted herrings, which I was told came from Dieppe. Near the Kitchen was a neat refectory for thirty Soeurs or Sisters, who manage the hospital, one of which showed it. Saw the quarter which was allotted for their Mad. It consisted of several long narrow courts with cells on each side. Most of them were loose; some confined in the cells; others chained on the outside. There were about 400 of these unhappy objects — a shocking sight. In another quarter were 8 or 900 women of the town of the lowest order, condemned to confinement and hard labour for a certain time by the magistrates. These are not to be seen. This Hospital is of a vast extent, and is divided into several courts; and is under the direction of the Hospital general.[171]

Cole visited this establishment in the same year, 1765:

Not far from hence [the Gobelins], on the Right, & inclining to the River Seine you discover an Hospital which covers as much space as a small Town: it is called *Le Salpetrière* & gives Food & Rayment to between 7 & 8,000 People of both Sexes: such the Sick, disabled, poor, disorderly Persons, Women of loose Lives, mad People & Beggars: in short all that can give no good Account of themselves are sent here, where, if in Distress & Sick, they are humanely taken Care of, tho' I think lodged too many in a Room, & too close together; if they are well, they are set to various Kinds of Work to earn their Livelihood. I went thro' many of their Wards & Apartments, which were full & kept very clean. Their Church is built on a new Construction, being a real Cross, having a vast heavy Dome in the Middle, with 4 Naves, fronting the High Altar which is immediately under the Dome, & serves for the 4 Churches, as they are in Effect: it being so contrived that the different Sexes & Sorts of Persons in the Hospital should not intermix with each other. It would seem that Cardinal Mazarine was a Benefactor to this institution, as his Arms in large are over one of the principal Gates into it. The Church is as gloomy withinside, as it is awkward & clumsy on the Outside.[172]

In his *Letters to a Young Gentleman*, which appeared in 1784, Andrews expressed approval of this institution, which he describes as 'an immense edifice, designed for the reception and support of the female poor, and for the confinement and correction of women of ill fame'. He was obviously full of admiration for what he saw there: 'It contains prodigious numbers who are kept in admirable order and neatness, and employed in the most useful and profitable manner: The rules are perfectly suited to those for whom they were made: sufficient indulgence and lenity are shewn, without relaxation of that necessary discipline, which is the only preservation of decorum in such places.' Hence his conclusion: 'A foundation of this kind is much wanted among us.'[173]

Two years later, while in Paris on his way into Spain, Townsend also thought this establishment worth a visit:

> The next day in the morning I visited the hospital called La Salpetriére, in which are maintained more than seven thousand foundling girls, with a few aged paupers, and about nine hundred prostitutes. This number is considerable, but these are only such as were guilty of other misdemeanours. On the list of the police are more than twenty-eight thousand of those abandoned and miserable women, who, in the dusk of the evening, swarm in every street. In this hospital they have eight hundred children employed in needlework and spinning, of which number many excel in most beautiful embroidery. When one of the old women dies, her husband leaves the hospital. The government is by a matron, fourteen priests, thirty-two sisters of a superior order, with fifty more, who are subordinate to these.[174]

As it was rather further from the centre of Paris, Bicêtre attracted fewer visitors. In his *Letters to a Young Gentleman* Andrews speaks of it as admiringly as he had of the Salpêtrière:

> At no great distance from the hospital just described stands one still larger, called Bicêtre. It is an ancient edifice of prodigious dimensions, a receptacle for characters of multifarious denominations, wild and disorderly young men, persons who can give no satisfactory account of themselves,

or are guilty of mal-practices, defrauders, cheats, pickpockets, criminals condemned to imprisonment, convicts for petty larcenies, in short, the whole catalogue of such as have committed misdemeanours, for which labour and hard fare are appointed.

There are also multitudes of vagrants, idlers, mendicants, and others of that stamp, people out of work, and poor of diverse sorts: for all these classes suitable employment is provided, and they are treated proportionably to their deserts.

Persons reduced through misfortunes and casualties to narrow circumstances, may for a moderate consideration find a maintenance here. This helps in no small measure to people it. Viewed in such a light, it is a very humane and useful institution, and with singular propriety situated near a metropolis where scantiness of means to support themselves is the fate of the many.

After adding that Bicêtre also housed the mentally ill, he speaks approvingly of the strict discipline maintained there: 'The strictest regularity and discipline are observed in the place. The least mutiny or disobedience is punished with unrelenting severity.' A spell there, he maintains, has reformed 'many a youth of whom small hopes at first were entertained'.[175]

In the autumn of 1788, Romilly relates in his memoirs, he visited Bicêtre together with the two Genevan publicists, Dumont and Mallet du Pan, Louis Sébastien Mercier and Mirabeau. He was so horrified by what he saw there that he took up Mirabeau's suggestion that he should write down his observations. Mirabeau then translated these into French and published them under the title of *Lettre d'un Voyageur anglais sur la prison de Bicêtre*. This pamphlet was suppressed by the police, but on his return to London Romilly published the English text, though he gave it out as 'taken from the French'.[176]

The tone of this essay is set in the opening paragraph, where Romilly writes indignantly of this institution: 'I knew, indeed, as every one does, that it consisted of an hospital and a prison, but I did not know that, at Bicêtre, an hospital means a place calculated to generate disease, and a prison, a nursery of crime.' He first substantiates his criticism of the hospital by describing what happened in its two sections, those for venereal diseases and mental disorders. He explains that the prison housed boys under twelve and males above that age. Some of the latter were housed, often for years on end, in underground dungeons, and the rest in what he calls a 'common room' where vices were practised which he has to have recourse to Latin to describe. He also points out that those confined in the 'common room' were 'not men convicted of atrocious crimes by regular tribunals, but those to whom are imputed petty offences against the police, who have quarrelled in the streets, who have abused the *guet*, or who have in any way offended even the most subordinate officers of justice'. The law reformer's verdict on Bicêtre is startlingly different from the other account of it just quoted.

While in the provinces, our travellers showed a similar appetite for visiting institutions ranging from hospitals in the medical sense to workhouses or even prisons. Thus at Boulogne Smollett viewed with approval what he himself describes as a workhouse:

> Among other public edifices at Boulogne, there is an hospital, or workhouse, which seems to be established upon a very good foundation. It maintains several hundreds of poor people, who are kept constantly at work, according to their age and abilities, in making thread, all sorts of lace, a kind of catgut, and in knitting stockings. It is under the direction of the bishop, and the see is at present filled by a prelate of great piety and benevolence, though a little inclining to bigotry and fanaticism.[177]

Peckham, who entered France from the Austrian Netherlands, was very impressed with the establishment he found in Lille: 'From the Citadel we visited the Hospital, which is as spacious as magnificent; it is founded for the support of old people and children, all of whom are employed according to their strength and years, in making shoes, lace, clothes, spinning yarn, and other manufactures, which require more art than strength.'[178] Burney's comments on this same institution were extremely critical:

> I visited the arsenal, citadel, and hospital, not only *des Enfans Trouvés* but also *des vielles et viellards trouvé* — for there seem to be as many of these two last as of the former. I suppose they are well fed and lodged but they are made to work too hard. The children are confined in rows, the girls at making lace — the boys as shoe makers, taylers etc., but I find their task masters allow them very little respit from 7 o'clock in the

morning to 8 at night. The room where the girls were so confined was very much crowded and too hot to be wholesome, if one may judge by the smell of stagnant and putride air which was so intolerable.[179]

In contrast, Rigby gives on the whole a remarkably favourable account of the institution which he encountered at Dijon in July 1789:

I called upon Monsieur Lerous, a surgeon, to whom I had sent one of my publications . . . He was not at home, but when I gave my name and requested to see the hospital, three of his pupils attended me. I was never more pleased with an establishment of this kind; charity and good sense seemed to have built this hospital. It is large and lofty, outside the walls of the city, receiving the pure air from the neighbouring mountains and hills. There are three hundred beds, all of iron, the coverings and furniture of white cotton, as clean and neat as any Quaker's in Norwich. I could detect nowhere the slightest impure or offensive smell. The wards are very wide, and at least thirty feet high. Some are for infirm old people and incurables, some, detached, for lunatics, and there are two wards for illegitimate children, called *enfans trouvés*, as is really the case, for they are always found at the gate of the hospital.

What follows reads as if it came from the pages of a utopian novel:

But what struck me most was a large ward full of beds, fitted up in the same comfortable manner, for the reception of the wandering stranger. Here the weary traveller may at once find an asylum and take his repose. He is permitted to stay three days, and is supplied with everything his situation requires, and if he is penniless a supply of money is given him at his departure. I never beheld a more interesting scene. Many of the beds were then occupied by sunburnt travellers, who were snoring away in perfect security, undisturbed by those apprehensions which in many cases must interrupt the sleep of those who are at a distance from home. I really envied the founder of this delightful establishment. I almost envied the persons who had the pleasing task of fulfilling his benevolent intentions. I am sure I had reason to praise them, for such an appearance of neatness, convenience, and comfort could not be kept up without the utmost attention . . . Even the kitchen was equally clean and neat, and the apothecary's shop or dispensary the neatest I have seen anywhere, but it was too small and not well lighted. The medicines also seemed principally vegetable, and the *materia medica* was not a good one — they give little bark or opium.[180]

Perhaps surprisingly, the famous Hôpital de la Charité at Lyons drew relatively little attention from our travellers. Pennant is one of the few persons to describe it in any detail:

Saw la Charité, a vast hospital, founded in 1533, for deserted children; those whose parents could not maintain them; for the aged of both sexes; in short, the poor of all sorts. In this place were about 4 or 5000; the children were employed in knitting stockings or in winding silk. The machine much resembled that at Derby, and was put in motion by two great wheels turned by men within each. In one room is kept in neat cases the archives, in which are kept in small bags a separate account of each child that they may be known if the Parent reclames them . . .

The Granary is very noble, consisting of two vast floors 365 French foot long and 65 broad; three feet deep in wheat. In each granary were about 8000 Anées of wheat — an Anée is a measure weighing 365 pounds, the word signifies, as much as an ass would carry. The floors of this granary are stone.

In one part of the hospital are les Cachots or places where young libertines of low rank are confined; those of a better sort are confined in another place.

In contrast Pennant has little to say about the Hôtel-Dieu: 'Saw the hospital; the front to the Rhone is very extensive; the center is adorned with Ionic pillars; it contains 7 or 800.'[181]

Some twenty years later, in 1784, Mrs Cradock has likewise very little to say about the Hôtel-Dieu except that she greatly admired the dispensary where she was able to buy such things as rose water of a better quality than any she had found elsewhere. She speaks very highly of La Charité, which she too describes in some detail:

Un autre hôpital, celui de la Charité, est un grand bâtiment carré, entourant une vaste cour plantée d'arbres. Un des corps du bâtiment est destiné aux femmes en couches, mariées ou non; un autre, aux petits enfants dont les parents sont trop pauvres pour les élever. Dans le troisième se trouve un moulin où la soie passe par toutes les préparations avant d'être livrée au tisserand. On y emploie des gens de tout âge et de tout sexe. Enfin, la quatrième aile renferme la chapelle très simple, la pharmacie fort bien aménagée, et les dépendances. On admet dans cet hôpital les pauvres dont l'âge ou les infirmités ne leur permettant plus de travailler. On ne les reçoit pas au-dessous de soixante-cinq ans; mais alors on les entretient complètement, et s'ils le peuvent encore, on les emploie à différents travaux. Enfin, on ne peut trop louer l'idée qui a présidé à cette institution dont l'ordre et la direction sont vraiment admirables; du reste, tous ceux que nous y avons rencontrés paraissaient gais et heureux.[182]

We are here far removed from the robust realism with which Burney described a similar institution at Lille.

However, four travellers in the 1780s have left behind their impressions of the Hôtel-Dieu. James Edward Smith, a doctor, formed a very unfavourable view of what he saw there and of the answer which he received to his criticisms: 'We accompanied Dr. Brun round the Hôtel Dieu, an hospital which has been more praised than it deserves. The beds have large thick woollen curtains, and each contains two or three patients. When we expressed our wonder that so absurd a practice should still be continued, we were told that hospitals must not be made too comfortable, as the poor would then be too fond of having recourse to them!'[183] Walker admired the building, but his contact with the surgeon who showed his party round was decidedly chilly: 'The Quay . . . is . . . faced with handsome buildings — one is the general Hospital, of great size, utility, and architecture. The Surgeon, in shewing it, asked if we had any hospitals in England! We answered him that England was the country of all others that might be said to possess an Hospital. The Surgeon shrugged up his shoulders with French infidelity; and we made our bows.'[184]

Muirhead, who visited Lyons early in 1789, gives more attention to the Hôtel-Dieu than to the Hôpital de la Charité when he writes:

The hospital and charity work-houses are said to contain

nearly one sixth of the population. The hôtel-dieu, a princely building, with a superb dome, and the chief charity-house, are supported by the produce of two ferry-boats which ply between the city and Dauphiny.

The stated fare is but one sol; yet from 1200 to 1500 livres will be collected on a sunday or holiday. — I failed not to visit the hôtel-dieu, a theme of ceaseless admiration in France. The kindly and pious nursing of the *soeurs de la charité*, one of the few orders of nuns which humanity will respect, may soothe the bed of languishing; but the cleanliness and comfortable accommodation of the wards by no means correspond to the grandeur of this edifice. The patients lie two or three in a bed, and surrounded by coarse woollen curtains and offensive odours.[185]

Rigby's impression of this institution, which he visited at the end of July 1789, a few days after his stay in Dijon, were much less favourable than those he had formed of the hospital there. It will be noticed that Muirhead and he fail to agree about the number of patients in a bed. He relates how, while his companions went to see the remains of a Roman aqueduct,

I preferred going to the hospital, the Hôtel-Dieu, being encouraged to this from the satisfaction I had experienced in seeing that of Dijon. But I was much disappointed. This is an enormous quadrangular building, having a square within, ill calculated to admit free ventilation, the front towards the Rhone, more than 400 yards long, and in a good style of architecture. There are 1,100 patients, one only in a bed. There were formerly more, but a late subscription has enabled them to increase the number of beds. The bedsteads are of iron, with linen furniture, but not clean. The wards are large, but too much crowded. A very large ward was appropriated for accidents, and it was very full: a proof of the populousness of the city and neighbourhood. There are 250 attendants, including physicians, surgeons, sisters of charity, priests, pupils, servants, etc. The *premier médecin* is an Englishman, he visits the hospital early in the morning and late in the evening. I was sorry I could not see him.[186]

Our travellers seem to have been so hypnotised by the extremes of poverty and wealth that they tend to offer relatively little about an important section of society, the middle classes. We have seen how Jardine found in France 'too few of those middle ranks which form the best bonds of society, and the strength of the nation'.[187] On their tours round hospitals and other institutions they had some contact with members of one of the liberal professions, physicians and surgeons. The excessive number of lawyers in Ancien Régime France is denounced in strong terms by St John:

> The multitude of the judges of all kinds, lawyers, attorneys, &c. attending to each of the provincial courts of justice in France, is truly astonishing, and an intolerable burthen on the state. They all more or less enjoy considerable emoluments, without being of any real benefit to the nation, without cultivating the earth, promoting manufactures, or in fact collectively or separately, being of any more utility to the interest of the community, than monks or friars; though they may flatter the ambition of some individuals, enrich themselves, and transfer the property of one person to another. One may judge the multitude of gentlemen belonging to the law in France, when in the city of Dijon alone, there are near eight hundred. In proportion, how many must they not be at Paris and in all the other cities of France?

Some of these observations seem rather wide of the mark. Even the judges of the *Parlements*, although they were men of substance, did not derive a large income from their posts, and the judges in the lower courts were poorly paid. Besides, by their very numbers many lawyers' earnings were bound to be small, despite what St John has to say on the subject in the next paragraph, which does, however, bring out clearly the extraordinary number of lawsuits in Ancien Régime France:

> A lawyer's fee in many of the provincial towns in France, does not exceed half a crown; and yet, although there are perhaps four times as many lawyers in France as there are in the British empire, many of them contrive to make fortunes. The fees being so inconsiderable, individuals are tempted to begin lawsuits for the most trifling affairs; and when once they commence, the lawyers frequently manage them in such a manner, that the parties grow irritated against one another; and finding it almost impossible to withdraw and extricate

themselves, plunge still deeper into a very gulph of memorials, clauses, attestations, *ad infinitum*. Besides, the natural fire and hastiness of the French render law-suits infinitely more common than among the graver inhabitants of England.[188]

Our travellers' contacts with shopkeepers must have been frequent. As we have seen,[189] these were not always greatly enjoyed, partly because they regarded as a form of cheating the common practice of asking high prices for goods and thus compelling them to haggle. Andrews establishes this distinction between *marchand* and *négociant*: 'Hence it may be that they in France who exercise what we call merchandize in England, conscious of the ignominy affixed to the word *marchands* from the base practices of those who bear it, have chosen to distinguish themselves by a more honourable title, and are known by that of *negocians*, while that of *marchands* is restricted to shopkeepers only.'[190]

Wealthy merchants, engaged not only in trade but often also in banking and the virtual employers of those occupied in domestic industry in both town and country, were encountered by our travellers on the eve of the Revolution. The author of anonymous *Notes on a Journey made into France* drew a contrast between the poverty of noblemen and the wealth of the middle class in Lyons in 1776: 'The distinction between noblesse & bourgeoisie in France, & the exclusion of the former from most means of acquiring wealth, have strong effects upon the national manners. They give the noblesse an exclusive right to pride with poverty: they give the bourgeoisie an exclusive right to wealth with grossiéreté.'[191] Such generalisations about these two classes are rather sweeping, but the author does bear witness to the existence of a wealthy section of the middle class.

For obvious reasons Mrs Piozzi looked with different eyes on the wealth enjoyed by some Lyons merchants by whom she was entertained in 1784. On one day she visited 'two villas belonging to some of the most opulent merchants of Lyons'. She was naturally impressed by her reception:

Such was the hospitality I have been witness to, and such the luxuries of the Lyonnois at table, that I counted six and thirty dishes where we dined, and twenty-four where we supped. Every thing was served up in silver at both places, and all was uniformly magnificent, except the linen, which might have been finer. We were not a very numerous company — from eighteen to twenty-two as I remember, morning and evening; but the ladies played upon the pedal harp, the gentlemen sung gaily, if not sweetly after supper: I never received more kindness for my part in any fortnight of my life, nor ever heard that kindness more pleasingly or less coarsely expressed. These are merchants, I am told, with whom I have been living; and perhaps my heart more readily receives and repays their caresses for having heard so.'[192]

In his account of his visits to French seaports in 1787 and 1788 Young repeatedly speaks of the wealth of their merchants. At Bordeaux he found that the merchants' mode of living was 'highly luxurious', that they lived and entertained 'on expensive scales'. The prosperity of this port as of Le Havre and Nantes inevitably brought with it the rise of a wealthy merchant class.[193] Yet the aristocratic prejudice against trade still obtained, as Adam Smith observed: 'The profits of trade, I have been assured by British merchants who have traded in both countries, are higher in France than in England; and it is no doubt upon this account that many British subjects chuse rather to employ their capitals in a country where trade is in disgrace, than in one where it is highly respected.'[194] Jervis writes of French merchants and manufacturers: They do not seem activated by the same principals, as people of the same Class in England; for after acquiring a moderate Fortune, they retire, and enter into the trifling folly and dissipation of the age, having always an Eye to the preservation of that Fortune they have with such difficulty acquired. From this description you may easily imagine how rare it is for a son in that Class to inherit an Overgrown Fortune.'[195]

It is notorious that for centuries the ranks of the nobility had been replenished and swollen by wealthy bourgeois. In an aristocratic society in which the *roturier* was despised, it was natural that those who could afford to do so should acquire noble rank for themselves and their children. 'Bourgeois', observed Andrews, 'is a term of reproach, which every man is sure to hear, who is daring enough to enter the lists of altercation, with any one that thinks himself by birth or office secured against the retortion . . . Whenever the word bourgeois is in the mouth of a French gentleman, it is always intended as a stigma, and never understood but as an expression of contempt.' Hence the rush of French merchants, as soon as they had acquired sufficient wealth, to acquire noble rank:

The French merchants are a very respectable and worthy class of men, no ways inferior to our own. They differ from them, however, in several instances, in nothing more than the prodigious hurry so many of them are in to exchange that sphere of life, for what may be called the hobby-horse of every Frenchman, the rank and privileges of a noble. These may be purchased here at no very high rate.[196]

This writer gives as an example the purchase of a post of *secrétaire du roi*, a sinecure which conferred noble rank. Another writer speaks of a different method — the purchase of an estate which carried a title with it: 'When a considerable fortune has been made, a great part of it is generally laid out in the purchase of an estate, to which a title is annexed, and though all merchants cannot become nobles, notwithstanding the great plenty of titles, yet any trader of eminence may have either that point, or an honourable alliance in view.' The acquisition of noble rank, as the author points out, had to be a long-term investment: 'It is true that the new-made nobility are not generally held in high esteem, but they comfort themselves by reflecting that, if they cannot boast an illustrious ancestry, their successors will probably have that advantage.'[197]

Swinburne indicates yet another way of acquiring noble rank. Though he points out that, owing to its situation on the Garonne, Toulouse 'seems destined to serve as a staple town between the upper and lower provinces, that line its shores for many hundred miles', he attributes the fact that it was not a great commercial city to the influence of its *Parlement* and to the noble rank conferred on the holders of the posts of *capitouls* who were responsible for the administration of the city:

The manufactures of Toulouse are of small importance, nor is its trade considerable. The genius of the citizens inclines more to letters than to commerce; the law draws to it every person, that can amass wealth enough to purchase a seat on the benches; the church also swallows up a large portion of the inhabitants; poverty and idleness seem the lot of the inferior class. Nothing contributes more to check the spirit of trade, than the temptation which the Capitoulat, or chief municipal magistracy, holds out to every wealthy merchant: this office imparts the rank and privileges of nobility, not only to the persons invested with the dignity, but also to their descendants, and is therefore the constant object of ambition to every thriving father of a family; when once attained, the channel through which the wealth flowed, is shut for ever, and thus the plant is left to wither on its stalk, just at the moment when it began to acquire strength and juices sufficient to secure a succession of useful fruit.[198]

Yet, if we look back from June 1790, when the Constituent Assembly abolished hereditary nobility and all titles, one feels that, in the last decades before the Revolution, many members of the wealthy middle class must have been losing that feeling of inferiority which made them seek noble rank for themselves and their children. In a remarkable passage, penned in the middle of the 1760s, Smollett had noted this change of attitude: 'Many of the commons, enriched by commerce and manufacture, grow impatient of those odious distinctions, which exclude them from the honours and privileges due to their importance in the commonwealth.'[199]

The collection of such indirect taxes as the *gabelle, aides, traites* and the duty on tobacco gave rise in Ancien Régime France to a wealthy class of tax-farmers. Their unpopularity is reflected by various of our travellers. Smollett, for instance, writes:

> Without all doubt they have reason to inveigh against the *fermiers généraux*, who oppress the people in raising the taxes, not above two thirds of which are brought into the king's coffers: the rest enriches themselves, and enables them to bribe high for the protection of the great, which is the only support they have against the remonstrances of the states and parliaments, and the suggestions of common sense, which will ever demonstrate this to be, of all others, the most pernicious method of supplying the necessities of government.[200]

Thicknesse too uses strong language to denounce the tax-farmers, contrasting the luxury in which they live with the hard lives of what he regards as the deserving poor:

> The *fermiers genereaux* oppress them beyond conception, and they toil from morning till night, exposed to the inclemency of all weathers, and yet lead a much more wretched life than any of the African slaves, in our colonies, or in their own. But their lively disposition bears them through all with

chearfulness, and they consider they are getting their own bread, while they are, in fact, toiling for wretches, who deserve not the name of men. The luxury in which the *fermiers generaux* live in France is scarce credible: the poverty and dirt of the poor is equally as offensive.

Elsewhere he writes: 'It is scarce possible to conceive in what voluptuousness the royal family, the princes of the blood, but above all, the *fermiers generaux* live; but then it is those, and those alone, who can afford to live so.'[201]

A more objective but none the less hostile account of the activities of the tax-farmers is provided by Adam Smith. He too criticises their excessive wealth and the way in which it was flaunted: 'In countries where the publick revenues are in farm, the farmers are generally the most opulent people. Their wealth would alone excite the publick indignation, and the vanity which almost always accompanies such upstart fortunes, with which they commonly display their wealth, excites that indignation still more.' He is particularly severe on the monopoly which the tax-farmers enjoyed of the sale of salt and tobacco, and the increasingly savage penalties which they obtained for those caught smuggling these commodities. 'The farmers of the publick revenue', he declares, 'never find the laws too severe, which punish any attempt to evade the payment of a tax. They have no bowels for the contributors, who are not their subjects . . . The smuggling of salt and tobacco sends every year several hundred people to the gallies, besides a very considerable number whom it sends to the gibbet . . . Those who consider the blood of the people as nothing in comparison with the revenue of the prince, may perhaps approve of this method of levying taxes.'[202] It is clear that Adam Smith strongly disapproved both of the great wealth of the tax-farmers and of some of the methods by which it was acquired.

In explaining why life annuities were taken up so much more frequently in France than in Britain and so formed a considerable part of the national debt, the same writer makes some interesting observations on the way of life of tax-farmers and other very wealthy members of the middle class:

> The people concerned in the finances, the farmers general, the receivers of the taxes which are not in farm, and court bankers, etc. make the greater part of those who advance their money in all publick exigencies. Such people are commonly

men of mean birth, but of great wealth, and frequently of great pride. They are too proud to marry their equals, and women of quality disdain to marry them. They frequently resolve, therefore, to live bachelors, and having neither any families of their own, nor much regard for those of their relations, whom they are not always very fond of acknowledging, they desire only to live in splendour during their own time, and are not unwilling that their fortune should end with themselves. The number of rich people, besides, who are either averse to marry, or whose condition of life renders it either improper or inconvenient for them to do so, is much greater in France than in England. To such people, who have little or no care for posterity, nothing can be more convenient than to exchange their capital for a revenue, which is to last just as long, and no longer, than they wish it to do.[203]

Collectively our travellers offer much detailed information about the life and economic activities not only of Paris, but of many provincial towns and cities in the closing decades of the Ancien Régime. We see something of the variety to be found there, from factories to men, women and children at work in their homes in the towns and the surrounding country, from the high living and aspirations to nobility of the wealthy sections of the middle class to the hospitals and workhouses for the desperately poor.

Notes

1. *A Tour, Sentimental and Descriptive*, vol. I, p. 213.
2. Rutt, *Life of Priestley*, vol. I, p. 237.
3. *French Journal*, p. 152.
4. *Music, men and manners*, pp. 2–3.
5. *Journal*, pp. 341–3.
6. *Letters from France*, vol. I, pp. 36–7.
7. *The Gentleman's Guide* (1788), pp. 84–5.
8. *A View of Society and Manners*, vol. I, p. 33.
9. *A Sketch*, p. 146.
10. *Sketch of a Tour*, vol. III, pp. 201–2.
11. *French Journal*, pp. 148, 101.
12. *Gentleman's Magazine*, 1798, p. 997.
13. *French Journal*, p. 101.
14. *Mrs Montagu*, ed. R. Blunt, vol. I, p. 328.
15. *Journal*, p. 50.

16. *Continental Excursions*, vol. I, p. 94.
17. *Gentleman's Guide* (1788), pp. 82–3.
18. *Travels through France and Italy*, p. 51.
19. *Journals and Correspondence*, vol. I, p. 146.
20. *Journal of a Visit to Paris*, p. 73.
21. *Tour on the Continent*, p. 36.
22. BL, Add. MS. 31192, f. 12.
23. From Cherbourg. See Young, *Travels in France*, vol. I, p. 551.
24. *French Journal*, pp. 178–9.
25. *Letters from Barbary, France etc.*, vol. I, pp. 244–5.
26. *Letters from France*, p. 23.
27. *French Journal*, pp. 180–1.
28. *Journal*, pp. 54–5, 77–8.
29. *A Sketch*, pp. 164, 177.
30. W. Sussex RO, Add. MS. 7236, f. 15. Extracts from this travel journal are reproduced by permission of Mrs B. E. Mitford and Miss S. M. Mitford.
31. *A Sketch*, pp. 164–5.
32. *A Tour, Sentimental and Descriptive*, vol. II, p. 93.
33. *Letters from France*, p. 13.
34. Rutt, *Life of Priestley*, vol. I, p. 238.
35. *Travels in France*, vol. I, pp. 87, 550.
36. *The Gentleman's Guide* (1788), p. 47.
37. *A Sketch*, pp. 130–1.
38. *Travels in France*, vol. I, pp. 90, 113, 550.
39. See below, pp. 100–1.
40. *A Year's Journey*, vol. II, pp. 93–4, 76.
41. *A View of Society and Manners*, vol. I, p. 151.
42. *Journals of Travels*, p. 150.
43. *Tour on the Continent*, pp. 43, 48.
44. *Journals and Correspondence*, vol. I, pp. 134–5.
45. *Observations and Reflections*, p. 30.
46. *Travels in France*, vol. I, pp. 555, 275.
47. *A Tour*, p. 132.
48. *Journal*, p. 91.
49. *Travelling Memorandums*, vol. I, p. 128.
50. *Diaries of a Duchess*, p. 213.
51. *Travels through France and Italy*, p. 330.
52. *A Year's Journey*, vol. II, pp. 50, 56–7.
53. *Journals and Correspondence*, vol. I, p. 145.
54. *A Tour*, p. 130.
55. *Travelling Memorandums*, vol. I, pp. 116–17, 119.
56. *Journey from Bayonne to Marseilles*, pp. 468–9. See also Muirhead, *Journals of Travels*, pp. 365–6.
57. *Letters*, pp. 151–99.
58. *Autobiography*, pp. 27–8.
59. *Letters from France*, pp. 8–9.
60. *Letters*, pp. 200–1.
61. *The Gentleman's Guide*, p. 83.
62. *Travels in France*, vol. I, p. 543.

63. *Letters*, pp. 209–10.
64. Somerset RO, DD/SH/67/19C/2480, p. 10.
65. *Travels through France and Italy*, pp. 89–104.
66. *Autobiography*, p. 35.
67. *The Gentleman's Guide*, pp. 71–2.
68. *Journals and Correspondence*, vol. I, pp. 138–9.
69. *Travelling Memorandums*, vol. I, pp. 209–10.
70. *Travels in France*, vol. I, p. 545.
71. *Journey from Bayonne to Marseilles*, pp. 370–1.
72. As at Lodève and Bédarieux.
73. *Travels in France*, vol. I, pp. 545–6.
74. *Journals of Travels*, pp. 272–3.
75. *The Gentleman's Guide*, p. 90.
76. BL, Add. MS. 31192, f. 43.
77. *Diaries of a Duchess*, p. 215.
78. *Pembroke Papers*, p. 458.
79. The text has '80,000'.
80. *Travels in France*, vol. I, pp. 59–61, 504.
81. *A Tour*, pp. 42–3.
82. *Travels in France*, vol. I, pp. 103–4, 505–6.
83. *A Tour*, vol. II, pp. 155, 172.
84. *Travels in France*, vol. I, pp. 91, 504–5.
85. See above, pp. 16–19.
86. *Travels through France and Italy*, p. 33.
87. *A Tour*, p. 221.
88. *Travels in France*, vol. I, pp. 548–9.
89. Ibid., p. 538.
90. Ibid., p. 553.
91. Ibid., p. 552.
92. Ibid., p. 553.
93. Ibid., p. 538.
94. Ibid., p. 540.
95. Ibid., p. 547.
96. Ibid., p. 542.
97. Ibid., pp. 548, 553.
98. Ibid., p. 542.
99. Ibid., p. 545.
100. Ibid., p. 552.
101. W. Sussex RO, Add. MS. 7237, ff. 10, 9.
102. *Travels in France*, vol. I, pp. 539, 569–70.
103. *Travels through France and Italy*, pp. 344–5.
104. *Travels in France*, vol. I, p. 553.
105. Ibid., p. 541.
106. Ibid., p. 92 (cf. p. 550).
107. *Journal*, pp. 39–40.
108. *Memoirs*, vol. II, p. 254.
109. *Travels in France*, vol. I, pp. 104–5, 552.
110. Ibid., p. 168.
111. *Contrôleur général* 1783–7.
112. *Travels in France*, vol. I, p. 554.

113. *Travels in France*, vol. I, p. 549.
114. *voie* = 'load'.
115. W. Sussex RO, Add. MS. 7237, f. 5.
116. *Gentleman's Magazine*, 1798, p. 197.
117. *Journals of Travels*, pp. 175–6.
118. Rutt, *Life of Priestley*, vol. I, p. 238.
119. *A Year's Journey*, vol. I, pp. 68–9.
120. *Journals of Travels*, pp. 159, 365.
121. *Travels in France*, vol. II, p. 105.
122. Ibid., p. 103.
123. *A Tour, Sentimental and Descriptive*, vol. I, pp. 204–5.
124. *The Courts of Europe*, vol. I, p. 303.
125. *Travels in France*, vol. II, p. 103.
126. Ibid., p. 104.
127. Ibid., pp. 103–4.
128. HMC 24, iii Rutland, p. 247.
129. *Travels in France*, vol. I, pp. 61, 535.
130. Ibid., p. 534.
131. Ibid., pp. 6, 535, 539.
132. Ibid., p. 536.
133. Ibid., pp. 87, 536.
134. Ibid., p. 536.
135. Ibid., p. 536.
136. Ibid., p. 93.
137. *Gentleman's Magazine*, 1797, p. 637.
138. *A Tour, Sentimental and Descriptive*, vol. II, p. 91.
139. *Travels in France*, vol. I, p. 537.
140. Ibid., p. 93.
141. *George Selwyn and his Contemporaries*, vol. IV, pp. 219–20.
142. *Travels in France*, vol. I, pp. 48–50.
143. *Letters from France*, p. 130.
144. *Useful Hints*, pp. 39–41.
145. *Letters from Barbary, France etc.*, p. 224.
146. *A Tour*, pp. 156–7.
147. *Observations and Reflections*, pp. 26, 18.
148. *Wealth of Nations*, vol. I, p. 108.
149. *Travels in France*, vol. I, pp. 562, 565–6.
150. Ibid., vol. I, p. 454.
151. *Journals and Correspondence*, vol. I, p. 135.
152. *Travels in France*, vol. I, p. 548.
153. BL, Add. MS. 31192, ff. 39–40.
154. *Tour on the Continent*, p. 45.
155. *Travels into France and Italy*, vol. I, p. 48.
156. *A Tour*, p. 228.
157. *Observations*, pp. 112, 53.
158. *Travels through France and Italy*, pp. 255–6.
159. *Tour on the Continent*, p. 11.
160. BL, Add. MS. 31192, f. 11.
161. *French Journal*, p. 184.
162. *French Journal*, p. 109.

The Towns, Trade and Industry

163. *Mrs. Montagu*, ed. R. Blunt, vol. I, pp. 325–6.
164. *Tour on the Continent*, p. 34.
165. *Useful Hints*, p. 255.
166. *The Gentleman's Guide* (1788), pp. 61–2.
167. *A Sketch*, pp. 150–1.
168. *A Journey through a part of France*, vol. I, pp. 35–6.
169. *Letters from France*, vol. I, pp. 196–7.
170. *Letters from France*, p. 24.
171. *Tour on the Continent*, p. 24.
172. *Journal of a Journey to Paris*, pp. 156–7.
173. *Letters to a Young Gentleman*, pp. 372–3.
174. *Journey through part of France*, vol. I, pp. 36–7.
175. *Letters to a Young Gentleman*, pp. 375–7.
176. *Memoirs*, vol. I, p. 97; *The Repository*, vol. II, pp. *9–*14.
177. *Travels through France and Italy*, p. 20.
178. *A Tour*, p. 127.
179. *Music, men and manners*, p. 6.
180. *Letters from France*, pp. 102–9.
181. *Tour on the Continent*, p. 45.
182. *Journal*, pp. 97–8.
183. *Sketch of a Tour*, vol. I, p. 141.
184. *A Sketch*, pp. 420–1.
185. *Journals of Travels*, pp. 155–6.
186. *Letters from France*, pp. 112–13.
187. See above, p. 118.
188. *Letters from France*, vol. II, pp. 35–7.
189. See above, pp. 76–7.
190. *An Account of the Character and Manners of the French*, vol. I, pp. 143–4.
191. BL, Add. MS. 12130, p. 49.
192. *Observations and Reflections*, pp. 31–3.
193. *Travels in France*, vol. I, pp. 60–1, 91–2, 104–5.
194. *Wealth of Nations*, vol. I, pp. 107–8.
195. BL, Add. MS. 31192, f. 38.
196. *An Account of the Character and Manners of the French*, vol. I, pp. 145–6, 144.
197. *Remarks on the Character and Manners of the French*, vol. I, p. 104.
198. *Journey from Bayonne to Marseilles*, pp. 359–61.
199. *Travels through France and Italy*, p. 313.
200. Ibid., p. 37.
201. *Useful Hints*, pp. 41–2, 54.
202. *Wealth of Nations*, vol. II, pp. 902–4.
203. Ibid., p. 919.

3
The Privileged Orders

The clergy

Compared with British travellers in the previous century, those who came to France in our period adopted a fairly mild attitude towards Roman Catholicism, even if none is known to have been a Catholic with the one exception of Swinburne, whose attitude was far from uncritical. The Reformation was now another 100 years away, and Britain was no longer faced with the danger of a Catholic king imposing his religion and absolute monarchy with the aid of Louis XIV.

Their dislike of Roman Catholicism and most of the things which it stood for does none the less peep out from time to time, even if it is no longer an obsession. The relics displayed in cathedrals and churches aroused a good deal of derision. Pennant, for instance, generally lists with obvious irony those which he encountered. Of the abbey of St Bertin in St. Omer he writes: 'The lower Jaw-bone of St. Paul and part of the leg bone of St. Peter was shewed me; also a piece of the blessed virgin's garment and a lock of her hair and a bit of one of the nails in the crucifixion.' In describing his visit to the abbey at St. Denis he mentions seeing 'the head of St. Dennis lodged in a golden case', and then continues: 'The Church of Notre Dame has in its treasury another head of St. Dennis. This gave rise to a famous Dispute between the Monks of the Abby and the canons of the Church, begun about 1191 and lasted till 1410, when the Parlement put an end to the suit by declaring one to be head of St. Dennis the Athenian, the other that of St. Dennis the Corinthian.'[1]

The Privileged Orders

The sight of such relics aroused stronger feelings in other travellers. The Scotsman, Blaikie, writes of his visit to St Omer: 'Saw the Cathedral where they showed us amongst other curiosities the head of St Omer which they pretended to be real; after went and Saw the Benedictins which Showed us another head of St. Omer — probably this was a Saint of Many heads.'[2] As St Denis was close to Paris, it was often visited, generally with the same incredulity, expressed briefly by Peckham: 'The treasures of the Abbey, if the jewels are not fictitious, must be immense, exclusive of saints bones, apostles fingers, pieces of the real cross, and such like trumpery, which superstition would purchase at a very high price.'[3] Villiers gives a more detailed account of what was exhibited there:

> We were shewn, amongst other sacred reserves, a piece of the true cross, a foot in length; a small crucifix, made of the same, and a nail that belonged to it. In a crown, composed of gold and precious stones, was exhibited a ruby, in which was preserved a thorn, from the crown that encircled our Saviour's head; there was also a bit of the pitcher that was used at the marriage of Cana; a bone from the arm of St. Simeon; bones of St. Hippolite, St. Placide, and many others of equal note. The chin of St. Louis; a tooth of St. Pancras; St. John the Baptist's thigh; St. Bartholomew's finger; St. Thomas's hand; some of the hair of the Virgin Mary; and, to crown the whole, a budget of bones belonging to the prophet Isaiah. The solemnity with which these pious lyes were detailed, was truly entertaining; and I could not help smiling at the idea which the monk must have been amused with, that of humming us.[4]

After crossing France Stanhope wrote to his mother from Berne;

> You have heard I dare say many very ridiculous Tales about the Relics of the Catholics, but most of them I believe to be litterally true. I myself was shown a Thorn, which was Part of the Crown upon our Saviour's Head, one of the Nails with which he was crucified, whole Loads of the Cross, and what is the most ridiculous of all, a large, black, double-grained Grinder from the Mouth of the Prophet Isaiah. The bloody Shirt in which our Saviour suffered kept in a golden Shrine at Bezançon, and exposed yearly to the Adoration of about 20000 Worshippers, who flock thither for that Purpose. To

increase the Solemnity some occasional Daemoniacs are generally miraculously healed.[5]

Mrs Cradock describes with mild irony what she and her husband were shown in the cathedral at Aix:

> Un prêtre nous fit entrer dans la sacristie et nous montra des reliquaires, des ostensoirs, des calices, des ornements et des vêtements d'une richesse merveilleuse. Quelques-uns de ces objets ne peuvent être touchés par tout le monde; aussi je crus m'apercevoir qu'en notre qualité d'hérétiques il nous tenait à une certaine distance, de peur, sans doute, que notre haleine même ne profanât ces objets sacrés. Il accepta cependant notre argent qui lui parut bon.[6]

Later on their travels, at Nantes, her husband describes a Sunday street scene in which relics were involved:

> In the afternoon, observing a man with a great concourse of people around him, apparently preaching, I went to see what it was, and found him holding forth on the great virtues of the relics which he had to sell, and which he disposed of in great numbers. The deluded people stood with open mouths to hear the wonderful things this man told them. I purchased one of the relics for two sous, and had one of his papers.[7]

In all these passages there is expressed, with varying degrees of vigour, a clear contempt for such superstitious practices.

Sometimes doubt is cast upon the depth of religious feelings among French Catholics. In commenting on the dullness of life in Boulogne, Smollett works in a satirical account of the way in which people there practised their religion:

> True it is, the only profane diversions of this place are a puppet-show and a mountebank; but then their religion affords a perpetual comedy. Their high masses, their feasts, their processions, their pilgrimages, confessions, images, tapers, robes, incense, benedictions, spectacles, representations, and innumerable ceremonies, which revolve almost incessantly, furnish a variety of entertainment from one end of the year to the other. If superstition implies *fear*, never was a word more misapplied than it is to the mummery of the

religion of Rome. The people are so far from being impressed with awe and religious terror by this sort of machinery, that it amuses their imaginations in the most agreeable manner, and keeps them always in good humour. A Roman catholic longs as impatiently for the festival of *St. Suaire*, or *St. Croix*, or *St. Veronique*, as a school-boy in England for the representation of punch and the devil; and there is generally as much laughing at one farce as at the other. Even when the descent from the cross is acted, in holy week, with all the circumstances that ought naturally to inspire the gravest sentiments, if you cast your eyes among the multitude that croud the place, you will not discover one melancholy face: all is prattling, tittering, or laughing, and ten to one but you perceive a number of them employed in hissing the female who personates the Virgin Mary.[8]

Mrs Thrale was shocked by the behaviour of the congregation at a church she attended in Rouen: 'I went to High Mass at one of the most considerable Churches in the Town, & was astonished at the Want of Devotion in the Audience; some were counting their Money, some arguing with the Beggars who interrupt you without ceasing, some receiving Messages and dispatching Answers, some beating Time to the Musick, but scarce any one praying except for one Moment when the Priest elevated the Host.' On her second visit to France she was equally upset by the failure to observe the sabbath: 'And surely I never knew till now, that so little religion could exist in any Christian country as in this, where they drive carts, and keep their little shops open on a Sunday, forbearing neither pleasure nor business, as I see, on account of observing that day upon which their Redeemer rose again.'[9]

The Cradocks were equally disconcerted by the behaviour of the congregation at a midnight mass which they attended on Christmas Eve in a church in Marseilles. Cradock writes:

The noise and loud talking of the people in the church was so great, it was not possible to hear the least word of the service; nor was there even the appearance of devotion among the congregation. Bargaining for chairs and places; some lighting and others putting out the candles, &c. &c. and other very improper conduct, rendered the whole a scene of confusion. At length the priests began to sing the *Gloria in excelsis Deo*, accompanied by the organ: this was solemn and fine; but to my great astonishment at the end of the first line I heard the song of Malbrooke echoed from the bottom of the Church by some of the mob there! As this was the case we thought it high time to retire, and did not go to any other Church.[10]

That by the 1760s there was in France a considerable amount of hostility to the Catholic Church and its clergy was noted by several travellers, though Hume's reference in a letter of 1765 to 'the almost universal Contempt of all Religion'[11] does seem wildly exaggerated. Smollett, writing at the same date, seems somewhat nearer the truth: 'All the learned laity of France detest the hierarchy as a plan of despotism, founded on imposture and usurpation.'[12]

Walpole's letters during his stay in Paris in 1765 bring out clearly the influence which the ideas of the *Philosophes*, including such radical thinkers as Diderot, D'Holbach and Helvétius, exercised on a small minority. He was scandalised by what he observed at a dinner at Baron d'Holbach's: 'I dined today with a dozen *savants*, and though all the servants were waiting, the conversation was much more unrestrained, even on the Old Testament, than I would suffer at my own table in England, if a single footman was present.' In another letter he wrote scornfully: 'The *savants*, I beg their pardon, the *philosophes* are insupportable. Superficial, overbearing and fanatic; they preach incessantly, and their avowed doctrine is atheism: — you would not believe how openly. Don't wonder therefore, if I should return a Jesuit. Voltaire himself does not satisfy them: One of their lady devotees said of him, *il est bigot; c'est un déiste.*' In another letter of the same period he wrote: 'Laughing is as much out of fashion as *pantin* or *bilboquet*. — Good folks, they have not time to laugh. There is God and the King to be pulled down first; and men and women, one and all, are devoutly employed in the demolition. They think me quite profane for having any belief left.'[13]

All these observations of Walpole's could obviously only apply to a tiny minority in Paris, and yet that the writings of the *Philosophes* did have some wider influence is attested by Thicknesse, writing only a few years later: 'Philosophy advances rapidly on this side the water, and tramples down a multitude of vulgar errors; nor is it in the power of the clergy, who are indefatigable in checking the progress of it, to turn the tide, which they perceive is rushing in upon them, and so likely to overthrow their best freeholds.' In another passage in the same work Thicknesse endeavours to account for the number of deists in France: 'The great misfortune of the Catholic religion is, that it renders the multitude superstitious and idolatrous, and leaves most men, who have sense enough to see through its errors, rather disposed to consider the whole Christian system founded on no better basis. There are more Deists in France than in all the Protestant countries of Europe.'[14]

By the time we come to the 1780s, various travellers detect a decline in the influence of the clergy, even at government level. In 1784 Andrews writes:

> Happily for the adherents to the notions that begin to prevail among some of the more enlightened individuals of the French nation, the clergy has lost much of the influence it once had among the great. The government supports them no longer with that blind subserviency, which characterised the eras of ignorance and superstition.
>
> The diminution of their credit appears in the diminution of their numbers. Much less considerable than twenty years ago, is the appearance of the secular and regular clergy at this day: one meets with fewer in the streets and places of public resort than formerly; one hears less about them; people also seem to think less of them; all this portends an inward decline, as it shews a visible decay.[15]

Though it ends with an extraordinarily rash prophecy, what St John wrote while in Burgundy in 1787 is certainly interesting:

> There is not, nor never was a nation in the world, who have less religion than the modern French. The lower class of people, and also the clergy, may keep up the shew of religion, but the generality of their genteel people make a scoff of the faith, and think it ridiculous to be a Christian. The Deistical works of Rousseau and Voltaire, are every where distributed through the kingdom, are universally read, and studied, and in my opinion have been the cause of undermining the whole structure of Christianity in France; and in the course of half a century more, in all human probability will totally erase all vestiges of revealed religion in the French nation.[16]

When Villiers left France in September 1788 and was tossing on the Channel 'on Board the Pacquet', he wrote down some reflections on his recent travels. He felt that the 'arbitrary power and blinded superstition' which he saw there were incompatible with 'the present refined and improved state of mankind'. Yet he found some satisfaction at the thought of the French clergy's loss of influence:

> It nevertheless gives me much pleasure to view the decay of ecclesiastical influence amongst the people, and to observe how much the priests are every where neglected and despised. They roam about the streets, drear and solitary; their visages pale and sallow, with the blush of health and youth destroyed; at once disregarded by the vulgar, and contemned by the wise.
>
> I do not much wonder at their being such a number of deists in this country: it is more a matter of surprise to me, that so many can sit down passive beneath the shade of superstition.[17]

However, if the clergy had lost their hold over a minority of the population, they still retained it over the great mass of the people, as travellers saw in the innumerable processions which took place on Church festivals, such as the one watched by Wharton in Dijon in 1775:

> There is here, to the Great Edification and happiness of the town, a hostie, which on being stabbed by an unbelieving Jew bled in three places, and the blood is still on it. Yesterday was the fête of this most holy Relic, which was carried in procession thro the town. First came a fellow bearing a Red silk banner embroidered with the figure of the Virgin & Child, then two other gentlemen with large torches lighted (observe it was 9 o clock in the morning and vastly hot), then an old fellow in a surplice with a chaplet of flowers on his head, carrying a large Silver Crucifix, and having on each side of him a little boy carrying a wax candle (not lighted) in a large silver candlestick, then came some little boys also in surplices & chaplets, then a great lubber, surpliced & chapleted carrying the Crucifix of the Minimes, of Brass; then 12 Minimes, then another such figure carrying the cross of the Cordeliers, of silver; then 12 Cordeliers, then a Capuchin in a long beard carrying a paltry wooden crucifix; then 12 Capuchins, then

another crossbearer chapleted & surpliced, then 12 Carmes, their crucifix was silver, then came some more little boys in red gowns, these were the enfans trouves, following, most likely their fathers, then came some priests in very rich embroidered robes, singing latin, then came the Chanoines of the Sainte Chapelle (to whom the Precious deposit belongs) in robes of white flowered satin Laced with gold, then some more little boys in surplices & chaplets with baskets of roses in their hands, which they strewed before the hostie, then 2 priests with pots of incense with silver chains, swinging them about to incense the hostie, which came after them, carried in a rich gold case in the midst of which was a Sun, the disk of 2 crystals between which was the cause of all this parade. I saw something like a dirty wafer which was it.[18]

Although this letter, addressed to a friend, an Anglican clergyman, is full of sarcasm, such a procession in a provincial city was typical of thousands which took place in any given year with the intention of impressing the mass of the population. Toulouse was notorious for its bigotry, and, as R.W.C., who arrived there at the end of December 1788, points out, there were endless religious processions:

There are Convents and Churches innumerable, adorned with a Profusion of Pictures, Images and Gilding, and you do not walk ten yards in the street but you are stopt by some Procession or other. I who did not wish to give offence, at first pulled off my hat, but I soon found that I might do nothing else if I pursued my original intention, so I pass them with as little ceremony as is due to 'the works of man's hands', although I frequently incur the curses of some old Devotees, who happen to be on their knees as *I wretched Heretic* pass by.[19]

A dozen years earlier the bigotry of Toulouse — especially the associations of Catholic laymen known as *Pénitents* — was too much for an English Catholic like Swinburne to stomach:

Besides a regular army of priests, friars, and nuns, Toulouse has a spiritual militia, animated with equal if not superior zeal for the interest of the church: this corps consist of a large number of laymen associated under the denomination of penitents: kings, statesmen, and generals, have thought it an honour to have their names enrolled on the list; but times are altered, and I believe men of sober judgment, and just notions of religion, wish these excrescences of the ecclesiastical trunk were lopped off, rather than encouraged.[20]

Pénitents were to be found in other towns in the South of France besides Toulouse. Mrs Cradock encountered *Pénitents blancs* at Aix and again at Montpellier. At the latter place she wrote on Maundy Thursday: 'Au coin d'une rue nous fûmes arrêtés par une procession des pénitents blancs. Des prêtres, psalmodiant et portant des crucifix, marchaient en tête; suivaient des hommes revêtus de grandes robes blanches avec des capuchons noirs rabattus cachant presque entièrement leur visage. On s'agenouillait sur leur passage. De jeunes garçons jouaient du cor et d'autres instruments. Du reste, aujourd'hui, jeudi saint, on ne rencontre que processions défilant par la ville.'[21]

Among secular clergy the parish priests, the *curés*, receive relatively little attention from our travellers. Smollett is mildly sarcastic when he writes: 'In some parts of France, the *curé* of the parish, on All Souls day, which is called *le jour des morts*, says a *libera domine* for two sols, at every grave in the burying-ground, for the release of the soul whose body is there interred.'[22] Pennant is purely factual when he records what he was told was the income of the incumbent at St Sulpice in Paris (an exceptionally high income for a *curé*): 'This Cure is worth 6000 £ per Annum or better, which rises from offerings at funerals buryings and christenings.'[23] Lord Gardenstone was much impressed with a *curé* whom he met at Remiremont in Lorraine: 'The Curè here is a primitive man, uniting the character of a true, uncorrupted, Christian pastor to the natural philosopher. He has been Curè of this parish for forty-one years, respected by all ranks. Upon a stipend of little more than sixty pounds Sterling a-year,[24] he has lived with decent hospitality; and, besides a choice library of books, has collected an excellent cabinet of natural curiosities.'[25]

One could well imagine Thicknesse denouncing in his robust style the nefarious activities of parish priests. But no, like Young,[26] he commends them for their moderation in levying their tithes: 'Though we complain so much of the Romish clergy, yet they are more moderate than ours in gathering their tythes, as they tythe corn, wine, and oil, not pigs, milk, and apples; they take here the great tythes only.' In other respects too he finds them superior to their English counterparts: 'It must be confessed, that the country clergy in France, attend to the functions of their duty (and have ten times the duty to perform) much better than in general it is done with us.' If only the Catholic clergy were allowed to marry ... He concludes his remarks with a page on the evils arising out of women going to confession.[27]

Young defends the French clergy against the view, commonly held in England, that they deserved their fate in the Revolution because of 'their peculiar profligacy'. So large a body of men, he argues, could not be wholly devoid of vices, but, he declares, 'they preserved, what is not always preserved in England, an external decency of behaviour'. There follows a splendid satire of some English country parsons:

> One did not find among them poachers or fox-hunters, who, having spent the morning in scampering after hounds, dedicate the evening to the bottle, and reel from inebriety to the pulpit. Such advertisements were never seen in France as I have heard of in England: — *Wanted a curacy in a good sporting country, where the duty is light, and the neighbourhood convivial.*[28]

On the whole the parish clergy escape much more lightly than their ecclesiastical superiors.

To be appointed a bishop or archbishop in France by the eighteenth century it was essential to be of noble birth. Although it takes one back to a slightly earlier period, an anecdote picked up by Muirhead when he visited Lyons in 1789 is revealing. The canons of the cathedral there, he writes, 'are counts of Lyons, must prove sixteen quarters of nobility, wear a cross of enamelled gold, surmounted with eight points and four coronets, and are little anxious to be reminded of the humble deportment of the early Christians'. Muirhead relates the following exchanges between a newly appointed archbishop of Lyons who lacked the necessary degrees of nobility to become a canon of the cathedral, and the haughty canons:

> When the abbé de Villeroi, who had made many unsuccessful attempts to become one of their number, was appointed by the king to the archbishopric, they waited upon him with the usual tribute of respectful compliments. While he received them with courtesy, he could not help remarking, that *the*

stone which the builders refused was become the head of the corner. Their spokesman instantly replied, *This is the Lord's doing, it is wondrous in our eyes.*[29]

Muirhead notes that the income from the see was 150,000 livres. Earlier the archbishop, Antoine de Malvin de Montazet, who occupied the see for thirty years to his death in 1788, had given Pennant a very polite reception.[30]

When Wraxall visited Auch, to the west of Toulouse, in 1775, he was much impressed both with the archbishop's palace and with his income: 'The revenues of the see of Auch, which is archiepiscopal, amount annually to three hundred thousand livres. The palace corresponds with these ample possessions, and is a very handsome building. The apartments are furnished with a voluptuous splendour, rather becoming a temporal than a spiritual prince; and in the chamber where the archbishop himself sleeps, I could not help smiling at a number of holy relics, which he has disposed around a bed, on which Heliogabalus might have reposed.'[31] Muirhead was in Auch in June 1789 and he too noted the handsome palace and the wealth of the archbishop: 'Adjoining [the cathedral] is the archbishop's palace, an ample mansion, and commanding a delightful range of variegated prospect. The income of this see is rated at 126,000 livres, and is worth a great deal more.'[32] His landlord did, however, tell him various stories about the generosity of the previous archbishop, Claude Marcel Antoine d'Apuchon.

Swinburne's impressions of Narbonne, the seat of another archbishopric, were decidedly unfavourable: 'The streets are narrow, and an air of poverty reigns throughout. The church alone seems to engross the wealth of the place; its archbishoprick is numbered among the richest benefices in the kingdom; the palace of the prelate resembles the gloomy fortress of an ancient feudatory prince, rather than the residence of a French archbishop in these days of peace and elegance.'[33]

The incumbent of this see always presided over the meetings of the Estates of Languedoc, and as Cornelia Knight was present with her mother when they met in Montpellier at the end of November 1777, her autobiography tells us a great deal about the archbishop from 1763 to 1801, Arthur Richard de Dillon. He was, she writes, 'of a commanding figure, and had a fine open countenance. By birth he was an Irishman, being brother to Lord Dillon, but he was brought up in France, and, while still very young, was present at the battle of Fontenoy. Subsequently he went into the Church, and became possessed of great benefices and considerable influence. He belonged to that class of prelates called "Evêques Administrateurs", but he was liberal-minded and charitable.'

Certainly the speech which he delivered at the opening of the Estates was decidedly liberal in tone. Its theme was 'the utility of commerce, in all nations and ages, towards the civilisation of mankind. Industry was the only true road to improvement.' The archbishop pointed to 'the flourishing state of the English navy, and the tranquil riches and peaceful security of the Dutch in the midst of powerful and envious nations'. Unfortunately France had followed a different path:

> The speaker then lamented that France, which possessed so many and such superior advantages, situated between two seas, in the centre of Europe, under the most favourable sky, and inhabited by a people of the most active disposition, was yet by no means as commercial as she ought to be. Louis XIV, he said, would have afforded encouragement to the commerce of his kingdom, had he not been hurried away by an ill-judged ambition, and thus compelled to leave that essential duty to the care of his minister, the great Colbert. That statesman, however, signally erred in laying restraints upon commerce, for it would have been far better to have suffered the trifling inconveniences resulting from certain commodities leaving the country and being useful to foreign nations, than to renounce the great advantages which arose from the communication of new discoveries and inventions, or from superior perfection in those already made. Instead, therefore, of laying the restraint he intended upon abuses, Colbert fostered the worst of all, monopoly.

In another speech to the Estates the archbishop denounced government intervention for the bad effects which it had in the province:

> Then with respect to commerce, if the unhappy laws, dictated by rigour rather than by prudence, were allowed to prevail, Languedoc would be utterly ruined, as the manufacturers, deprived of all power of extending their views, would necessarily give up all emulation and desire of impovement. He then observed that, although the neglect of public statutes

was injurious to a country, even that perhaps was a less evil than the observance of pernicious ones. As an example, he mentioned the manufacturers of woollen cloths, who, perceiving that the dyes of France were inferior to the texture while the reverse was the case in the Levant, had acquired and introduced into this province the beautiful hue which is in use among those nations. This, strictly speaking, was contrary to law, but it had been of infinite benefit to France.

Not content with expounding the liberal economic principles which were now fashionable, in his opening speech he even ventured, in a province with a large Protestant minority, to criticise their persecution in the last two reigns and to express the hope that something would soon be done to redress this wrong:

> The archbishop then reverted to the unhappy fanaticism which had driven so many industrious citizens to seek refuge in the open and liberal arms of England and Holland, which nations were amply repaid for their generosity by the stimulus given to their commerce, and the improvements introduced into all useful arts, by these grateful exiles. Louis XV had proper views on these subjects, but was prevented from carrying them into execution by the troubles of the times and the narrow-mindedness of his ministers. Under the present government, however, everything might be hoped for from the known good disposition of the king towards his people, and especially in this province, where his Majesty's gracious intentions were so well understood and seconded.[34]

It was to be another ten years before a very modest improvement in the legal position of Protestants was to be achieved:[35]

The Archbishop of Narbonne proved a faithful supporter of Étienne Charles Loménie de Brienne, the Archbishop of Toulouse, when the latter held power in the critical period from May 1787 to August 1788. During their long stay in Toulouse, Lady Knight and her daughter had an opportunity of observing Brienne though he was not often in his diocese, a point which Cornelia Knight illustrates with an anecdote:

> He visited his diocese every year, but did not remain long at a time. He was there while we were at Toulouse to receive the Emperor of Germany, Joseph II, who travelled in the most

unostentatious manner, under the title of Count Falkenstein. At his departure he thanked the archbishop for his hospitality, but declined his offer of accompanying him to the next place whither he was going, saying 'I cannot think of taking you from a city where your duty requires your presence.' The emperor knew very well what he was saying, and the archbishop answered him with a bow.

Before discussing Brienne she makes a generalisation: 'The high clergy was very tolerant, very charitable, and very delightful in society; perhaps not always sufficiently strict to the rules of that exact morality which is expected in the profession to which they were devoted.' Indeed she adds: 'It was said that Louis XVI would not allow Monsieur de Brienne to be Archbishop of Paris on account of his connection with a certain lady.' After pointing out that his period in government did not 'come up to the expectations which had been formed from his talents in the administration of his diocese and in society', she goes on: 'He had a sensible countenance, an active person, and great facility of expression. By all accounts his quickness of comprehension was such as hardly to give time to others to explain themselves, for he seemed to understand every subject more clearly than the person whom it chiefly concerned.' Elsewhere Cornelia Knight wrote of Brienne:

> His manners were elegant, but not conciliatory, and his effrontery appeared to me astonishing . . . He was of an ancient and distinguished family, and, probably, had he been brought up to a military profession, would have been a man of honour and agreeable to society. I believe he was liberal, and in many respects useful in his diocese. He was at the head of those who were called 'Evêques Administrateurs', in opposition to the 'Dêvots', or pastoral bishops: both had their defects, and helped on the Revolution in different ways; for the first were too often libertines, and the second intolerant and illiberal.[36]

It could scarcely be said that our travellers looked with favour on the large numbers of regular clergy, male and female, which they came across in France. When he arrived at Lille in 1782, Pennington noted: 'In few towns of its size, have superstition and bigotry erected more altars to religion than at Lille. There are eighteen Monasteries of men and seventeen of women.'[57]

On the other hand travellers also observed that many of these religious houses were under-occupied and that few members of the various orders were to be seen abroad. Already in 1765 Cole discussed this point with Walpole and ended by wondering whether the regular clergy would be allowed to survive:

> To such a Pitch of Assurance was the French Philosophy risen, that I was told by Mr Walpole, on observing to him the few regular Clergy one saw in the Streets of Paris, that they had Orders from their Superiors to keep more within their Cloistres, not to give Offence to their Enemies, by their too open Appearance in the World: & their Ridicule had this Effect, that many of the younger Monks of St Germain's & other Convents, had actually petitioned the Parliament for Leave to quit their religious Habit: but as the older Part of their Convents had disavowed what the others had done, it was not yet judged proper to proceed to those Lengths taken on the same Conjuncture in Henry 8th's Time. Things were not quite ripe for that yet: However there is a Restraint laid upon receiving Religious of both Sexes under such an Age, & beyond such a Number: & so far, I think, they judge very rightly: but whether they will end as prudently, God only knows for certain; tho' one may be allowd reasonably to presume, that they will not: considering the Temper, Disposition, & Principles of those who are likely to be the Reformers.[38]

Drastic measures were not taken against religious orders until the Revolution, but these observations are part of Cole's view that France was already on the verge of a civil war.

Six years later Walpole wrote from Paris a letter in which he expressed his own views on the depressed state of the religious orders:

> It is very singular that I have not half the satisfaction in going into churches and convents that I used to have. The consciousness that the vision is dispelled, the want of fervour so obvious in the religious, the solitude that one knows proceeds from contempt, not from contemplation, make these places appear like abandoned theatres destined to destruction. The monks trot about as if they had not long to stay there; and what used

to be holy gloom is now but dirt and darkness. There is no more deception, than in a tragedy acted by candle-snuffers.[39]

Other travellers note more prosaically the small numbers to be found in religious houses. To Pennington, an abbey at Amiens presented 'a desolate appearance, as there are not above four or five monks in it: the rest are generally in Paris'. A footnote added later reads: 'Surely no one can blame the policy of suppressing monastic institutions, when this, and similar instances so frequently occur, of their quitting their monastery.'[40] In September 1787 St John noted a general fall in numbers; 'The religious houses here have declined very much within the space of this latter century. I have been told, that the convent of Cordeliers at Dijon, that had in it nearly thirty friars about thirty years ago, has at present but seven; and that many other religious have fallen away in the same proportion.'[41]

One religious order, the Society of Jesus, had in fact already been dissolved in France. Shortly after his arrival in Paris in March 1762, Sterne was convinced that the progress of the Seven Years War interested the French less than the proceedings being taken against the Jesuits:

> I could never have been in France at so critical a period, as this, when two of the greatest Concerns that ever affected the Interest of this kingdom are upon the Anvil together — the Affair of the Jesuits — & the War — for, much of this kingdoms future glory & wellfare seems to be depending upon these two points — the first takes up the attention of the french, much more than the last — & well it may — for in this city alone, the Society have a rent of 95,000 pounds a year — what must their revenue be from the whole kingdom? — it will end, I trow, like our Henry the 8^{ths}, in a general Resumption.[42]

Slightly later travellers saw something of the consequences of the action taken by the *Parlements* against the Society. Thus at Dijon at the end of September 1763 an anonymous writer noted: 'The poor Jesuits were to take their departure the very day we arrived without, I think, much regret on the side of the People.'[43] In Paris Pennant found that what had been for over a century a great tourist attraction was visible only from the outside: 'The Jesuits' church Rue St Antoine is now shut up.' Earlier at St Omer he had found that the College of the English Jesuits, the ancestor of Stonyhurst College, was in a poor way, like many other colleges in France which the Society had been compelled to leave: 'Visited Mr. Talbot, Brother to Earl of Shrewsbury, who very obligingly shewed me the College of which he was president. It lately belonged to the English Jesuits but is now in possession of the seculars. It was in a flourishing state when the former had it, but is now almost deserted by students.'[44]

Cole was clearly disconcerted by the existence of commendatory abbots who drew a considerable part of the income of a religious house without taking vows. He was particularly nonplussed by the Comte de Clermont, a prince of the blood who followed a military career and was at the same time commendatory abbot of the rich Benedictine monastery of St Germain des Prés in Paris. At Walpole's, Cole met an army officer of Irish descent named Dromgold:

> Having a Commission in the Count de Clermont's Regiment, he now resides in the Abbey of St Germain des Prez, of which the said Count is Commendatory Abbot, tho' a Military Man; but being a Prince of the Blood Royal of France, this rich Abbey was given him to support his Dignity: yet I have several Times met this Lay Abbat in his Coach, dressed in a Clerical Habit, having a Cassock & Cloak over it, in his own short Hair, with a Cross before his Breast, as a Prelate; being a fat, jolly, well looking man. As Mr Dromgold is a Favourite of his, he is lodged in the Abbey, & attends him also when he goes to his Regiment. This mixing religious & military Characters together, let the Persons who bear them be ever so unexceptionable, can never be for the Credit or Advantage of Religion: it must at length undermine all Notions of the use of religious Societies: better surely, if the Riches of the Endowment are a Temptation to give it in this Manner, to reduce the regular Abbat's Income.[45]

Young's comments on the wealth of this abbey, which he visited in 1787, were blistering: 'To the benedictine abbey of St. Germain, to see pillars of African marble, &c. It is the richest abbey in France; the abbot has 300,000 livres a year (£13,125). I lose my patience at such revenues thus bestowed; consistent with the spirit of the tenth century, but not with that of the eighteenth. What a noble farm would a fourth of this income establish!'[46]

The Privileged Orders

Our travellers found that certain wealthy abbeys provided lavish hospitality which reflected the very comfortable way of life which the monks enjoyed. The Scottish gardener, Blaikie, who held the post of inspector of the gardens of the Comte d'Artois, accompanied a French colleague on a visit to a monastery at Passy from which they passed to the Abbey of St Germain des Prés:

> We Breakfasted with the Prior of the Convent where we was well treated with white wine and oisters; those poor Monks lives in a rich stile which, as Mr. Bressy told me I should see better by going and dining with the Benedictins in the Abbay St. Germains des Prez where he knew one Don Dreouin who was professor, so we agreed to go there to dinner and in arriving the Monks had just finished dinner but the monk with whom he was acquainted went and ordered us dinner, where we dinned and was served like princes with the best of every thing and the Superiore of the monks knowing that we belonged to the Comte DArtois came to our table to see if we wanted for any thing, so that not only the Princes in this country is honnoured but those belonging to them; after being thus served in splendour after dinner Dom Drouen took us to his apartement where in the midle of his room he oppened a trape door where he had a little cellar full of the choicest wines of all sorts; there we continued drinking untill the poor monk lay across the cellar door and his two compagnons little better; however we made shift to get out of the convent which way I know not.[47]

Equally lavish, though rather more decorous hospitality was available in the provinces. Wharton found himself splendidly entertained when in 1775 he went from Dijon to the abbey of Cîteaux, the original house of the Cistercians, an order dedicated to solitude and simplicity of life.[48]

Ten years later the Cradocks were much impressed with the 'douceur de vivre' enjoyed by the Benedictines at Vendôme. After describing the wonderful supply of freshwater fish from which the monks could 'order whatever they chose for their fast-days' dinner', Cradock goes on:

> We then entered their fine summer apartments, for they have a set for each season, and here, to our surprise, we saw cardtables; and the servant informed us, that, in one very large

room, they received and entertained all the ladies of the neighbourhood. We afterwards walked in their sumptuous gardens, and, from a shady terrace, saw the castle, with the tranquil river Eure at the foot of it; the city and all its environs; and returned again through the abbaye. Having expressed our astonishment at seeing female servants in the kitchen as we passed, the attendant said, as the kitchen was very large, and well fitted up, perhaps we should like to walk into it. This was what was wanted; and, indeed, we had never seen its equal since we examined that of the Prince de Condé at Chantilly. It was neatness itself, and possessed every possible convenience. We counted sixty stew-pans, and every other article was in the same abundance.[49]

More fortunate than the Cradocks, R.W.C. tasted what the kitchens and cellar could produce at another Benedictine abbey, one on the outskirts of Bordeaux, where he was entertained in December 1788, not long before all religious orders were abolished in France:

We were favoured with a letter of introduction to the Prior of the Convent by the Abbé Mc.Dermot, a native of Ireland residing in Bourdeaux and deservedly respected there, who takes all occasions of evincing his civility to his Countrymen. We arrived at the Convent about a quarter of an hour before dinner was served. It was a maigre day. We were not expected, yet I have seldom seen a repast at once so superb and elegant. There was no Meat, yet we had, in the different courses, at least Forty dishes, exclusive of the Desert which consisted of sweetmeats, a variety of fruits and half a dozen different kinds of exquisite Cheese. The dinner consisted of white Soups, a species of aquatic wildfowl, vegetables and eggs dressed in various manners. The Abbé of . . . is a younger brother of one of the first families in France. The man of birth, of education and breeding is conspicuous in his every action — polite, easy and genteel; and although above fifty, yet such is the tranquillity and good cheer he enjoys as Monarch of the Convent that he appeared to me not more than thirty. He invited, with the Prior, half a dozen of his subjects to dine at his table with his English guests. In all we made the number of the Muses, with Apollo at our head. If brilliant wit flows from sparkling Wine, ours was of the first

The Privileged Orders

quality. The Symposium Dei, as described by the antient Poets, was rather a boisterous club. Ours was 'the feast of reason, and the flow of Soul'. This Convent is one of the richest of its order, and their revenues are very large, and arise principally from the exquisite Wines made upon the land contiguous to and belonging to the convent. Besides White, he gave us seven different kinds of Red Claret with each of which Bacchus himself might have deigned to purple his mouth. The noble Abbé drank moderately, but seeing the wild Englishmen smack their lips after each glass, he had the happy talent of inducing his guests to imbibe cheerfully. His discourse was so powdered with attic salt that it excited thirst. His look was so benign, yet friendly, he would beg us so earnestly to taste yet another and another glass; he was so desirous that such good judges should give him their opinion of the comparative value of his several kinds of Wine, he had such an art of exhibiting a better and still better bottle that we were fain to oblige our noble host . . .

After Coffee, the Abbé very politely pressed us to take a bed and stay a few days at the Convent, saying he would give us meat for supper, which we should have had at dinner if he had known of the honor we intended him.

Before leaving the monastery they were shown round the buildings:

The Benedictines retain only the rational part of devotion; they clog not the way to Heaven with useless restraints. They have for relaxation a Tennis Court and even a Billiard Table. They are Lords of many villages and large tracts of land in the environs. They go a shooting, and have proper sporting apparatus for the use of their visitors. They again insisted on our staying two or three days in their retirement. Having an indispensable engagement, we made polite excuses to the Abbé and, promising to visit on our return home, we rode back to Bourdeaux.[50]

Clearly such monks must have lived quite unaware of the hostility towards most religious congregations which was so soon to lead to their total abolition.

A very different monastery, the Grande Chartreuse, attracted a surprising number of travellers, even though the journey up into the mountains was tiring, difficult and even at times dangerous. Romilly, who made the journey in 1781, writes of his visit: 'Though it was early in September, we had so deep a fall of snow, and which lasted so long, that the roads became impassable, and for three days we were obliged to prolong our stay with the hospitable fathers against our will.' In a letter written during this enforced stay Romilly relates his impressions on waking up on his first morning:

> The next morning, after a slumber of nine hours without interruption, — except once, indeed, that I was waked by the melancholy bell which summons the fathers to the midnight service, — I found myself lying on a small wooden bed, in a little cell paved with tiles, and furnished only with two wooden chairs, and a desk for prayer, over which hung a very indifferent print of the passion of our Saviour. My window looked over the spacious court-yard before the house, which was vast, but solitary; the grass grew between the stones, and in the midst stood two fountains, the melancholy splashing of whose waters alone interrupted the deep silence. The aspect of the country was well suited to the building, and presented to the view a dreary mountain rising above, one end wholly covered with woods of gloomy pine. I quitted my little cell to walk about the house of this solitary community. Every object struck me with awe and respect. As I walked through the long cloisters, nothing broke the profound silence of the convent but the sound of my steps on the pavement, faintly echoed by the vaulted roof. The cloister led me by a small burial ground in the midst of the building, where a number of tombstones in the form of crosses were placed in a kind of irregular order, — some high, some low; some new, others mouldering away and broken or fallen down, and with inscriptions scarce legible. This is the burial-place of the Generals; and they are never permitted to be far distant from it after their elevation to the supremacy of their order; for the General must not step beyond the precincts of the monastery. I began to read the inscriptions; and while I was remarking the very advanced age to which a life abstemious even to excess had been prolonged by these venerable fathers, and was observing the slight distinction which some of them derived from the addition of a few years to their uniform lives, or by having died, some in the present century, and some three hundred

years ago, I heard the distant steps of some person in the cloister. I quitted the cemetery to see who it might be; a white figure at a considerable distance was advancing towards me; it was one of the fathers. I walked to meet him, and should have spoken to him; but he had arrived at the door of his cell, which opened into the cloister; he entered and shut-to his door. I reproached myself for having forgotten that the fathers are not permitted to speak, and for having exposed him to the temptation of opening his lips; for he seemed in that instant to regret that the laws of his order imposed silence on him. The falling-to of the heavy door rang through the building, and left an awful impression on my mind.[51]

Different travellers naturally took away different impressions of the Grande Chartreuse. Romilly's awe at such austerity was not shared by Wilkes, who visited it in 1765 during his exile. Although struck with the wildness of the landscape — 'Nature sits here indeed in great gravity, on a sublime craggy throne; but the situation, I think, inspires horror rather than pensiveness' — Wilkes views everything in the monastery from a practical, down-to-earth point of view:

Hospitality is a very steady and extensive virtue among these good monks. All strangers are well received, but their stay is supposed not to exceed three days. A German, to whom the excellence of their Burgundy, no less than the exemplariness of their piety, was thought to suggest a longer abode in that holy retreat, found over his cell, *Triduanus est, jam soetet* [sic]. I continued with them a day and a half, was greatly edified, and extremely well accommodated, as well as my servants and horses. They are not allowed meat, but have excellent fish of various sorts, garden stuff, butter, cheese, bread, and fruit in perfection. The rule of their order enjoins silence, but a *père coadjuteur* has a dispensation to receive strangers, and to do the honours of the convent. The *père général* is likewise exempt from the rule. The fathers are allowed to drink wine, and the *père général* sent me a present of the best Burgundy I ever tasted. There are separate apartments for the French, Spaniards, English, &c. with a large hall to dine, for the building is immense. At a distance are small houses and sheds for all sorts of workmen — carpenters, joiners, smiths, masons, &c. The fathers have each a bedchamber, an anti-chamber, a cabinet, and a small garden, with a variety of iron and wooden instruments to make their own chairs, boxes, &c. to cultivate their gardens, and to amuse themselves. Many of them are men of great families in France and Germany, and appeared of high breeding, as I observed in a variety of little circumstances, when I attended their evening devotions. Five of them had given up to their relations large family estates to retire to that dreary solitude. The *père coadjuteur* and the *père général* were really fine gentlemen, of easy and polite conversation. They had both lived much in the gay world. From satiety and disgust they had retired from it, to that internal peace and tranquillity which they told me they had found only in those deserts. This *guilty* world however they did not seem quite to forget, for I saw on the table of the *père général* the Mercure Historique, printed at Amsterdam, and the Journal Encylopédique of Bouillon, and they asked me a thousand questions about the late war, and the affairs of England.[52]

In the second half of this letter Wilkes describes a visit to Voltaire at Ferney where the atmosphere was no doubt more congenial to him.

Nuns naturally attracted their share of attention. While Lord Clive and his party were staying in the bishop's palace of Lodève — a favour which they enjoyed because he had presented the bishop with one of his horses which had been particularly admired — they met many priests. Lady Clive's female companion, who wrote an account of their journey, relates how they came to inspect a neighbouring convent:

The Vicar in the Bishops absence was the head of them, and had the government of a neighbouring convent. At our request [he] used his interest to permit Lady Clive and myself to be admitted within the grate, and to visit every part of the Convent: we found the poor nuns of whom there were about 30 beside noviciates, delighted to see us, and ready to answer any questions we put to them relating to their way of life; they seemed thoroughly satisfied with their lot, and such is the effect of Enthusiasm that they are persuaded the enjoyment of freedom and society here are inconsistent with the persuit of future happiness. I should give them more merit on this account were their profession a voluntary one, but it is generally an act of necessity. Be that as it will, the poor women certainly deserve pity. This convent was much the neatest house which I have seen in France.

The writer rounds off her account of the visit with a somewhat surprising sentence: 'Lord Clive was invited to accompany us on this visit, a very particular compliment to his Lordship, which he however declined.'[53]

Various travellers noted how the division between nobles and *roturiers* obtained in convents as well as among the male clergy. The author of *Travels into France and Italy* observed at Lyons that the rigid requirement of noble birth for admission to the cathedral chapter was paralleled in a neighbouring convent:

> Near the city is a house of Royal Chanoinesses, the same proofs of birth are required for their admission as the canons. They are educated for this scheme of life very young, but do not engage by vows till twenty-five; before that time they are at liberty to marry; and when the engagement is made, they do not spend their lives like other religious orders: they visit, go to concerts and all amusements, as women of the world, except for the theatre; which the confessors prohibit to the sex, though they are not attended to often in this point. Some fortune is requisite to these ladies, as they do not live in the common style of convents.[54]

Pennington encountered another such convent in Flanders, and although he was quite satisfied with his reception ('The apartments and gardens are neat, and the inhabitants were very polite in conducting us over them'), he wrote sarcastically: 'The nuns must all prove their *noblesse*, unmixed with the *canaille* for many generations.'[55] At Épinal, Muirhead encountered in 1787 a similar establishment: 'Besides other religious houses, Epinal has a noted abbey of canonesses, with a yearly revenue of 12000 livres. The nuns are all noble, and wear a broad blue ribband, with a golden cross, surmounted with eight points, and representing the Virgin and St. Goëri!'[56]

The exemption from direct taxes such as the *taille* enjoyed by the French clergy is occasionally criticised because of the extra burden which it threw on the *roturiers* who were compelled to pay more than their fair share. In his chapter on the Revolution, as we have seen, Young asks: 'What must have been the state of the poor

The Privileged Orders

people paying heavy taxes, from which the nobility and the clergy were exempted? A cruel aggravation of their misery, to see those who could best afford to pay, exempted because able!'[57] In his account of the French taxation system, Smollett does mention the relatively modest contribution which the clergy made to the Treasury: 'The French king draws considerable sums from his clergy, under the denomination of *dons gratuits*, or free-gifts', but on the whole the privileges of the clergy in the matter of taxation are little emphasised. One matter to which Smollett twice refers is the time lost each year in France through the celebration of Church festivals. The French, he declares, 'are very slothful with all their vivacity, and the great number of their holidays not only encourages this lazy disposition, but actually robs them of one half of what their labour would otherwise produce'.[58]

Since the revocation of the Edict of Nantes in 1685, reinforced by a royal declaration of 1724, the Huguenots had officially ceased to exist. A man found guilty of attending their illegal assemblies out in the country ('le désert') was liable to be sent to the galleys for life, and a woman to life imprisonment, while the penalty for an officiating pastor was death. Only a Catholic form of marriage was recognised, and children had to be baptised by the *curé* of the parish or else to be held to be illegitimate and unable to inherit from their parents. Huguenots continued to be excluded from all official posts. These laws gradually came to be used less harshly, yet even as late as 1762 a Protestant pastor was hanged at Toulouse and three Protestant noblemen who had tried to rescue him were decapitated. It was in the same year and in the same city that the Protestant, Jean Calas, was broken on the wheel for the alleged crime of murdering his son to prevent him from abjuring Protestantism, a case which Voltaire took up in a masterly propaganda campaign which led to Calas's rehabilitation.

Toulouse had a reputation for religious fanaticism which was acknowledged even by an English Catholic like Swinburne when he visited the city in 1776:

> This was the birth-place of the Inquisition; and in our days, the proceedings that attended the condemnation of John Calas prove that the seeds of the fanaticism, which produced that cruel tribunal, are not yet destroyed in this province. The true state of this melancholy event is still hidden behind

clouds of doubt and conjectures, nor have I been able to procure any satisfactory lights on the subject. A sensible uninterested spectator of the whole transaction assured me, that he had strong reasons for suspecting that John Calas had, by some unlucky blow or push, been the innocent cause of his son's death: the expressions uniformly made use of by that unfortunate parent, agree with this surmise.

When Swinburne moved on to Montpellier, he noted that by this date the persecution of the Huguenots was giving way to 'the milder arts of toleration', which leads him to make a plea for Catholic Emancipation in Britain.[59]

In 1763 Smollett noted the strict letter of the law as it concerned Protestant pastors convicted of officiating at secret conventicles: 'Certain it is, the laws of France punish capitally every protestant minister convicted of having performed the functions of his ministry in this kingdom, and one was hanged about two years ago, in the neighbourhood of Montauban.'[60] Yet he also noted that even at this date the severe laws against conventicles were not strictly applied in the neighbourhood of Montpellier and Nîmes:

> There are many protestants in this place, as well as at Nismes, and they are no longer molested on the score of religion. They have their conventicles in the country, where they assemble privately for worship. These are well known, and detachments are sent out every Sunday to intercept them; but the officer has always private directions to take another route. Whether this indulgence comes from the wisdom and lenity of the government, or is purchased with money of the commanding officer, I cannot determine.[61]

That by this date the idea of toleration was gaining ground is shown by a remark of Pennant in describing his visit to the library of the abbey of Ste Geneviève in Paris. There he was shown the famous medal struck to glorify the Massacre of St Bartholomew. He writes: 'I must do justice to the Abbé that was with me, as well as the Monk who shewed me this that they spoke with the utmost horror of the fact as well as the medal.'[62]

Writing also in the 1760s, Thicknesse gives a somewhat mixed view of the Catholic attitude to Protestants. He was living in St Germain en Laye, and he thus describes his dealings with a local prior:

When he found I was not *a sheep* for his *fold*, he did not think it politic to be over civil or familar with *an heretic*. Two or three Protestants who have died in this town since I have been here, he would not permit the carpenters to make coffins for, and they were buried naked in shallow graves in the forest, and their bodies soon after were turned out of the earth by the wild boars! One of those spectacles, I was informed, came under the King's observation at the hunt, who expressed his abhorrence at such *religious* brutality.

He has another story to tell of intolerance, this time once again at Toulouse:

When colonel Forrester[63] died at Toulouse, they required his servants to pay thirty *louis-d'ors* for permission to bury him even in his own garden; and, upon their making remonstrances against such an imposition, the principal magistrate of the town sent them notice, if the money was not forthwith paid, he would cause his dead corpse to be dragged naked about the town!! The king, however, was so much offended with the magistrate's conduct, that he caused him to be forthwith degraded, and, together with his son, banished the city.

What truth these two stories contain is uncertain.

After pointing out that Protestants were much more numerous in the South of France than in the Paris region, Thicknesse too remarks on the difference between the letter of the law on their conventicles and the actual practice of the authorities:

Some thousands . . . assemble and hear divine service every Sunday in those parts of this kingdom, though the priests who are detected, are instantly hanged up! But what is more singular is, that a party of horse are sent out every Sunday, with *public orders* to apprehend all those persons who unlawfully assemble in the fields to serve God their own way; but as they constantly take a direct contrary route from that which they know the Protestants are gone, it is past all doubt they have *private orders* not to *find* them. The ignorant rabble, however, are amused by these pursuits, and they are too ignorant to perceive the deception.[64]

Some years later, in 1775, when he visited the South of France on his way to Spain, Thicknesse wrote at Nîmes:

The greater part of the inhabitants are Protestants, who meet publickly between two rocks, at a little distance from the city, every Sunday, sometimes not less than eighteen thousand, where their pastors, openly and audibly, perform divine service, according to the rites of the reformed church; such is the difference between the mild government of Louis XVI and that which was practised in the reign of his great grand father. But reason and philosophy have made more rapid strides in France, in these last few years, than the arts and sciences.[65]

Slightly earlier the author of *Travels into France and Italy* had heard a Protestant pastor preach at a service held outside Nîmes, though he does not seem to have formed a high opinion of the intellectual level of the congregation: 'His language was good and his subject adapted to the congregation; had the one been fine, and the other elevated, the rocks amidst which he was placed, would have understood as well as the audience.' He found that the Protestants there were conscious of a decided improvement in their position, though the reason they gave for it seems rather too simple:

At Nismes they think their present state very free; for though the same laws which formerly persecuted them remain in force, they are seldom put in execution, except by the bigotry of some inferior magistrate, of which I have known an instance, with regard to two gentlemen; but they had immediate redress upon application to the court; this liberty and tranquillity the Protestants impute to the expulsion of the Jesuits.[66]

Writing in her diary in April 1773, the young Lady Harriet Spencer, who had been in Montpellier for several months with her parents and elder sister, describes an encounter with Protestants outside the town:

In coming back we saw the road full of people, very much dress'd, some on foot, but most on asses or mules, with umbrellas of different colours that made it look very gay & pretty. They told us it was the Protestants coming from their assemblies, which they hold in a garden or field near here. It was what they call their catechumen, to prepare for the first communion, which is always done by questioning them in publick, and their minister takes great pains with them, both with what they ought to do, and the difference between them & the Roman Catholic religion, that they may know how to defend themselves, or if necessary suffer persecution, which they are constantly threatened with, for the laws are very severe against them.

Here she relates an interesting story about the reaction of the Commandant of the province to her mother's request for permission to attend one of these conventicles. This illustrates the difficulties facing the authorities, saddled with severe laws and yet wishing to show some degree of toleration: 'When mama asked Mr. de Perigord leave to go to one of their meetings, he begg'd her not, as he said his orders were so strict to prosecute and even put to death any minister who held a congregation, if he discovered them; that he was obliged to pretend not to suppose such a thing could be, but that if any body as much known as mama went, it would be impossible for him to pretend not to know it.' The child goes on: 'The day of communion is kept with great solemnity, all the relations, many leagues round, are invited, & even on the common church-days they assemble in all weather, and pray & listen to their preachers, in rain & wind, & through every danger.' Her father's comment closes the entry: 'Papa bid us observe how much persecution encreas'd zeal for the religion so oppress'd, which he said was a lesson against oppression, and for toleration, which the catholics give in a despotic monarchy against their will.'[67]

Our travellers are almost always extremely sympathetic towards the French Protestants. An exception is provided by Cornelia Knight in her autobiography. After declaring that at Montpellier relations between Catholics and Protestants were much less hostile than at Nîmes, and that during the Revolution the lives of many Catholic priests were saved there by Protestants, she makes some very critical remarks about a pastor, Rabaut de Saint-Étienne. No doubt her attitude was partly coloured by the part he was to play in the Revolution: 'I am sorry to say that M. de St. Etienne, who was a pastor here, did not do credit to his cloth in this respect, for he was very violent, and worthy to have belonged to Cromwell's Independents.' Even his wife is not spared: 'I remember we were much struck by the showy dress and variegated plume of feathers worn by a young woman at a concert at which we were present, and we were told that she was the wife of a Protestant minister — in fact, of M. de St. Etienne himself.'[68]

By 1785, if the Cradocks are to be believed, the Protestants at Montpellier no longer met completely in the open air, but had now some protection from the weather. Cradock recounts their attendance at one of the Sunday services.

> To the Protestants assembly. A church not being allowed here, the meeting was held about a mile and a half out of the city. The field was spacious, and in the middle of it was a place something like a barn, in which were a reading desk, and a pulpit. A large space, however, adjoining was covered with an awning. It was supposed that sixteen hundred Protestants were present, and this was considered but as a small assemblage. The service was in French. There was afterwards a sermon, that was plain and judicious; two psalms were then sung by all the congregation, which had a fine effect, and a liberal collection was made for the poor.[69]

Shortly afterwards in Bordeaux Mrs Cradock found that there the Protestants had to make do with services held secretly in private houses: 'A onze heures, j'assistai à un service protestant célébré dans la plus grande intimité, car il n'y a pas le moindre lieu de réunion destiné spécialement à ce culte.'[70]

In the same year Bishop Bennet and his party travelled from Béziers to Toulouse on the Canal du Midi. One of their companions on the boat offered to show them round the city:

> He was dressed in white as a Layman, but was in reality the Minister of the Protestant Congregation at Bourdeaux, where he is going to proceed next Sunday. He is well known, but, as it is death to exercise his profession, he does not appear openly as a Clergyman. The Protestants are still numerous in the Southern Provinces and Government connives at, without tolerating them, only now and then hanging an old Priest by way of checking their progress, but of late has omitted even this sanguinary method of pleasing the bigoted Catholics.[71]

Meanwhile other travellers penned accounts of conventicles held outside Nîmes. A certain Cage attended one in the spring of the same year:

> Being Sunday, attended the assembly of the Protestants at the place of public worship in a valley half a league from the

town. The service was decently performed by two persons one of whom also preached & was in the habit of a clergyman, and devoutly & sincerely attended to by near two thousand spectators, a small part of the total number which is reckoned at thirty thousand or half the inhabitants of Nismes. The audience was seated on heaps of stones on the declivity of a hill opposite the preacher.

This writer adds to his account: 'The protestants here are a quiet people & neither give or receive any molestation. They have applied to government for leave to build a church, & their prayer has been seconded by the Archbishop of Narbonne.'[72] Such a petition was, as we shall see, doomed to failure, though it is interesting that the tolerant attitude of Dillon, the Archbishop of Narbonne, should have reached so far as to support it.

In May 1787 Lord Gardenstone came to Nîmes. He speaks of the stir caused by the presence at a conventicle of one of George III's younger brothers, the Duke of Cumberland, who had disgraced himself by marrying without the king's consent:

> One half of the people are Protestants. They have three very respectable ministers, who perform divine worship in a delightful situation, near the romantic rock which fronts the fine fountains and curious old Roman baths. On solemn occasions they assemble to the number of from twenty to thirty thousand people, who are watched by military troops, but unmolested, as they are always decent and inoffensive, never tumultuary. There was such a numerous meeting, very lately, when our Duke of Cumberland was one of the audience. An honest burgess, in relating the circumstances of this assembly to me, said 'O! Sir, we wept for joy to see such a meeting, and at the same time a prince among us!![73]

In that same year, on 19 November, the government edict which made a modest improvement in the lot of the Protestant minority was issued at last. The Catholic Church retained its monopoly of public worship; Protestant pastors were not allowed to describe themselves publicly as such, to wear a distinctive costume, or to register births, deaths and marriages. Considerable restrictions were maintained on the professions which Protestants might enter. All that the edict really gave them was the right to have their births, deaths and marriages officially registered, either by the *curé* or by a local judge. The edict was registered, with modifications, by the Paris *Parlement* on 29 January 1788.

Reactions of our travellers to this modest improvement in the position of the Protestants are difficult to find. As they were still not allowed their own churches, in August 1789, near Montélimar, Young stumbled upon one of their conventicles: 'Yesterday . . . we passed a congregation of protestants, assembled, Druid-like, under five or six spreading oaks, to offer their thanksgiving to the great Parent of their happiness and hope.'[74] So strong was the resistance to the granting of equal rights to Protestants that it needed a revolution to bring it about; on 24 December 1789 the Constituent Assembly passed the necessary decree.

The nobility

A fair number of our travellers were members of the peerage or the gentry. Several of them were presented at Court and many of them mixed in the high society of Paris, or for one reason or another had contacts with its members. Although merely a younger son of a British prime minister who had been dead for twenty years, in 1765 and later years Walpole was invited to dine or sup by the aristocratic hostesses of the capital. When the young Lord Herbert arrived in Paris in 1780, he soon went boar-hunting with the Duc de Chartres, the future Philippe-Égalité, and a few days later he was admitted to all sorts of fun and games at the duke's property at Mousseaux: 'After the Hunt the Duke of Chartres carried me to his petite Maison at Moussow, where we dined a pretty numerous, noisy Company, there being some Females of the Party. After Dinner we amused ourselves in flinging one another into the Water, at last by stripping naked & hunting the Hare through Wood, Water, etc. etc.'[75]

There was, of course, a fundamental difference between the English and French nobility. Whereas in England only peers and peeresses enjoy noble rank, in France before the Revolution the number of persons enjoying noble rank, whether of the *noblesse d'épée* or the more recent *noblesse de robe*, was extremely large, totalling perhaps something of the order of 200,000 or 300,000. As titles of nobility were relatively rare in Britain, some British travellers who regarded themselves as being among the 'top people', felt rather left out in the cold on social occasions, as Smollett explains: 'The French, as well as other foreigners, have no idea of a man of family and fashion, without the title of duke, count, marquis, or lord, and where an English gentleman is introduced by the simple expression of *monsieur tel*, Mr. Suchathing, they think he is some plebeian, unworthy of any particular attention.'[76]

The gap between *noble* and *roturier* in France was one of which our travellers were fully conscious. We have already seen the comments of Andrews and James Edward Smith on the subject.[77] 'Nobility of France', wrote Jervis, 'so distinguished for Servility to their Prince, exact an equal degree of submission from their Inferiors; under an exterior of complaisance and condescension, they conceal great pride and haughtiness.'[78] 'The distinction between the *noblesse* and *roturiers*', declared Young, 'is nowhere stronger, more offensive, or more abominable than in Bretagne.'[79] A revealing story is related by one of our travellers who happened to be in Rouen on the day of the patron saint of the city. To commemorate his killing a dragon, 'the canons of the cathedral have a right to demand the release of one person capitally convicted. A gentleman, who killed his servant in a passion, received the benefit of this anniversary.'[80]

Jervis not only disapproved of the pride and haughtiness of French noblemen; he also formed a poor opinion of their upbringing:

> The Education of the Nobility is extreemly superficial, the Graces of the Body being much more attended to, than those of the Mind. That part of Youth call'd Adolescence, employ'd by us in cultivating the Mind and enculcating Principles by which we are to be guided thro' Life, is by them on the contrary, consum'd in trifling dissipation. At twelve Years old and oft before they commence Petit Maitres, are let loose among the Women whom they court, and attend, on all occasions. From the Beau sex they learn all their futile Vanity which however becoming in them weakens the Mind of Man, and renders him incapable of great Actions. One great disadvantage from this Mode of Education, is their early and excessive Polution. A French Woman of Pleasure always expresses surprize at your Wish to lie with her; and many of them have assured us that Young Frenchmen of Fashion rarely propose it to them, which is sufficiently Visible in their puny Proginy.

He also has a good deal to say about the army, *the* career for members of the *noblesse d'épée* and also for some of the scions of the *nobless de robe*. He does not fail to point out some of the drawbacks of the profession:

> Military passion being so essential to the Government of France, it is very politically deemed dishonourable for a person of any Fashion not to have served, or for a person of middling Rank to retire without the Croix de St Louis, or some public Testimony of faithful Service. This wise principle inspires the Nation with Military Ideas, and is of infinite consequence to it as a Military Government, by making them immediately dependent on their Prince. Notwithstanding the Military Character is thus held up, it seems to have lost much of its lustre, and Credit among the Trading people, which appears to arise from the frequent distress of the inferior Officers who, replete with every expensive Vice and Dissipation, have such inconsiderable appointments, that even with the strictest Economy, they find a difficulty to support their Character without assistance from their Friends. — Add to this the extreeme Indigence of many Chevaliers de St Louis, who, tho' Coverd with accumulated Wounds, in addition [to] their Croix perhaps have not received a farthing of the Pension annex'd to it (trifling as it is) for some Years past & you shall not wonder at its declining in the eyes of the people.

He also noted that for the majority of officers the prospects of promotion were small: 'It seldom happens that a Man without protection gets higher than the rank of Captain — after twenty Years good service receives the Croix and may retire without disgrace.'[81]

In the section on the peasantry we have already seen what our travellers have to say about such matters as the nobility's exemption from the *taille* and about feudal dues, signorial justice and the *droit de chasse*. Although they perhaps over-emphasise the poverty of the peasants, they certainly did not imagine that all noblemen were rich. The anonymous author of *Travels into France and Italy* declares that the nobility of Nivernais were 'much distressed', but, he continues, 'the most shocking sight I ever saw in this subject, was a gentleman travelling in la Beauce, walking with his wife, who was barefooted'. The man, we are told, had 'sword, shoes and stockings', and 'he had, as they called it, deroged, by marrying his servant'.[82] The town of Auch, Young noted, 'is supported chiefly by the rents of the country'. 'But', he continues, 'they have many of the noblesse in the province, too poor to live here; some indeed so poor, that they plough their own fields, and these may possibly be much more estimable members of society, than the fools and knaves that laugh at them.'[83]

Noblemen and their families spent at least part of the year in provincial towns, large and small. We have seen that was the case in Toulouse.[84] Smollett found many in Boulogne and makes them the butt of his satire:

> The noblesse have not the common sense to reside at their houses in the country, where by farming their own grounds, they might live at a small expence, and improve their estates at the same time. They allow their country-houses to go to decay, and their gardens and fields to waste, and reside in dark holes in the Upper Town of Boulogne, without light, air, or convenience. There they starve within doors, that they may have wherewithall to purchase fine cloaths, and appear dressed once a day in the church, or on the rampart. They have no education, no taste for reading, no housewifery, nor indeed any earthly occupation, but that of dressing their hair, and adorning their bodies. They hate walking, and would never go abroad if they were not stimulated by the vanity of being seen.[85]

In Brittany, 'at the little town of Lamballe', wrote Young, 'there are above fifty families of nobles that live in winter, who reside on their estates in the summer. There is probably as much foppery and nonsense in their circles, and for what I know as much happiness, as those of Paris. Both would be better employed in cultivating their lands, and rendering the poor industrious.'[86]

For those who could afford it (or who thought they could), Paris was naturally the ideal place of residence for a nobleman. On her way from Boulogne to Chantilly Mrs Piozzi noted: 'The very few gentlemen's seats that we have passed by, seem out of repair, and deserted. The French do not reside much in private houses, as the English do; but while those of narrower fortunes flock to the country towns within their reach, those of ampler purses repair to Paris, where the rent of their estate supplies them with pleasures at no very enormous expense.'[87] The attitude of the court nobility in these matters is well described by R.W.C.:

Paris abounds in superb palaces for the Nobility, they cover a great deal of ground, are elegantly and gorgeously furnished and being built of fine white stone, form, I think, one of the principal beauties of Paris. The Palais de Bourbon, belonging to the Prince of Condé, hanging upon the Seine, would be thought a princely residence for any crowned head in Europe. The reason is obvious why the town houses of the French Nobility are, in general, upon a larger scale than those of the like description in England. It is the fashion for the nobility of England to spend a certain portion of the year upon their domains in the country, where they have much more elegant houses than any the French nobility possess, and where they enjoy their freedom and rank in a higher degree than at Court. On the contrary, the French noblemen and men of Fortune live (as I am told) the year round at Paris, where they deem themselves à portée to Versailles, having little villas contiguous to the capital, where they sometimes dine or give a petit soupé to a few choice friends, and return the same evening to town. A Frenchman is never truly happy out of the court atmosphere, and they have here a Punishment, which is termed a banishment to your own Estate; and altho in general a French Nobleman is looked up to by the hinds round his Chateau with an air of adoration, yet, if not at Versailles, he is unhappy.[88]

A similar contrast between the habits of the English and French aristocracies is drawn by Gibbon in his account of his visit to Paris in 1763: 'The splendour of the French nobles is confined to their town-residence; that of the English is more usefully distributed in their country-seats; and we should be astonished at our own riches, if the labours of architecture, the spoils of Italy and Greece, which are now scattered from Inverary to Wilton, were accumulated in a few streets between Marybone and Westminster.'[89]

In the course of his travels through the provinces of France, Young several times loads curses on absentee landlords who neglected their estates. Sometimes he does this in rather vague terms, as in his account of his journey southwards from Orleans, where he found that the fields were 'scenes of pitiable mismanagement'. 'Yet', he goes on, 'all this country is highly improveable, if they knew what to do with it; the property, perhaps, of some of those glittering beings, who figured in the procession the other day at Versailles. Heaven grant me patience while I see a country thus neglected — and forgive me the oaths I swear at the absence and ignorance of the possessors.' Much more precise is his comment on part of his journey north from Bordeaux:

> In this thirty-seven miles of country, lying between the great rivers Garonne, Dordogne, and Charente, and consequently in one of the best parts of France for markets, the quantity of waste land is surprising; it is indeed the predominant feature. Much of these wastes belonged to the prince of Soubise, who would not sell any part of them. Thus it is whenever you stumble on a Grand Seigneur, even one that was worth millions, you are sure to find his property desert. The Duke of Bouillon's and this Prince's are two of the greatest properties in France, and all the signs I have yet seen of their greatness are wastes, *landes*, deserts, fern, ling. — Go to their residence, whatever it may be, and you would probably find them in the midst of a forest, very well peopled with deer, wild boars, and wolves. Oh! if I was the legislator of France for a day, I would make such great lords skip again!

The only thing which could drive a great noble to live on his estates, Young noted, was being exiled from the court. In 1770 Louis XV exiled his chief minister, the Duc de Choiseul, to his estate at Chanteloup on the Loire which Young visited on his travels. He was very critical of some features of the estate, particularly of the way in which, during the Duke's lifetime, the forest 'had the mischievous animation of a vast hunt, supported so liberally as to ruin the master of it'. 'Great lords', he adds, 'love too much an environ of forest, boars, and huntsmen, instead of marking their residence by the accompaniment of neat and well cultivated farms, clean cottages, and happy peasants.' Yet he did find some things to praise at Chanteloup:

> As a farmer, there is one feature which shows the Duke de Choiseul had some merit; he built a noble cow-house; a platform leads along the middle, between two rows of mangers, with stalls for seventy-two, and another apartment, not so large, for others, and for calves. He imported 120 very fine Swiss cows, and visited them with his company every day, as they were kept constantly tied up. To this I may add the best built sheep-house I have seen in France, and I thought I saw from the pagoda part of the farm better laid out and ploughed

than common in the country, so that he probably imported some ploughmen.

Young is quick to draw the moral of the story: 'This has merit in it; but it was all the merit of banishment. Chanteloup would neither have been built, nor decorated, nor furnished, if the Duke had not been exiled.'

He refers the reader to his account of the estate of another exiled minister, the Duc d'Aiguillon, Louis XV's last foreign minister, who was dismissed at the beginning of the new reign. The construction of the main part of the chateau and its unfinished state were due, Young points out, first to the Duke's banishment and then to him receiving permission to return to Paris and the court: 'This edifice is a considerable one, built by the present Duke; begun about twenty years ago, when he was exiled here during eight years; and, thanks to that banishment, the building went on nobly; the body of the house done, and the detached wings almost finished; but as soon as the sentence was reversed, the Duke went to Paris, and has not been seen here since, consequently all now stands still.' This produces the usual comment: 'It is thus that banishment alone will force the French nobility to execute what the English do for pleasure — reside upon and adorn their estates.'

Young did, of course, encounter one exception which proved the rule. Although the Duc de Liancourt held a high post at court, he did reside for periods on his estate at Liancourt and had carried out various agricultural improvements there. It is true that it was less than forty miles from Paris and that the Duke had been in England. Young spent over three weeks at Liancourt and found to his surprise that 'the mode of living, and the pursuits, approach much nearer to the habits of a great nobleman's house in England than would commonly be supposed'.[90]

It has long been maintained by British travellers that a Frenchman would be prepared to live in a garret and eat and drink abstemiously in order to appear in expensive clothes. *The Gentleman's Guide* puts this somewhat sarcastically: 'Their vanity makes them more extravagant in their dress than in their eating and drinking: for though a Frenchman eats nothing but soup-meagre every day in the week, you will rarely see him without his laced coat, silk stockings, powdered hair, and laced ruffles, which are often tacked upon either false sleeves, or a shirt as coarse as a hopsack.'[91] Smollett made this claim in dealing with the nobility at Boulogne; he returned to the point, somewhat unexpectedly, in his account of Genoa. He praises the abstinence of the Genoese which had enabled them to build palaces and churches, whereas 'a Frenchman lays out his whole revenue upon tawdry suits of cloaths, or in furnishing a magnificent *repas* of fifty or a hundred dishes, one half of which are not eatable, nor intended to be eaten. His wardrobe goes to the *fripier*, his dishes to the dogs, and himself to the devil, and after his decease no vestige of him remains.'[92]

This is obviously Smollett at his most satirical. There is more of interest in Swinburne's expression of alarm at the excessive cost of equipping a bride from the French aristocracy. In January 1788 he wrote:

> The extravagance of the French is scarcely credible, and nothing in England ever equalled it, at least that I ever heard of. The trousseau of Mademoiselle de Matignon, who is going to marry the Baron de Montmorency, is to cost a hundred thousand crowns (about 25,000 l. sterling). There are to be a hundred dozen of shifts, and so on in proportion. The expense here of rigging out a bride is equal to a handsome portion in England; five thousand pounds worth of lace, linen, and gowns, is a common thing among them.[93]

And this was just eighteen months before the fall of the Bastille and the end of the 'douceur de vivre' enjoyed by the upper classes in the closing decades of the Ancien Régime.

On the whole what our travellers have to say about the second order in the state is not very satisfying. Those who were of high enough rank to move in aristocratic circles in Paris tend to take their way of life for granted and simply to enjoy the hospitality on offer. Those who moved in less exalted circles occasionally note instances of the friction which existed between noblemen and *roturiers*, but naturally they have no inkling of the violent clash between them which was imminent. They were well aware of the extraordinary range of wealth and poverty inside the order, from the great noblemen leading a luxurious existence in the capital to the poverty-stricken *hobereau* or the pensioned-off army officer; but they cannot be said to offer more than a few insights into the very varied lives led by different sections of the nobility.

Notes

1. *Tour on the Continent*, pp. 3, 22.
2. *Diary of a Scotch Gardener*, p. 189.
3. *A Tour*, p. 183.
4. Ibid., pp. 201–2.
5. West Yorkshire Archive Service, Sp St 6/1/115. Extracts from this collection are reproduced by permission of the Archive Service, Bradford.
6. *Journal*, p. 109.
7. *Memoirs*, vol. II, p. 317.
8. *Travels through France and Italy*, pp. 27–8.
9. *French Journal*, p. 84; *Observations and Reflections*, pp. 27–8.
10. *Memoirs*, vol. II, p. 299.
11. *Letters*, vol. I, p. 497.
12. *Travels through France and Italy*, p. 313.
13. *Correspondence*, vol. 10, p. 176; vol. 14, p. 144; vol. 40, p. 385.
14. *Useful Hints*, pp. 93–4, 178. (On the last point see also p. 137.)
15. *Letters to a Young Gentleman*, p. 84.
16. *Letters from France*, vol. II, pp. 233–4.
17. *A Tour*, p. 318.
18. *An Englishman's Impressions*, p. 92.
19. *Letters from France*, p. 8.
20. *Journey from Bayonne to Marseilles*, pp. 363–4.
21. *Journal*, pp. 110, 139.
22. *Travels through France and Italy*, p. 173.
23. *Tour of the Continent*, p. 10.
24. Even this was roughly double the amount to which the stipend of the worst-off *curés* (those à portion congrue) had been raised in the previous year, 1786.
25. *Travelling Memorandums*, vol. II, p. 64.
26. See above, pp. 58–9.
27. *A Year's Journey*, vol. I, pp. 71–2.
28. *Travels in France*, vol. I, p. 608.
29. *Journals of Travels*, pp. 154–5.
30. *Tour on the Continent*, p. 46.
31. *A Tour*, p. 85.
32. *Journals of Travels*, p. 283.
33. *Journey from Bayonne to Marseilles*, pp. 372–3.
34. *Autobiography*, vol. I, pp. 40–1, 37–9.
35. See below, pp. 176–7.
36. *Autobiography*, pp. 29–31.
37. *Continental Excursions*, vol. I, p. 26.
38. *Journal*, pp. 95–6.
39. *Correspondence*, vol. 35, p. 127.
40. *Continental Excursions*, vol. I, p. 75.
41. *Letters from France*, vol. II, pp. 140–1.
42. *Letters*, p. 160.
43. Nottingham University Library, Me 244/2a, p. 8.
44. *Tour of the Continent*, pp. 12, 2.
45. *Journal*, p. 66.

46. *Travels in France*, vol. I, p. 77.
47. *Diary of a Scotch Gardener*, pp. 177-8.
48. *An Englishman's Impressions*, pp. 91-2.
49. *Memoirs*, vol. II, pp. 326-7.
50. *Letters from France*, pp. 5-6.
51. *Memoirs*, vol. I, pp. 60, 171-3.
52. *New Elegant Extracts*, pp. 249-50. There are several other accounts of the Grande Chartreuse, for instance, in Pennant, *Tour of the Continent*, pp. 52-6, and in William Beckford, *Travel-Diaries*, ed. G. Chapman, London, 1928, 2 vols, vol. I, pp. 277-310.
53. Somerset RO, DD/SH/67/19C/2480, pp. 20-1.
54. *Travels into France and Italy*, vol. I, p. 150.
55. *Continental Excursions*, vol. I, p. 52.
56. *Journals of Travels*, pp. 74-5.
57. *Travels in France*, vol. I, p. 598.
58. *Travels through France and Italy*, pp. 311, 45 (cf. p. 29).
59. *Journey from Bayonne to Marseilles*, pp. 364-5, 389.
60. In Toulouse. He was arrested near Montauban.
61. *Travels through France and Italy*, p. 105.
62. *Tour on the Continent*, p. 18.
63. Among the deaths announced in the *Gentleman's Magazine* (1765, p. 46) is that of 'Col. Forrester, late Gov. of Belleisle in France'. See also *The Gentleman's Guide*, p. 15.
64. *Useful Hints*, pp. 136-7.
65. *A Year's Journey*, vol. I, pp. 86-7.
66. *Travels into France and Italy*, vol. II, pp. 21, 23.
67. *Lady Bessborough and her Family Circle*, pp. 26-7.
68. *Autobiography*, p. 44.
69. *Memoirs*, vol. II, p. 192. Cf. Mrs Cradock, *Journal*, pp. 154-5.
70. *Journal*, p. 206.
71. Bodleian, MS. Eng. Misc. f. 54, f. 161.
72. Ibid., f. 55, pp. 86-7.
73. *Travelling Memorandums*, vol. I, pp. 210-11.
74. *Travels in France*, vol. I, pp. 185-6.
75. *Pembroke Papers*, pp. 473, 479.
76. *Travels through France and Italy*, p. 334.
77. See above, pp. 75, 137.
78. BL, Add. MS. 31192, f. 36.
79. *Travels in France*, vol. I, p. 98.
80. *Travels into France and Italy*, vol. I, p. 19.
81. BL. Add. MS. 31192, ff. 36-38.
82. *Travels into France and Italy*, vol. I, p. 124.
83. *Travels in France*, vol. I, p. 58.
84. See above, p. 89.
85. *Travels through France and Italy*, p. 26.
86. *Travels in France*, vol. I, p. 98.
87. *Observations and Reflections*, p. 7.
88. *Letters from France*, p. 2.
89. *Memoirs*, p. 125.
90. *Travels in France*, vol. I, pp. 12, 62, 66-7, 59, 71.

91. *The Gentleman's Guide*, p. 109.
92. *Travels into France and Italy*, p. 213.
93. *The Courts of Europe*, vol. II, p. 41.

4
Justice

Our travellers do not appear to have become personally involved with either the civil or criminal courts while on French soil. Curiously enough, several of them got quite worked up about a problem which really did not exist. Shortly after his arrival in France Smollett wrote:

> If a foreigner dies in France, the king seizes all his effects, even though his heir should be upon the spot; and this tyranny is called the *droit d'aubaine*, founded at first upon the supposition, that all the estate of foreigners residing in France was acquired in that kingdom, and that, therefore, it would be unjust to convey it to another country. If an English protestant goes to France for the benefit of his health, attended by his wife or his son, or both, and dies with effects in the house to the amount of a thousand guineas, the king seizes the whole, the family is left destitute, and the body of the deceased is denied christian burial.[1]

Poor Cole flew into a passion on learning in Paris that the *droit d'aubaine* — 'that inhospitable, barbarous, & Gothic Law' — had been applied to the estate of the Dowager Countess of Sandwich who had spent a great part of her life in France and died there in 1757:

> By this *Droit d'Aubaine*, the Personal Effects of most Strangers, (for some Nations are exempt) who happen to die in the King of France his Dominions, fall of Right to that Sovereign. So that it behoves every Foreigner, Englishmen in particular, to

be very cautious how their Effects are deposited, in Case of Accident which may threaten their Life: & great Pity it is, considering the Inhospitality of such a singular & barbarous Law, that so many of this Nation, who generously spend their Money among them, to the great Enrichment of their beggarly Country, should be tempted to hazard the Loss of what may be very considerable to their Families in England, by crouding in such Numbers to see a City much inferior to what they left behind them, & a Country & People highly ridiculous . . . This Law seemed to me to be so unjust & inhuman, that it in a Manner determined me to get out of their Country as fast as I could.[2]

In 1768 *A Sentimental Journey through France and Italy* opened with a passage in Sterne's usual bantering style on the dire effects of this French law; after arriving in Calais,

by three I had got sat down to my dinner upon a fricassed chicken, so incontestibly in France, that had I died that night of an indigestion, the whole world could not have suspended the effects of the *Droits d'aubaine*; my shirts, and black pair of silk breeches, portmanteau and all must have gone to the King of France, even the little picture which I have so long worn, and so often have told thee, Eliza, I would carry with me into my grave, would have been torn from my neck. Ungenerous! to seize upon the wreck of an unwary passenger, whom your subjects had beckon'd to their coast. By heavens! SIRE, it is not well done . . .

In the very same year, however, Thicknesse politely contradicted what Smollett had to say on the subject, though he admits that it was widely believed by Frenchmen as well as English people resident there that the *droit d'aubaine* was rigorously enforced:

Mr. Smollett somewhere says, if a stranger dies in France, all his effects are seized for the King's use. This assertion alarmed me exceedingly, for though I have not much to be seized, I have more than I can in justice to my family risque upon my own life. I therefore made it my business to enquire strictly into this matter, and have reason to believe it is never done but when a stranger dies possessed of houses or land, and that their personal effects are not meddled with. Indeed

> I bought a second-hand coach, that was the property of an English gentleman who died in France, at the Hotel of the Duke of Richmond, where it was sent till properly claimed, and it was sold for the benefit of his English heirs, not the King of France. Besides I am well assured that one of our ambassadors procured an exemption from this law in favor of the English subjects who die here.[3]

What Thicknesse wrote was, broadly speaking, correct, as we see, for instance, from the official correspondence of the secretary of the British embassy a few years later. British subjects were exempted from the *droit d'aubaine* under the Treaty of Utrecht, confirmed by a royal declaration of 1739. There were, it is true, occasional difficulties when British citizens died in the provinces.[4]

State prisons and the use and abuse of *lettres de cachet* naturally struck British travellers in France. Writing after the Revolution had begun, Young discusses *lettres de cachet* fairly temperately on the whole. While he accepts as true the legend that blank *lettres de cachet* could be bought, he does point out that the abuses 'were reduced almost to nothing, from the accession of the present King'. The great mass of the people, he argues, suffered far more from other forms of oppression. None the less the very sight of state prisons clearly upset him, as it did most British travellers. The Bastille does not occupy much space in his travel diary — 'another pleasant object to make agreeable emotions vibrate in a man's bosom', he writes sarcastically — but his feelings come out much more strongly at the sight of the prison at Lourdes:

> Take the road to Lourde, where is a castle on a rock, garrisoned for the mere purpose of keeping state prisoners, sent hither by *lettres de cachet*. Seven or eight are *known* to be here at present; thirty have been here at a time; and many for life — torn by the relentless hand of jealous tyranny from the bosom of domestic comfort, from wives, children, friends, and hurried for crimes unknown to themselves, — more probably for virtues, — to languish in this detested abode of misery, — and die of despair. Oh, liberty! liberty! — and yet this is the mildest government of any considerable country in Europe, our own excepted.[5]

As the Bastille was a very prominent building in the east end of

Paris, it drew the attention of many travellers besides Young. Pennant describes it as 'a large square ancient castle, very lofty with round towers on the sides and at the ends; a wide ditch round it. The drawbridge is drawn up, the windows are strongly grated and the watch houses on the battlements render it horrible to look at.'[6] Apparently tourists were sometimes allowed inside the walls, as we see from Cole's description of it a few months later:

> Close to [the Porte St Antoine] almost stands the great, heavy & clumsy Castle of the Bastille, which consists of a sort of Square Building, with 8 roundish high Towers about it, & none or few Windows from it: so that it must be a very gloomy Habitation for the unhappy People who live in it: except the Court within-side is better lighted. It was built as a Fortress & Defence of the City in the 14 Century, & now serves as a Prison for State Criminals. Monsr the Comte de Lally was confined therein when I was admitted into the outward Courts of it.[7]

Wharton uses the same epithet as Pennant to describe this prison: 'I have seen the Bastille which looks horrible indeed.'[8] In August 1788 Villiers penned an extraordinary passage on the Bastille as a symbol of arbitrary power:

> As I looked upon the gloomy walls, my soul shuddered within me. I beheld that terrific engine of arbitrary power, with horror and detestation. I feared to tread upon the ground that encircled it: — all was horrible and dreary. Accursed mansion! I exclaimed; thou hast been the dungeon and the tomb of many, whose breasts have burned with the sacred love of liberty, and whose hearts have been warmed with the holy flame of virtue! — Would that I were an enchanter! — that thy ghastly walls might tumble to the ground![9]

They were, of course, to begin to do so less than a year later.

Much more interesting is a conversation with Malesherbes which Walpole recorded in a letter written shortly after his return to England in October 1775. Earlier in the month at a dinner party in Paris he had met Malesherbes who had recently succeeded the Duc de La Villière (earlier known as the Comte de Saint-Florentin) as Secrétaire d'État de la Maison du Roi and as such responsible for the state prisons:

> Monsieur de Malesherbes, in the most simple and unaffected manner, gave me an account of his visitation of the Bastille, where he released the prisoners, half of whom were mad with their misfortunes, and of many of whom he could not find even the cause of their commitment. One man refused his liberty; he said he had been prisoner fifteen years, and had nothing in the world left; that the King lodged and fed him, and he would not quit the Bastille unless they would give him half his pension. M. de Malesherbes reported it to the King, who replied, *C'est juste*, and the man has fifteen hundred livres a year and his freedom. This excellent magistrate, who made my tears run down my cheeks, added that what the prisoners complained of most, was the want of pen and ink. He ordered it. The demons remonstrated and said the prisoners would only make use of the pen to write memorials against the ministers; he replied, *Tant mieux*. He is going to erect a court of six masters of request to examine the petitions of those who demand *lettres de cachet* for their relations. Under the late Duc de la Vrilliere, his mistress, Madame Sabatin, had a bureau of printed *lettres de cachet* with blanks, which she sold for twenty-five louis apiece.[10]

Walpole's last sentence cannot surely be part of what Malesherbes told him about the Bastille.

Another state prison, that of Pierre-Encize near Lyons, also attracted some attention. In 1772 the Duchess of Northumberland, on one of her visits to France, drove out of the city in her coach to a point from which she had a view of the prison.[11] Her account of what went on inside the fortress is obviously secondhand, but Ayscough claims to have been inside its walls and therefore to be able to provide a most vivid description of the various categories of prisoners detained there. He begins with a sarcastic account of the prison, which is somewhat modified by his description of what he saw when he visited it:

> There is here a very famous state prison called Pierre-Encise . . . It is built on a very high rock, and you ascend to the outer gate by two hundred and twenty two steps. It is here the noblesse who offend the king or his mistress, or the minister or his mistress, or her dependants, are confined during pleasure, without the least trial, or perhaps even reason assigned for their punishment; nay, young men are often sent

hither from Paris on the most trivial complaints from their relatives.

I own I had a great inclination to view not only the *chateau*, but its inhabitants, and as I was acquainted with the governor, I asked his permission, who gave it me most freely, and at the same time requested my company to dinner.

When he was admitted to the fortress, he soon discovered that some prisoners, while confined there for an indefinite period, could look forward to being released one day:

To my utter amazement I found no immediate marks of sorrow, no weeping or wailing, but an excellent dinner prepared in an excellent *salle à manger*, at which the governor and about ten *gentlemen prisoners* were present, all of whom were in as high spirits as if they had been at a *bal masqué* at Paris. The mere confinement appeared indeed the greatest evil, for they had all tolerably convenient apartments; they were allowed the freedom of a little garden; the air they breathed was pure and healthful, and the prospect from so great an eminence as delightful as it was extensive. But these were most of them shut up only for a certain period, and were to be released when it was imagined they had had sufficient time for reflection and repentance. Two of them were sent there (as they told me) on account of their having had duels with their superior officers; and one, who was a youth of about twenty, and a person of considerable rank, was secured because he paid his addresses in an *honorable manner* to a Parisian barber's fair daughter.

Very different was the lot of some other prisoners:

But if these poor birds were lively and warbled in their cages, there were others whose conditions were truly deserving of pity: they were, literally speaking the *state* criminals, and were in rooms in a tower with walls at least fifteen feet thick, through which the light entered only by an aperture of six inches wide. These wretches were never permitted to come out of their cells, and no one was allowed access to them except the man who twice a day brought them their meals, and they were prohibited the use of fire and candles, even in the midst of winter.

They could hold converse with no mortal being, had no employment or amusement, and there was one (as I was informed) who having been treated with all this rigour for the space of twenty years, had fallen by degrees into *melancholy madness*. But of that I saw a still more shocking instance. There was an old man who I thought appeared remarkably pensive, and on my addressing myself to him, he answered me very incoherently. This child of misery was in his *seventieth* year, and his crime was no other than that of having had an intrigue with the mistress of a former minister; for this he had been confined forty years; despair had at length turned his brain: there he remained neglected and forgotten, but an eternal reproach to the author of this evil, and an object that excited pity in the heart of every beholder. This man you say was cruelly and unjustly punished, almost without the shadow of a crime.

This prisoner's lot is contrasted with that of a great nobleman who was definitely confined for life. Though guilty of a crime 'at which human nature recoils', he 'escaped the rigour of the law, merely because he was a man of quality'. With the aid of his servant, he had killed another man in a duel. The servant died while being tortured on the rack:

The traitorous master, doubtless the most guilty of the two, was only confined for life in this prison, where he had every accommodation wealth could bestow in such a situation; and he had there a weekly concert by the best performers, saw a great deal of company, had *amours* with opera-dancers sent from Paris, and, instead of affecting any contrition, was all gaiety, and immersed as much as he was in every kind of luxury and dissipation.[12]

The administration of justice receives relatively little attention from our travellers. In his chapter on the Revolution, Young, basing himself on the *Cahiers* of 1789, delivers a violent attack on the manorial courts:

Nothing can exceed the complaints made in the *cahiers* under this head. They speak of the dispensation of justice in the manorial courts, as comprising every species of despotism;

the districts undetermined — appeals endless — irreconcilable to liberty and prosperity — and irrevocably proscribed in the opinion of the public — augmenting litigations — favouring every species of chicane — ruining the parties — not only by enormous expences on the most petty objects, but by a dreadful loss of time. The judges commonly ignorant pretenders, who hold their courts in *cabarets*, and are absolutely dependent on the seigneurs.

The manner in which civil cases were tried by the *Parlements*, the highest courts in the land, is denounced as 'partial, venal, infamous'. He is referring here in particular to the established custom of soliciting one's judges:

The conduct of the parliaments was profligate and atrocious. Upon almost every cause that came before them, interest was openly made with the judges; and woe betided the man who, in a cause to support, had no means of conciliating favour, either by the beauty of a handsome wife, or by other methods. It has been said, by many writers, that property was as secure under the old government of France as it is in England; and the assertion might possibly be true, as far as any violence from the King, his ministers, or the great was concerned; but for all that mass of property, which comes in every country to be litigated in courts of justice, there was not even the shadow of security, unless the parties were totally and equally unknown, and totally and equally honest; in every other case, he who had the best interest with the judges, was sure to be the winner.[13]

St John is rather more precise in his criticism since he claims to have been present at the trial of civil cases by the Paris *Parlement*:

I have repeatedly seen in the Parliament house, or rather court of judicature at Paris, several of the judges huddled up in their cloaks, and absolutely asleep and snoring on the bench, while the lawyers would make the hall re-echo to their vociferous harangues in their clients' causes: and the one half of the judges would appear to know nothing of the affair, until roused by their companions to give their votes to the verdict!

St John admits that he had never seen this happen in a criminal trial, but he makes a fierce attack on the criminal procedure followed by French courts. The Inquisition, he declares, has been abolished in France.

> Yet if we consider their *procès criminel*, it must appear altogether a real inquisition. From the time the prisoner is apprehended, until he is examined by the judge, he is confined *in secret*, is not permitted to write to his friends, nor to a lawyer, nor receive any letter, nor have any communication with any one whatever. Thus he is deprived of the means of making his defence, of procuring his witnesses, of consulting a lawyer; and his antagonists in the mean time have every opportunity to attack and circumvent him without being opposed face to face to him and his witnesses. If one considers that the judges are not men chosen for their integrity and virtue, but mercenaries who buy and sell their employments, their criminal jurisdiction must appear horrible to a man born in liberty and independence.

After his swipe at sleeping judges in the Paris *Parlement* during the hearing of civil cases, he continues:

> I cannot say that I ever saw this in a criminal trial; for it is not as in England, where the accusers and the accused appear face to face in open court, in the face of day, of all the world; but the whole affair is carried on in the darkest secrecy, and the public know nothing of the proceedings, but all is covered with a veil of mystery and darkness. One cannot expect so much impartiality in such judges, as in the breasts of a jury composed of his equals, and who are acquainted with the life and morals of the accusers and accused.

The use of torture to extract a confession from persons against whom there was insufficient evidence to secure a conviction — the so-called *question préparatoire* — had been abolished in 1780, but another form of torture continued to be practised, as St John points out in another passage:

> Though they do not at present put a man to the torture on suspicion alone, yet they frequently put their criminals to the rack after condemnation, to force them to allow the justice of their sentence and inform against others; and the unhappy

Justice

wretches seldom hesitate to own and declare every thing proposed to them, hoping the sooner to be relieved by a kind death from their sufferings. I am told, that it is not an uncommon thing to see criminals carried to execution here, incapable of either walking or sitting up, having all their limbs dislocated by the torture.[14]

Only a few months after the time St John appears to have been writing these travel notes, a royal edict of 1 May 1788 abolished this form of torture.

Smollett relates a story of a gross injustice which, as historians of Boulogne confirm, had taken place there some years before:

There is a substantial burgher in the High Town, who was some years ago convicted of a most barbarous murder. He received sentence to be broken alive upon the wheel, but was pardoned by the interposition of the governor of the county, and carries on his business as usual in the face of the whole community. A furious *abbé*, being refused orders by the bishop, on account of his irregular life, took an opportunity to stab the prelate with a knife, one Sunday, as he walked out of the cathedral. The good bishop desired he might be permitted to escape, but it was thought proper to punish, with the utmost severity, such an atrocious attempt. He was accordingly apprehended, and, though the wound was not mortal, condemned to be broke. When this dreadful sentence was executed, he cried out, that it was hard he should undergo such torments, for having wounded a worthless priest, by whom he had been injured, while such-a-one (naming the burgher mentioned above) lived in ease and security, after having brutally murdered a poor man, and a helpless woman big with child, who had not given him the least provocation.[15]

Of the two criminal cases which aroused a great deal of controversy in the 1760s — those of Jean Calas and the Chevalier de La Barre — the first attracted a fair amount of interest from our travellers, who were generally favourable to the accused,[16] while the second is discussed only by Thicknesse. He is surprisingly hostile to this youth, who was executed in 1766 for allegedly mutilating a crucifix. To this writer the matter was very simple: 'However trivial the crime of the young man executed at Abbeville may appear in the eyes of us protestants, he was certainly guilty of a high offence against the religion and laws of his country, and therefore merited punishment.' He defends Louis XV's refusal to grant a pardon, expressing indignation at 'the many cook'd up stories which are continually in the English news-papers reflecting so often on the severity and injustice of so humane a prince as the King of France'. He concludes his defence of Louis XV with the rather odd sentence: 'If judges are corrupt, that is a king's misfortune, not his fault; and judges may be corrupt in all kingdoms.'

On his return journey to Boulogne, he recorded a conversation about the affair with the landlady of an inn at Abbeville:

> While I breakfasted, I made some enquiry about the young man executed here not long since, whose execution I mentioned in a former letter to you. She told me that the minute he came upon the scaffold, his head was cut off, and afterwards his body burnt; she also assured me, that he was a very bad man; and she looked so good herself, that I was inclined to believe every word she said, and I am persuaded she declared the sentiments of every individual in the whole town.

That would seem a somewhat rash conclusion. To this he adds: 'As I passed over the market where he was executed, I saw the remaining ashes of a large fire, and near it, the pavement much stained with blood; which I concluded (for I asked no question about it) was the blood and ashes of this unhappy youth.'[17]

Inevitably the fear of being robbed either in Paris or on their journeys across France looms larger in our travellers' accounts than concern about the workings of the French system of justice. 'Be careful on the road', Walpole warned Cole, when his friend was about to set out to join him in Paris. 'My portmanteau with part of my linen was stolen from before my chaise at noon while I went to see Chantilly. If you stir out of your room, lock the door of it in the inn, or leave your man in it.' A fortnight later he had to report to another correspondent not only this theft, but another in his Paris hotel: 'At Chantilly I lost my portmanteau with half my linen, and the night before last I was robbed of a new frock, waistcoat and breeches, laced with gold, a white and silver waistcoat, black velvet breeches, a knife and a book.'[18]

Inevitably Walpole was less pleased with the policing of the capital than was Thicknesse, who speaks highly of it despite what he calls 'the infinite number of rogues, whores, and murderers, which Paris abounds with'. He maintains that it is 'the safest of all great cities to pass through, even at midnight. The guards are so alert, and so numerous, that it is next to an impossibility for a street-robber to escape with his booty; and if he does, and you can describe his dress or person, the *police* will find him the next day.'

Thicknesse was even more impressed by what he calls 'the interior police of Paris', the surveillance of the population by means of a multitude of spies (*mouchards*). He declares that, if he leaves St Germain and spends a night in Paris, 'though no questions are asked me at my entrance, the lieutenant of the *police* has my name and my abode the next morning in his book, and most likely knows the business on which I went, and at whose hotel I had visited'. Later he points out that this is perhaps not as surprising as it sounds, since this surveillance is little concerned with what he calls 'the *Burgoise* and fixed inhabitants of the city', but is concentrated on 'the intrigues of the bettermost people of their own country, and manoeuvres of all strangers residing within the city and kingdom'. Hence the proliferation of police spies, placed even in the British embassy:

> For this purpose they continually keep spies, from five louis-d'ors a week, who ride in their coaches, down to the common *laquais*, at thirty sols each, and from which no family is exempt. Lord Rochford[19] knows that two or three of his present servants are spies, and paid by the police. All the *laquais de place*, who trade in waiting upon strangers, understand a little English, Dutch, German, &c. but pretend not to know one word. These fellows hear your conversation, read your letters, examine your books, and give in once a week (or oftener if matters arise) every particular about you to the *police*! . . . Most of the coffee-houses have a waiter or two who understand English; I am convinced the head waiter does of the Coffé de Conti; and I have remarked, that when the English gentlemen assemble together up stairs at that coffee-house, there is always an odd Frenchman, affecting to be asleep, and totally ignorant of what is said, who is a spy.[20]

Naturally the *mouchards* were highly unpopular with the inhabitants of Paris, and as the Revolution approached, they were sometimes physically assaulted.[21]

On journeys from town to town highwaymen were particularly feared, especially as travellers continued to believe that, whereas English highwaymen were normally content with taking their victims' money and other valuables, in France, as Peckham put it, 'if you are robbed on the highway, you lose both your money and your life'. However, he does add that thanks to a special police force with the more familiar name of *gendarmerie*, which it was given during the Revolution, 'this seldom happens, as there is in every large town a maréchaussée established, which is a horse patrol of six or eight persons, whose sole employ is to patrol the roads and protect the traveller'.[22] Smollett took a very optimistic view of the safety of travel in France: 'The highways seem to be perfectly safe. We did not find that any robberies were ever committed, although we did not see one of the maréchaussée from Paris to Lyons.' This last remark was hardly surprising as one of the demands of the *cahiers* of 1789 was that this thinly-spread police force should be greatly increased. Smollett lamented the absence of any such protection for travellers in England: 'You know the *maréchaussée* are a body of troopers well mounted, maintained in France as safe-guards to the public roads. It is a reproach upon England that some such patrol is not appointed for the protection of travellers.'[23] Cayley too would have liked to see the equivalent of the *maréchaussée* on the roads of England:

> The cruel executions in France cause the robbers and banditti generally to kill the travellers they meet, before they rob them — tho' now, through the good police of France, in keeping a constant horse patrolle on the roads, there are very few robberies committed. Some of these guards I saw on the road. I wish this were imitated in England where robberies are very frequent, tho' seldom murders, unless resistance is made.[24]

Thicknesse offers a rather grim picture of the number of murders committed on French roads, though he maintains that both the murderers and their victims mostly went on foot:

> Travelling in France is, in general, secure. I say, in general; for there are, nevertheless, murthers committed very frequently upon the high roads in France; and were these murthers to be made known by newspapers, as ours are in England, perhaps it would greatly intimidate travellers of their own, as well as other nations. But as the murthered,

and the murtherers, are generally foot-travellers, though the
dead body is found, the murtherer escapes; for as nobody
knows either party, nobody troubles himself about it.

Thicknesse points out how leaving prosecution of criminals to the
manorial courts in the country often led to such murderers remaining unpunished:

> The *Seigneur* on whose land a murthered body is found, is
> obliged to pay the expence of bringing the criminal to justice.
> Some of these lordships are very small; and the prosecuting of
> a murtherer to punishment, would cost the lord of the manor
> more than his whole year's income; it becomes his interest,
> therefore, to hide the dead body, rather than pursue the living
> villain; and, as, whoever has property, be it ever so small, has
> peasants about him who will be glad to obtain his favour, he is
> sure that when any of these peasants see a murthered body,
> they will give him the earliest notice, and the same night the
> body is for ever hid, and no enquiry made after the offender.

He shares the common view that in France highwaymen always
murder or attempt to murder their victims: 'As they always
murther those whom they attack, if they can, those that are
attacked should never submit, but defend themselves to the utmost
of their power.' Although convinced that 'road murthers are ten
times more common in France than in England', as British tourists
seldom travelled on foot, this cannot have sounded particularly
alarming to them. In any case he adds that the *maréchaussée* is
always there to protect them: 'People of condition may, neverthe-
less, travel through France with great safety, and always obtain a
guard of the *Maréchaussée* through woods, forests, or where they
apprehend there is any danger.'[25] Certainly although our travellers sometimes express apprehension at journeys on the roads of
France, actual instances of attacks by highwaymen are not to be
found in the writings studied here.

In general our travellers found the punishments inflicted by the
French penal code on the harsh side. An exception is provided by
something the Duchess of Northumberland observed in Bordeaux:
'On my way home I saw a Woman punish'd for stealing. She was
tyed to a stake in such a manner that she could not hold down her

Head over which was placed a paper inscribed in large Letters: "Une Voleuse". Surely if this Shame did affect her it is a more politic as well as a more merciful punishment than either Death or Transportation.'[26]

As in the previous century, the galleys which could be seen in such ports as Marseilles, Toulon and Rochefort were a great draw for our travellers. By this date these ships had ceased to form part of the French navy and were simply penal establishments. The convicts were a very mixed bag; they included Huguenots who had been caught attending secret conventicles, men guilty only of offences against the game laws or of attempting to smuggle salt or other goods, deserters from the armed forces, and those who had committed crimes not considered quite serious enough to merit the death penalty.

Wharton made his first contact with galley slaves at Lyons where he saw a group being conducted to Marseilles to serve their sentence, 'chained 2 & 2 by the Neck & a great Chain passed through the middle of the whole train between every Pair'. He also noted that people in Lyons 'were very compassionate as they generally are to prisoners', and gave them soup, bread and money.[27]

As Marseilles was more frequented by our travellers than Toulon or Rochefort, there are many accounts of the galleys and the convicts to choose from. We have already seen Armstrong's sarcastic comments on the breaches of the game laws which brought this harsh punishment on many offenders.[28] One of the longest accounts of the galley slaves is provided by Boswell, who was in Marseilles at the end of 1765:

> It was curious to see a row of little Booths, with signs, all occupied by Slaves, many of whom look'd as plump and contented as any decent tradesman whatever. I went into one of The Galleys where the Slaves were mostly working in different ways in order to gain some little thing. I was told that many of them make rich, as they are allowed a great deal of time for themselves when lying in the harbours. I talked with one who had been in the galleys twenty years. I insisted with him that after so long a time custom must have made even the Galleys easy. They came about me, several of 'em, and disputed my proposition. I maintained that custom made all things easy, and that people who had been long in prison did not chuse to come out. 'Ah', said the Slaves, 'Il est autrement

ici. C'est deux prisons. Si nous pourrions échapper, nous le ferons certainement. Un oiseau renfermé dans une cage désire sa liberté, et de plus forte raison un homme doit le désirer. Au commencement nous pleurons, nous gémissons, mais toutes nos pleurs et nos gémissements ne font rien.' I was touched with the misery of these wretches, but appeared firm, which made them not shew much grief. Mallet,[29] who used to joke me on being an eternal Disputer, might now say, 'Le Baron dispute même avec les esclaves des galères.' One of them gave me a very full account of their manner of life. When he would tell me of their being out at sea, He said, 'Quand nous sommes en campagne.' This, it seems is a Galley phrase. I could not but smile at it. They said, 'Nous aimerons mieux les Campagnes des Bois.' I was much satisfied with having seen a Galley. I gave the slaves something to drink.[30]

Better informed than Boswell, Wraxall correctly noted that 'the gallies themselves, useless and neglected, rot peaceably in their respective stations; and it is said that no others will ever be constructed to supply their place, as they have long ceased to be of any utility to the state, and are scarcely even navigable in severe weather'. He felt, however, that Marseilles would be even more attractive, 'if the chains of galley slaves heard among the hum of business, did not tincture it with the hateful idea of slavery'.[31] Lady Mary Coke, on the other hand, took a rather complacent view of the galleys and concluded that something of the kind ought to be tried in England as an alternative to the death penalty:

> I was quite glad to find the Galley Slaves were not such miserable beings as I had represented them to myself; they are not chain'd to the Galleys, and are allowed to Work for themselves, & as most of them have some trade, they gain a very comfortable subsistence: there are numbers of little shops on the side of the Port where they sit at work with a chain to their leg: others who walk about are chain'd together: their allowance from the Government is only a loaf of coarse bread, dry beans, & water, & they are all Obliged to lie aboard the Galleys, of which there are seven close to the side of the Port, with one Guard Ship where there are always such a number of Soldiers, which are relieved from time to time; their business is to keep a watch over the Slaves to prevent

their making their escape: they are not all condemn'd for life, but for such a term of years, which is shorter or longer according to the Nature of their offence; a very trifling one sends them to the Galleys for a certain number of Years: the smuggling anything tho' not worth a shilling is a sufficient crime: there are at present many thousands, & Mr Birkbeck told me they were brought some times hundreds together: something of this kind less rigid wou'd be a good thing in Our Country for the trifling crimes instead of death.[32]

One cannot help feeling that Thicknesse exaggerates somewhat when he writes of the galley slaves in their little shops, that they 'appear happy and decently dressed; some of them are rich, and make annual remittances to their friends'.[33]

The author of *The Gentleman's Guide*, who had earlier visited Toulon, declared that the galley slaves at Marseilles were better off because of their freedom to run such little shops, and for this he offers a somewhat cynical explanation: 'I am told, this indulgence proceeds more from pecuniary views, than humanity; as it puts a considerable sum of money annually into the admiral's pocket; be that as it may, I was glad to see it.' He had been shocked by what he saw at Toulon, where the galley slaves were employed in the naval dockyard:

> It is impossible for an Englishman to see, without the greatest pity and compassion, those poor unhappy men called galley-slaves, chained by the leg together, and their chains of a merciless weight, many of whom have been guilty of no other crime than smuggling three or four pounds of tobacco, or salt, or perhaps killed a partridge, pheasant, or hen (to hinder their families from starving) on the estate of some tyrannical despotic seigneur. Cruelty of this nature, for such slight offences, is certainly flying in the face of our merciful Creator, and most profanely prostituting the power he has been pleased to invest in the great, over the rest of their unhappy fellow-creatures; and to add to their misery and affliction, they are obliged to do all the slavery in the king's yard that the horses do in ours; and have no other food to support their hard labour, than a pint of pease, or calisanders, per day, with a pound of bread, and water to drink, and at night they are crammed into a galley, which lays afloat, and contains (as they told me) fourteen hundreds of them; so we

Justice

may suppose, they have as little rest in the night as the day.[34]

The Cradocks both offer an interesting account of the galley slaves at the naval port of Rochefort, which they visited in August 1785. Cradock writes:

> Their hour of rest being over, we saw them march, fifty in a company, to their respective occupations, each company guarded by two soldiers. They were chained two and two together by the leg, all clothed tolerably well, and taken great care of, each man being allowed a pint of wine every day. They have a building set apart for them; they sleep upon straw mattresses, two together, for, except in cases of sickness, they are never unchained. In this building are several small houses, in which those of any trade who behave well are permitted to work for themselves, at such times as the Governor gives leave. Many, by so doing, with great industry, contrive to accumulate considerable sums of money; and they are allowed to come out, accompanied by a guard, into the town to dispose of their merchandice.[35] The King's expense for these galley slaves is clothing, and a certain allowance of food besides from 4 to 14 sous in money. The different colours of their dresses bespeak the nature of their crimes: red signifies theft; green, smuggling; brown, desertion; those who are condemned for life have a cap of the same colour as their dress, while those for a term of years wear a white one. They are strictly watched, as the love of liberty, and natural aversion to such a species of slavery, induce many of them to attempt to escape. To prevent the guards from being bribed for that purpose, they are liable to the pain of becoming slaves for life if any should escape, and not be retaken.[36]

Capital punishment by hanging was the penalty for so many crimes in eighteenth-century Britain that British travellers could hardly have been surprised that it was much in use in France. What was new to them was the barbarous punishment of breaking on the wheel; they were also — men, women and children — struck as they travelled round France by the practice of leaving the bodies of those executed by either method at the place where they had undergone this penalty. Thus Thicknesse writes: 'I saw hang on the roadside, a family of nine, a man, his wife, and seven children, who had lived many years by murther and robberies.'[37] More squeamish, Blaikie was shocked when, walking from Orleans to Paris, he came across such a spectacle for the first time:

> About a league from the toun begines the forest which is about two Leagues to pass. There is no doubt of roberys being committed here; there is six remains of bodys upon wheels where they have been brock, this was the first time I had ever seen this horrid spectacle; this was not all for upon a large oak there was twelve others hanging and some more upon another tree some of whom seemed not to have been long there. Left this horrid scene.[38]

The woman in Lord Clive's party noted in her diary on leaving Toulouse: 'At about two miles from the Town we saw the shocking spectacle of 23 bodies of criminals which were still fresh and exposed by the roadside. Many of them were hanging on a Gallows between four pillars, and the rest exposed upon a wheel as they were executed.'[39] Children who accompanied their parents on their travels were not spared such sights. On the way from Étampes to Orleans, Lady Harriet Spencer had her first experience of such a spectacle: 'The road ugly, except one great forest, but there was a shocking sight coming out of it, 7 or 8 dead bodies broken upon the wheel a few days ago, so that the bodies are quite fresh. It was for a shocking murder of a young woman who was going to have a child, and whom they cut to pieces.' A fortnight or so later, she met with a similar spectacle: 'On our way to Thoulouse we saw a most shocking sight, 19 or 20 dead bodies hanging on a triangular gallows, and three or 4 more broke on the wheel, all close to the road.'

The custom of executing criminals at or near the spot where their crimes had been committed could prove extremely disagreeable to British travellers. The Spencer family had an unfortunate experience in Montpellier just after Lord Spencer had had an operation and could not be moved, as Lady Harriet explains:

> There was a horrible thing today. Just before the Salle de Comédie a great gallows was put up, and a poor young man of 18 hung upon it, for having robbed his master, and squandered away what he had got in very bad company at a house near the theatre, at the door of which he is to be hung.

Mama says it is nearly like the story of an English play which she will read to us, called George Barnwell. The shocking thing is we see the gallows from all our windows, and papa is not well enough for us to go away.[40]

Reactions to these executions varied greatly. Garrick's diary contains some strong reflections on an execution which had taken place shortly before he and his wife arrived in Lyons: 'I must only Mention one thing, a Criminal was broke upon the Wheel three days before our Arrival & he was upon the rack for twelve hours before he dy'd & all his Crime was robbing a Smith of 7 Livres — the French can't bear Murder upon the Stage but rack Criminals for Small thefts, we can bear any Butchery upon the Stage & hang only for the Greatest Thefts & Murder. The french delicacy & Sensibility extends only to Dramatic Executions. I think that Both carry their way of thinking too far.'[41]

Other travellers were much less squeamish. While in Paris, Pennant seems to have quite enjoyed attending executions. Those which he saw at two days' interval he describes without the slightest emotion. On the first date he entered in his diary:

> In the Evening went to see an execution of two men for breaking open a house and stealing three silver Tumblers. They were executed about half past eight by torch light; it was late as numbers of the accomplices were brought to confront them. One was hanged on a low gallows; the executioner jumped on his neck and swung on him for a considerable time; the other was broken on the wheel, I was told, alive, but I did not hear him cry. He was attended by a Doctor of the Sorbonne, who kneeled by him after he was broke. The scaffold was very ordinary and without rails; near it was a wheel on which the body was to be placed. There was a small number of guards, 24 of whom had lighted flambeaux, during the execution.

He appears to have come upon the second execution by accident:

> Going to Notre Dame, found that a criminal was about to make the Amende honorable before the great door of that church. He was a baker's lad who had murdered his master and mistress, robbed their house and attempted to set it on fire. He was brought in a sort of Cart or tumbril in his shirt,

bareheaded and barefoot, a haltar round his neck, a writing on his back and breast the words Assassin et Voleur. In the tumbril were the Executioner and confessor. He was taken out of the Cart and on his knees holding a large taper in his hand asked pardon of God, the King and Justice. Thence was conducted to la Greve, where he was broken and placed alive on the wheel, there to die; the confessor standing by him as long as there was life in him. He lived eleven hours. The Confessors are always of the Sorbonne and are chosen by the house. There are two who attend alternatively at each execution for a year.[42]

Thicknesse seems to have been even less squeamish, judging by the horrible detail into which he enters in his blow-by-blow account of a criminal being broken on the wheel at Dijon. This leads on to his discussion of the hazards of travelling in France, which begins — one feels somewhat illogically — 'It is such examples as these, that render travelling in France, in general, secure.'[43] Neither the executions themselves nor the custom of leaving the bodies of criminals where they had been put to death seem to have proved an effective deterrent.

What is surprising to the modern reader is that rather more sensitive travellers, who were obviously horrified by this brutal punishment, insisted none the less on seeing it carried out. There was, after all, absolutely nothing to compel them to be present at such a grim spectacle; and yet they were somehow irresistibly drawn to it. The last surviving letter of R.W.C. (it breaks off at the point where the criminal had just made the *amende honorable*) is concerned with just such an execution at Toulouse in April 1789. His account opens with the words: 'I was present last evening at a most tragic spectacle, rendered more strikingly so by being exhibited after dark and enlightened by the funeral gloom of Torches.'[44] St John's feelings of revulsion were even greater when he writes: 'I have been to see a most dreadful spectacle, a man broke alive upon a cross: which they call breaking on the wheel.'[45]

On his way from Paris to Lyons in 1765 Pennant describes a sight which he saw on leaving Dijon: 'About a mile from the city was a sort of gibbet formed of several pillars connected to each other by long beams. On one was hung a malefactor, and on the bank on which this gibbet was erected was a wheel with a body on it, broke

Justice

about ten months before for sacrilege.'[46] Although no Ancien Régime law laid down a specific penalty for sacrilege, which could include the theft of a chalice or a ciborium, as late as 1780 a man was condemned by the Paris *Parlement* to be burnt at the stake for this crime. It is true that none of our travellers mentions any such happening, but a passage in Thicknesse reminds one of the most barbaric of all punishments imposed by this court, that inflicted on Robert Damiens in 1757 after he had stabbed Louis XV. It may be that Thicknesse's account of the king's answer to the relatives of the Chevalier de La Barre, who pleaded for his life, is apocryphal, but it takes one right back into the atmosphere of the time: 'No! Was not Damien torn to death by horses for assaulting me, an earthly King; and shall I pardon those who insult the King of Kings?'[47]

On 25 July 1789, Babeuf, writing to his wife from Paris, endeavoured to describe to her the extraordinary events taking place there. He was obviously revolted by the barbarous way in which a number of prominent people, starting with the governor of the Bastille, had been put to death and their heads carried on pikes through the streets. 'Je comprends que le peuple se fasse justice', he writes, 'j'approuve cette justice lorsqu'elle est satisfaite par l'anéantissement des coupables, mais pourrait-elle aujourd'hui n'être pas cruelle? Les supplices de tout genre, l'écartellement, la torture, la roue, les bûchers, le fouet, les gibets, les bourreaux multipliés partout, nous ont fait de si mauvaises moeurs!'[48]

Notes

1. *Travels through France and Italy*, p. 9.
2. *Journal*, pp. 83–4.
3. *Observations*, pp. 71–2.
4. See G. G. Butler, *Colonel St. Paul of Ewart, Soldier & Diplomat*, London, 1911, 2 vols., vol. I, pp. 197–8, 205–7.
5. *Travels in France*, vol. I, pp. 597–8, 77, 55.
6. *Tour on the Continent*, pp. 17–18.
7. *Journal*, p. 215.
8. *An Englishman's Impressions*, p. 78.
9. *A Tour*, pp. 127–8.
10. *Correspondence*, vol. 28, pp. 226–7.
11. *Diaries of a Duchess*, pp. 163–4.
12. *Letters from an Officer in the Guards*, pp. 45–51.
13. *Travels in France*, vol. I, pp. 600–1, 602–3.
14. *Letters from France* vol. II, pp. 20–2, 27.
15. *Travels through France and Italy*, pp. 25–6.

16. See above, pp. 170-1.
17. *Observations*, pp. 77, 74-5, 100-1.
18. *Correspondence*, vol. 1, p. 98, vol. 39, p. 17.
19. Ambassador in Paris from 1766 to 1768.
20. *Useful Hints*, pp. 160-1, 166-7.
21. See below, p. 287.
22. *A Tour*, pp. 229-30.
23. *Travels through France and Italy*, p. 68.
24. *A Tour*, pp. 86-7.
25. *A Year's Journey*, vol. I, pp. 52-7.
26. *Diaries of a Duchess*, pp. 214-15.
27. *An Englishman's Impressions*, pp. 85-6.
28. See above, p. 61.
29. A Genevan who acted as travelling tutor.
30. *Boswell Private Papers*, vol. 7, p. 43.
31. *A Tour*, p. 130.
32. *Letters and Journals*, vol. III, p. 188.
33. *A Year's Journey*, vol. II, p. 50.
34. *The Gentleman's Guide*, pp. 64, 60-1.
35. Mrs Cradock relates how at breakfast the following day two galley slaves, escorted by soldiers, came to their hotel selling their wares. Out of pity they bought some of their cotton yarn. (*Journal*, p. 231.)
36. *Memoirs*, vol. II, pp. 313-14.
37. *A Year's Journey*, vol. I, p. 57.
38. *Diary of a Scotch Gardener*, p. 100.
39. Somerset RO DD/SH/67/19C/2480, p. 23.
40. *Lady Bessborough and her Family Circle*, pp. 22, 23, 26.
41. *Journal*, p. 10.
42. *Tour on the Continent*, pp. 23, 25.
43. *A Year's Journey*, vol. I, pp. 47-52.
44. *Letters from France*, p. 12.
45. *Letters from France*, vol. II, p. 10.
46. *Tour on the Continent*, p. 41.
47. *Observations*, p. 74.
48. *Pages choisies*, ed. M. Dommanget, Paris, 1935, pp. 74-5.

5
Popular Amusements

Many of our travellers were assiduous theatre-goers, and both in Paris and the provinces they found ample opportunity to satisfy their taste for comedy and tragedy as well as for opera and *opéra-comique*. Many frequented the leading Paris theatres — the Opéra, Comédie Française and Théâtre Italien — as well as other independent theatres which gradually emerged in these years. With the revival of the provincial theatres they found more or less satisfactory companies performing in most of the towns which they visited. The theatre at Lyons was one of the attractions which the city presented for tourists, while they found theatres even in much smaller towns such as St. Omer and Rochefort because they had garrisons. Ayscough, an officer in the Guards, noted with some disgust at Lille the reason for the presence of theatres in garrison towns: 'The officers are ordered to attend merely (like children) to keep them out of mischief.'[1] No doubt a careful examination of all notes on performances attended both in Paris and the provinces would throw fresh light on the history of the French theatre in this period; but as this chapter is mainly concerned with the leisure pursuits of the great mass of the population, few of whose numbers were assiduous theatre-goers, this question will be left on one side.

There were other forms of entertainment in Paris which drew in members of virtually all social classes. This was particularly the case with those offered by the Boulevards. In April 1765 Pennant drove along them in a cabriolet which he had just bought for his journey beyond Paris. He writes rather briefly: 'At the porte St Antoine went on the Boulevards, where in summer there is a vast appearance of company in coaches. Here all the entertainments from the Foire de St Germain are transferred; these Boulevards are shaded on each side by high trees; on the left is the city, on the right the country.'[2] *The Gentleman's Guide* gives much more detail about what went on there:

> Paris being walled in, the *Boulevarts* or ramparts are adorned with four rows of stately trees, in the centre of which is a broad road for coaches, and on each side very fine stately walks. Upon their ramparts are to be seen, every fine evening, many of the people of fashion in their coaches, which are often gaudy, but oftener truly elegant, and painted in an exquisite manner; not with *arms*, *crests*, or *initial letters*, but with a variety of pastoral scenes. On the margin of these walks are a great number of coffee-houses, and places of public entertainment, where are exhibited a variety of amusements, something in the way of Bartholomew-fair, but, you may imagine, better executed, by a people whose characteristic is to laugh and be merry. The coffee-houses, &c. are finely decorated, and in most of them are musicians; and there the Bourgeois, with their wives and children, enjoy a little fresh air, and the view of the adjacent country, which is to be seen in great variety from the different parts of these ramparts.[3]

When she came again to France in May 1770 as a guest at the Dauphin's wedding, the Duchess of Northumberland hurried back to the Boulevards the day after she arrived in Paris. Her lively account of the scene shows what a variety of people from different social classes were drawn there:

> In the Evening I went to the Old Boulevard where I was always pleased with the chearfulness & whimsical variety of the spectacle, the confusion of Riches & poverty, Hotels & Hovels, pure Air & stinks, people of all sorts & conditions, from the Prince of the Blood to the *Crocheteur*. The common people in their sprucest dress walking or junketting, fine Equipages, dirty Fiacres with five or six people squeezed into them. Beaux parading on Horseback, People of fashion sitting on Chairs in little parties of 5 & 6 . . .
> The Sides of the Walks are almost cover'd with Prints & border'd with Women selling Eggs, Loaves, Apples, Nosegays, Cakes, &c., others of both sexes running about among the Voitures, & mounting on the Steps of them, offer for Sale Fans, Oranges Sweetmeats, Dogs, &c. Here a group of little

Boys fighting, there a sett of Footmen round a Table drinking Beer, old Soldiers smoaking, Shopwomen & Abigails, bien Coiffée, with their Chintz Sacks & Lappels, (gallanted by *Les Garçons friseurs, Chapeau bas*), Puppet Shews, Raree Shews, Monsters, dancing Dogs &c &c &c, & Crowds incredible.⁴

Peckham confirms this impression of the very mixed clientele which the Boulevards attracted when he describes what went on in the coffee-houses and the very varied places of entertainment: 'Singing and musick both French and Italian, dwarfs and giants, conjurors and drolls, plays and rope-dancing, with a thousand other articles of merriment to amuse both the eye and the ear . . . These different species of entertainment continue and are frequented from five in the evening till two or three in the morning. — The hard-working artizan soon disappears, and the industrious tradesman in an hour or two after makes way for the people of fashion, who call midnight the polite hour for the business of the Boulevards.'⁵

Mrs Thrale, Bentley and Mrs Cradock were among those who visited the Boulevards and enjoyed the spectacle. More developed and of greater interest is Villiers's account of a visit there in the crisis month of August 1788 which saw the government compelled to promise to summon the Estates General for May 1789 and the resignation of Loménie de Brienne:

> The evening was spent very pleasantly, with a large party on the *Boulevards de St. Martin*, where an immense number of people were collected. Spacious rows of trees, that extended to a vast length on either side, formed the walks; — whilst the roads, equally spacious, were filled with carriages . . . The buildings [are] very good; the walks delightful; and most of the places of amusement adjoin. A number of *caffés* present the company with opportunities of resting and refreshing themselves; and gardens, and tents before them, are filled with parties sitting at their respective tables. Within the *caffés* are small concerts, and the rooms very brilliantly lighted, towards the evening. On every side of the walks are displayed some entertainments; and the humours of Punch, the pleasantries of a puppet-show, and the *petites comedies* are exhibited for the relaxation of the meaner sort. They may be well accommodated with seats in the boxes and see five comedies, for sixpence. I was entertained with some very

good wax-work, at the expence of two sous, where was a piece very well executed; and they say taken from the original of the late King of Prussia.[6]

Evidently people were not put off their usual amusements by the political crisis.

The succession of fairs held in Paris at different seasons of the year also attracted a broad cross-section of the population. The most famous of these was the Foire St Germain, held near the abbey of that name in the early part of the year. In March 1762 Sterne wrote to his wife and told her of the disastrous fire which had caused an estimated loss of six million livres. He also gives a brief account of the fair: 'This fair of St. Germain's is built upon a spot of ground covered with tiles, as large as the Minster Yard, entirely of wood, divided into shops, and formed into little streets, like a town in miniature. All the artizans in the kingdom come with their wares — jewellers, silversmiths, — and have free leave from all parts of the world to profit by a general licence from the Carnival to Easter.'[7]

The damage to the building must have been fairly quickly repaired. In March 1765 Pennant went to the fair on two successive days and offers a vivid account of what went on there:

29th. In the afternoon went to the Foire de St Germain, vastly crowded with company of all sorts. Abundance of Shops with toys, goods for apparel, mode &ca and all kinds. Very large coffee houses with musicians and singers to allure company. Puppet shews, tumblers and shews of animals; Guards kept to preserve order here as well as every other public place. Saw a tall Italian, a Chamois, a horned Cock, a bottle nose Whale, a fine striped Tiger cat, a Porcupine and a Cassowary.

30th. At La Foire again in the evening. Went to the Sr[8] Nicholet's Booth; the Tumbling much better than in England; a man that danced most surprisingly on the tight rope in great Jack boots; another with a sort of braces fastened on his legs which he danced on instead of his feet, — the first danced on the slack rope in a wonderfull manner; a woman ballanced herself on wires, ballancing different things on the nose and chin, — she ballanced a small dog that stood on the top of a stick; a little pantomime of children from 4 to 6 years old, and a petit piece.[9]

Ten years later Wharton seems to have been mainly attracted by the theatrical performances offered at the fair. He too emphasises that these drew people of quite high rank:

> The Foire St Germain is a large place full of Booths and temporary buildings in which there are two theatres neat enough. At one they represent little pieces, pantomimes &c. The actors here are children, some of 6 or seven years old, others nearly 15 or 16. Some of them act very prettily, particularly a young speaking harlequin about 12 or 13 years old. This theatre is always full of company, and when the great theatres are shut (which they are for the fortnight before Easter & the Easter week), one sees the best company in Paris, come to see these childrens performances. The other Theatre is equally Frequented but not by so good company tho numbers of genteel people go to it every night. The diversions of it are a farce, rope dancing, the tight & slack rope, and a pantomime like our English ones. In short it is a Sadlers Wells. The price of the first Theatre is three Livres the Boxes, 2 l. the pit (which has benches in it & is called here the Parquet, tho it is the same place as the Parterre at the great theatres) and 1 L 10 the high gallery. The price of the second is, 2 l. 10 the boxes or pit. The rest I know not. The foire is divided in to several streets full of shops of all kinds of toys, coffee houses, &c are full of people equally trifling with the wares which are there sold. This is the Great amusement and resource while the other spectacles are quiet.[10]

In February 1784 Mrs Cradock went to the fair with her husband; she gives a varied account of what went on, and in passing expresses her surprise at finding the best people there too:

> Après avoir dîné à trois heures, nous sommes allés voir la fameuse foire Saint-Germain. On y vend de tout: des bijoux, des étoffes, de la lingerie et bien d'autres choses. Les marchandises sont disposées avec un goût parfait dans de petites boutiques. Çà et là, des cabarets où se font entendre des musiciens et des chanteurs, et où j'ai été surprise d'y trouver des dames de la société; mais il paraît que c'est admis. Partout des spectacles, des théâtres en plein vent, des bals, des saltimbanques, des marionnettes, etc. etc., des expositions de bêtes sauvages vivantes ou empaillées. Les oiseaux sont

surtout fort bien réussis et montés de façon à produire un joli effet. Nous sommes entrés voir des figures de cire. Un des groupes représentait le roi, la reine et le dauphin, assis sous un baldaquin, et un peu plus loin devant eux, accoudés à une table, trois personnages. Ceux-ci figuraient M. de Voltaire, M. Rousseau et le Dr Franklin; ils étaient si bien reproduits qu'on avait su donner à chacum de ces hommes illustres, mais funestes, le caractère de sa physionomie.

When she returned a month or so later, with some other English women, she came away with a much less favourable opinion of the fair: 'Il y faisait sale, froid et désagréable. Nous sommes entrées dans plusieurs boutiques: tout y était horriblement cher et de mauvais goût; aussi n'y restâmes-nous pas longtemps.'[11]

On 30 May, when the Foire St Laurent opened, the Cradocks were there. They inspected, among other things, the *Redoute chinoise*, a garden laid out with psuedo-Chinese ornaments. They went back again at the end of July to the same fair 'où', as she puts it, 'il est de bon ton de se promener'. They paid great attention to a seal, apparently a creature relatively unknown at that time, which was exhibited there. After eating waffles prepared on the spot and viewing a model in glass of the fair at Venice, she goes on: 'Pour continuer notre soirée, nous entrâmes dans un café rempli du public le plus varié, depuis le petit bourgeois jusqu'au grand seigneur.' Thirty musicians performed on a stage, among them two girls to whom the Cradocks had earlier given a present. For their benefit 'God save the King' was played.[12]

Yet another fair — the Foire St Ovide — took place in the autumn in what is now the Place de la Concorde. Mrs Thrale, accompanied among others by Johnson, went to see it at the end of September 1775:

> At night we drove round the Foire St Ovide which exhibited a Show totally new to me: there stands in the middle of a large open Place an Equestrian Statue of Lewis 15th: & round it — but at a considerable distance — are Shops which form a Circus of the gayest Appearance I ever saw and perfectly singular — the Shops are temporary, & slight enough of course, but adorned with a sort of Frippery Finery, Ribbons, Looking-Glasses, Cutlery, Pastry, every thing one can imagine that is at once brilliant & worthless — but which when illuminated with numberless Lights gives an Air of

Festivity which not even the Philosophy of an Englishman can despise nor the Stupidity of a Dutchman neglect. Lamps formed into Pyramids surround the Statue, & the Circus of Shops at a proper distance, glittering in the Eyes of a Crowd of Spectators, who walk round the gay Place every Evening, tempt some to buy & some to talk, and brought to Johnson's Mind the Image of Cranborn Alley[13] on a Saturday Night.[14]

The last remark would seem to suggest that this fair attracted fewer of the best people.

Townsend describes vividly in 1786 scenes in which they presumably did not participate — those which in Paris marked the end of the Carnival on Ash Wednesday:

In the evening of february 28, being the last day of the carnival, when Catholics bid adieu to festivity and mirth for forty days, all Paris was in motion, and some thousands were in masks, men in the dress of women, and women in the dress of men; all assuming characters, and many sustaining those characters with spirit. Popes, cardinals, monks, devils, courtiers, harlequins, and lawyers, all mingled in one promiscuous crowd. In the street of S. Honoré alone were assembled more than one hundred thousand souls.[15]

Cradock records similar scenes at Marseilles:

Ash-Wednesday. — To the Plain Saint Michel, to bury the sins of the Carnival. This was a tumultuous meeting of all sorts of people, some in masks, some without; men in women's clothes, and women in men's; some drinking, some quarrelling, some dancing, and some appeared to be seriously devout. Harlequins, scaramouches, mock-doctors, and other buffoons abounded . . . We found that many by purchase had lengthened the Carnival, and that the fast with them did not begin till late the next day.[16]

In 1787 an anonymous army officer also had an opportunity of observing the carnival in the provinces. At Rouen he 'walked upon the quay where there was a great deal of Merry Andrew work going on on account of the Carnival'. He saw and heard more of it at Dieppe where he had to wait some time for a boat back to England. On his arrival he noted: 'The Streets are full of racketing and noise from Blaguards & sailors in Masks running about with Speaking trumpets and dressed in ludicrous dresses, being the last week of Carnaval.' Three days later he wrote with some irritation: 'The Carnaval being allmost at an end the Streets are crouded with Masks and every sort of Foolery is practised in the Streets, roaring & hollowing the whole night.' The next day's entry is rather more tolerant: 'The whole night the streets full of Confusion and a roar of noise with the Maskers every sort of foolery — was most entertained from my window with seeing the fishermen; they have a long rod and line and put a large shugar almond upon it and walk allong with it hanging before them and a croud of boys with extended jaws and eager eyes strive to catch it.'[17]

In their wanderings round Paris our travellers often saw something of other popular entertainments. Cole, for instance, describes how 'after admiring the Louvre I walked to the Side of it fronting the River, & back to the Pont-Neuf, all the way being crouded with People listening to Montabanks on Horseback, & on Sort of Stages, with Curtains & small Apartments behind them, acting Farces & Interludes, for their own Profit, & diversion of the People'.[18] The Cradocks derived considerable amusement from watching, from the windows of their hotel in the Rue Jacob, the strange mixture of secular and religious spectacles in the street below on a Sunday afternoon. In April 1784, after noting their presence in the morning at a sermon by 'a celebrated preacher' at St Sulpice, Cradock writes:

> In the afternoon the succession of amusements under our balcony was much more extraordinary than usual: first, a concert by Savoyards; then ball and battledore; then a grand religious procession; and immediately afterwards, a camel, with a monkey dancing on its back; then bears, tumblers, mock-doctors, street-orators, and scaramouches. Our milkman was in the crowd, well-dressed, in a fashionable coat, embroidered waistcoat, silk breeches, and worked ruffles; yet next morning appeared again entirely in his own character.[19]

At Marseilles the Duchess of Northumberland observed a similar street scene: 'The End of the Place which my Window looks to was all This morning cleared from the little Stalls and Stands which make it look like a Fair on Week Days & the space they usually occupy was fill'd by Jugglers who collected together great circles or rather Ovals of people before whom they perform'd all their Tricks with Cups, Balls, Cards &c in the open air.'[20]

Another scene described by Cradock took place on the Seine, also on a Sunday:

> Observed one of the Sunday evening amusements of the common people. It is a manly exercise in boats on the water, and those who are engaged in it must be expert swimmers. They encounter each other with a staff, like a lance, and the man who pushes the greatest number into the water gains the prize, has a flag given him; and is saluted with firing of cannon, and warlike music. The whole is concluded with fireworks.[21]

Not all the entertainments which our travellers met with in Paris won their approval. Pennant's account of his visit to the bear garden one Sunday in 1765 is scathing:

> Attended the Ambassador's chapel, and his Levée. In the afternoone went to Les Combats des animaux, or bear garden of Paris, rue de Sevre. It has a large area covered with sand; on each side are places for the spectators, — those on the ground are guarded by rails, above are seats for the better sort of company, of which there was a numerous and gentile set; all seemed more pleased with the horrid cruelties exercised on the beasts than was consistent with humanity. The beasts baited were a bear, 2 wolves, a wild boar, stag and hind, horse, two bulls and an Ass, besides many combats between dogs. A swiss bull was very expert in defending itself; the ass excellent, for by rolling or kneeling on, biting and kicking the dogs, never suffered them to fasten on him; the hind and horse despised the dogs, but the other animals were cruelly treated. The rough English were the only people here that expressed any feeling.[22]

Some twenty years later Andrews was no more polite in his account of 'a bear-garden, where dogs, bulls, lions, tygers, bears, and other beasts are baited and worried to death':

> This savage pastime is as much frequented as any at Paris, and is exhibited in winter as well as in the middle summer; which is the more remarkable, as this scene of blood and

carnage passes in an open arena, surrounded by seats which, though covered over head, leave one otherwise exposed to all the inclemencies of the weather . . . You will, I doubt not, rejoice that so vulgar and base a diversion is now in England abandoned to the meanest of the populace, and is not as in France licensed by public authority.[23]

The Cradocks both provide interesting accounts of the festivities in Bordeaux on Midsummer Eve and Midsummer Day; both note the element of superstition associated with the celebrations on what was on paper a religious festival. Cradock writes:

Thursday the 23rd. — The eve of St. John. Preparations innumerable for lighting up the city, though we were almost suffocated with heat; old pitch-barrels brought out, which were to be set fire to all along the quay; immense faggots to blaze likewise for three miles at least, along the banks of the river; and all this we found was merely to burn out the old witches of the last year! However, when it grew dark, I think I never saw a more brilliant illumination.

Friday the 24th. — Was ushered in with music of every kind. The lowest of the multitude were all decorated with flowers: I even saw a beggar opposite to our windows pay fourpence for a large bunch of pomegranate and a few roses, to wear on the outside of his tattered garment.

In the afternoon the commander of the troops gave a grand treat to the military; all the standards were covered with poultry and provisions, which were to be distributed amongst the victors, after the games were concluded. There were many hogsheads of claret to be delivered out, but the sport itself was rather new to us, till our attendants, shocked at our ignorance, whispered to us, that it was 'Prison bars'.[24] The soldiers all exerted themselves in white decorated dresses, and when victory on one side was at last proclaimed, we were stunned with the noise of 'guns, drums, trumpets, blunderbuss, and thunder'.

We were greatly delighted, however, to find, that amidst this immense concourse, with wine flowing on every side, no outrage whatever was committed, nor any real mischief done.

Next morning early, I walked about the city, and saw that many were busily engaged in nailing horse-shoes at their doors to keep some particular old witch out; and I greatly lamented that, after so much trouble and expense, this additional labour should be found to be absolutely necessary . . . I felt puzzled to know what was, or was not intended to be kept holy.[25]

The magnificent art collections of the Duc d'Orléans drew many of our travellers to the Palais Royal. They also frequented its gardens, some before the Duc de Chartres, later Philippe Égalité, savaged them to put up, between 1781 and 1786, buildings round three sides, and others after the transformation was completed. In 1776, for instance, Bentley admired the old gardens; only in his last sentence does he hint at the somewhat mixed company which they attracted:

> In the evening at the Jardins du Palais Royal. These gardens furnish a charming and a very rational amusement. They consist of long walks separated by rows of trees, and those over some of the walks are bent into an arch. These walks are often extremely full of well-dressed people, and there are common chairs under the trees on each side the walk. Where any of the company are disposed to sit, a party draw their chairs into a circle and enter into lively, gallant, or philosophic conversations as they are disposed, and they all seem very sociable and happy. Everything here seems to lead to sociability and the pleasure of conversation as *the chief end of Man*. I stayed here till about 10, and company were still coming in, but I fancy of the gayer kind.[26]

Ten years later Mrs Piozzi (formerly Thrale) visited the new Palais Royal and noted how the popular fury aroused at first by the building plans of the Duc de Chartres[27] had subsided. The new buildings certainly drew the crowds in a way which it is difficult to imagine nowadays as one walks through the thinly occupied garden or along its silent arcades. The Piozzis met a very different spectacle:

> In the evening we looked at the new square called the Palais Royal, whence the Duc de Chartres has removed a vast number of noble trees, which it was a sin and shame to profane with an axe, after they had adorned that spot for so many centuries. — The people were accordingly as angry, I believe, as Frenchmen can be, when the folly was first committed: the

court, however, had wit enough to convert the place into a sort of Vauxhall, with tents, fountains, shops, full of frippery, brilliant at once and worthless, to attract them; with coffee-houses surrounding it on every side; and now they are all again *merry* and *happy*, synonymous terms at Paris, though often disunited in London; and Vive le Duc de Chartres![28]

Villiers, who visited the Palais Royal two years later, was decidedly more enthusiastic and he also gives a clearer impression of the scene there:

> After the termination of the opera, we walked to the Palais Royal, a very fashionable and most lovely place of resort. It is the property of the Duc d'Orleans, and was some time since a private palace: — it is now decorated around with shops, the best in Paris, which produce a prodigious rent to the duke. Every thing that is rich, brilliant, and beautiful, is exposed to sale, at these different *boutiques*; the splendor of which, together with the pleasantness of the walks, and the croud of well-dressed company, make this place truly enchanting and delightful. The company are dispersed in various parts, and at different entertainments; — some walking; — some sitting without doors *sub dio*; — and some under tents; — while the *caffés* beneath piazzas are equally filled. In the center of the garden is a long building, newly and grotesquely erected; it is encircled with water, and small fountains, that are continually playing.
>
> We supped in an elegant apartment above stairs; and, sitting in the balcony, fancied ourselves in a kind of paradise. In addition to the light of the lamps, the moon towered above, and through the fleecy and thin clouds diffused her softened radiance, which, like that of a modest fair, shone more lovely, from being half concealed beneath the thin cover of a veil.[29]

That was in August 1788. Very soon, with the approach of the Revolution, the Palais Royal was to become a very different place.

The gardens of the palace at St Cloud, which also belonged to the Duc d'Orléans, attracted many of our travellers as they did crowds of people, particularly on Sundays. Peckham noted how stalls were set up to satisfy the varied tastes of those who frequented the park: 'In these gardens are temporary stalls for the sale of ribbands, toys, cakes, fruit &c. with moveable pamphlet shops, where (this being a privileged place) you may buy books, which are either from their immorality or irreligion prohibited elsewhere.'[30] After describing the palace, Bentley continues:

> But the most striking thing we saw here and all the way was the immense crowds of people, and the manner of their Sunday amusements. Many kinds of shops were open as on other days; everybody was taking the air in their holiday clothes; close to the terrace leading to the gardens of St Cloud under the shade of a grove a large party of young men and women clean and decently dressed were dancing country dances and minuets of 3 couples alternately with all the ease and decorum of a genteel assembly.[31]

During their long stay in Paris the Cradocks inevitably visited St Cloud, and Mrs Cradock offers a lively account of what they saw there on a Sunday in September when the festival of the saint after whom the town is named was celebrated:

> Nous arrivâmes à Saint-Cloud vers cinq heures et demie. Des milliers de personnes se promenaient dans le parc. Les grandes eaux jouaient; partout des boutiques disposées avec goût, des tentes sous lesquelles on prenait des rafraîchissements, des bals en plein air, des théâtres de marionnettes, des saltimbanques, des balançoires, etc. etc. Tout le monde gai et en train.

At seven the Comte and Comtesse d'Artois and the Duc d'Orléans's children put in an appearance in their carriages, accompanied by guards and a band, and paraded slowly up and down the main avenue four times. 'Après leur départ', Mrs Cradock continues, 'on fut admis avec des billets dans une autre partie du parc où l'on avait établi des tribunes circulaires au milieu desquelles on dansait. A huit heures se tira un feu d'artifice, et à dix heures et demie nous étions à la maison, contents de notre soirée, et heureux d'échapper a la poussière inévitable produite par une foule aussi compacte.'[32]

There are many other references in our travellers' accounts to the popularity of dancing all over France. On a brilliantly fine day in 1787, while travelling from Pont-à-Mousson to Nancy, Muirhead noted: 'The meanest peasant seemed to partake the blessings of returning spring. Too many symptoms I certainly could perceive of poverty and depression — few, I think, of fretfulness or discontent . . . The female villagers tript lightly on the grass, in a circular dance: the young men seemed to prefer parties at nine pins — a separation not quite consonant to our ideas of French gallantry.'[33] Wharton describes a characteristic scene at a small inn between Mâcon and Bourg-en-Bresse: 'There were in the Kitchen 5 or 6 peasants & a Jolly Bressance Girl. A Fellow came in with a Cymbal. One of the peasants took out the Girl and they began dancing & skipping about to the great delight of the Beholders & you may easily imagine to my no small Entertainment.'[34]

Mary Berry was most impressed with the dancing in the streets which she saw on a Sunday in 1785 at a small town which she passed through on the way from Nîmes to Aix:

> At St. Rémy all the young people of the town were dancing in the faubourg. For the first time in my life I saw small bourgeois servants [sic] and peasants dancing with natural grace and signs of real gaiety: they wanted no dancing-master to show them the figures. For half an hour they danced the figure of a quarrée, and were never wrong in a single step, and always with a grace and gaiety that one sometimes vainly looks for in our dress-ball rooms. Their band was a tambourine and a fife; they danced quarrées, a Pérégordine, and a dance they called the matelot, which was very like our English country dances.[35]

A very different kind of entertainment was available to British travellers who happened to be in Paris in 1783 and 1784 when that great triumph of French technology, the balloon, was being demonstrated. On 1 December 1783 Cradock went with his wife to see the physicist, Charles, and the younger of the Robert brothers make the first ascent in a hydrogen balloon:

> At eleven o'clock set out for the Thuilleries, to see the balloon go off; we soon quitted the coach, and it was with the greatest difficulty we got through on the Pont-royal to the little garden door. It was not long afterwards, that the Duke of Cumberland[36] was in danger of being squeezed to death, as announced in all the public journals. The Queen of France sat in the balcony in front of the Thuilleries . . .
> As soon as the aeronauts had taken their flight, I quitted

the gardens, passed the Seine in a small boat, and arrived at the hotel time enough to send off a letter by that night's post to Leicester, in conformity with a promise previously made to the Rev. Mr. Ludlam. In this I gave him a rough sketch of all that I had just seen. This he directly copied out, and communicated the whole to some of his friends in London, and I found, on my return to England, that this was the fullest (if not the earliest) account of this sort of balloon, that had then been printed. A Montgolfier passed over my head soon after I arrived at Paris.[37]

On 2 March of the following year, as her husband had returned to England for two months, Mrs Cradock did not go to see the ascent made by Blanchard from the Champ de Mars, though she allowed her maid to see it with their manservant.[38] On 7 June they met Charles by chance on the boat coming back from Sèvres:

Was introduced to Mons. Charles, who returned with us, and much interesting conversation took place on the subject of balloons. He very obligingly told me that if I did not object to sitting up all night, he would give me a ticket of admission to see the process of that which was then filling at the Tuilleries. This invitation I gladly accepted, and never was any thing more surprising to me, than the enthusiasm that seemed to rage in this assembly of daring aeronauts. I confess from all I had before witnessed, I would not have ascended with any of them, for 'all beneath the moon'.[39]

Not all the ascents of these early balloons went according to plan, as the Cradocks found when they went in an Anglo-French party to be present at the ascent of Abbé Miolan and Janninet from the Luxembourg Gardens at 10.30 a.m. on Sunday, 11 July:

This day a balloon, on a new construction by the Abbé Miolan, was to have ascended from the Luxembourg gardens, but after waiting several hours, an apology was made, that from an accident, it would not fill. As some thousands had assembled, and each person had paid three livres for admittance, there was rather an appearance of riot; but after destroying some tents, tables, and chairs, the police interfered, and being reduced to order, we all went home again very quietly.[40]

We have two very different accounts of the ascent made on Sunday 19 September by the Robert brothers and a third man (not Charles) from the Tuileries gardens. Mrs Piozzi, who was passing through Paris on her way to Italy with her new husband, provides a version which tells one more about what she considered the excellent behaviour of the vast crowd than about the actual ascent:

> All Paris I think, myself among the rest, assembled to see the valiant brothers, Robert and Charles, mount yesterday into the air, in company with a certain Pilâtre de Rosier, who conducted them in the new-invented flying chariot fastened to an air-balloon. It was from the middle of the Tuilleries that they set out, a place very favourable and well-contrived for such public purposes. But all was so nicely managed, so cleverly carried on somehow, that the order and decorum of us who remained on firm ground, struck me more than even the very strange sight of human creatures floating in the wind: but I have really been witness to ten times as much bustle and confusion at a crowded theatre in London, than what these peaceable Parisians made when the whole city was gathered together. Nobody was hurt, nobody was frighted, nobody could even pretend to feel themselves incommoded. Such are among the few comforts that result from a despotic government.[41]

Mrs Cradock too, in describing the same occasion, gives more attention to what was happening on the ground than in the air, but her account is radically different:

> Après déjeuner, M. Cradock sortait voir l'ascension du ballon; à onze heures, je me dirigeai sur le quai dans la même intention avec ma femme de chambre et notre laquais. Je fus assez heureuse pour trouver de très bonnes places. Le temps était superbe: sur les quais et les ponts une foule énorme, en habits de fête, attendait avec curiosité. Je jouissais de cette scène animée, lorsqu'un grand cri se fit entendre; tournant la tête, je vis une grosse pierre lancée du haut d'une maison. La pierre tua sur le coup un homme qui se trouvait non loin de moi et en blessa plusieurs autres. Grande fut d'abord la consernation; puis, presque aussitôt le monde s'amassa autour du malheureux et à grand'peine la garde, qu'on était allé quérir, put-elle arriver jusqu'au cadavre qu'on emporta sur

une civière. Je ne puvais quitter ma place sans risquer d'être écrasée, aussi fus-je forcée d'assister aux sauffrances des pauvres blessés, dont les gémissements me brisaient le coeur. Moins d'une demi-heure après l'accident, l'ascension commençait: en un instant, tout sembla oublié et, lorsque le ballon s'éleva au-dessus des maisons, les acclamations du public ne connurenn plus de bornes. Je revins assez fatiguée de l'émotion et de la chaleur.[42]

These travellers' notes offer a lively account of the spectacles other than public executions available to the masses and of the amusements such as open-air dancing which they organised for themselves in Ancient Régime France.

Notes

1. *Letters from an Officer in the Guards*, p. 18.
2. *Tour on the Continent*, p. 36.
3. *Gentleman's Guide* (1788), pp. 70-1.
4. *Diaries of a Duchess*, pp. 105-6.
5. *A Tour*, pp. 135-6.
6. *A Tour*, pp. 129-31.
7. *Letters*, p. 154.
8. Jean Bapiste Nicolet ran at this date a company of rope dancers. The text has 'St'.
9. *Tour on the Continent*, p. 31.
10. *An Englishman's Impressions*, p. 82.
11. *Journal*, pp. 5-6, 11.
12. *Journal*, pp. 35, 68-70.
13. A London market for cheap goods and clothes.
14. *French Journal*, p. 92.
15. *A Journey through a part of France*, vol. I, pp. 39-40.
16. *Memoirs*, vol. II, p. 172.
17. W. Sussex RO, Add. MS. 7237, ff. 9, 13, 16, 17.
18. *Journal*, pp. 154-5.
19. *Memoirs*, vol. II, pp. 54-5.
20. *Diaries of a Duchess*, p. 212.
21. *Memoirs*, vol. II, p. 296.
22. *Tour on the Continent*, p. 31.
23. *Letters to a Young Gentleman*, pp. 550-1.
24. 'Prison (or prisoners) bars': 'A game played in a variety of ways, chiefly by boys; the players are divided into two parties, they occupy distinct demarcations, "bases", or "dens", the aim of each side being to make prisoner by touching any player of the opposite side who runs out from his enclosure' (*OED*).
25. *Memoirs*, vol. II, pp. 227-8.

26. *Journal of a Visit to Paris*, p. 31.
27. He succeeded his father as Duc d'Orléans in 1785.
28. *Observations and Reflections*, p. 13.
29. *A Tour*, pp. 92–4.
30. *A Tour*, p. 181.
31. *Journal of a Visit to Paris*, p. 34.
32. *Journal*, pp. 83–4.
33. *Journals of Travels*, p. 70.
34. *An Englishman's Impressions*, p. 90.
35. *Journals and Correspondence*, vol. I, pp. 143–4.
36. A younger brother of George III.
37. *Memoirs*, vol. II, pp. 38–9.
38. *Journal*, p. 10.
39. *Memoirs*, vol. II, pp. 67–8.
40. Ibid., pp. 84–5. Cf. Mrs. Cradock, *Journal*, pp. 62–3.
41. *Observations and Reflections*, pp. 22–3.
42. *Journal*, pp. 86–7.

Part Two
The Collapse of Absolute Monarchy

6
The Last Years of Louis XV

What most impressed Moore when he arrived in France in 1772 was the difference between British and French attitudes to monarchy. 'It must be acknowledged', he writes, 'that monarchy (for the French do not love to hear it called despotism, and it is needless to quarrel with them about a word) is raised in this country so very high, that it quite loses sight of the bulk of the nation, and pays attention only to a few, who, being in exalted stations, come within the court's sphere of vision.' Though he also declares that a considerable minority took a very different attitude to monarchy, he felt that the average Frenchman still remained devoted to his king and indeed to all the members of the royal family:

> A Frenchman, while he knows that his king is of the same nature, and liable to all the weaknesses of other men; while he enumerates his follies, and laughs as he laments them, is nevertheless attached to him by a sentiment of equal respect and tenderness; a kind of affectionate prejudice, independent of his real character.
>
> *Roi* is a word which conveys to the minds of Frenchmen the ideas of benevolence, gratitude, and love; as well as those of power, grandeur, and happiness.
>
> They flock to Versailles every Sunday, behold him with unsated curiosity, and gaze on him with as much satisfaction the twentieth time as the first.
>
> They consider him as their friend, though he does not know their persons; as their protector, although their greatest danger is from an Exempt or Lettre de Cachet; and as their

benefactor, while they are oppressed with taxes.

They magnify into importance his most indifferent actions; they palliate and excuse all his weaknesses; and they impute his errors or crimes, to his ministers or other evil counsellors; who (as they fondly assert) have, for some base purpose, imposed upon his judgement, and perverted the undeviating rectitude of his intentions.

The mass of the people, Moore goes on, are interested in the most trivial details concerning their king and, when he appears in public, they have eyes for nobody else:

At a review, the troops perform their manoeuvres unheeded by such of the spectators as are within sight of the king. They are all engrossed in contemplation of the prince. — Avez-vous vu le roi? — Tenez — ah! — voilà le roi. — Le roi rit. Apparemment il est content. — Je suis charmé, — ah, il tousse! — A-t-il toussé? — Oui, parbleu! et bien fort. — Je suis au désespoir.

At mass, it is the King, not the Priest, who is the object of attention. The Host is elevated; but the people's eyes remain fixed upon the face of their beloved Monarch.

This affection for their king seemed to Moore sincere even though the great mass of the people, far from having any expectation of receiving any of his favours, were totally unknown to him. They had no conception of a king being accountable to his people for his acts.

The French seem so delighted and dazzled with the lustre of monarchy, that they cannot bear the thoughts of any qualifying mixture, which might abate its violence, and render its ardour more benign. They chuse to give the splendid machine full play, though it often scorches and threatens to consume them and their effects.

They consider the power of the king, from which their servitude proceeds, as if it were their own power. You will hardly believe it; but I am sure of the fact: They are proud of it; they are proud that there is no check or limitation to his authority.

They tell you with exultation, that the king has an army of near two hundred thousand men in the time of peace. A

The Last Years of Louis XV

Frenchman is as vain of the palaces, fine gardens, number of horses, and all the paraphernalia belonging to the court of the monarch, as an Englishman can be of his own house, gardens, and equipage.

Instead of being mortified, Moore goes on, by the degree of liberty enjoyed on the other side of the Channel, the average Frenchman is quite shocked to be told of it:

When they hear of the freedom of debate in parliament, of the liberties taken in writing or speaking of the conduct of the king, or measures of government, and the forms to be observed, before those who venture on the most daring abuse of either can be brought to punishment, they seem filled with indignation, and say with an air of triumph, C'est bien autrement chez nous: Si le Roi de France avoit affaire à ces Messieurs-là, il leur apprendroit à vivre. And then they would proceed to inform you, that, parbleu! their minister would give himself no trouble about forms or proofs; that suspicion was sufficient for him, and without more ado he would shut up such impertinent people in the Bastile for many years. And then raising their voices, as if what they said were a proof of the courage or magnanimity of the minister — Ou peut-être il feroit condamner ces drôles là aux galères pour la vie.[1]

Moore, it is true, proceeds in his next letter to qualify this view of the political outlook of the French, pointing to the growth of opposition to absolutism and mentioning, for instance, the influence of Montesquieu's writings; but though no doubt somewhat exaggerated, his account of the attitude of the great mass of the people towards their king contains a considerable amount of truth.

Louis XV, fifty-three in 1763 and with eleven more years to reign, was seen in the flesh by quite a number of our travellers. Some observed him as mere tourists, going to Versailles along with ordinary French people, to see him at mass or dining in public. A number of the men were formally presented at court, whether because of their high birth or simply because of their status as gentlemen, which included officers in the armed forces. Women from the British aristocracy on their travels were not presented at court, but were made welcome there. In June 1763 Lady Holland wrote to her sister, the Countess of Kildare:

> I have also been at Versailles, where I went to chapel; saw the whole Royal Family, coming from mass; in the antechamber the Queen and the Dauphin stopp'd to speak to me very graciously which was very *polie* [*sic*], as we English ladies are not presented. But the Dauphin said so much to me that in the meantime the King passed by, who I'm told intended speaking to me, and I lost the opportunity of seeing him near, which I regret, for at a distance he appears to me the handsomest man I ever saw.[2]

A few months later Hume, as secretary to Lord Hertford, the British ambassador, was presented at court. He was quite dazzled by the reception he met from the courtiers, male and female, at Fontainebleau but, as he explains amusingly in a letter to Adam Smith, he was rather taken aback by Louis XV's coldness: 'The King said nothing particular to me, when I was introduced to him, and (can you imagine it) I was become so silly as to be a little mortify'd by it, till they told me, that he never says any thing to any body, the first time he sees them.'[3] Two years later, when Walpole was presented to the different members of the royal family, he noted wrily: 'The Queen took great notice of me; none of the rest said a syllable.'[4]

Earlier that year Pennant had visited Versailles as an ordinary tourist. He saw the king and queen go to mass and later 'sup in publick or at a Grande Covert, a Maigre supper, but very sumptious. When the King or Queen called for drink it was tasted by two before it was presented. Behind stood cardinal de Laines [Luynes], with a red Calotte, and several gentlemen to whom he talked a good deal.' Louis XV, he noted, 'is a very good looking man; rather short; appears young of his years; great lover of hunting'. He drew a sketch showing the seating arrangements at the table and indicated the position from which it was taken — 'myself in a window, standing in a tub of cinders, which very luckily the Femme de chambre left there, or I should have been excluded from the sight without that advantage'. This is followed by various observations, starting with: 'His Majesty had an excellent stomach, Her Majesty seemed thirsty; the rest of the Company only piddled.' He also observed that security had been tightened up since Damiens's attack on the king; the French nobleman whom he accompanied had twice to answer for him. 'The King', he writes, 'as he passed from mass eyed me for a considerable time, seeing I was a new face.'[5]

Thicknesse, if one accepts the dates given to the letters printed in his first two travel books, resided at St Germain from May 1766 to August 1767 with a break of some three months in the middle. He claims to have been presented at court and to have been allowed to follow the royal hunt. On the whole he was rather more impressed by Louis XV than some other travellers, although he does admit that he 'would have made a much better country gentleman with twenty thousand pounds a year, than a sovereign prince'. He was also struck by his outward show of piety. When Thicknesse attended mass in the chapel at Versailles, he was greatly taken with the music: 'Nothing can be conceived more becoming the dignity of a great king offering up his prayers to the King of Kings, than his heavenly choir inspires, which the King of France does in the most solemn manner; and at the elevation of the host, strikes his breast, and frequently crosses himself.'

He found the king 'a remarkable handsome man', though later he rather qualifies this when he draws his portrait:

> Lewis XV then is fifty-seven years of age, has large, full, prominent, black, piercing eyes, and a Roman nose. Upon the whole, his countenance betrays a handsome goodliness, and is certainly the remains of a manly beautifulness. His person is of a middle stature, rather too bulky for a young man, but what gives grace to one of his years: he walks well, rides better; though he begins to bend a little over the shoulders. When he is thoughtful, and not disposed to speak, he is apt to open his mouth, fix his eyes upon some one object, and let his chin drop; and to such who only see him at such times, his looks are rather unfavourable. He is extremely affable and well bred, many instances of which I perceived at the hunt, even to myself, though without speaking. I mention this as singular, because neither he nor his subjects are much prejudiced in favour of Englishmen. He is extremely fond of women; nor has any man been more indulged that way. He is also fonder of wine than is the present fashion of France. He finds the saddle the seat of health, and spends more of the day on it than off. He is particularly addicted to asking trifling questions, such as How old are you? Or to say, You are

seventy; you can't live long; and the like. In short, Lewis XV is neither that wit his flatterers represent him, nor has he that weakness which his own countenance sometimes bespeaks.

Thicknesse was somehow convinced that Louis XV was 'a humane and generous prince'; he even goes so far as to maintain that, if it had not been for the pressure exerted upon him, he would have spared the life of Damiens.[6]

The anonymous author of *Travels into France and Italy* (the letters are undated) picked up at Rouen another story of the king's goodness of heart: 'Passing by la Plaine des Sablons, he saw the troops assembled for the execution of a soldier; asking the cause, was answered the man highly merited the punishment, for he was a coward, and not willing to serve his majesty. The king replied, Poor fellow; want of courage is a misfortune; let him live, and serve me some other way.'[7] It is difficult to imagine that either of these stories of the king's goodness of heart could have any foundation in fact.

In 1769 Walpole, now back again in France, returned to Versailles with the main object of seeing the new mistress, Mme Du Barry, at mass. After describing her appearance he adds: 'In the tribune above, surrounded by prelates, was the amorous and still handsome King; one could not help smiling at the mixture of piety, pomp and carnality.'[8] The Duchess of Northumberland, who came to France in May 1770 for the Dauphin's wedding, was much involved with Mme Du Barry; indeed she was put up at the Hôtel de Luynes, the mistress's house in Versailles. At the wedding she noted the king's dress and appearance: 'The King's Coat was neither of those I had seen, but a red very much embroidered with Gold, not pretty, but the Loop which held his Ribbon was of 7 Diamonds of a prodigious Magnitude. He is like the Duke of Kingston but is outjaw'd, & looks a great deal older.'

After the ceremony the duchess was presented to Mme Du Barry and she thus had accidentally a somewhat abortive conversation with the king: 'After I had been there a little while the King came in & looking toward me ask'd her who I was & then said to me, "Parler vous francois?" to which I reply'd, "Une peu Sire", & there the Conversation dropt & the Prince D'Henin gave me a sign to retire.'

Two days later, after attending various festivities, including an opera, in connection with the wedding, she was again with Mme Du Barry when the king returned from the hunt. 'In his Hunting

Dress & his Slippers I thought he look'd much better than when he was full dress'd. He ask'd me with a Look of great Good humour if I had liked the Opera & then said to me "La Chasse m'a menée un peu Loin aujourdhuy, mais il faisoit un Temps delicieuse"; then turning to Mme. de Barrie he told her that the Dauphin was much pleas'd with the Chasse.'

Before leaving Versailles on 21 May, the duchess was invited to dine with the mistress. Although she did not see the king on this occasion, she was privileged to taste some coffee which he had prepared with his own royal hands: 'I had a dish of Coffee & the Servant asking me how I liked it & I told him I thought it the best I had ever tasted in my Life, to which he reply'd that it was the Kings own roasting, grinding & preparing. Mme. du Barri told me the King had order'd it on purpose for me & had charged her not to tell me who had made it till I had given my opinion of it, adding she would tell him when he came from the Chasse & she was sure he would be highly pleas'd to hear that I liked it.'[9]

By this date the queen and Louis's only son were both dead. Marie Leczinska made a good impression on those travellers who frequented the court, starting, as we have seen, with Lady Holland. When Walpole was presented, he described her as 'the good old Queen' and speaks of the rather embarrassing attention which she paid to him: 'The Queen called me up to her dressing-table, and seemed mightily disposed to gossip with me; but instead of enjoying my glory like Madame de Sévigné, I slunk back into the crowd after a few questions. She told Monsieur de Guerchy of it afterwards, and that I had run away from her, but said she would have her revenge at Fontainebleau ... The King, Dauphin, Dauphiness, Mesdames ... did not say a word to me.'[10] Thicknesse gives a very favourable account of the old queen (Louis XV was seven years younger than his Polish wife):

> The Queen is a little cheerful looking woman, and though she was but just recovered from a dangerous fit of illness, she condescended to walk through the apartments (her sedan chair following her) that those who had not seen her, might have an opportunity; and that those who knew her, might rejoice, and congratulate her upon her recovery; for she is a good woman, and much beloved.[11]

She died in June 1768, two and a half years after her only son, Louis.

The Dauphin, Hume was told when he was presented at court, 'declares himself on every Occasion very strongly in my favour', and when later he went to Versailles with the ambassador to be presented to the Dauphine and her children, he had to face a panegyric from three future kings of France which, he was also informed, was delivered on the express instructions of the Dauphin:

> When I was presented to the Duc de Berry [Louis XVI], a child of ten years of age, he said to me 'Monsieur, vous avez beaucoup de réputation dans ce pays-ci: votre nom est très bien connu; et c'est avec beaucoup de plaisir que je vous vois.' Immediately upon which his brother the Comte de Provence [Louis XVIII], who is two years younger, advanced to me and said, with great presence of mind, 'Monsieur, il y a longtemps que vous êtes attendu dans ce pays-ci avec beaucoup d'impatience; je compte avoir bien du plaisir quand je pourrai lire votre belle histoire.' But what is more remarkable, when we were carried to make our bows to the Comte d'Artois [Charles X], who is about five years of age, and to a young Madame of between two and three, the infant prince likewise advanced to me in order to make his harangue, in which, though it was not very distinct, I heard him mumble the word *Histoire*, and some other terms of panegyric. With him ended the civilities of the royal family of France towards me; and I may say it did not end till their power of speech failed them; for the Princess was too young to be able to articulate a compliment. You may see, by this instance alone, what you could not fail to remark in many other instances, how much greater honour is paid to Letters in France than in England.[12]

Pennant went to Versailles in March 1765 and he observed of Marie Leczinska and her son: 'The Queen looks very old, plain and sickly; . . . the Dauphin, tall, thin and sickly.'[13] When in October of that year Walpole was presented at court, he wrote of his reception by the Dauphin: 'He scarce stays a minute; indeed poor creature, he is a ghost and cannot possibly last three months.' At the very end of the month he wrote to another correspondent: 'The Dauphin will probably hold out very few days. His death, that is, the near prospect of it, fills the *philosophers* with the greatest joy, as it was feared he would endeavour the restoration of the

Jesuits.'[14] On the same day his friend, Cole, who had only just arrived in Paris, decided, in anticipation of the Dauphin's death, that he must do something about providing himself with mourning: 'My Taylor, one Mr Schelling, a Brandenburgher established at Paris, measured me for a Suit of black Cloaths, & a Pompadour-Coloured Great Coat, by way of Morning Gown. As the Dauphin's Death was expected every Day, I ordered my Coat not to be full trimmed with Buttons, that it might serve me without making up fresh Mourning.'

In fact the Dauphin lived until 20 December. Cole took a great interest in his fate. When he later wrote up his account of his visit to Paris, he mentions the disease ('a confirmed dropsy') which brought his life to an end at the age of thirty-six, and speaks of him as 'a most amiable Character, an excellent Husband, tender and good Father & Dutiful Son'. He too speaks of the unseemly joy which the *Philosophes* expressed at the Dauphin's impending disappearance from the scene:

He was a great Freind to the Church, a Protector, as much as laid in his Power, of the Jesuits; consequently maligned, hated & abused by the Deistical Philosophers & their Faction to such a Degree, as it was a shameful Sight to observe the Joy on their Countenances, as fresh Advices came every Day from Fontainbleau confirming the little Hopes of his Recovery. Nay, notwithstanding the great Silence imposed, & generally observed by the French, on any public Calamity, or any Thing respecting the Court, or Politics; where one is presently sent to the Bastille, or some Place of Confinement, for it, yet in private Society this Restraint was less, & People could not help expressing their Hopes & Fears upon this alarming Occasion: for it was presumed, should the Dauphin survive his Father, the Banishments of the Jesuits would be repealed, and their Enemies, with those of Christianity, would be disgraced.[15]

Another prominent figure at the court of Louis XV, Madame de Pompadour, vanished from the scene in April 1764, so that there is little mention of her in the writings of our travellers. When in the previous year Hume was presented at court, he relates, 'all the Courtiers who stood around when I was introduc'd to Me de Pompadour, assured me that she was never heard to say so much to any Man . . . However, even Me Pompadour's Civilities were, if possible, exceeded by those of the Dutchess de Choiseul, the Wife of the Favourite and Prime Minister.'[16]

The next *maîtresse en titre*, Mme Du Barry, attracted a good deal of attention from our travellers from the time of her presentation at court in April 1769. In September Walpole went to Versailles to satisfy his curiousity about her. As he and his companions arrived too early for mass, they went to see the Dauphin and his brothers at dinner:

> You may imagine, this royal mess did not detain us long. Thence to the chapel, where a first row in the balconies was kept for us. Madame du Barri arrived over against us below, without rouge, without powder, and indeed *sans avoir fait sa toilette*; an odd appearance, as she was so conspicuous, close to the altar, and amidst both court and people. She is pretty when you consider her; yet so little striking that I should not have asked who she was. There is nothing bold, assuming or affected in her manner. Her husband's sister was along with her. In the tribune above, surrounded by prelates, was the amorous and still handsome King; one could not help smiling at the mixture of piety, pomp and carnality.[17]

When the Duchess of Northumberland came to France in May 1770, she had much closer contact with the royal mistress. At this stage in her life the duchess was not exactly a beauty (little Harriet Spencer wrote of her two years later: 'She is very fat and has a great beard almost like a man').[18] She offers this portrait of Mme Du Barry when she was presented to her:

> I own I expected her to be handsomer. She had nothing on her head, but 7 fine Diamond Pins, a negligée of Chintz with very little Gold. She is rather of a tall, middle size, full breasted, and is pretty but not to be call'd handsome, very like the print but not as well, & has a strong Look of her former profession. Her Complexion is fair & clear & her skin very smooth, but her Bloom is entirely gone off, she wears Rouge but in a very small Quantity & of a faint Colour. Her Face is oval, rather long, her Forehead high but her Hair which is very fine & in great quantity grows very well upon it.
>   Her Eyes are of a lively light Blue & she has the most wanton Look in them that I ever saw. Her Eyebrows are well form'd, and so is her Nose; her mouth is pretty, her Lips very

red & her Teeth fine, but she has a kind of artificial smirk which also savours strongly of her old trade. Her Chin is very pretty, her Voice loud, her Air very good, & her manner obliging & civil, but vulgar. Her Behaviour extreamly free & chearful, Her Disposition Benevolent, good natured, generous and charitable, but her Temper I imagine as warm as her Constitution, her Language very rough & indelicate when she is angry. She is lodged in parts of the Kings apartment in the Attic.

She received me very civilly and was rather kind than polite, insisting on my sending to her Stables, Kitchen & Cellar as tho they were my own.

Later on the same day she saw Mme Du Barry again, this time together with a prince of the blood (Comte de la Marche), a great nobleman who was one of the king's intimate circle (Prince de Soubise), the longest-serving Secretary of State (the Comte de St Florentin), the Abbé Terray (*Contrôleur général*) and other ministers. Her behaviour and language, though natural enough, seemed somewhat out of place in such company: 'She had 4 Femmes de Chambre, 2 on their Feet & 2 on their Knees. She seem'd in a very bad Humour & call'd them a great many Betes & scolding one of them in particular, she said she believ'd never *Truye* [sow] produced a "Cochon si Bete". The Comte de St. Florentin said to her, "N'Impatientez vous pas, Madame", she replied with great fierceness, "Taisez vous, cela savouroit beaucoup des Porcherons."'

Two days later in a conversation with the mistress the duchess was told that 'the King himself was the best Man in the World but that many of his Ministers were great Rogues'. Before leaving Versailles she was invited to dine with the mistress and two other women: 'We had a small Dinner but perfectly good & neatly served. There was a very small plate of pease which cost 4 Louis. Upon my saying I loved Strawberrys she (without saying anything to me) immediately sent for some & made me eat up almost the whole dish & would not touch one herself. She would have persuaded me to stay & see the Bal masquee but it was not in my power as I had left my Women in Paris.'[19] On returning there she picked up various pieces of gossip about Mme Du Barry and her family, but these are of less interest than her account of her face to face encounters with the mistress.

Lady Mary Coke, who arrived in Paris in April 1771 in the

midst of the turmoil caused by Maupeou's reforms, noted: 'The power of Madame de Barry increases every day: nothing is done without her approbation.'[20] Later in the same year Walpole, who in Paris had moved in the same aristocratic circles which were hostile to Maupeou, wrote scathingly on his return to England of both Louis XV and his mistress:

> The besotted old *Bien-aimé* neither desires this increase of power, nor feels for the sufferings it occasions; but shudders for his own life, and yet lets Abigail, who has still less sense than himself, plunge him into all these difficulties and shame. This street-walker has just received the homage of Europe. The Holy Nuncio and every ambassador but he of Spain, have waited on her, and brought gold, frankincense and myhrr. Fuentes alone would neither bend the knee to her or to the Chancellor.

'The *vive le Roi*', he wrote in the same letter, is 'certainly extinguished at present; . . . an old King, like Hercules betwixt virtue and vice, torn different ways by a bigot daughter [Louise, a Carmelite nun] and an idiot bunter.'[21]

Moore, who arrived in France with the young Duke of Hamilton in 1772, noted the loss of prestige by Louis XV, but also points out how respect for him was not yet totally destroyed:

> Although the enthusiastic affection which the people of this nation once felt for their present monarch be greatly abated, it is not annihilated. Some of the courtiers indeed, who are supposed to administer to the King's pleasures, are detested. The imprudent ostentatious luxury of the mistress, is publicly execrated; but their censure of the King, even where they think themselves quite safe, never bursts out as it would in some other nations, in violent expressions, such as, Curse his folly, — his weakness, or — his obstinacy. No: Even their censure of him is intermingled with a kind of affectionate regret. — Naturellement il est bon, they say. — And when they observe the deplorable anxiety and disgust in his countenance, which are the concomitants of a constitution jaded by pleasure, and of a mind incapable of application, they cry: Mon Dieu, qu'il est triste! — il est malheureux lui-même; — comment peut-il penser à nous autres?[22]

The year of Peckham's visit to France cannot be precisely stated (all we know is that the first edition of his *Tour* appeared in 1772), but it obviously portrays Louis XV in his last years. He provides a description of the king out shooting:

> He has a manly countenance, a penetrating eye, and fine features, rather corpulent, and so helpless, that matter of state, in being assisted to get out of his carriage and upon his horse, was in fact, a matter of necessity.
>
> ... He was attended by about two hundred horsemen, and forty or fifty chasseurs on foot, with guns in their hands, the Prince de Soubise, and the Count de March, son of the Prince de Conti, were the only nobles permitted to shoot; they fired on horseback ...
>
> The moment the King had fired, another gun was put into his hand, which was instantly discharged. I had the curiosity to observe his first thirty shots, in which number, he only missed twice.
>
> He is proud of being esteemed the best shot in the kingdom, a most royal accomplishment! Nature certainly intended him for a game-keeper, but as a satire on mankind, let him be King.[23]

At Senlis, on his journey to Paris, Peckham had earlier run into one of the king's shooting expeditions:

> The king was hunting in the neighbourhood, and was to return through the town to Versailles in the evening. So careful were the inhabitants of their *Grand Monarque* that all the signs were removed, lest peradventure they might fall on his royal pate. There were relays of carriages and guards, at the distance of every six miles, waiting on the road, which was covered with his numerous retinue. It had more the appearance of a triumphal entry than a return from partridge shooting.[24]

Peckham obviously enjoyed writing down his version of the well-known epigram on Bouchardon's equestrian statue of Louis XV which was set up in what is now the Place de la Concorde:

> Bouchardon est un animal
> Et son Ouvrage fait pitié

> Il met le vice à cheval,
>   Et les quatre vertus à pie.[25]

On 6 November 1772 the Spencer family was at Versailles. 'We went to the *partie de chasse*', writes Lady Harriet. 'It is St. Hubert's day, who is the saint of hunting. They told us the Royal Family alone had 1500 horses out, and there was a great crowd besides . . . Such numbers of people in red, blue, & green gold, glittering in the sun with their *piqueurs*, servants, horses & carriages, made it a fine sight.' In the evening they saw a performance given by actors from the Comédie Française, including Lekain. 'All the Royal Family were there on one side, and Mad. du Barry in a great box on the other. The King is a handsome old man, but he seemed to sleep the greatest part of the play.'

In the following year the family spent some time in Paris on their return journey. On 7 May they visited Mme du Barry's château at Louveciennes (sometimes known as Lucienne). On the following day Lady Harriet made the following entry in her diary:

> Here is mama's account of Lucienne, which mama told me I had better copy as it is such a curious place and is so much talk'd of for belonging to the King's great favourite. The house of Lucienne is very small but beautifully furnished with clouded lutestrings and a profusions of glasses, bronzes, gilding & china. It formerly belonged to the Countess de Thoulouse, an old princess of the blood, to whom the King gave it for her life. Since her death he has given it to Mad. du Barry for ever . . . The expense & luxury with which these rooms are fitted up is carried to the utmost height, and must be seen not to exceed belief. Everything even to the handles of the doors, not only of the finest materials, but finished like a snuff box. Most of the furniture is white lutestring or sattin richly embroidered to suit the hangings of the rooms. The gradual degree of splendour from the vestibule to the boudoir is well kept up, increasing in each room till the King's cabinet, where it is poured out *à pleines mains*.

Then comes some of the gossip which Lady Spencer had picked up about the mistress's extravagance:

> In short the sum she costs is so enormous, & the King so infatuated, that I cannot help putting down some circumstances

that I have heard on the best authority. The pension is at present 1,500,000 (£62,000) besides unlimited credit on the Treasury. She sends drafts for whatever she wants, and sometimes gratifies her friends with a blanc seing. She has most valuable jewels and great services of plate with her own arms (Lord Barrymore's) to an immense amount, and it is said refused all title, hoping to get her husband created an Irish peer, meaning to retire to England on the king's death. He passes almost all his time with her. She reads all his letters. He received some not long ago at a *souper de cérémonie*, one from one of his daughters, she put her arm around his neck & read it over his shoulder, opening another soon after and reading it before him. She always sits by him, walks on his right hand, precedes every one but the King's family.[26]

On 30 April 1774 Swinburne wrote to his brother to describe how on 26 April he had been to Versailles with the ambassador and the Duke of Dorset to be presented:

About eleven, the introductors gave notice of the king's levee being ready, and so, in company of a German baron, we trudged up stairs, and surprised his most Christian majesty in his waistcoat: for none but the family ambassadors can see him in buff.
After staring at us, talking about the opera with some few of the crowds of courtiers, and saying about one minute's prayer with his cardinal,[27] he drew towards us, who were ranged near the door in rank and file. All he said was, 'Est-il fils du vieux Duc de Dorset, que j'ai connu autrefois?' and so marched off.

After being presented to the younger members of the royal family, Swinburne and the others made their way up to the mistress's apartment:

After all these perambulations up stairs and down stairs through the royal family, we climbed up a dark winding staircase, which I should have suspected would have led to an apartment of the Bastile, rather than to the temple of love and elegance. In a low entresol we found the favourite sultana in her morning gown, her capuchin on, and her hair undressed; she was very gracious, and chatted a good deal, as every body else seemed to do at Versailles, about the opera. I could hardly refrain from laughing at an involuntary exclamation from my brother presentee, the Duke, whose mistress, Mrs. Parsons, has you know, been long out of her teens. 'Good heavens!' said his grace in a whisper to me, 'why, her bloom is quite past.'

She is of a middling age, just plump enough, her face rather upon the yellow leaf, her eyes good, and all her features regular; but I cannot think her a pleasing figure now, whatever she may have been, or may be still, when made up and decked out in her pride.

Her reign, like that of the king, was almost at an end. Swinburne's letter contains towards the end the words. 'This morning news came of the King having the small-pox.' On April 27 Louis XV had begun to feel unwell; by 10 May he was dead, and in the night of 12–13 May Mme Du Barry was arrested and locked up by *lettre de cachet* in a convent. On 11 May Swinburne could write to his brother: 'It was my lot to be the last person to be presented to the king and Madame du Barré.'[28]

Even at the beginning of our period, two of our travellers saw trouble ahead for Louis XV's successor from the new spirit of freedom which they detected in the air. Writing allegedly from Nice in March 1765, Smollett vaguely predicted some future upheaval in France:

There are, undoubtedly, many marks of relaxation in the reins of the French government, and, in all probability, the subjects of France will be the first to take advantage of it. There is at present a violent fermentation of different principles among them, which under the reign of a very weak prince, or during a long minority, may produce a great change in the constitution. In proportion to the progress of reason and philosophy, which have made great advances in this kingdom, superstition loses ground, antient prejudices give way; a spirit of freedom takes the ascendant.[29]

He foresees a variety of sources of conflict — the alienation of enlightened laymen from the Catholic Church, the grievances of the Protestant minority, the dissatisfaction of the wealthy section of the middle class with its lowly position in society, and the challenge which the *Parlements* presented to the royal authority.

In the same year Cole saw a grim future ahead for France: 'In short, the present Situation of France has much the Appearance of being soon the Theatre of a civil War.' Though the Dauphin, whose final illness he had followed very closely while in Paris, did not die until Cole was back in England, when he came to write up his journal, he declared that God 'took him to Himself . . . at the same Time releasing him of his Pains & delivering him from the Troubles & Uneasinesses preparing for him by a factious & turbulent Spirit forming among his Subjects, had he lived, which, in all Probability, will end in downright Rebellion, Anarchy & Confusion'.[30]

Thicknesse agrees with Smollett's remark about the 'many marks of relaxation in the reins of the French government'. Indeed, he puts the matter even more bluntly: 'He might have gone farther, and have said, "there are very few marks of any permanent government at all"!' Elsewhere he maintains that France is too large a country to be governed effectively: 'The springs of government lose their elasticity by being too remote from the first mover; they would do so, in a great measure, were the first movements ever so well regulated; at present it has no regulation at all.' Although in many ways he admired Louis XV, he had no illusions about his ability to govern:

> The king has three million sterling in his private purse, which makes him easy let what will happen; for he esteems that more than any thing.
>
> He hates the duke de C[hoiseul]; but does not change hands, because he says he is convinced all men and ministers are alike. In short, H.M.C.M. is one of those few kings who has born that high title near half a century, and consequently it is not to be wondered at, if he be not tired both of governing, and *being governed*; and therefore he minds, at this day, little else but gratifying his passions, which neither loss of family, *favourites*, or even of part of his dominions, deprive him from pursuing every day.[31]

Whether or not Thicknesse was right about Louis's attitude to Choiseul, the duke was undoubtedly the most powerful minister of the period down to his dismissal at the end of 1770. He was made Secretary of State for Foreign Affairs in 1758 and three years later became Secretary of State for both War and the Navy; although he gave up Foreign Affairs in 1761 and the Navy in 1766 when he took back Foreign Affairs, both these posts were held by his cousin and he remained the dominant figure in the government. Walpole, who had much closer contacts with him than Thicknesse could have, had no high opinion of him. His first impression was obtained on the day he was presented at court in 1765: 'After dinner [I] was presented by Monsieur de Guerchy to the Duc de Choiseul ... The first minister is a little volatile being, whose countenance and manner had nothing to frighten me for my country. I saw him but for three seconds, which is as much as he allows to any body or thing.'[32] Four years later he saw much more of him as through Mme de Deffand he became very friendly with the duchess: 'I spent five evenings in a week with the Duchesse de Choiseul and her select friends in the summer of 1769. The Duke often of the party.' He gives as an example of the minister's fatuity an incident in the war between Turkey and Russia. For his own reasons Choiseul had consistently urged the Turks to go to war. Catherine astonished everyone in Western Europe by sending a fleet into the Mediterranean against the Turks for whom the war was to end disastrously. 'But few days before this intelligence reached him, he had the vain levity, as I was supping with him in his own house, to send for the last Paris Gazette, which he had dictated himself, to prove the late victory of the Turks, and read it to the company.'[33]

Our travellers frequently comment on the continuing clash between the Crown and both the Paris and the provincial *Parlements* which were bent on asserting the power which they wielded owing to the restoration to them by the Regent of their right to make remonstrances before registering royal edicts and thus giving them force of law. Smollett had noted how 'all the parliaments, or tribunals of justice in the kingdom, seem bent upon asserting their rights and independence in the face of the king's prerogative, and even at the expence of his power and authority'.[34] Travellers who came to France slightly later have more to say on this subject as the clash between the monarch and the Paris *Parlement*, by far the most important of these courts, became entwined with what is known as 'l'affaire de Bretagne'.

Down to our own day Brittany has been noted for its particularist tendencies. In addition to a *Parlement* at Rennes, it also had Estates which met every two years and often gave the central government a good deal of trouble. A great nobleman, the Duc

The Last Years of Louis XV

d'Aiguillon, who was Commandant of the province (that is, the representative, along with the *Intendant*, of the central government) had repeated difficulties with the Estates and the *Parlement*. Matters came to a head in 1764 when the *Parlement* registered a financial edict only with various reservations and made strong criticisms of d'Aiguillon's administration of the province. The duke and La Chalotais, the *procureur général* (attorney general) of the *Parlement*, were on particularly bad terms, and when a deputation of the *Parlement* was summoned to the court, Louis XV took La Chalotais aside and warned him about his future conduct.

The deputation returned to Rennes, and far from showing remorse for its past behaviour, it drew up fresh remonstrances in which it maintained that only the Estates General could approve new taxes. Later in the year it backed up the Estates of the province in resisting new taxes, and when the government issued an edict quashing its ban on the levying of the new taxes in the province, the judges suspended the administration of justice. Finally, in May 1765, encouraged in its stand by the other *Parlements*, all the judges except twelve resigned their posts.

Thicknesse may take up the story at this point. He sympathised strongly with the *Parlements*' struggle for 'that birthright of all men, LIBERTY', and he declares that they and particularly the *Parlement* at Rennes 'have immortalized themselves by their resolution, wisdom and sufferings'. This is how he introduces the story of the arrest of La Chalotais and his son, who had been appointed his successor:

> In May, 1765, the parliament of Bretagne were, by a short note sent them, signed by the king, suspended from their functions, and ordered to remain in the town of Rennes till they were further informed with his pleasure; and the month following Mr. Belongelais [de la Bellangerais], a gentleman of Bretagne, was arrested and sent prisoner to the Bastile in Paris; and at the same time two engravers were arrested, their papers seized, and imprisoned in the town of Vitre, where they were closely examined relative to the publication of certain *libels*! *libels, I say*, for *libels* are not the *growth* of England *alone*.[35] The next person arrested was madame la marquise de la Roche, who was also conducted to the Bastile, accompanied by her *femme de chambre*. I should have told you, a little before this appeared at Rennes, a print, on which was engraved the names of those officers of parliament who had

249

not signed the act of their dismission. This print was decorated with a great number of initial letters, namely d'J. et de F. at the top of which was a medallion, whereon was cut several large J.F.'s and on it a crown of JFs. Round the medallion was the following motto, *nunc & ab omni aevo*. These J's and F's, no doubt, stood for *Judex Fidelis*.[36] But what rendered this rather too serious a joke is, that there was engraved on them also, that the marquise de la Roche and monsieur de la Belengerais were the authors and distributors of them.

After relating how a canon of Quimper cathedral was arrested and imprisoned in Paris and a young man arrested for allegedly sending an anonymous letter to the Comte de St Florentin, he comes at last to the fate of La Chalotais and his son:

> Some time in July the *procureur du roi*, who brought an arret of parliament to Rennes, received by the post, addressed to him, several pieces of paper, whereupon many things were wrote in prose and verse, of a libellous nature, though perhaps composed of true matter, one of which was a parody of a letter of Monsieur le comte Florentin's. Another was an epitaph on the *deceased* parliament of Bretagne. Some of these papers were also engraved; on one of which was wrote *Coniat, seneschal de Rouen* [Rennes]. On another was wrote *de votre feu parlement*. In short, these papers, embellished with a great number of devices, that were well understood by the inhabitants of Bretagne, and severely *resented* by the *courtiers* at Versailles, occasioned a great number of innocent people, and all perhaps well meaning, to suffer imprisonment under many cruel aggravations.

Thicknesse was convinced of the innocence of La Chalotais, father and son, who were arrested in November 1765:

> Poor Monsieur de la Chalotais and his son, were confined in separate and wretched apartments in the castle of St. Maloes, without being permitted to see each other, or partake of the benefit of the air or exercise, which had brought the old gentleman's health to a dangerous state. And what renders it still harder, he and his son too, both protest their innocence, and that they neither directly nor indirectly were the authors or publishers of the papers in question.

After quoting a letter of La Chalotais to the king in which he protested his innocence, Thicknesse works in an allusion to British politics of the 1760s: 'In short, France has its butes* to shoot at [*Bute signifies, in French, a butt, to shoot at for a prize] as well as other countries, and every soil produces a W[ilke]s, a Ch[urchi]ll, and a C[hatha]m.'[37]

A special court was set up to try La Chalotais and his son and a new *Parlement* installed at Rennes. This produced indignant protests from both the Paris and the other provincial *Parlements*. In accordance with its claim that the different *Parlements* of France were merely branches of one body, the Paris *Parlement* drew up repeated remonstrances protesting against the treatment of their Breton colleagues. Finally the king's patience gave out, and in March 1766 he went in person to the Palais de Justice and held a *séance royale*, known as the 'séance de flagellation' because of the scathing terms in which he spoke of the political claims of the *Parlement*. He reaffirmed — only two decades before 1789 — the absolutist principle that the monarch was the source of all power, including legislative power.

Walpole, who was in Paris at this moment, followed developments closely. On 10 March he wrote to a former ambassador in Paris:

> There has been a violent clap of thunder here. Tother morning the King, with all his lightnings about him, appeared suddenly in the parliament, ordered four privy councillors, not peers, to follow him into the chamber and sit at his feet, where he bid them read a *Discours*, in which he informed the giants, that they were nothing but magistrates and rebels, and that he alone is Jupiter Omnipotent and Omniscient. He forbids union with the Titans of other parliaments, and prohibits their forging and printing any more remonstrances in Aetna. They may whisper in his divine ear, but no more murmurs. He then dispatched a courier to Roan [Rouen], for three presidents, whom he sent back again still more haughtily, only referring them to his *Discours*.

Walpole then relates an incident which illustrated the king's outward piety: 'As he crossed the Pont Neuf, he met his neighbour the Bon Dieu, lighted from his eagle, kneeled down in the dirt, and as Trincale says in *The Tempest*, acknowledged the Viceroy over him'. Walpole then resumes his narrative of events in the same bantering style:

The new god's back was no sooner turned, than Messieurs les Titans appointed a committee to consider what was to be done. They sat seven days and nights — and what do you think was the first thing they determined — to send three of their body, now shrunk like Milton's devils to pygmies, to condole on the death of King Stanislas [Louis's father-in-law]. A voice from a cloud said, 'Je n'ai que faire de vos condoléances.' Well, they sent again to beg to know when the god might be approached: 'What have you to say?' 'We don't know.' 'Return and bring me word.' They went, came, and said: 'Our soul is humbled to the dust, hear us, good Lord, hear us!' Jupiter named seven o'clock last night; forty-two commissioners went with a collect of repentance, to which, it is said, they have tacked a remonstrance, ten times stronger than their former; and thus have stolen a march upon omniscience.[38]

The last remark is scarcely accurate, though the Paris *Parlement* did continue to protest against the imprisonment and trial of La Chalotais and his Breton colleagues; when proceedings against them were quashed, the *Parlement* continued to protest against the exile into which they had been sent. Finally, in 1768, D'Aiguillon resigned his post as commandant, and in the following year the *Parlement* of Rennes was reinstated.

In the meantime the Paris *Parlement* continued to oppose the financial measures to which the government was driven by the financial needs of the Treasury; clearly the 'séance de flagellation' had had no effect. What led directly to the bold reforms undertaken in 1771 by a new chancellor, Maupeou, was once again the 'affaire de Bretagne'. When the king curtly rejected the petition of the *Parlement* of Rennes for the recall of La Chalotais and his son from their exile, it opened proceedings against D'Aiguillon. These were quashed by the government, but the duke insisted on being allowed to defend himself. For a peer the appropriate tribunal was the Paris *Parlement*, or rather the most august form of that body, the *cour des pairs*, which required the attendance of the princes of the blood and the *ducs et pairs*.

The trial opened at Versailles in April 1770 and dragged on until the end of June, when the king held a *lit de justice* and quashed the whole proceedings. The *Parlement* was furious and forbade D'Aiguillon to fulfil any of the functions of a *duc et pair* until he had cleared himself before the *cour des pairs* of the charges brought against him. The king quashed these proceedings too, but the *Parlement* did not give way. On 11 July Stanhope wrote to his mother from Paris in terms which show what violent passions this case aroused:

> The Principal Topic of Conversation here at present is the Affair of the Duke d'Aiguillon. The Parliament have already published one Edict of Condemnation against him, which the King out of the Plenitude of his Power has thought proper to annull; And this Day it is expected we shall have something of the same Nature published by the Parliament, which perhaps the King may treat in the same royal Manner. One thing however his Majesty who seems to be his only Friend, can not do; he can not reinstate him in the good Opinion of the World; who as far as I can see, seem generally to condemn him, and to think that tho' his Head may remain on his Shoulders and his Estate in his Possession, it is no Proof he does not deserve to loose both. He was Governor of low Bretagny, and is accused of almost all sorts of Crimes that a Governor can commit.[39]

The Paris *Parlement*'s refusal to give way led it straight on to its doom and that of the provincial *Parlements*. A new government team was being formed which would take a much stronger line with the *Parlements* than Choiseul had done. Since the installation, in 1768, of a new chancellor, René Nicolas Maupeou, and the presentation of Mme Du Barry in the following year, the chief minister's days were numbered, especially as in 1769 Maupeou was joined in the government by a new *contrôleur général*, Abbé Terray, who was also hostile to him. In December 1770 Choiseul was relieved of all his offices and exiled to his estate at Chanteloup.

The Paris *Parlement* continued to intervene in the dispute between the Crown and the *Parlement* at Rennes. At the end of November Maupeou sent for registration a royal edict forbidding the *Parlements* to claim to act as one body, to correspond with one another and to suspend the administration of justice, under penalty of confiscation of their posts. The *Parlement* was faced with an awkward dilemma: either to obey and renounce all its political claims or to risk a head-on collision with the government. When it met on 3 December, it decided to make representations against the edict. At a *lit de justice* held at Versailles, Maupeou declared that once the king had rejected the remonstrances of the *Parlement* against a new edict, the matter was closed. The *Parlement*'s answer was to suspend the administration of justice and offer fresh remonstrances which the king refused to receive until the judges had resumed their functions. On 13 December Gilly (George James) Williams wrote from Paris:

> There is the devil to pay here between the King and the Parliament. The King held a *lit de justice* last week, in order to cause an edict to be registered, which the Parliament has refused to register. The edict was to restrain the privileges of remonstrating in Parliament. They yesterday sent the *premier Président* to desire the King to annul the edict, or accept of all their resignations. The King's answer is not yet known.

The letter has a postscript: 'The King has refused to give an answer till the Parliament *ait repris ses fonctions*.[40]

As the judges repeatedly refused to obey this command, Maupeou acted. During the night of 19–20 January 1771 each received a *lettre de cachet* ordering him to resume his functions and to state in writing whether, *oui* or *non*, he was prepared to do so. The great majority refused and received *lettres de cachet*, declaring their posts confiscated and exiling them to various parts of the provinces. To take the place of the *Parlement* one of the royal councils was installed in the Palais de Justice, but the *avocats* and *procureurs* refused to recognise the new court and justice was at a standstill.

Despite the opposition of the other Paris sovereign courts and the provincial *Parlements* Maupeou went ahead with his reforms. As the area of jurisdiction of the Paris *Parlement* was notoriously too large, new courts were set up in six provincial towns to judge all the civil and criminal cases previously dealt with in Paris. The Paris *Parlement* was kept, but restricted to judging cases concerning the Crown and the peers of the realm; its right to register laws and present remonstrances against them was also preserved. The same edict contained two further reforms — the abolition of the buying and selling of judicial posts and of all charges to litigants. In April the king installed a new *Parlement* in Paris, and when the provincial *Parlements* protested, they too were reformed. Two of them were replaced by lesser courts, and although they kept the title of *Parlement*, the rest were reduced in size, and both the sale of their posts and the charging of fees to litigants were abolished. Very often a great many of the existing judges refused to continue to serve; they were replaced by new men and sent into exile. When in November 1772 Lady Harriet Spencer passed through Toulouse, the seat of one of the most important provincial *Parlements*, she noted: 'The few people of consequence in the town do nothing but lament their Parliament being nearly destroyed, and some of their Magistrates sent into banishment.'[41]

The furious opposition encountered by Maupeou's reforms offered a kind of dress rehearsal for the aristocratic revolt of 1787 and 1788. The princes of the blood, who since the Fronde had been kept silent by the Crown, won popularity by their protests against these arbitrary acts. The nobility, especially in those provinces which had estates, proclaimed its solidarity with the judicial members of its order. Nor was opposition by any means confined to the aristocracy although many of the changes made by Maupeou were to the advantage of the general public. Matters were made worse by the unpopular financial measures which the sorry state of the royal finances compelled Terray to take.

Lady Mary Coke, who arrived in Paris in April 1771, observed of the political situation there: 'Every thing with regard to Politicks is in great confusion: everybody thinks the Chancellor a bold man, & 'tis not easy to say what turn things will take.'[42] When Walpole returned to Paris in the following July, he heard nothing but cries of woe in the aristocratic circles in which he moved. In his *Memoirs of the Reign of King George III* he declares that during this visit he 'was witness to the final overthrow of their constitution' and proceeds to offer a very unflattering portrait of Maupeou:

> I never saw character written in more legible features than in those of Maupeou. He was sallow and black, with eyes equally penetrating, acute, and suspicious. His complexion spoke determinate villainy; his eyes seemed either roving in quest of prey for it, or glaring on snares that he apprehended. His parts were great and his courage adventurous. Power was his object, despotism his road, the clergy his instrument; but the hardness and cruelty of his nature showed that severity was as agreeable to his temper as to his views.

Looking back on the situation that he found in Paris, he mentions both the continued popularity of Choiseul who in his exile at Chanteloup attracted numerous admirers of the highest rank, and the financial expedients adopted by Terray to deal with the crisis in the royal finances. These included reductions in the pensions paid by the Treasury:

To the city of Paris, and to the ruined counsellors of the Parliaments, the Duke remained still dear. They coupled his cause with their own, from the unity of time. The Chancellor adopted the same idea to incense the King against both. The depopulation of Paris ensued. So many families were undone by the new edicts and stoppages of payments, and so many persons attached to the late Parliament had quitted the capital, that in less than twelve months one hundred thousand persons were computed to have retired into the provinces, and such as could escape into other countries. The King's servants were unpaid; trade at a stand; distress and dissatisfaction in every countenance. Daggers threatened the King and Chancellor: the Comptroller-General threatened to plunder every body else to prevent a national bankruptcy.[43]

Shortly after his arrival in Paris at the end of July 1771, he wrote a long letter on the political situation in which he stresses not only the continued popularity of Choiseul but also that of the Duc d'Orléans and the Prince de Condé who drew large numbers of visitors to their estates at Villers-Cotterêts and Chantilly while the court at Compiègne was deserted:

> The distress here is incredible, especially at Court. The King's tradesmen are ruined, his servants starving, and even angels and archangels cannot get their pensions and salaries, but sing Woe! woe! woe! instead of Hosannas. Compiègne is abandoned; Viller-Coterets and Chantilly crowded, and Chanteloup still more in fashion, whither everybody goes that pleases, though, when they ask leave, the answer is, *Je ne le defends ni le permets*. This is the first time that ever the will of a king of France was interpreted against his inclination. Yet, after annihilating his parliament and ruining public credit, he tamely submits to being affronted by his own servants.

Yet much as he tended to adopt the views of his aristocratic friends, Walpole was too clear-sighted to fail to see that their opposition would not last long: 'Madame de Beauveau and two or three high-spirited dames defy this czar of Gaul. Yet they and their cabal are as inconsistent on the other hand. They make epigrams, sing vaudevilles against the mistress, hand about libels against the Chancellor, and have no more effect than a sky-rocket; but in three months will die to go to Court, and to be invited to sup with Madame du Barry.'

Walpole then proceeds to speak of the rivalry between Maupeou and the newly-appointed Secretary of State for Foreign Affairs, the Duc d'Aiguillon, the former Commandant of Brittany:

> The only real struggle is between the Chancellor and the Duc d'Aiguillon. The first is false, bold, determined, and not subject to little qualms. The other is less known, communicates himself to nobody, is suspected of deep policy and deep designs, but seems to intend to set out under a mask of very smooth varnish, for he has just obtained the payment of all his bitter enemy La Chalotais's pensions and arrears. He has the advantage too of being but moderately detested in comparison of his rival, and what he values more, the interest of the mistress.

Of the third important member of the government (these three ministers were known as the Triumvirate) Walpole writes:

> The Comptroller General serves both, by acting mischief more sensibly felt; for he ruins everybody but those who purchase a respite from his mistress. He dispenses bankruptcies by retail, and will fall, because he cannot even by these means be useful enough. They are striking off nine millions from the *caisse militaire*, five from the marine, and one from the *affaires étrangères*; yet all this will not extricate them.

He concludes this gloomy picture of the state of France in the summer of 1771 with the remark: 'You never saw a great nation in so disgraceful a position.'[44]

Early in the next month he wrote in similar grim terms to another correspondent:

> New *arrêts*, new retrenchments, new misery, stalk forth every day. The Parliament of Besançon is dissolved; so are the *Grenadiers de France*. The King's tradesmen are all bankrupt, no pensions are paid, and everybody is reforming their suppers and equipages. Despotism makes converts faster than ever Christianity did. Louis XV is the true *Rex Christianissimus*, and has ten times more success than his dragooning great grandfather.

Back at Strawberry Hill in September, Walpole felt rather freer to express himself about the king, his ministers and the state of France:

> For the misery of his people, and for the danger of his successors (if he escapes himself) the King, I think, will triumph over his country — a victory which most kings prefer, not only to peace, but to foreign laurels. The Princes of the Blood are firm without spirit or sense: the nobility have as little of either — the vigour of parliamentary remonstrances are hushed by the English remedy, bribery, and the people curse the King, the Chancellor, the mistress, and starve. Besançon, Douay, Toulouse, Grenoble, and by this time Bordeaux, have lost their parliaments, or accepted new ones. In some are erected superior councils. This variety proves how wrong the system is, or how incomplete.

Of Maupeou he writes: 'The Chancellor does as much hurt *against* all law, as any of his profession ever did *by* law. He is very able, very enterprising, and after being the most servile flatterer, proves the most inhuman tyrant.' He also expands his earlier remarks on the Duc d'Aiguillon: 'He is very gracious, but very dark, *and by some circumstances*, I believe so great a politician that he is a very little one; that is, he will spring a mine to blow up an ant hill.' There is the usual tale of the ruin inflicted by Terray's policies — 'Every body is pillaged, and numbers ruined' — but surprisingly he now seems to find these policies effective, for he goes on: 'The army is much reduced, and if corruption does not prevent it, their finances will soon be in good order.'

Although he again mentions how popular Choiseul remains, he judges him severely: 'The Duc de Choiseul acts joy, spirits, happiness: receives all the world, treats all the world, and thinks himself not only the greatest minister, but the most beloved that ever was; not reflecting how foolishly he threw away his power; and insensible to the ruin he is drawing on his friends, and on himself too.' After repeating the king's answer to requests for permission to visit Chanteloup, he goes on:

> This has passed for permission; but the King has said he would remember those who should go — and he will not want remembrancers. In short, the proscription is already commenced. The Prince of Beauvau is removed from the government of Languedoc, worth 103,000 livres a year, under

pretence that having opposed the fate of the Parliament of Paris, he could not be proper to dissolve that of Toulouse. The Duc de Duras is to lose the government of Bretagne, and I know from very good authority that not one person placed by Choiseul but will be removed within a year. His own Swiss guards are to be taken away, *bongré, malgré*.[45]

Moore arrived in Paris in the following year. In *A View of Society and Manners*, which appeared in 1779, he expresses great admiration for the courageous struggle which the old *Parlements* had conducted against the royal power. He praises in particular the Paris *Parlement*: 'Some of these remonstrances display not only examples of the most sublime and pathetic eloquence, but also breathe a spirit of freedom which would do honour to a British House of Commons. The resistance which the members of the parliament of Paris made to the will of the king does them the greatest honour.' He was correspondingly shocked by the treatment it had received from Maupeou, though he was realist enough not to be surprised at the way the mass of Frenchmen quickly recovered from their first indignation:

> The security, and even the existence, of the parliament of Paris, depending entirely on the pleasure of the king, and having no other weapons, offensive or defensive, but justice, argument, and reason, their fate might have been foreseen — the usual fate of those who have no other artillery to oppose to power: — The members were disgraced, and the parliament abolished. The measure was considered as violent; the exiles were regarded as martyrs; the people were astonished and grieved. At length, recovering from their surprise, they dissipated their sorrow, as they do on all occassions of great calamity, — by some very merry songs.[46]

Despite the outcry raised by Maupeou's reforms, things soon settled down; the new *Parlements* and other courts got into their stride fairly rapidly. Although Terray did little to improve the financial situation which was to weigh so heavily on Louis XV's successor, he did manage to keep the government afloat. But the whole future of the reformed courts of justice and the continuation of the Triumvirate in power hung on the life of Louis XV. When he was carried off by smallpox in May 1774, Maupeou's reforms were rapidly undone and all three men were sent into exile.

That Louis XV was not mourned by his subjects was clearly seen by two of our travellers. The day after the king's death Swinburne wrote to his brother: 'I never, indeed, saw joy more visible than it appears to be on the loss of this same Louis *le bien aimé*, whose illness was once the object of so much alarm and anxiety. Indeed, never did a king deserve more than he did to lose the affection of his people.'[47] Lady Mary Coke was also in Paris during Louis XV's last illness. She visited the royal vault at St Denis and on the way back encountered the funeral cortège coming from Versailles: 'I thought it indecent to see them go so fast; for the Guards who follow'd the Coach gallop'd. The mob was very great & very indecent; so far from showing the least concern they hoop'd & hollow'd, as if they had been at a horse race instead of a funeral procession; never was a King less regretted.'[48]

Notes

1. *A View of Society and Manners*, vol. I, pp. 33–4, 38–46.
2. Duchess of Leinster, *Correspondence*, vol. I, pp. 379–80.
3. *Letters*, vol. I, p. 408.
4. *Correspondence*, vol. 35, p. 112 (cf. vol. 39, p. 13).
5. *Tour on the Continent*, pp. 27–8.
6. *Useful Hints*, p. 62; *Observations*, pp. 48–9; *Useful Hints*, pp. 201–2; *Observations*, p. 49.
7. *Travels into France and Italy*, vol. I, p. 12.
8. *Correspondence*, vol. 10, p. 292.
9. *Diaries of a Duchess*, pp. 111, 117, 127, 128–9.
10. *Correspondence*, vol. 35, p. 112; vol. 39, p. 13.
11. *Observations*, p. 57.
12. *Letters*, vol. I, pp. 414–15, 417; *New Letters*, pp. 75–6.
13. *Tour of the Continent*, p. 28.
14. *Correspondence*, vol. 35, p. 113; vol. 39, p. 22. Later, in his *Memoirs of the Reign of King George III* (vol. II, pp. 241–2), Walpole argues, most implausibly, that the Dauphin was really a *Philosophe*.
15. *Journal*, pp. 93–4.
16. *Letters*, vol. I, pp. 407–8.
17. *Correspondence*, vol. 10, pp. 291–2.
18. *Lady Bessborough and her Family Circle*, p. 19.
19. *Diaries of a Duchess*, pp. 116–17, 118, 127, 128.
20. *Letters and Journals*, vol. III, p. 397.
21. *Correspondence*, vol. 23, pp. 330–2.
22. *A View of Society and Manners*, vol. I, pp. 106–7.
23. *Tour*, pp. 130–1.
24. Ibid., pp. 144–5.

25. Ibid., p. 171.
26. *Lady Bessborough and her Family Circle*, pp. 22, 27–8.
27. Cardinal de la Roche Aymon, the *grand aumônier*.
28. *The Courts of Europe*, vol. I, pp. 9–10, 12–13, 15, 22.
29. *Travels through France and Italy*, p. 313.
30. *Journal*, pp. 96, 240–1.
31. *Useful Hints*, pp. 93, 206–7.
32. *Correspondence*, vol. 39, p. 14.
33. *Memoirs*, vol. IV, p. 6; vol. III, p. 386.
34. *Travels through France and Italy*, p. 313.
35. Thicknesse had been sentenced to three months imprisonment and to a fine of £300 for libel.
36. This was a Latin euphemism for the coarse French *jean-foutre* which was obviously meant.
37. *Useful Hints*, pp. 208–12.
38. *Correspondence*, vol. 39, pp. 55–6.
39. West Yorkshire Archive Services, Sp St 6/1/115.
40. *George Selwyn and his Contemporaries*, vol. III, p. 2.
41. *Lady Bessborough and her Family Circle*, p. 23.
42. *Letters and Journals*, vol. III, p. 398.
43. *Memoirs*, vol. IV, pp. 331, 342–3.
44. *Correspondence*, vol. 39, pp. 143–4.
45. Ibid., vol. 35, p. 126; vol. 23, pp. 320–2.
46. *A View of Society and Manners*, vol. I, pp. 109–9, 111.
47. *The Courts of Europe*, vol. I, p. 23.
48. *Letters and Journals*, vol. IV, p. 350.

7
Louis XVI and Marie Antoinette

The picture of the reign of Louis XVI which is provided by the accounts of British travellers, from his accession in 1774 to the collapse of absolute monarchy in 1788, is somewhat distorted by the War of American Independence. Hostilities between Britain and France from 1778 to 1783 did not prevent a small number of British subjects from visiting enemy territory, but they were very much fewer than those who came to France either before or after the war.

We get our first glimpse of the future Louis XVI when the nine-year-old prince, known then as the Duc de Berry, recited his piece to Hume on the latter's presentation to the Dauphine and her children at Versailles in 1763.[1] Two years later, when Walpole was presented at court, he noted that the Duc de Berry 'looks weak and weak-eyed'. This was only two months or so before he succeeded his father as Dauphin. In 1769 Walpole was back at Versailles, this time to satisfy his curiosity about the new mistress. Before mass he saw the Dauphin and his brothers at dinner. Once again he was not impressed by the appearance of the heir to the throne. 'The eldest is the picture of the Duke of Grafton, except that he is more fair and will be taller. He has a sickly air and no grace.'[2]

The Duchess of Northumberland, who was present at the wedding of the Dauphin (not yet sixteen) and the even younger Marie Antoinette (fourteen and a half), writes of the bridegroom in a very different style: 'The Dauphin disappointed me much, I expected to have found him horrid, but on the contrary his figure pleased me very well. He is tall & slender with a Countenance *tres interessant* & a look of good Sense, his Complexion is rather pale & his eyes are large. He has a great quantity of fair Hair which grows very well to his Face & his figure appeared very genteel, but I am told he is not so well in his own Cloths.' Can this be the youth of whose appearance Walpole had spoken so disparagingly less than a year before? The duchess also noted that during the marriage ceremony 'the Dauphin appear'd to have much more Timidity than his little Wife. He trembled excessively during the service & blush'd up to his Eyes when he gave the Ring. When Mass begun & they presented him with a Book, he look'd quite relieved to have an excuse for not looking about him.' Later she adds: 'The Dauphin as he pass'd by look'd quite fatigued, he seems very delicate & to have the appearance of a Boy who had out grown his strength.'

Marie Antoinette naturally drew the duchess's attention: 'The Dauphine was very fine in diamonds. She is very little & slender. I should not have taken her to be 12 Years Old. She is fair & a little mark'd with the Smallpox, the Corps of her Robe was too small & left quite a broad stripe of lacing & Shift quite visible, which had a bad effect between 2 broader stripes of Diamonds. She really had quite a Load of Jewells.'[3]

When Walpole came back to France in 1771, he considered the country, as we have seen, to be in a sorry plight. 'Their next prospect', he declares, 'is not better: it rests on an *imbécile*, both in mind and body.' Back at Strawberry Hill, he wrote contemptuously of the old king and found the Dauphin 'more unpromising'. In the same letter in which he speaks of the diplomatic corps, headed by the Papal Nuncio, paying court to Mme Du Barry, he notes that Marie Antoinette had refused to follow their example: "The Dauphinesse, who is governed by her husband's aunts, paid no regard to her good mother's instructions, and would not speak to the mistress at her presentation."[4]

In 1772, before the Spencer family moved to the South of France, they visited Versailles. Lady Harriet reports rather briefly: 'The Dauphiness is so fair & so handsome, it is impossible not to admire her . . . The Dauphin is better looking than we expected.' In the following summer, on their way north, they visited Versailles again; this time the child's impressions are more developed: 'We went to Versailles to see the King at High Mass . . . We went afterwards to see the Dauphiness at dinner. She is not regularly handsome, but her complexion and countenance are beautiful, and she has so much grace & dignity. She is very lively

& her eyes sparkling. She spoke to mama, kiss'd my sister & me, & gave us flowers. The Dauphin looks stupid but good natured, and would be handsome if he was not so heavy.'[5]

Swinburne gives a lively account of the Dauphin and his brothers, whom he saw first at the king's levee when he was presented at court towards the end of April 1774, just a fortnight before Louis XVI ascended the throne:

> The Dauphin is very awkwardly made, and uncouth in his motions. His face resembles his grandfather's, but he is not near so handsome, though he has by no means a bad countenance. His nose is very prominent, his eyes are gray, and his complexion is sallow. He seemed cheerful and chatty, and I think his aspect bespeaks a good-natured man. The second brother is a pretty figure, and so is the third, only his mouth is rather wide, and drawn up in the middle to the top of the gums.
>
> They are not yet quite formed as to legs and strength, and have all a good deal of that restless motion, first upon one leg and then upon another, which is also remarkable in some members of the English royal family.
>
> The questions they ask seem very frivolous and puerile. I believe they find their time hang very heavy on their hands, for they ran with great glee to tickle one of the king's valets de chambre, as he was carrying out the king's dirty clothes.

On the other hand Swinburne was bowled over by Marie Antoinette: 'The Dauphiness . . . quite won my heart. I can give you no account of her particular features; but her air, eyes, shape, motion, her *tout ensemble*, were most charming. She spoke so cheerfully, and so easily, *comme si elle se sentait*, as the French say:

> Elle avoit une grace,
> Un je ne sais quoi qui surpasse
> De l'amour les plus doux appas.[6]

When Priestley was in Paris later in 1774, he did not obtain a high opinion of the new king from the circles in which he moved: 'The king is, on all hands, agreed to have nothing at all in him.'[7] In the following year Wharton visited Verailles as a tourist and saw the king and queen. Louis XVI's physical appearance did not impress him: 'The king is not tall, inclinable to En Bon Point, his Nose Aquiline, his eyes not very Piercing, his Complexion dark without much Colour. He has by no means the Air Fier & Majestueux of his Grandfather & the Bourbon Family.' Marie Antoinette attracted far more of Wharton's attention:

> The Queen is the most Amiable person by far of the whole Family, she is tall Enough, genteel, & Handsome. Her Air is exceedingly Agreeable and at first prejudices one in her favor, lively & good natured. Her Complexion is light, her forehead high, her Eyes blue, her nose rather aquiline than otherwise, her mouth, especially when she smiles, very pretty. She was Elegantly but not very Splendidly dressed. The King was in a Suit of light Velvet slightly Embroidered.[8]

When later in the same year Walpole attended a ball given at Versailles for the wedding of the king's sister, Louis is rapidly disposed of with the old comparison with the Duke of Grafton; but Walpole was dazzled by Marie Antoinette: 'What I have to say, I can tell your Ladyship in a word, for it was impossible to see anything but the Queen! Hebes, and Floras, and Helens, and Graces, are street-walkers to her. She is a statue of beauty, when standing or sitting; grace itself when she moves. She was dressed in silver scattered over with laurierroses; few diamonds, and feathers much lower than the Monument. They say she does not dance in time, but then it is wrong to dance in time.'[9]

In the autumn of the same year Mrs Thrale saw the queen for the first time at a performance at the Comédie Française: 'The Queen of France was at the Play tonight sitting in one of the Balcony Boxes like any other Lady, only that she curtsied to the Audience at going out & they applauded her in Return. She is wonderfully pretty, & I fancy perfectly amiable; for She clapped the Players when they pleased her, & chatted with her Maids in a Manner most engaging, free & lovely.' The next day she saw the queen again at a race held in the Plaine des Sablons just outside Paris between horses belonging to the Comte d'Artois, the Duc de Chartres and two noblemen. 'The Queen', she wrote, 'is still handsomer by Day than by Night, tho' dressed with the utmost Simplicity: She praised the Jockey who won, & stroked the Horse: She & her Ladies clapped their Hands, & almost shouted when the Winner came in.'

However, Mrs Thrale was very shocked by a story which she picked up there:

But the most surprizing thing I heard of in this Respect was the Riot raised at the Course today by forty three Fishwomen who surrounded the Queen, & with the loudest Voices and frantic Gestures uttered a thousand Gross Obscenities in her Ears till She was forced to give 'em Money to be rid of them. When I expressed my Astonishment at such Things being permitted; Ah, says a French Gentleman with great Composure, que ces Gens la scachent bien la Methode d'attraper les Ecus! & another presently informed me that these were the Women who kissed Louis quinze one Day in a fit of riotous Madness, & that they had this very Morning forcibly saluted the King's Brother, Comte d'Artois, who happens to be a pretty Young Man & pleas'd their Fancy.

A fortnight later Mrs Thrale went to Fontainebleau with her husband, her daughter, Queeney, Johnson and Banetti. Johnson's account of the expedition is extremely laconic, but Mrs Thrale's journal is full of detail about the royal family and especially the queen. They toured the various rooms in which the members of the royal family were at dinner:

The King & Queen dined together in another Room. They had a Damask Table Cloth neither course nor fine, without anything under, or any Napkin over. Their Dishes were Silver, not clean and bright like Silver in England — but they were Silver: their Plates, Knives, Forks & Spoons were gilt. They had the Pepper & Salt standing by them as it is the Custom here, & their Dinner consisted of five Dishes at a Course: The Queen eat heartily of a Pye which the King helped her to, they did not speak at all to each other, as I remember, but both sometimes turned & talked to the Lord in waiting: The Queen is far the prettiest Woman at her own Court, & the King is well enough — like another Frenchman.

She then passes to their inspection of the Comte and Comtesse de Provence at dinner, offering the comment:

It is a mighty silent ceremonious Business — this dining in publick. They likewise sat like two people stuffed with straw; and only spoke to enquire after our Niggey [Queeney], about whom the Queen had likewise before been very inquisitive. She would have our Names written down, & was indeed very condescending but troublesome with her Enquiries. I got to another Corner of the room & heard a Gentleman say: That is the pretty English Woman I am sure by her blushing.

The next day they saw the queen mount her horse to go hunting in the forest, and in the evening, with the help of the ambassador, managed to obtain seats for a performance in the palace theatre where she noted that 'the Queen had no mind to dress after her Morning's ride they told us — so sat upstairs incog'.[10]

In the following year Bentley also paid the usual visit to Versailles: 'Saw his Majesty walk through the rooms, and at Mass; afterwards the Queen; and then their Majesties at dinner, being very near and directly facing them . . . Their Majesties talked and laughed much at dinner. The Queen is young and very handsome. She appears to be extremely lively and gay, without the forms and attentions that might be expected from her high rank.' Later he was privileged to see some of the royal pictures kept in a house away from the palace, but the visit was cut short by the arrival of the queen on the same errand. One thing about her dress surprised Bentley: 'We saw the Queen again in her carriage coming to this place, when she was dressed in a *hat* a l'anglaise. A very rare thing here. The French women in general from the lowest to the highest are always without hats.'[11] Cornelia Knight relates how her mother and she went to Versailles 'and took our stand among many others in the great gallery to see the King and Queen and their attendants pass to their chapel. I was not so much struck with the beauty of Marie Antoinette as with the gracefulness of her person, and the very pleasing smile with which her salutation was accompanied, for she noticed us as she passed. Louis XVI appeared grave and rather melancholy '[12]

The Scotsman, Blaikie, who was in France from 1776 to 1792 as *Jardinier anglais* to the Comte d'Artois, gives in his eccentric spelling a vivid account of Louis XVI and his queen at Choisy-le-Roi in 1777:

Mr Brown . . . conducted us to the Pailas to see the King &c at Breakfast who was to go a hunting; this Breakfast might pass for a dinner as it seemed not of tea or coffe but of good solid meat; the King was dressed almost like a country farmer a good Rough stout man about 25, the Queen which is a very handsome beautifull woman sat opposite with Mme Elizabeth by her, which is young and handsome; the whole company seemed exceeding free and gay with an open cheerfulness which is not common to be seen amongst the higher Ranks in England.[13]

In normal times Lord Herbert would have been presented at the French court as he had been at others on his very extensive grand tour; but when he was in Paris in 1780, Britain and France were at war, and there was no ambassador to present him. The first glimpse he had of the king and queen was at a military review held in the Plaine des Sablons. 'The King', he writes, 'looks much like a Castrato, the Queen I saw only at a distance, very like her Brother.' A few days later when he was taken to Versailles, he penned a most unflattering account of Louis XVI, the future Louis XVIII and Marie Antoinette: 'The King and Monsieur are very much like Eunuchs in their figure & neither of their Countenances forbode much Sense. The Queen is handsome & her behaviour excessively indecent.'[14] Could it be that these contemptuous references to Louis XVI and his queen were inspired by Lord Herbert's acquaintance with the Duc de Chartres, the future Philippe Égalité?[15]

Another wartime traveller in France was Romilly who in 1781 returned to England from Switzerland via Lyons, Paris, Lille and Ostend. He too paid the usual visit to Versailles which he describes in a letter prudently written, not from Paris, but from Ostend:

At Versailles I assisted at the mass. The service was very short, though it was on a Sunday; for kings are so highly respected in that country that even Religion appoints for them less tedious ceremonies than it imposes on the people. The moment his Majesty appeared, the drums beat and shook the temple, as if it had been intended to announce the approach of a conqueror. During the whole time of saying mass, the choristers sang, sometimes single parts, sometimes in chorus. In the front seats of the galleries were ranged the ladies of the court, glowing with rouge, and gorgeously apparelled, to enjoy and form a part of the showy spectacle. The King laughed and spied at the ladies; every eye was fixed on the personages of the court, every ear was attentive to the notes of the singers, while the priest, who in the mean time went on in the exercise of his office, was unheeded by all present. Even when the Host was lifted up, none observed it; and if the people knelt, it was because they were admonished by the ringing of the bell; and even in that attitude, all were endeavouring to get a glimpse of the King. How can a king of France ever be brought to regard his subjects as his equals, when, even before the throne of heaven, he maintains so high a superiority over all around him? What an idea must he not conceive of his own importance, when he thus sees his God less honoured than himself?

Later, writing this time from London, he comments on an event which occurred while he was in Paris. After eleven years of marriage Marie Antoinette had at last produced a Dauphin:

You know that the Queen of France was brought to bed at the time that I was at Paris; but I never had time to give you any account of the rejoicings on that occasion. What seemed to me most extraordinary was, that they were commanded. The day the Dauphin was born, an order was posted up in all the streets, enjoining the citizens to illuminate their houses for three successive nights, and to shut up their shops, and commanding the officers of the police to look to the execution of this order. Who would have thought that a people so famous for their fond attachment to their kings would have needed such an order!

He was certainly not greatly impressed by what he saw of the festivities:

At night I walked about Paris to see the illuminations; the streets were crowded with people, and the public edifices were well lighted up; but in many of the private houses there appeared only one glimmering lamp at each window, hung up, not in token of joy, but of reluctant obedience to the Sovereign's will; and some of the citizens were daring enough not to illuminate their houses at all. In many of the squares were little orchestras with bands of music playing to the populace, some of whom danced about in wild irregular figures. But it was at the Place de Grève that the greatest crowd was assembled. The Town-house there was richly illuminated, a fire-work was played off, and afterwards the people were invited to dance to the music of four bands in different orchestras. The company, which consisted of the very lowest and dirtiest rabble of Paris, soon began to dance in a ring; but they were noisy rather than merry, and none seemed happy, unless happiness can be found in a tumultuous oblivion.

Romilly was depressed by the thought of the bloody executions carried out in the same Place de Grève, and also by 'the ragged and miserable appearance of the people, the sight of the guards drawn up on every side, the frequent appearances of the horse-guet, who came upon one every now and then unexpectedly'.

In his memoirs he records a conversation with D'Alembert who compared the present rejoicings with those for the birth of Louis XVI's father in 1729: 'He contented himself with observing what an effect philosophy had in his own time produced in the minds of the people. The birth of the Dauphin afforded him an example. He was old enough, he said, to remember when such an event had made the whole nation drunk with joy* [*On était dans une ivresse de joie]; but now they regarded with great indifference the birth of another master.'[16]

With the ending of the war of American Independence by the Treaty of Paris of 3 September 1783 there came a fresh flood of British travellers. At the end of October the Cradocks began their lengthy stay in France which was to last until the spring of 1786. In December they caught a glimpse of Marie Antoinette at the ascent of the first hydrogen balloon from the Jardin des Tuileries: 'The Queen of France', wrote Cradock, 'sat in the balcony in front of the Thuilleries, appeared serious, and our party remarked that she looked like a very handsome English woman.' In the following June they were present at the Opéra when Marie Antoinette accompanied France's ally, Gustavus III of Sweden, to a performance of *Didon*: 'Madame de St^e huberti was Didon; and it was remarked, that neither the Queen of France, nor the Queen of Carthage, appeared to wear either powder or paint.' A month later he noted: 'At the apartments in the Tuilleries. The Queen of France passed through them, full dressed, handed by the King of Sweden, and accompanied by Madame, sister to the King of France. They were all to dine with the Lieutenant of Police.'[17] 'Elle est jolie, très blonde et d'une taille moyenne', wrote Mrs Cradock. 'Toute sa personne respire un air natural de dignité sans fierté. Sa toilette, pleine de distinction, était très simple.' After describing how the queen was dressed, she adds: 'Peu de rouge. Mme Élisabeth et la dame d'honneur, bien moins jolies que la reine, sont plus fortes.'

In the following month she and her husband made the usual pilgrimage to Versailles. They were exploring the gardens when they were invited to visit the château while the king was out hunting. To their surprise Mme Élisabeth suddenly passed through one of the apartments which they were in, and though their guide assured them that they would not encounter the queen,

> quelques minutes s'étaient à peine écoulées, que nous entendions announcer: 'La Reine!' Nous nous rangeâmes de côté, tandis que Sa Majesté se retourna gracieusement par trois fois vers nous, et nous fit comprendre, par un sourire et une légère inclination de tête, que nous étions les bienvenus et que nous pouvions continuer notre visite. Je ne sais comment dépeindre l'émotion et l'étonnement de ma femme de chambre, qui nous accompagnait, en apprenant que cette dame était la reine.[18]

Jane Parminter's comments on the king and queen when she visited Versailles are much briefer: 'We saw the King a corpulent man not strikingly agreeable; the Queen is tall & elegant small features.'[19]

A much livelier account of Louis XVI and his queen is provided by Walker, who visited Versailles at about the same date in 1784. His description of the procession through the Galerie des Glaces for St Louis's day gives for once pride of place to the reigning monarch:

> To these succeeded the King, a short thick dumplin of a Monarch, the very picture of peace and plenty. He rolled along, with an air as perfectly disengaged from thought or care, and bore this great kingdom with so much ease upon his shoulders, that I could not but think him a jolly eating-and-drinking English 'Squire, perfectly at his ease, and without any other ideas coming across his thinking faculties than what must be next for his dinner! he has got the true Bourbon nose, and is really a well-looking man upon the whole.
>
> After the King followed the Queen — very handsome, and well-painted. She is very like the pictures I have seen of her in England, if they had a little dash of the Vixen thrown into them . . . Her train was borne by a Gentleman, and she was richly dressed, but much in the same way, and little better than a lady of quality in England.[20]

Two year later, James Edward Smith, whose account of his travels was written up some time afterwards and published in 1793, gives what is in part a doctor's verdict on Louis XVI:

> Sunday being the best day in the week for seeing Versailles, Mr. Broussonet accompanied me thither . . . We saw the royal family go to chapel, with young maids of honour painted of a rose colour, and the old ones crimson. We saw the crowd adoring their grand monarque, little thinking how soon that adoration would cease. The king's countenance seemed agreeable and benignant, by no means vacant; his ears, which his hair never covered, were remarkably large and ugly, and he walked ill. He had some very fine diamonds in his hat. The queen received company in her chamber, not having been out of it since her lying-in.[21]

In December of the same year an English army officer was presented at court by the ambassador, the Duke of Dorset:

> Went to Versailles (with Mr Coxe the famous Traveler) in a Coach & four. Met the Duke of Dorset in the Salle des Ambassadeurs. Lord Pembroke,[22] Lord Fielding, Mr Coxe and myself & two other english Gentlemen were Presented to the King, Monsieur, Madame, Count & Countess D'Artois and all the Court except the Queen who was indisposed. Dined with Monsr Vergennes and a great Number of Ambassadors & after dinner the Duke of Dorset asked me & Mr Coxe to go with him [to] the Duchess of Polignac were [sic] we saw the Queen who made an Apolygy [sic] for her not receiving the presentations. Afterwards her Majesty sat down to trick track, and afterwards went to Billiards. Her Majesty asked me if I could play. I answered no. She plays very well. She was dressed in a large blue bonnet and brown silk great Coat exactly à L'Angloise.[23]

Evidently the queen's indisposition was not very serious.

Though by 1787 we have reached the crisis which brought about the collapse of absolute monarchy, nothing of this was to be seen at the court where the ceremonial followed its usual course. On Whitsunday Young, who had just begun the first of his lengthy tours in France, was present in the chapel at Versailles when the Duc de Berry, the younger son of the Comte d'Artois, was invested with the *cordon bleu*: 'During the service', writes Young, 'the King was seated between his two brothers, and seemed by his carriage and inattention to wish himself a hunting. He would certainly have been as well employed, as in hearing afterwards from his throne a feudal oath of chivalry, I suppose, or some such nonsense, administered to a boy of ten years old.' After the ceremony Young could observe the queen talking with members of the procession: 'Her Majesty who, by the way, is the most beautiful woman I saw today, received them with a variety of expression. On some she smiled; to others she talked; a few seemed to have the honour of being more in her intimacy. Her return to some was formal, and to others distant. To the gallant Suffrein[24] it was respectful and benign.' Young was then present when the royal couple dined in public, a custom of which he strongly disapproved: 'The ceremony of the King's dining in public is more odd than splendid. The Queen sat by him with a cover before her, but ate nothing; conversing with the Duke of Orleans, and the Duke of Liancourt, who stood behind her chair. To me it would have been a most uncomfortable meal.'[25] A month or so later another English traveller, Garmston, who visited Versailles on his way to Italy, also censured Louis XVI's behaviour at mass: 'His brother sat with him & they talked & laughed most of the time Mass was said.'[26]

On 25 August 1788, the very day on which Loménie de Brienne resigned after the financial débâcle, Villiers witnessed the usual St Louis's day procession in the palace. After the queen and the king's brothers with their spouses and their sister came Louis XVI:

> Next proceeded the high and illustrious orders of the *Cordon Rouge*, and the *Cordon Bleu*; and afterwards, the king. Her majesty is a fine portly looking woman, and on this day assumed one of her most pleasant countenances, of which I am informed she keeps a wardrobe. Monsieur very much resembled the king, though he has considerably the advantage of him. All the portraits, that I have seen of the king are likenesses of him notwithstanding they in general exhibit his worst part, which everyone, I believe, allows his head to be. The person of the Comte d'Artois is genteel and graceful;[27]

An anonymous English clergyman was another traveller to find fault with the king's behaviour at mass when he visited Versailles two months later, on Sunday 26 October:

At 12 o'clock the king passed to the chapel. He was preceded by the counts de Provence and D'Artois. He is of a middle stature, inclined to be corpulent; his nose is aquiline, and his eye beams goodness and affability. We followed him to mass. Here his demeanour did not conciliate our veneration. Except at the adoration of the host, he was during the whole mass, employed in the most jocular conversation with the Comte d'Artois.[28]

Another English traveller, R.W.C., decribes a visit to Versailles about the end of November. This shows how, despite the gathering storm, the same ceremonial routine continued to be followed:

We saw their Majesties at Chapel, as well as the grand couvert. Judging from the lines of his face, the King will not be supposed a shining genius, but, what is much preferable, a very good man. He possesses in a high degree the virtue of oeconomy, a very great, because a useful virtue for a Prince. I have heard some anecdotes of this Prince, which gave me the highest opinion of his goodness and integrity of heart, and I confess the sight of him was not one of the smallest pleasures I received at Versailles.[29]

These remarks, if somewhat naïve, do concentrate attention on the king; what is unusual is that the writer says nothing whatever about Marie Antoinette.

Relatively little can be gleaned from British travellers' accounts about the events and personalities of the reign of Louis XVI until we reach the crisis years of 1787–8. When in Paris in 1774, Priestley, for instance, must certainly have met Turgot. According to a friend he performed some of his experiments before a select audience in the minister's house, but he never mentions him by name. In a letter of October 1774 he gives a very vague account of the new government which was formed at the beginning of the reign and in which Turgot held, first, the post of Secretary of State for the Navy and then, from 24 August, that of *contrôleur général*:

I have here had opportunity of seeing many of the men who have the chief lead in the direction of affairs, which gives me some pleasure, as I shall have a better idea of them when I read of them in the papers. They are a set of philosophical men, whose object is freedom of commerce, and universal peace. But there is another set out of the ministry, whose object is the very reverse. At present, however, it is not thought that they have any chance of getting the upper hand; and there are every where such luxury and dissipation, as must make a state of war very irksome, even to the officers. In other respects, if the present ministry continues in power for a few years, this country will be in excellent order for commencing a war; for they are bent upon economy, and improving the riches and strength of the nation.

The reference to the Duc de Choiseul is clear, but it is difficult to see how the ideas attributed to the ministers in power could fit anyone except Turgot himself. Another of Priestley's letters (undated) again refers to his contacts with 'several of the present leading statesmen of France' whom he describes as 'in general philosophical people, very honest and economical, friends of commerce and of peace'. If the king has 'nothing at all in him, . . . while he is in good hands, all will do well'. However, Priestley refers once again to opponents of the new ministry and reaches a gloomy conclusion about the prospects for peace, whatever happens: 'There are many persons, disaffected, intriguing, lovers of war, and violent enemies of England. If these get into power, which is far from being impossible, we shall certainly have a war, and the economy of the present ministers will have brought the nation into excellent order for it.'[30]

Early in the new reign Maupeou's reforms were undone and the *Parlements* recalled. The Paris court was reinstated in November 1774 and the provincial *Parlements* rather later. Swinburne offers a vivid description of the reinstallation of the *Parlement* in Bordeaux in March 1775. His account shows clearly what a hold a *Parlement* had over the city in which it was established; and this was to be demonstrated once again in the revolt of the *Parlements* in the critical years 1787–8.

Swinburne begins his account with a description of the arrival of the Comte de Noailles, who had been sent from Versailles to reinstate the *Parlement*. He then writes of the Premier Président's triumphant return to the city on 28 February:

In the afternoon all the parliament men and women were assembled at the Chapelle de Barbet, a mile from the town, to receive the premier president at a grand banquet. A triumphal arch and the feast were prepared by the freemasons, who distributed invitations printed on satin, with various devices: he afterwards proceeded to Bordeaux, escorted by one hundred and sixty coaches full of all the town contains of people of fashion, besides many young men on horseback, and the Maréchaussée, each side of the road, every house-top, every window being crammed as full as could be with spectators. It was an animated spectacle. He was received at his own house by music, garlands and triumphant mottoes, and the mob filled the house so that it was midnight before he got rid of them.

When the *Parlement* was solemnly reinstalled, there were once again scenes of great rejoicing:

We went next day to the palace, where M. de Noailles arrived with his guards *en habit de cérémonie*. The return of the exiles was applauded by a most numerous populace without, and a large assembly of gentlemen within, the hall. The *Manants*, or such as remained in 1771, were hissed and hooted at by the mob. One of the *présidents à mortier*, M. d'Augeard, brought us by a side-door into the salle de conseil, where he placed us close to M. de Noailles. There were not above twenty strangers admitted. The whole parliament was there, attired in red gowns. M. de Noailles opened the assembly with a short and proper speech, expressive of his joy in being the instrument the king had chosen to employ in restoring the parliament of Bordeaux to his people, recommending union, &c. The premier president then rose, and pronounced a good discourse, but very severe on the ministers of the late king, and replete with a greater spirit of resolution and freedom than the *Grand Monarque* might have liked to hear. The edict of re-establishment was then read, which is similar to that of Paris. The doors were then thrown open, and it was again read to the multitude.[31]

The Premier Président's speech offered a foretaste of the trouble which this *Parlement*, like several others, was to cause the monarchy in the coming years down to the final clash in 1787–8.

Walpole was again in France from August to October 1775. After describing to Lady Ossory the ball at Versailles at which he had been present, and various other festivities for the marriage of Louis XVI's sister, he adds: 'and there end the spectacles, for Monsieur Turgot is *oeconome*'. In another letter to the same correspondent, dated 3 October, he sums up the political situation in a half serious, half bantering style:

> Messieurs de Turgot and Malesherbes are every day framing plans for mitigating monarchy and relieving the people; and the King not only listens to, but encourages them. Their *philosophes* tell folks, that the age is enlightened — but don't repeat this, Madam; I should be laughed at in England, where we are wiser, and have adopted all the notions which the French are so silly as to relinquish. However, things do not seem fixed here; there are two parties, if either of which prevailed, Dame Vertu would return to her rags. The charming Queen is eager to reinstate Monsieur de Choiseul, and then Madame Gloire would blaze out in full *éclat*. If Monsieur and Madame (the latter, a very artful Italian) get the ascendant, then the Princess de Marsan (Monsieur's governess) would bring back the Jesuits, persecution, the Church and the devil knows what — everything, but a Madame du Barry, who must wait for the reign of the Comte d'Artois, till when there will be no naughty doings in this country.

In a postscript Walpole interrupts his account of the political situation to discuss the latest *opéra-comique*, but he does make it clear that the return of Choiseul was considered a serious possibility in the Paris circles in which he moved:

> Huge news! — yet not quite ripe. Monsieur de Choiseul is come suddenly to Paris — They say he goes back on Saturday, but his friends look in great spirits; and as the Queen has lately committed some acts of authority, and as Madame de Marsan has retired without a pension, the family compact — but perhaps your Ladyship had rather hear about *La Réduction de Paris*.

Three days later he wrote more seriously to a male correspondent:

> The Duc de Choiseul, I said, is here; and as he has a second time put off his departure, *cela fait beaucoup de bruit*. I shall not

be at all surprised if he resumes the reins, as (forgive me a pun) he has the *Reine* already. Messieurs de Turgot and Malesherbes certainly totter — but I shall tell you more when I see you.[32]

Choiseul never, of course, regained power. Malesherbes, who only joined the government in July 1775, resigned in May 1776, at which date Turgot was dismissed.

As we have seen,[33] during his 1775 visit to Paris Walpole heard from Malesherbes himself what he had found when in his ministerial capacity he visited the Bastille. In this same letter, written shortly after his return to Strawberry Hill, he declares: 'I . . . was not a little edified by my journey. I saw a King who accords everything that is asked for the good of his people, and I saw two ministers, Messieurs de Malherbes [*sic*] and Turgot, who do not let their master's benevolent disposition rust.' He then refers to Turgot's plans for replacing the *corvée* by a tax paid by all landowners, but adds gloomily: 'The *country gentleman*, that race of interested stupidity, will baffle him.' When in the following April he received a copy of the recent proceedings of the Paris *Parlement* which had strongly opposed this measure, he was indignant at 'such renegade conduct in a Parliament that I was rejoiced had been restored'. 'These profligate magistrates', he declares, 'resist happiness for others, for millions, for posterity! — Nay, do they not half vindicate Maupeou, who crushed them?'[34]

In practice though not in title, Turgot's successor was Necker; as a foreigner and a Protestant he could not hold the post of *Contrôleur général*, but was finally appointed instead *Directeur général des finances*. British travellers, both before and after his tenure of office from October 1776 down to 1781, had social relations with him and his wife who had a famous salon. Thus in 1775 Walpole and in the following year Mrs Montagu were frequently entertained there during their time in Paris,[35] while some ten years later Sir John Sinclair was often at their house just before the marriage of their daughter to the Swedish ambassador, Baron de Staël. Sinclair has a fair amount to say about the ex-minister who was not to return to power for another two and a half years:

> On the same day I was asked to dine with the celebrated Necker. His appearance was heavy, and there was no spirit or

vigour in his eye. He was very reserved, as might be expected from an ex-minister, in a very delicate situation. When I pressed him to come to England, he said that he never expected to revisit that country. It is unfortunate that the marriage between Mademoiselle Necker and Lord Rivers' son did not take place, as it would have detached him from French politics.

Sinclair maintains that the choice of Baron de Staël as a husband for his daughter was connected with Necker's desire to return to power:

Mademoiselle Necker was then preparing for her marriage with the Swedish ambassador, Count Stael. It is understood that she was not overfond of the match; but it was a court affair, and entered into by Monsieur Necker, in hopes of his being again placed at the head of the financial department. Count Stael was much connected with Count Fersen, a Swedish nobleman of Scotch extraction, his name being properly Macpherson, who had much influence at Court; and it was supposed that the marriage would greatly promote an event of which M. Necker was passionately desirous, namely, his return to power.[36]

Fersen's name was, of course, linked with that of Marie Antoinette.

One British traveller who did frequent the Necker household during his first period in office was Gibbon. Some twenty years earlier in Switzerland he had fallen in love with Suzanne Curchod, but his father forbade the match. During his stay in Paris from May to October 1777 he was a frequent guest at the Neckers' house, as he explains in a mildly humorous letter about his social contacts in Paris:

You remember that the Neckers were my principal dependence and the reception which I have met from them very far surpassed my most sanguine expectations. I do not indeed lodge in their house (as it might excite the jealousy of the husband and procure me a letter de cachet), but I live very much with them, dine and sup whenever they have company which is almost every day, and whenever I like it for they are not in the least *exigeans*.[37]

That British travellers should have little to say about Necker's financial and other policies is scarcely surprising as they were few and far between during the American War of Independence. The only comments so far discovered concern the publication of Necker's famous *Compte rendu au roi* on the state of the country's finances in February 1781 and his resignation in the following May. These comments came from Ellis who, after spending the winter at Marseilles 'in the enemies country', was now at Spa where he felt himself free to discuss French affairs. On 10 May 1781 he wrote:

> The state of the French Finances, published by Mr. Neckar, produced a very great sensation at first, not only in France, but in other parts of Europe, and gave a high idea of the resources of that Kingdom, and of the candour and ability of its Minister. But the sentiments of the publick in these respects are mightily changed since it has been known that he prohibited the publication of a review of his performance, after having appealed to those in office to confirm or refute it. A very enlightened friend of mine, who was in the Bureau of Monsieur de Turgot, has assured me that he could point out above 150 millions of debt, in one shape or another, concealed from the public.

It is generally accepted that this best-selling production contained a somewhat optimistic account of the French finances. In the following month the same writer had this comment on Necker's departure from the government: 'You see the fate of M. Necker; the circumstances which produced his disgrace I suppose you are not ignorant of, otherwise I might, in a few words, suggest them to you; the principal, indeed, were his designs against the Parliaments and the Intendants of the Provinces, whom he looked upon as in the way to obstruct the operation of his new system of Finance; and his ambition to force himself into the Council.'[38]

Pennington, another British traveller who was in France during the war, from March to September 1782, notes at this early date the influence which that war had produced on the outlook of Frenchmen. After giving a long account of the Bastille, he continues:

> It is said, however, that the French are asserting their liberty, and having endeavoured to obtain it for the Americans, next

mean to take care of themselves; if so, the King and Ministry are rightly punished for their interference in the American war . . . There certainly never prevailed a greater freedom of speech than at present. Military and civil men, who formerly dared not avow their sentiments, now speak them openly, and without the least caution.

The same writer speaks highly of the resistance which the Paris *Parlement* offered to government measures: 'The remonstrances of the parliament now breathe the spirit of Englishmen, jealous of their freedom and government.'[39]

After Necker's resignation, two more *contrôleurs généraux* came and went before the appointment of Calonne, a controversial figure who held the post from November 1783 to his dismissal in April 1787 when the financial crisis came to a head. Although Calonne is seldom named, accounts of government subsidies to encourage the setting up of new factories in the mid-1780s, which we have already encountered,[40] were part of the expansionist policy which he pursued. The queen and the other members of the royal family, along with the courtiers, were found the money they wanted; important public works were undertaken. All this was made possible by a succession of loans. Despite the opposition of the *Parlements*, to begin with these were over-subscribed. However, by 1786 Calonne was in difficulties and was forced to offer exorbitant terms in order to borrow money.

In August of that year he finally put before the king a programme of sweeping reforms to deal with the critical financial situation. As well as effecting economies he aimed to raise extra revenue by a new land tax (the *subvention territoriale*), payable by all sections of the community including the nobility and the clergy, and by raising and extending the existing stamp duty. His proposed reforms were not merely fiscal; they affected the whole administration and the economic life of the nation. He sought to free French trade and industry from the restrictions imposed upon them by abolishing the internal customs barriers, by relaxing government controls over the grain trade, and by a reform of the *taille, gabelle* and the *corvée*.

To present such a programme of reforms to the Paris *Parlement* was to invite strong opposition, and at this moment to summon the Estates General was unthinkable. Calonne hit upon an expedient last used in the reign of Louis XIII as an alternative to a meeting of the Estates General: this was to summon an Assemblée des Notables, consisting of the princes of the blood, great noblemen, archbishops and bishops, judges of the *Parlements* and high civil servants — 144 in all. The first meeting took place on 22 February 1787.

When the Assemblée des Notables met, Calonne immediately ran into difficulties which ended with his dismissal on 8 April. A few days before Calonne's fall Swinburne entered in his diary an anecdote which illustrates the low reputation which Calonne enjoyed at the time in certain quarters:

> The Archbishop of Narbonne (Dillon) was conversing with the contrôleur-général, Calonne, on the deficit in the finances, which is now the great subject of discourse and surmises, and he expressed a desire to know when and how this deficit was to be prevented for the future. Calonne, very cross at being pressed on this subject, said he could not tell, but that it was no such mighty matter if the king remained in debt a few years longer; 'for who is there that is not in debt?' said he; 'there is scarcely a nobleman who is not overwhelmed with a load of it. *Et vous-même, Monseigneur, vous devez plus que vous n'êtes gros.*' '*Pour vous, Monsieur de Calonne*', replied the prelate, '*vous deviez, mais vous ne devez plus.*'[41]

Power then passed to one of Calonne's main critics in the assembly, Laménie de Brienne, the archbishop of Toulouse. On 1 May he was made *Chef du Conseil Royal des Finances* and on 26 August *Ministre principal*; and in January 1788 he was translated to the archbishopric of Sens. Despite his earlier criticisms of Calonne's proposals, he was compelled to adopt them in a modified form, and in his turn he found himself up against the intransigence of the Assemblée des Notables. On 25 May, after it had rejected his revised proposals for a land tax, it was dissolved. Brienne was thus left to face the opposition of the *Parlements* to his proposals.

When in July the edicts for the *subvention territoriale* and the stamp duty came before the Paris *Parlement*, they encountered stiff resistance; it declared that it was not competent to deal with new taxes and that only a meeting of the Estates General could cope with the financial situation. In remonstrances presented on 26 July it boldly demanded the summoning of the Estates General. It was supported in its resistance by other sovereign courts in Paris, the Cour des Aides and the Cour des Comptes, as well as by many provincial *Parlements*. When on 6 August the king held the customary *lit de justice* to force through the new edicts, the Premier Président repeated the demand for the Estates General to his face. On its return from Versailles the *Parlement* declared illegal the government's publication of the tax edicts whereupon it was transferred to Troyes. Excitement ran high in Paris, where public opinion was behind the *Parlement*'s demands. For several days riots and all manner of disturbances took place there.

Swinburne, who was living just outside Paris at this time, records in his diary a number of items which give a vivid impression of the atmosphere in the capital, even if the printed version (the only one now available) gives some oddly jumbled dates:

6 July [August]. All at court are in a bustle, because the parliament of Paris will not hear of new taxes, till the king lays before them a state of his debts and expenses, that they may be convinced of the necessity of fresh impositions. Calonne, who has fled to Rotterdam, has written to the king that he is gone off to have liberty to prepare for his defence, as the Archbishop of Toulouse is doing all he can to deprive him of the means of justifying himself.

19. At the Chambre des Comptes the other day, where the Comte d'Artois went to register by force the *edit du timbre et de l'impôt territorial*, he was hissed and hustled, but on somebody calling out '*aux armes!*' the cowardly mob fled in an instant, and many people were lamed. The first president, Nicolai, made a very vigorous speech, ending by these remarkable words: *On veut nous forcer à passer une loi la plus oppressive, mais jamais nous ne le ferons*; then raising his head and voice, he repeated: *Non, monseigneur, nous ne le ferons jamais!*

Monsieur was accompanied by loud acclamations, from the Luxembourg to the Cour des Aides. After the princes had retired, each court remained assembled, and the Chambre des Comptes came to a determination to address the king for the return of his parliament, to declare the edicts illegal, and to forbid their execution; since which the king sat at Versailles, *en lit de justice*, or *Séance*, and had the edicts registered before him. The parliament was sullenly mute, and the king angry. As soon as they returned to Paris, the parliament assembled and came to very strong resolutions, containing a doctrine of fundamental rights and primitive contracts, and national consents, that the kings of France seem long to have lost sight of. On the 15th they were exiled. The day had been fixed for the 17th, but the parliament being convoked to assist at the anniversary of the vow of Louis XIII on the 15th, it was apprehended there might be some riots so their exile was hastened by two days. They were sent to Troyes.

The abuse bestowed on the king and queen and the Archbishop of Toulouse is incredible. It was proposed in parliament that the deputies should return *en corps*, and, throwing themselves on their knees before the king, implore him to have pity on his people, and recall the odious taxes, and perhaps they might touch his heart and convince his reason. It is said that clubs and salons are prohibited.

20. La Cour des Aides is as stiffnecked as the other courts. The populace have given the king the nickname of *Louis le timbré*.[42] The parliament of Rouen[43] was ordered to go into exile at Libourne, but the people have risen and kept them by force in the city. The parliament of Rouen, being summoned to Paris, have returned for answer, that they have upon their hands business of the highest importance, which they cannot leave.[44]

At this moment affairs in the Netherlands had brought England and France to the brink of war, but in September Young noted in his travel journal that the state of the French finances ruled this out: 'The preparations going on for a war with England are in the mouths of all the world; but the finances of France are in such a state of derangement, that the people best informed assert a war to be impossible.'[45]

In the meantime Brienne succeeded in working out a compromise with the Paris *Parlement*; the government withdrew the edicts for the *subvention territoriale* and the stamp duty, in return for which the *Parlement* registered an edict prolonging the two existing *vingtièmes*. Thereupon it was recalled and returned in triumph to the capital.

On 13 October Young recorded a conversation at dinner at the Hôtel de La Rochefoucauld about the political situation:

The feeling of every body seems to be that the Archbishop will not be able to do any thing towards exonerating the state from the burthen of its present situation; some think that he has not the inclination; others that he has not the courage; others that he has not the ability. By some he is thought to be attentive only to his own interest; and by others, that the finances are too much deranged to be within the power of any system to recover, short of the states-general of the kingdom; and that it is impossible for such an assembly to meet without a revolution in the government ensuing. All seem to think that something extraordinary will happen; and a bankruptcy is an idea not at all uncommon. But who is there that will have the courage to make it?

Four days later he gives a more detailed account of the state of opinion in Paris at this critical moment:

Dined today with a party, whose conversation was entirely political. Mons. de Calonne's *Requête au Roi* is come over, and all the world are reading and disputing on it. It seems, however, generally agreed that, without exonerating himself from the charge of the agiotage, he has thrown no inconsiderable load on the shoulders of the archbishop of Toulouse, the present premier, who will be puzzled to get rid of the attack. But both these ministers were condemned on all hands in the lump; as being absolutely unequal to the difficulties of so arduous a period. One opinion pervaded the whole company, that they are on the eve of some great revolution in the government: that every thing points to it: the confusion in the finances great; with a *deficit* impossible to provide for without the states general of the kingdom, yet no ideas formed of what would be the consequence of their meeting; no minister existing, or to be looked to in or out of power, with such decisive talents as to promise any other remedy than palliative ones; a prince on the throne, with excellent dispositions, but without the resources of a mind that could govern in such a moment without ministers; a court buried in pleasure and dissipation; and adding to the distress, instead of endeavouring to be placed in a more independent situation; a great ferment amongst all ranks of men, who are eager for some change, without knowing what to look to, or to hope for: and a strong leaven of liberty, increasing every hour since the American revolution; altogether form a combination of circumstances that promise ere long to ferment into motion, if some master hand, of very superior talents, and inflexible courage, be not found at the helm to guide events, instead of being driven by them. It is very remarkable, that such conversation never occurs, but a bankruptcy is a topic; the curious question on which is *would a bankruptcy occasion a civil war, and a total overthrow of the government?* The answers that I have received to this question appear to be just: such a measure, conducted by a man of abilities, vigour, and firmness, would certainly not occasion either one or the other. But the same measure, attempted by a man of a different character, might possibly do both. All agree, that the states of the kingdom cannot assemble without more liberty being the consequence; but I meet with so few men who have any just ideas of freedom, that I question much the species of this new liberty that is to arise. They know not how to value the privileges of THE PEOPLE: as to the nobility and the clergy, if a revolution added any thing to their scale, I think it would do more mischief than good.[46]

In the last part of this long analysis of opinion Young expresses the fear that the privileged orders who were leading this assault on the monarchy could be those who profited most from any changes which might take place.

James Edward Smith who, on returning from Italy, spent some six weeks in Paris in September and October 1787, also has some interesting remarks to make about the state of opinion there in that period. Already a year earlier he had noticed a distinct change, compared with what he had observed on an earlier visit, in the freedom with which people discussed political matters:

I was surprised, on being introduced into various Parisian circles in 1786, to hear much unreserved political talk, and that of a nature which I had supposed would infallibly lead to the Bastille. Its prevailing tenour was, that neither the finances nor the authority of the government could long be supported; that the people would not long bear the excessive taxes and excessive oppression under which they groaned; and that the French in general were ardently desirous, and strongly flattered themselves with the hopes of being, in a very few years, governed as we were. This was the conversation of people of consideration and property, even connected with the court, and shining in the elevated walks of life.

A year later, when Calonne had given way to Brienne, he found even more agitation and freedom of speech, as illustrated by the treatment meted out to a police spy in a well-known café:

> In October 1787 the public sentiments began to be greatly agitated. The banishment of the Parliament of Toulouse[47] was much talked of, and when the people's tongues were once let loose, they began with one accord to hunt out all persons suspected of being spies of government, and to treat them with great indignity. One of these people being in the Caffe de Chartres leaning his head and arms on a marble table, was known to a gentleman, who believed him to be listening to the conversation of the place, and without any ceremony gave him a violent blow on the back of the head, which drove his nose against the table, and sent him bleeding out of the room. The company starting with surprise and indignation, the person who gave the blow coolly said, 'Ce n'est qu'une mouche.' It is but a fly. Alluding to the term *mouchard*,[48] by which such people were distinguished from their manner of blowing the nose as a signal to each other. Upon this the company were perfectly satisfied, and the poor *mouchard* never returned.[49]

The reconciliation between the government and the Paris *Parlement* proved short-lived. On 19 November the king held a *séance royale* to secure the registration of an edict for a series of loans to be spread over the next five years to help to overcome the government's financial problems. This was on the understanding that the Estate General would meet before 1792. The edict encountered outspoken opposition from certain of the judges, one of whom demanded the summoning of the Estates General in 1789. When the king brought the long proceedings to an end by ordering the registration of the edict without a vote being taken, the Duc d'Orléans (Philippe Égalité) protested that such a registration was illegal. The next day Swinburne entered in his diary: 'The Duc d'Oréans is exiled.'[50] The government also had two of the judges arrested. As usual, the provincial *Parlements* supported their Paris colleagues and also came into conflict with the government on their own account.

The affair dragged on during the winter until finally a fresh crisis, graver than any of its predecessors during the century because it involved not only the *Parlements*, but the whole power of the privileged orders in revolt against the monarchy, was unleashed in April 1788 by the drawing up of the Paris *Parlement*'s remonstrances against the *séance royale* of the previous November. Swinburne noted on 4 May that the king and Marie Antoinette were far from popular: 'The king and queen were at the review of the Gardes Françaises yesterday, in great splendour, bowing to every one, notwithstanding which there was no *vive le roi*! All was silent till the old Maréchal de Biron mounted his horse at the head of his regiment, when he was received with the loudest acclamations.' The *Parlement* had got wind of the severe measures which the government intended to take against it, and on 3 May, the very same day as the review, it drew up a list of the fundamental laws of the kingdom which included both the nation's right to vote taxes through regular meetings of the Estates General and the right of the different *Parlements* to register royal edicts only when they were satisfied that they were in conformity with these fundamental laws and with the laws of a particular province. The government promptly annulled this declaration and ordered the arrest of two of the judges who took refuge in the Palais de Justice.

Swinburne made interesting diary entries on this critical situation, even though he proved a rather bad prophet:

5 May. The arrêté of the day before yesterday was like our Bill of Rights; strong and declaratory of the just claims of the people . . . Wednesday is to be the day of destroying the parliament. I believe all this will end in *gasconnades*, either by the court eating its words, or that fear of chastisement will bring the parliamentarians on their knees. We shall see whether violence and despotism will prevail. I do not think there is steadiness, spirit, or union requisite for a revolution, to be found in the French nation. All will depend on the perseverance of the ministry, and the temper of the army.

The entry for the following day describes the arrest of the two judges:

Messrs. D'Espresmenil and Gollard[51] were ordered to be arrested by *lettres de cachet*; the first for urging the parliament to make the *arrêté*, and laying before it copies of the Garde des

Sceaux's plans (which he had procured by stealth from the king's press at Versailles): the other for denouncing the amplification of the vingtième. Both made their escape and came to the parliament house, which was soon after invested by three thousand five hundred Swiss and French guards, who locked the gates, and kept all within prisoners for twenty-four hours. Eleven peers, two archbishops, and all the parliament passed the day and night in the halls, with all the spectators who chanced to be there. Then M. d'Agoult, aide-major (senior adjutant) of the guards, came in and demanded the two members, who were refused him. At last the two obnoxious gentlemen got up, and after protesting against this unheard-of violation of this most sacred asylum, surrendered themselves to M. d'Agoult, and were hurried away to l'hôtel de police, from whence one was sent to l'Isle de St. Marguerite, the other to Pierre Encise near Lyons. A rescue was attempted, but the two members themselves opposed and prevented it.

'Monsieur d'Agoult', Swinburne added later, 'is universally reprobated for his officiousness in this business.'[52]

On 8 May the king held another *lit de justice* at Versailles at which Lamoignon, the *garde des sceaux*, announced a complete reform of the judicial system, a revised version of Maupeou's reforms which had been undone at the beginning of the reign. The first edict created forty-seven *grands bailliages*, courts whose competence was sufficiently wide to leave the *Parlements* very little work, either in criminal or civil cases. Other edicts reduced the number of judges in the *Parlements*, and, most important of all, decreed that in future all royal edicts were to be registered by only one court, the *cour plénière*, which would be presided over by the king and have as its members the princes of the blood, peers, senior judges of the Paris *Parlement*, and a great number of dignitaries, lay and ecclesiastical. The next day Swinburne summarised the proceedings thus:

> The parliament was summoned to Versailles, and all the inferior chambers of it broken up. The grande chambre was retained to form part of a *cour plenière*, composed of officers of state, &c., where the king has passed a number of edicts, whereby he changes the whole order of magistracy, amplifies the powers of lower jurisdictions, and, *en attendant les états*

généraux, reserves to this *cour plenière* the power of enregistering all acts. The parliament unanimously refused its acquiescence. A prorogation is proclaimed, to give time to make up the new tribunals, &c.

The Chatelet, *unâ voce*, has refused to act instead of the parliament, so the king and his ministers will be finely hampered.[53]

After the *lit de justice* of 8 May the so-called aristocratic revolt entered upon its most violent phase. The Paris *Parlement* had been sent on holiday, but the provincial *Parlements* led the resistance, supported by many great nobles and even by the clergy. The Assemblée du Clergé which had begun its sittings on 5 May, refused to come to Brienne's aid in the desperate financial position and granted less than a quarter of the sum asked for as its contribution to the Treasury (the *don gratuit*). What is more, it demanded the maintenance of its fiscal immunities, the reinstatement of the *Parlements* and the summoning of the Estates General. Swinburne has two references in his diary to the meetings of the assembly. In the first he describes how when its president, Dillon, the archbishop of Narbonne, made the usual speech to the king at the head of the deputation of the clergy, 'Louis, contrary to custom, answered by heart, but his memory failed him, and, after two attempts to recollect himself, he gave it up.' The second entry concerns the failure of Dillon, who was a loyal supporter of Brienne, to prevent the assembly from taking part in the aristocratic revolt: 'The clergy have in their assembly, at the instance of the Bishop of Blois, instituted a committee to remonstrate with the king, and to petition for a speedy convocation of the états généraux. The Archbishop of Narbonne opposed it.'

Up and down the country the *Parlements* sought the support of the nobility and of all the members of the enormously large legal profession, and in several places turned resistance to the edicts of 8 May into riots and disorder. The position was particularly serious in Brittany, where the *Parlement* at Rennes was supported by the nobility which occupied a dominant position in the provincial estates and enjoyed great privileges in such matters as taxation. On 7 June, shortly before he returned to England, Swinburne noted in his diary:

> Accounts from Brittany state that a deputation of four hundred gentlemen waited upon Monsieur de Thiers [Comte

de Thiard, the commandant], requesting him to forward their memorial to the king, and their circular letter to the princes and peers. He promised to do so, but expostulated with them upon the illegality of their assembling in such a manner, and expressed how much the king would be offended by it. To this they replied, that when the English landed at St. Cast,[54] they assembled in a similar manner, and had been thanked for doing so by his majesty. 'That was a different case', said Thiers, 'it was against the enemies of your country.' — 'The case is the same now', they boldly answered.[55]

Swinburne's wife, who stayed on in Paris until November, has some interesting comments on the political situation in her letters, particularly in July and August. On 24 June she wrote: 'The number of discontented provinces increases every day, Franche-comté, Provence, Burgundy, Lorraine. The parliament of Grenoble had letters of Exile, but the people will not let it go. Mr de Tonnerre [the commandant] was very near being killed. Mr. de Jaucourt has refused to take Mr de Tonnerre's place. The King is worse in his affairs; one day he proposes to set matters to rights, the next day the Queen undoes every thing.'[56] Although Mrs Swinburne had won the favour of Marie Antoinette (her account of her last interview with the Queen in May 1789 is a well-known document),[57] she was critical of her political activities. Five days later she reported on happenings in another province: 'The day before yesterday there arrived a courier from Pau with very disagreeable intelligence. The Mob had obliged all the members of the Parliament, even the first President who was ill in bed, to put on their robes & take their seats in the Courts of Justice.'[58]

On 1 July a deputation of twelve Breton noblemen arrived in Paris to agitate against the reforms; on the night of 14–15 July they were arrested and sent to the Bastille. In the following month, after his diatribe against this state prison, Villiers noted: 'The deputies from Brittany were then airing themselves upon the ramparts.'[59] In a letter of 17 July Mrs Swinburne has some interesting references to the general situation, in particular to the sanctions taken against those court noblemen who had shown support for the Breton protests, to the troubles in Dauphiné, and to the unreliability of numbers of noble officers in this crisis. The Duc de Praslin, she writes,

is forbid to appear at Court. The Duke of Charost for having offered to sign (which the Bretons would not agree to) is disgraced, so is abandoned by both parties. The Duke of Chabot is deprived of his position, the Marquis de La Fayette of his Command of a Brigade for the same reason. Many other persons are disgraced. They sent troops into Dauphiny, while they were amusing the people with hopes of an accommodation. The Inhabitants have assumed the colours of their Ancient Sovereigns & say they are strong enough to support their pretensions. The Vivarais have offered to join them. They are armed. The Nobility of Languedoc to the Amount of 150 have signed an Association to defend their rights. Bearn is in the same humour. Four regiments are sent there. Britany however gives the most trouble. They pretend they have 200,000 Men & it is feared they will get arms & ammunition from England . . . The Regiment of Bassigny has signed a declaration *En Corps* that they would not have a hand in these operations & 2 other Regiments now in Britany have adhered to the resolution of Bassigny . . . Many officers of every Rank are resolved to quit the Service if they are ordered against their Countrymen.[60]

When Young arrived in the great Breton port of Nantes on 21 September, after the release of the prisoners from the Bastille by Necker who had by now succeeded Brienne, he noted the revolutionary sentiments there and made his famous prophecy:

Nantes is as *enflammé* in the cause of liberty, as any town in France can be; the conversations I witnessed here prove how great a change is effected in the minds of the French, nor do I believe it will be possible for the present government to last half a century longer, unless the clearest and most decided talents be at the helm. The American revolution has laid the foundation of another in France, if government do not take care of itself. Upon the 23rd one of the twelve prisoners from the Bastile arrived here — he was the most violent of them all — and his imprisonment has been far enough from silencing him.

Earlier on his second tour of France Young had noted signs of the conflict between the king and the *Parlements* backed by other members of the privileged orders. On 13 August at Rouen he wrote:

The parliament house here is shut up, and its members exiled a month past to their country seats, because they would not register the edict for a new land tax. I enquired much into the common sentiments of the people, and found that the King personally from having been here, is more popular than the parliament, to whom they attribute the general dearness of every thing.

He provides a very interesting account of the situation at Rennes, the seat of the *Parlement* of Brittany, which had seen violent disorders as soon as the news of the edicts of 8 May arrived. He spent several days there at the beginning of September and made the following notes on the situation:

The parliament being in exile, the house is not to be seen . . . The object at Rennes most remarkable at present is a camp, with a marshal of France (de Stainville), and four regiments of infantry, and two of dragoons, close to the gates. The discontents of the people have been doubled, first on account of the high price of bread, and secondly for the banishment of the parliament. The former cause is natural enough; but why the people should love their parliament was what I could not understand, since the members, as well as of the states, are all noble, and the distinction between the *noblesse* and *roturiers* no where stronger, more offensive, or more abominable than in Bretagne. They assured me, however, that the populace have been blown up to violence by every art of deception, and even by money distributed for that purpose. The commotion rose to such a height before the camp was established, that the troops here were utterly unable to keep the peace.[61]

It will be noticed that already here Young touches on a theme to which he was to recur again and again in his travel journal for 1789 — that the high price of bread was one of the immediate causes of the Revolution, or, as he puts it, 'that the *deficit* would not have produced the revolution but in concurrence with the price of bread'.[62] It is also clear that he did not share the views of most earlier British travellers on the conflict between the *Parlements* and the Crown which they generally regarded as a struggle for liberty against despotism. Nor had Villiers, who spent most of August in Paris, any illusions about the motives behind the actions of its *Parlement*. In his long-winded way he has some shrewd comments to offer:

> In France, the impositions are peculiarly oppressive to the poor, and burdensome to the middle ranks of people. The poor pay heavy taxes for every trifling article of life; the mechanic and the merchant are subject to the capitation; the houses of the inhabitants are burdened with the vingtieme, whilst the rich have their estates and their lands in the country free and unencumbered.
>
> Under these circumstances there could be no tax more just and proper, than one that should apply to the richer part of the community, and leave the poor free from any additional burden. Of such a nature was the *Territorial Impost*; it was an equal tax on the landed possessions of every man, levied in just proportions; a tax that would have been at once equitable and productive.
>
> This was the cause of all the opposition and disturbance of the parliament; and avarice was the leading motive. The members of it belonging to the law, a body always aspiring and ambitious, jealous of their own rights, and encroaching upon those of others, were possessed of the largest property, and the first landed interest in the kingdom. Finding the old mode abolished, that of making the poor always the supporters of the public burdens; edicts which they have ever willingly registered, and that they are now to be the contributors, they determined upon resistance, and adopting methods which they knew they could justify to the multitude, till, by repeated acts of opposition and contumacy, they at once nullified the intentions of the king, and annihilated their own existence.

After this reference to Lamoignon's reforms Villiers goes on to criticise the policy pursued by Brienne's governments: 'The proceedings of the court seemed to be dictated more by resentment than by prudence; as they should have first considered their inability to raise supplies, in direct opposition to the parliament.'

That the *Parlement* enjoyed a good deal of popular support is noted by Villiers:

> The people, different from what they were in time past, had now begun to conceive a relish for liberty; whether taught by the growing progress of refinement, imbibed from their connection with their American friends, or encouraged by their commerce with England; they now began to be clamorous,

and openly to espouse the side of parliament; conceiving that every tax must ultimately fall upon them, they regarded the opposers of this new imposition, as patriots and friends. Riots and disturbances took place in different parts of the city; blood was spilt; the guards were doubled; and the number and vigilance of the spies increased.

But he remains sceptical as to whether the aims of the *Parlement* and of their supporters among the mass of the population coincided:

> Did it appear that the sacred flame of liberty, or the love of their country, were the principles of the resistance of parliament; or, was it probable that this suspicious moment was seized for the glorious purpose of liberating the people from the bondage of arbitrary power, solely on account of opportunity; I would be the first to weave a wreath of glory for their heads. But the probability is far different. Acts much more arbitrary, impositions much more unjust, have been seconded and sanctioned by their authority. It was self-interest alone, that gave birth to their resistance.[63]

Travellers who happened to be in Paris during Brienne's tenure of office provide little information about his efforts to grapple with the pressing financial problems confronting the government. Among the many economies which he effected in order to reduce the deficit in the national accounts was the closure of the Paris École Militaire. In August 1788 Villiers noted:

> I went yesterday to view the *Ecole Royale Militaire*, which is a large and fine building, where the youth were educated for the military. It is well laid out for the purpose; but, owing to the poverty of the king, is now obliged to be given up; and all the furniture is advertised for sale on Sunday next.[64]

What he gives much more attention to is the financial crisis of that month which swept away Brienne and his attempts at reform and brought about the return of Necker.

By the beginning of August the coffers of the Treasury were empty. On 8 August, in order to try to restore the government's credit, Brienne was compelled to announce that the meeting of the Estates General would take place on the following 1 May and that until then the establishment of the *Cour plénière* would be suspended.

Circumstances ruled out raising an ordinary loan; the only possibility that remained was a forced one. An *arrêt du Conseil* of 16 August replaced most government payments in cash by *billets du Trésor* bearing interest at 5 per cent. Villiers was so impressed by this event that he reproduces the French text of the *arrêt du Conseil* as well as offering the following comments on it:

> Amidst this disorder of affairs, on the 16th instant, the court, finding itself to the last degree embarrassed and restrained; its resources exhausted, and its power of adding to them withheld, was obliged to have recourse to a means the last to be adopted, as operative to the contrary of its design; being calculated still more to depress the falling state of public credit. The king, by the edict of the 16th of August, had acknowledged himself under the necessity of stopping payment of a part of the interest of the national debt for the ensuing year, as a temporary resource, till further means could be adopted; and had given by way of security, to each creditor, a *billet* for their respective amounts; payable, with interest, at the expiration of the term.

Villiers comments sarcastically on the embarrassed tone of this royal edict: 'It is entertaining to observe how invariably arrogance and vanity, at one time, are succeeded by meanness and dejection at another. The low and embarrassed state in which the court of France has publicly declared itself to be, and the humble language it now makes use of, form a striking contrast to the haughtiness and insolence of its deportment not long since.'

The immediate effect of the issue of this edict was to create a panic in Paris among those who held government bills, as Villiers explains:

> It was said and believed, (not without some reason) that the *Caisse d'Escompte* had not escaped the general ravage, amid the difficulties that government laboured under. This idea was received abroad, anxiety and fear sat upon every countenance; the public funds confessed the alarm, and every billholder immediately rushed forward with his demands. The conflux of people to the *Caisse d'Escompte* was so great, and the demands on it so large, that it was unable to provide sufficient for the discharge of the bills that were presented. After this alarm had continued, and the demand increased for a day, it

was found necessary to shut up the *Caisse d'Escompte*; and to refuse payment, for want of money, and to apply to his Majesty for the royal interference, which on the 18th took place.

This took the form of two more *arrêts du Conseil* which, Villiers notes, 'had the desired effect; and the more prudent, finding this alarm at present groundless, chose rather to rest themselves on the security of so large an establishment, than to trust to that of any individual, however respectable or opulent'.

This financial débâcle led a week later to Brienne's resignation and the recall of Necker:

> In this embarrassment of circumstances, when not only popular tumult was raised to so high a pitch; but the commercial part of the community, ever the touch-stone of a nation, began to be interested, and alarmed; in order to stem the tide of such an ocean of difficulties, the king was driven to a measure the most conciliatory that could possibly be adopted, namely, that of recalling M. Neckar to the head of affairs; and of displacing the present administration, who had made themselves as odious to the nation, as M. Neckar was beloved; the people having long been in the habit of looking up to him with the utmost veneration.[65]

Writing on 26 August, Mrs Swinburne offers the following account of Brienne's fall:

> Every thing is in the most dreadful confusion. Bread is increased from 4 to 8 sous. The people are quite mad and talk of nothing but hanging the principal minister. The King's brothers went to him & told him that he was tottering on his throne, that Sens had overturned the whole kingdom and would end by overturning him. Eh bien, renvoyons le said he. The archbishop was sent for; he threw himself at the King's feet, wept bitterly & told him every thing he had done was for the best. — The consequence was that he was to stay, but the Archbishop finding himself in so perilous a situation sent an express for the Abbé de Vermond[66] . . . who was gone to his Abbey and upon his return yesterday was insulted in the gallery. M[de] Adelaide[67] has had an interview with the Queen who was seen with her eyes red as if she had been crying.

The Nation is Outrageous & the Sovereigns are now convinced of it. Last night at 8 o'clock the Archbishop gave in his demission. The King treated him remarkably well . . . Mr Necker is at the head of the Finances.[68]

Necker's return to power was greeted with enthusiasm, according to Villiers: 'The joy was great and universal on the return of M. Neckar; on the news being circulated through the *palais-royal*, the general rendezvous of the politicians, every one seemed wild with rapture, and, running and embracing each other, congratulated them on the happy event.' Yet the immediate consequence of Brienne's departure was more rioting in Paris:

> But the head of the populace was too much kindled to be allayed by lenient and temperate restoratives. They had tasted something of the sweets of liberty, in the riots of licentiousness; and having once made themselves formidable, were not willing to give up their glimpse of consequence. They had learnt to look upon the man who assumed an arbitrary control over them with disgust and jealousy; they had learnt to despise and to insult the military, which once they revered and trembled at; in short, their minds were embittered, their spirits roused; nor could general fermentation be allayed, but by the introduction of some more predominant and specific quality.
>   At the same time that they evinced their zeal for M. Neckar, and their joy at his return, they endeavoured to vent indignation and inveteracy towards the old administration, and their hatred and resentment towards the soldiers. For several successive nights riots took place in different parts of the city, and particularly about the Place Dauphine which they forced to illuminate, and there the effigy of the Archbishop was repeatedly burnt, in the midst of the enraged mob.

There follows an eye-witness account of the riots:

> On Thursday the 28th, and Friday the 29th of August, the last evenings I was in Paris, the riots seemed increasing to a very alarming degree; it was impossible to pass, at night, over the Pont-Neuf. I walked out in the evening, and saw the whole of the Place Dauphine in a blaze, from the burning of

the Archbishop, and the illumination of the windows; one huge sea of heads covered the whole *Place*, and thousands, and tens of thousands, were wrapt in confusion, noise, and violence. The guards were parading about the streets, doubled ten deep, some on foot, and some on horseback, fighting with the furious populace, who repelled their drawn swords with clubs and showers of stones.

Villiers's final comment on Brienne is that 'though the tide of popular prejudice runs high against him, there are some silent individuals who think highly of his character'. He also records a typically French reaction to his fall: 'A Frenchman will have his witticism on any occasion: a friend of the Archbishop was observing the other day, in company, on his being burnt night after night by the populace: "Qu'il sortoit de ses cendres, comme un Phoenix!" one of the opposite party replied "qu'il bruloit comme un diable!"' [69]

Our travellers do not offer any detailed comments on events in France after Necker's recall. On 14 September Lamoignon resigned and fresh riots broke out in the streets of Paris. On 23 September the government recalled the *Parlements* and withdrew all the reforms put forward by Lamoignon on 8 May. On 25 September the Paris *Parlement* demanded that the Estates General should be composed 'suivant la forme observée en mil six cent quatorze'. As this meant that since the three orders should meet and vote separately, the two privileged orders would always be able to outvote the Third Estate, this decree lost the *Parlement* a great deal of popular support; there was an increasing demand for the doubling of the number of deputies of the Third Estate and for all the deputies to sit and vote together in one national assembly. The government recalled the Assemblée des Notables to seek its views on the form which the Estates General should take. This meeting lasted from early November until 12 December and ended with the rejection, by a large majority, of the proposal to double the number of the deputies of the Third Estate. However, on 27 December, Necker finally persuaded the government to agree to the doubling of the number of its deputies. The question of whether the deputies of each order should meet and vote separately or in one national assembly still remained to be decided when the Estates assembled at Versailles in May 1789.

As Villiers reflected on the riots which he had recently observed in Paris (he was writing allegedly 'On board the Pacquet,

2 Sept.'), he penned these comments on the situation in France:

> So much perturbation and heat will not easily subside; and it will be found a matter extremely difficult, if practicable, to reduce their minds, as before, to the yoke of subjection. In fact, the whole kingdom seems ripe for a *Revolution*; every rank is dissatisfied: they despise their king; they detest their queen; the public walks are now filled in every corner with sets of politicians, and every one seems eager to have some share in the business: in private companies, the chief topic now is politics, and they are as much interested and as much agitated, as in the most troublesome times in England. That fear, which once tied their tongues, and that reverence which restrained their thoughts, is now no more; and where they are not afraid of spies, they can condemn their government, and abuse their king, with as much freedom and as little ceremony as Englishmen; though with fifty times the reason. They begin now to see that so large and so rich a territory was never made for the service and the pleasure of one man; and they learn from their increased acquaintance with our country, how much the happiness, the prosperity, and the refinement of a people, depend upon well-regulated laws.[70]

Romilly relates in his memoirs how he spent the law vacation of 1788 in France; he only managed by the skin of his teeth to arrive back in England in time for a court engagement early in October as he was held up in Boulogne for nearly a week by contrary winds. On 10 August, the day after they arrived in Paris, he and his companion went to Versailles for the presentation of the ambassadors of the sultan of Mysore, Tippoo Sahib: 'Though we could only procure a place in one of the rooms through which the ambassadors passed, yet we had an opportunity of seeing all the splendour and gaiety of the court; and its dazzling magnificence has often occurred to my imagination, when I have read of the horrible scenes which were, soon afterwards, acted on the same theatre.' His comments on the political situation in France in the summer of 1788 are rather brief, but they do contain some points of interest:

> The state of public affairs, during this our visit to Paris, was highly interesting. The administration of the Archbishop of Sens had become extremely unpopular, and there were some

trifling commotions in the streets. Crowds assembled on the Pont Neuf, and obliged all the passers-by to take off their hats, in token of respect, before the equestrian statue of Henry IV. In the coffee-houses of the Palais Royal, the freest conversations were indulged; and in the midst of the public ferment which prevailed, a change of ministry was announced, and M. Necker was recalled to the administration.[71]

Another Englishman, a clergyman, who landed at Calais on 19 October, observed on his arrival in Paris the rapid changes which had taken place in recent months in the political situation. On visiting the Palais de Justice on 24 October he wrote:

Astounding are the revolutions which a few days can produce! In the summer, the gates were lined by the king's guards, and the parliament exiled: now, in the shops which swarm in the Palais, political squibs against the minister under whose direction that event took place, and even against majesty itself, are openly sold, and bought with avidity. The king's want of resolution is the principal cause of these frequent changes of system, which diminish the public veneration, and presage a reign of turbulence and troubles.[72]

There is a striking passage in Romilly's memoirs in which he contrasts the high expectations of many French people as they entered the year 1789, with the violent changes which were to take place in the next quarter of a century:

The best and most virtuous men (and I place the Duke de la Rochefoucauld and M. de Malesherbes amongst the foremost of them) saw in it the beginning of a new era of happiness for France, and for all the civilized world. The ambitious rejoiced at the wide field that was opening to their aspiring hopes, and the men of letters began to entertain a higher opinion of their own importance than even they had before conceived. There was not, however to be found, a single individual, the most gloomy, the most timid, or the most enthusiastically sanguine, who foresaw any of the extraordinary events to which the assembling the States was to lead. Who, indeed, could in that single measure, have discovered the seeds of what followed? — the abolition of the monarchy; the public execution of the king and queen; the destruction of the nobility; the annihilation of all religion; the erection of a petty but most sanguinary tyranny in almost every town of France; a succession of wars, all contributing to increase the martial glory of the nation; and, finally, the establishment of a military despotism, the subjugation of almost all the rest of Europe, and the nearest approach that is to be found in the history of modern times to universal empire![73]

Notes

1. See above, p. 238. Hume got the boy's age wrong.
2. *Correspondence*, vol. 35, p. 112; vol. 10, p. 291.
3. *Diaries of a Duchess*, pp. 111–13, 115.
4. *Correspondence*, vol. 39, p. 144; vol. 23, pp. 322, 321.
5. *Lady Bessborough and her Family Circle*, pp. 22, 29.
6. *The Courts of Europe*, vol. I, pp. 10–12.
7. Rutt, *Life of Priestley*, vol. I, p. 256.
8. *An Englishman's Impressions*, p. 87.
9. *Correspondence*, vol. 32, p. 254.
10. *French Journal*, pp. 98–101, 124–8.
11. *Journal of a Visit to Paris*, pp. 43–4.
12. *Autobiography*, p. 26.
13. *Diary of a Scotch Gardener*, p. 133.
14. *Pembroke Papers*, pp. 473, 478.
15. See above, p. 177.
16. *Memoirs*, vol. I, pp. 177–8, 180–1, 64.
17. *Memoirs*, vol. II, pp. 38, 68, 80.
18. *Journal*, pp. 58, 79–80.
19. *Notes of Travel*, p. 269.
20. *A Sketch*, pp. 185–6.
21. *Sketch of a Tour*, vol. I, p. 69. The queen had just given birth to her fourth child, a girl, who died in the following year.
22. Henry, the 10th Earl, the father of Lord Herbert.
23. W. Sussex RO, Add. MS. 7236, ff. 10–11.
24. Pierre André de Suffren (1729–88), an admiral who had scored several successes in Indian waters during the recent war.
25. *Travels in France*, vol. I, pp. 9–10.
26. BL. Add. MS. 30271, f. 8.
27. *A Tour*, pp. 161–2.
28. *Gentleman's Magazine*, 1798, p. 462.
29. *Letters from France*, p. 3.
30. Rutt, *Life of Priestley*, vol. I, pp. 257n, 253, 256.
31. *The Courts of Europe*, vol. I, pp. 48–50.
32. *Correspondence*, vol. 32, pp. 257, 266, 268; vol. 39, pp. 270–1.
33. See above, pp. 191–2.
34. *Correspondence*, vol. 28, pp. 225–6; vol. 41, pp. 346–7.

35. Ibid., vol. 32, pp. 259-60; *Mrs. Montagu*, ed. R. Blunt, vol. I, pp. 318, 321, 332.
36. *Correspondence*, vol. II, pp. 88-9, 91.
37. *Letters*, vol. II, p. 150.
38. HMC 55, vi, pp. 176, 178.
39. *Continental Excursions*, vol. I, pp. 113-15.
40. See above, pp. 81, 106-7.
41. *The Courts of Europe*, vol. II, p. 19.
42. A pun on *timbre* (stamp) and *timbré* (crack-brained).
43. A mistake for Bordeaux. The *Parlement* there was exiled to Libourne some twenty miles away in mid-August. The story of the revolt in Bordeaux was quite untrue; it was obviously one of the wild rumours current in the capital.
44. *The Courts of Europe*, vol. II, pp. 23-6.
45. *Travels in France*, vol. I, pp. 72-3.
46. Ibid., vol. I, pp. 76-7, 80.
47. A mistake for Bordeaux.
48. *Mouchard* derives from *mouche* (police spy).
49. *Sketch of a Tour*, vol. III, pp. 206-8.
50. *The Courts of Europe*, vol. II, p. 32.
51. Goislard de Montsabert.
52. *The Courts of Europe*, vol. II, pp. 53-6.
53. Ibid., vol. II, pp. 55-6.
54. In 1758.
55. *The Courts of Europe*, vol. II, pp. 56-7, 67.
56. BL, Add. MS. 33121, f. 5.
57. *The Courts of Europe*, vol. II, pp. 78-9.
58. BL, Add. MS. 33121, f. 5.
59. *A Tour*, p. 127.
60. BL. Add. MS. 33121, f. 6.
61. *Travels in France*, vol. I, pp. 105, 90, 97-8.
62. Ibid., p. 151. See also pp. 118-19, 137-8, 142-3, 144, 149, 155.
63. *A Tour*, pp. 290-4.
64. Ibid., p. 143.
65. Ibid., pp. 294-6, 302, 307-8.
66. *Lecteur* to Marie Antoinette. He had been largely responsible for Brienne's appointment.
67. One of Louis's aunts.
68. BL, Add. MS. 33121, f. 7.
69. *A Tour*, pp. 309-13, 315.
70. Ibid., pp. 312-13.
71. *Memoirs*, vol. I, pp. 96, 99.
72. *Gentleman's Magazine*, 1798, p. 198.
73. *Memoirs*, vol. I, pp. 99-100.

Conclusion

It has been generally accepted that the observations recorded by foreign travellers provide a far from negligible source for the history of the country which they were visiting. Obviously all the accounts provided by foreigners weigh very little against the home-produced material stowed away in the country's own libraries and archives. None the less they have some value. Travellers often wrote down details about ordinary life which the inhabitants took too much for granted to notice and put on paper. Some were present at striking events or at critical moments in the history of the country and wrote down what they saw. In their dealings with the natives they noted views and attitudes which help to assess the state of public opinion. They often encountered interesting people of all classes of society as well as men and women who played a prominent part in the political or intellectual life of the country.

Historians concerned with France in the period 1787–90 still continue to quote Young's *Travels in France*, to discuss the value of the work, sometimes to refute it on points of detail and sometimes to confirm its findings. Young takes up a good deal of space in the first half of this book, since he offers a far fuller account of the state of French agriculture and industry just before the Revolution than any other British traveller. Yet the accounts of France produced by numerous other travellers do at times confirm, amplify, modify or contradict what he has to say on these topics. Moreover Young did not start on his first French tour until May 1787, when the final crisis of the Ancien Régime had already began. We must turn to other writers for information about what was going on in France from 1763 onwards, and the fairly numerous group of British travellers who were also there in 1787 and 1788 add considerably

Conclusion

to what he has to say about the crisis.

In recent years one has occasionally noticed a rather sneering attitude towards travellers' accounts, perhaps, one suspects, because they sometimes fail to confirm fashionable historical views. One sign of this is that such travellers are often dismissed as mere 'tourists'. It is true that many of the writers considered here travelled for pleasure and often spent only a short time in France, indulging in a trip from London to Paris which lasted altogether only about a month, or else making a fairly rapid crossing of the country on their way to or from Switzerland or Italy. But when such men and women took the trouble to write down interesting observations about what they saw and heard, does it matter if they were just 'tourists'?

At least a score of those travellers for whose journeys more or less precise dates can be established, spent a year and sometimes substantially longer in France. Can Adam Smith, who was there for two and a half years and made a lengthy stay in the provinces as well as in Paris, be written off as just a 'tourist'? Can Wraxall, who deliberately visited 'the unfrequented provinces of France', or Swinburne, who received part of his education there, lived for several years altogether in various parts of France and, with his wife, moved in court circles? Can such travellers as Walpole and Lady Mary Coke, who on their frequent visits to France had the *entrée* to aristocratic circles in Paris and were thus able to record their reactions to current events, be similarly dismissed? Can Gibbon, or Hume, or Sterne?

One noticeable difference since the seventeenth century is the increase in the number of women whose impressions of life in France have come down to us. As might be expected, they are almost all women of the upper classes, from a duchess and other titled women to the wives of a wealthy colliery owner and a London brewer. To these women travellers this book owes a substantial debt, not least to the future Lady Bessborough who between the ages of eleven and twelve produced an interesting record of the family's travels in France.

The men ranged from members of the aristocracy and those of sufficient social status to be presented at court and to be received in the high society of Paris to the barely literate Scottish gardener, Blaikie, who made a successful career for himself in France until he was driven out by the Revolution. Many were academics (some engaged as 'bearleaders' to youths doing the grand tour), doctors, lawyers and clergymen as well as some of the most famous

Conclusion

writers of the age — Hume, Gibbon, Smollett, Sterne and Boswell. There were also some army and navy officers as well as young men — some of them distinguished in later life — travelling on their own or in pairs on the Continent.

Many of them confined their travels to a limited number of commonly-followed routes — from the Channel ports to Paris and then via Chalon-sur-Saône to Lyons and on to Italy or Switzerland or else down the Rhône valley either to Italy or else to Nîmes and Montpellier and often on to Toulouse and Bordeaux. Collectively they covered a much greater area of France than travellers in the previous century. Various parts of the Pyrenees were explored, together with a number of towns south of Bordeaux. Alsace and the newly acquired province of Lorraine attracted some visitors. Brittany drew a few travellers besides Young, and although the mountainous region in the centre and south of France was little frequented, a few did penetrate into Auvergne.

An important qualification for recording anything worthwhile about the country one is visiting is a knowledge of the language. The way French words are spelt and French expressions and whole sentences are transcribed often gives one a poor opinion of a traveller's knowledge of the language, but correct spelling in one's own tongue was not yet regarded as important. Some of the male travellers' spellings of common English words are decidedly odd. On the whole one gets the impression that their command of French was better than that of their predecessors 100 years earlier. What could have occasionally aided communication is that a knowledge of English was less rare in France than it had been in the seventeenth century.

While they encountered difficulties in those parts of the country where French was virtually a foreign language, they did succeed in communicating with members of a wide range of social groups, from members of the aristocracy in Paris and Versailles to provincial *hobereaux*, and from wealthy merchants in such cities as Lyons, Bordeaux and Nantes to shopkeepers and artisans in the towns and to peasants, male and female, at work in the fields.

Clearly these travellers do not by any means answer all the questions which a modern reader would have liked to put to them seeing that they after all had the advantage of actually being in France in these years. If they fail by a long way to answer all our questions, such answers as they do offer come from men and women who were in closer contact with the realities of French life on the eve of the Revolution than anyone today can possibly be. In

Conclusion

a work of this kind one must look less at the overall picture which these seventy-six travellers offer of the France of their day than at the host of significant details about all sorts of aspects of life there which they provide. While what they have to tell us needs to be related to the findings of historical scholarship over the last 200 years, they do contribute something of value to our understanding of what France was like just before the great upheaval.

Appendix A
Notes on Travellers Whose Writings Have Been Quoted

Anonymous writers

The Gentleman's Guide in his tour through France. The title-page states that the author was a naval officer, and it has been suggested that he could be PHILIP PLAYSTOWE (*Factotum*, Oct. 1984, pp. 12–13). The date of the tour described is not clear; what is apparently the first edition is undated. The third edition appeared in 1768. The author claims to have spent eighteen months in France. The tour described takes in Calais, Paris, Chalon, Lyons, Avignon, Antibes, Marseilles, Montpellier, Toulouse and Bordeaux.

A Journal of a Tour to Italy. The first ten pages describe the journey from Calais via Paris and Lyons to Turin; this lasted from 19 September to 10 October 1763.

Notes made in a journey into France, chiefly relating to the picturesk circumstances of the country. The author landed at Dieppe on 17 October 1776 and went via Rouen to Paris, Dijon, Lyons, Avignon, Nîmes, Aix and Marseilles to Nice. He was in Nice from 11 December 1776 to 26 February 1777 and then returned to Calais via Marseilles, Lyons, Nevers, Orleans and Paris.

Remarks on the characters and manners of the French, in a series of letters. This work, published in 1769, consists of a series of letters dated between September 1766 and September 1767. No information is offered about the author's travels in France except that the letters are said to have been written 'during a residence of twelve months in Paris and its environs'.

Sketch of a Trip to Paris in 1788. The author describes himself as a clergyman and claims that 'much of my youth has been spent in France'. He landed at Calais on 19 October and reached Paris on 22 October. The *Sketch* continues until 27 October, at which point a note explains that the account breaks off.

A Tour, Sentimental and Descriptive, through the United Provinces, Austrian Netherlands, and France. No dates are given for the journey. The book was published in 1788. France is dealt with in vol. I, pp. 204–28, and

Appendix A

the whole of vol. II. The author visited French Flanders, Paris and Normandy, returning home from Le Havre to Southampton.

Travel Diary. The author appears to have been an army officer; he included quite a number of sketches in the two little volumes of his diary. Some of these, especially those of fortifications on the coast near Dieppe, were possibly of military value. He was in France from 29 October 1786 until 21 February 1787. He spent most of his time in Paris, but also made stays in Rouen and then Dieppe, where he had a long wait for a boat back to England.

Travels into France and Italy, in a series of letters to a lady. This work, published in 1771, offers no indication as to when the journey was made. The French travels occupy the whole of vol. I and pp. 1–64 of vol. II. The writer made a fairly extensive tour of France from Dieppe to Paris and then via Lyons to Marseilles where he embarked for Italy.

List of authors

ANDREWS, Dr John (1736–1809), historian and pamphleteer. Although his two works show a good knowledge of France, particularly of Paris, they offer no information about where or when he resided there.

ARMSTRONG, Dr John ('Lancelot Temple') (1709–79) MD Edinburgh, 1732. He practised in London, but was also a poet and essayist. In April 1770 he set out by sea for Genoa and, after travelling in Italy, returned via Marseilles, Lyons and Paris. There is no information about his journey from Paris.

AYSCOUGH, George L. (?–?), an officer in the Guards. (The work was published anonymously, but the last letter is signed.) Pp. 1–91 and 229–34 are concerned with France, but they offer no information about the date of his two journeys which took in Calais, Paris, Lyons and Marseilles in both directions on his way to and from Italy.

BENNET, Dr William (1746–1820). BA Cambridge, 1767. Fellow of Emmanuel. Bishop of Cloyne, 1794. The journal begins with his arrival at Calais on 20 June 1785 and ends with his sailing from Calais on 30 October. The tour began with a journey through Lille into the Austrian Netherlands and Germany (ff. 8–69). Re-entering France at Strasbourg, he made a journey through Switzerland, Geneva and Savoy (ff. 73–130). The rest of the MS is devoted to a journey through Lyons, Montpellier, Bordeaux, Orleans, Paris and Rouen.

BENTLEY, Thomas (1731–80), Josiah Wedgwood's partner. The part of his journal which survives covers his stay in Paris from 25 July to 13 August 1776. The most interesting section is his account of a meeting with Jean-Jacques Rousseau.

BERRY, Mary (1763–1852). She made a continental tour with her father and sister which included travels in France from February 1784 to June 1785. These took in Lyons, Montpellier, Aix, Marseilles, Paris and Calais. She and her sister Agnes are remembered today for their friendship with the aged Horace Walpole.

Appendix A

BLAIKIE, Thomas (1750-1838), a gardener. He crossed France into Switzerland via Boulogne, Paris and Lyons in April 1773 and returned via Roanne and Paris in December. Apart from two short visits to England he spent the whole of the period 1776-92 in France as gardener to the Comte de Lauragais and later to the Comte d'Artois.

BOSWELL, James (1740-95). He arrived at Antibes from Genoa on 16 December 1765 and travelled via Marseilles and Lyons to Paris which he left for Calais with Thérèse Levasseur on 31 January 1766.

BURNEY, Dr Charles (1726-1814). He visited France twice in the 1760s in connection with his daughters' education. He left accounts of his journeys through France on his way to Italy (7 June-3 July 1770) and of the return journey (30 November-23 December) as well as of his journey from Calais into the Austrian Netherlands on his second musical tour (July 1772).

BYRON, Isabella, Countess of Carlisle (1721-95). The widow of the 4th Earl of Carlisle. Several letters to George Selwyn, written from the South of France (Aix, Beaucaire, Montpellier, etc.) in 1779-80 have been printed.

R.W.C. The writer was in France from November 1788 to at least the end of April 1789, at which point the copies of the letters suddenly break off. They begin with an account of Paris. He then appears in Bordeaux on his way to Montpellier for his health. He moved on to Toulouse, from where he made a trip to Béziers along the Canal du Midi. The last letter was written after his return to Toulouse.

CAGE, —. The probable author of a travel diary covering a journey from Lyons to Antibes (22 October-7 November 1784). After a stay in Nice he travelled (6-25 March 1785) from Antibes to Castelnaudary where the diary breaks off.

CAYLEY, Cornelius (1729-80?), religious writer. In 1772 he sailed from Hull to Holland, then passed through the Austrian Netherlands and returned home via Dunkirk, Gravelines and Calais.

COKE, Lady Mary (1726-1811). In 1747 she married Viscount Coke, but they separated in 1749 and shortly afterwards she was widowed. A great traveller, she was several times in France: 1. In June 1764 she crossed to Calais on her way to Hanover. 2. In July 1767 she made the same journey on her way to Germany and then re-entered France via Alsace and travelled to Paris (26 August-12 September). 3. After travelling from Lyons to Geneva she went to Marseilles and back via Paris to Calais (October 1769-April 1770). 4. Returning from Vienna, she travelled from Strasbourg via Paris to Calais in April-May 1771, and in September of that year she travelled from Calais to Strasbourg. 5. Returning from Vienna, she travelled from Strasbourg via Paris to Calais in May-July 1772. 6. Returning from Italy, she crossed France via Paris to Calais in April-June 1774. She probably made later journeys to France.

COLE, Rev. William (1714-72), antiquary, one of Walpole's correspondents. BA Cambridge, 1736. He made his way from Calais to Paris and back between 17 October and 2 December 1765. His stay in Paris coincided with one of Walpole's visits there.

CRADOCK, Joseph (1742-1826) and Anna Francesca (?-1816). They

Appendix A

were married in 1765 and lived on his estate at Gumley near Market Harborough. They landed at Calais on 30 October 1783 and left France for the Austrian Netherlands on 24 April 1786. Mrs Cradock spent the whole of this period in France, but her husband twice returned to England, from February to April 1784 and from October 1785 to the beginning of April 1786. They spent nearly a year in Paris before beginning a tour of the provinces which lasted almost the same length of time. They spent part of the winter 1784–5 in Marseilles and then gradually returned north via Montpellier, Toulouse, Bordeaux, Nantes and Blois, reaching Paris on 12 October 1785.

ELLIS, Henry (1721–1806). After being successively governor of Georgia and Nova Scotia, from about 1770 onwards he seems to have spent the rest of his days on the Continent, sometimes wintering in Marseilles and then moving on to Spa. He died in Naples.

ESSEX, James, FSA (1728–84), architect. The main object of his journey was to visit the Austrian Netherlands. He travelled there via Calais, Gravelines and Dunkirk, and came back via Lille and St Omer in August and September 1773.

GARDEN, Francis, Lord Gardenstone (1721–93), a Lord of Session and a Lord of Judiciary. Founder of the town of Laurencekirk. He travelled on the Continent from September 1786 to the summer of 1788. Between September 1786 and May 1787 he travelled extensively in France, from Calais via Paris, Lyons and Marseilles to Hyères where he spent the winter, then on to Montpellier, Avignon and Lyons on his way to Geneva. He also made a short journey from Basle to Plombières, Nancy and Metz on his way to Luxembourg from 25 June to 13 July 1787.

GARMSTON, Richard (?–?). In his journal he describes briefly his journey from Calais via Paris and Lyons to Geneva (19 June–9 July 1787). (A fresh title-page to the MS announces the continuation of the journal for his travels in Savoy and Italy, then on to Antibes and the South of France, Normandy and Flanders, but it breaks off while he was still in Rome.)

GARRICK, David (1717–79). After his trip to Paris in 1751 he made a second journey to France on his way to Italy in September–October 1763, travelling from Calais via Paris and Lyons into Savoy. On his return journey he spent longer in France, from the end of October 1764 to the beginning of April 1765.

GIBBON, Edward (1737–94). Apart from crossing France in 1753 and 1758 on his way to and from Lausanne, he made two stays in France. He landed at Calais on 25 January 1763 and, after three and a half months in Paris, he went on to Lausanne. He returned to Paris in 1777 and spent from May to November there.

HERBERT, Lord George (1759–1827), 11th Earl of Pembroke. He went on a mammoth grand tour which lasted from 1775 to 1780 and which took him as far afield as Russia, Sweden and Italy. Apart from a trip into Switzerland, he spent the period from November 1775 to the summer of 1777 in Strasbourg. His diary relates his return through France from Turin between 18 March and 3 June when he left Paris for Ostend. In this short period he travelled via Lyons, Montpellier

Appendix A

and Bordeaux to Paris where he spent over a month.

HOBHOUSE, Sir Benjamin, Bart. (1757–1831). BA Oxford, 1778. MP from 1797 to 1818. Created a baronet in 1812. He was in France from 6 October 1783 to 13 September 1784 when he sailed from Marseilles for Leghorn. He spent only six days in Paris, and after two months in Marseilles he stayed mainly in Montpellier and the surrounding region.

HOLLAND (FOX), Lady Caroline (1723–74), eldest daughter of the 2nd Duke of Richmond and wife of the politician, Henry Fox. When her husband was created Baron Holland in April 1763, he took her and their son, Charles James, to the Continent for four months, first to Paris and then to Spa.

HUME, David (1711–76). He spent the period from 1734 to 1737 in France, first at Rheims and then at La Flèche. From October 1763 to January 1766 he was in Paris, first as secretary to the ambassador, then as secretary to the embassy, and finally as chargé d'affaires.

JARDINE, Lt.-Col. Alexander (?–1799). His travels in France are found in vol. I, pp. 183–487 of his *Letters from Barbary, France, etc.* and are said (p. 271) to have taken place in 1776 and 1777. They included (p. 476) a journey from Paris to Bordeaux and back.

JERVIS, John, 1st Earl St Vincent (1735–1823), admiral and later First Lord of the Admiralty; created Earl St Vincent after his victory over the Spanish fleet in 1797. His French journal begins on 31 October 1772 and ends with his return to Paris on 17 May 1773. After a few weeks in Paris he moved to Lyons where he stayed until the end of April. He then returned to Paris via Avignon, Montpellier, Bordeaux and Tours.

JOHNSON, Dr Samuel (1709–84). He spent the period from 12 September to 11 November 1775 in France, mainly in Paris, with the Thrales and Baretti.

KNIGHT, Ellis Cornelia (c.1757–1837). She spent from the spring of 1776 to February 1778 in France with her mother, Lady Philippa. They travelled from Calais to Paris and then spent about a year in Toulouse. They arrived in Montpellier in November 1777 and in Marseilles in January 1778. They sailed from there for Italy but were driven back into Toulon and did not finally leave France until mid-February.

KNIGHT, Lady Philippa (1727–99), widow of Admiral Sir Joseph Knight who died in 1775, and mother of Cornelia (q.v.). As she did not receive a pension, she decided to live abroad. She died in Palermo.

LATHAM, Mrs (attr. to) (?–?), a relative of Lady Clive. She accompanied Lord and Lady Clive on a tour of France which lasted from 24 January to 27 June 1768. After ten days in Paris, they moved south via Lyons to Montpellier. For two months they divided their time between Montpellier and Pézenas and then returned to Paris via Toulouse, Cahors, Limoges and Orleans. The journal ends on 28 June at Brussels.

MONTAGU, Mrs Elizabeth (1720–1800), a famous bluestocking, author of an *Essay on the Writings and Genius of Shakespeare* (1769). In July 1763 she crossed the north-eastern corner of France on her way from

Appendix A

Calais to Brussels and Spa. In 1776 she spent nearly four months in France, mainly in Paris, arriving at Calais on 23 June and leaving there on 15 October.

MOORE, Dr John (1729–1802). In 1747–8 he worked in a military hospital in Flanders and then studied medicine in Paris. He returned to Glasgow and practised as a surgeon. From 1772 to 1777 he accompanied the young Duke of Hamilton on his grand tour. The exact dates of their stay in France are not clear, but the journey began there and took them from Paris to Dijon and Lyons on their way to Geneva. Moore was back in Paris in 1792 and in 1793–4 he published *A Journal during a Residence in France from August to December 1792*.

MUIRHEAD, Lockhart (1766–1829). Matriculated Glasgow, 1779. University Librarian, 1796. First professor of natural history, 1807. On his travels he made two journeys in France. 1. In 1787 he entered France at Longwy on 12 April and travelled via Metz, Épinal, Nancy, Plombières and Besançon to Pontarlier where he entered Switzerland on 21 April. 2. In 1789 he entered France through the Pays de Gex on 30 January and proceeded via Lyons, Avignon, Montpellier, Barèges, Toulouse and Aix to Marseilles where he sailed for Italy on 6 October.

PARMINTER, Jane (?–?), a Devonshire woman who was in France in the summer of 1784, travelling from Calais to Paris and on to Dijon.

PECKHAM, Harry (1740–87), a barrister, KC. BA Oxford, 1769. Fellow of New College. The first edition of his *Tour* appeared anonymously in 1772. The work gives no dates for the journey. He entered France from the Austrian Netherlands and proceeded via Lille and Péronne to Paris. After a trip to Rouen he returned from Paris via Amiens and Abbeville to Calais.

PENNANT, Thomas (1726–98), naturalist and traveller. He began his continental tour at Calais on 20 February 1765 and travelled via St Omer and Péronne to Paris. After six weeks there he set out for Geneva which he reached on 29 April, travelling via Montbard where he was put up by Buffon, Lyons and the Grande Chartreuse. On his return journey he arrived at Dunkirk on 15 August and sailed from Calais three days later.

PENNINGTON, Rev. Thomas (1761–1853). BA Cambridge, 1780. Fellow of Clare. Rector of Kingsdown, Kent (1786–1853) and of Thorley, Herts (1798–1853). He made several journeys in France: 1. March–November 1782. He entered France from Ostend and travelled via Lille and Amiens to Paris, returning through Brussels, Dunkirk and Calais. 2. September 1787. From Boulogne he travelled via Paris and Lyons to Geneva. 3. October 1787. He called in at Strasbourg and then returned from Ghent via Lille and Calais. 4. February–May 1789. He crossed France via Lille, Paris, Bourges and Lyons on his way to Geneva. 5. June 1789. He called in at Strasbourg on his way down the Rhine and passed through the Austrian Netherlands to Calais.

PERCY, Elizabeth, 1st Duchess of Northumberland (1716–76). A great traveller; her diaries record the following visits to France: 1. In March–April 1769 to attend the wedding of the Duc de Chartres. 2. In May–June 1770 to attend the wedding of the Dauphin. 3. In April

Appendix A

1772 she was at Lyons on her way to Geneva from where she visited Voltaire at Ferney. 4. In April–May 1774 she travelled down the Rhône to Marseilles and then went on to Bordeaux.

PIOZZI, Mrs Hester Lynch (1741–1821). She made two journeys to France. 1. As Mrs Thrale she spent nearly two months there (17 September–11 November 1775), travelling from Calais via St Omer, Amiens and Rouen to Paris and Fontainebleau, returning via Lille and Dunkirk to Calais. 2. As Mrs Piozzi she travelled via Paris and Lyons to Italy (7 September–1 October 1786).

PRIESTLEY, Joseph (1733–1804). He made a continental tour with his patron, Lord Shelburne, in 1774. They landed at Calais towards the end of August and travelled via St Omer and Lille into the Austrian Netherlands. They re-entered France on 20 September and travelled from Strasbourg to Paris which they reached by 29 September. Priestley spent a month there and met a number of French scientists including Lavoisier.

PULTENEY, Daniel (1749–1811). Entered King's College, Cambridge, 1769. Fellow, 1772. MP for Bramber, 1784–8. He was in Lille on his way to and from Brussels in August–September 1784.

RIGBY, Edward (1747–1821). He practised medicine in Norwich, but also farmed 300 acres five miles away. He and his party were in France from 3 July to 2 August 1789; they travelled from Calais to Paris via Lille and then on to Lyons, Avignon, Nîmes, Marseilles and Antibes into Italy. They also travelled from Basle to Strasbourg on 22 August before crossing the Rhine into Germany at Kehl.

ROGET, Mrs Catherine (?–?), the sister of Sir Samuel Romilly (q.v.). After her husband's death, her brother accompanied her and her children from Lausanne to London in September–October 1783. They entered France via Basle and Mulhouse and made their way to the Austrian Netherlands via Arlon.

ROMILLY, Sir Samuel (1757–1818), lawyer and law reformer. Solicitor General, 1806. He left accounts of three journeys to France. 1. He spent two months there in September–October 1781 on returning from Geneva, travelling via the Grande Chartreuse, Grenoble and Lyons to Paris and returning via Ostend. 2. In September–October 1783 he travelled via Paris to Geneva and Lausanne and crossed France with his sister and her children from Lausanne (see ROGET, Mrs Catherine). 3. In the law vacation of 1788 he travelled via Dieppe and Rouen to Paris where he spent nearly two months, returning via Boulogne.

ST JOHN, James, MD (?–?). He practised in Waterford and wrote poetry and the libretto of an opera. His first letter from Paris is dated 1 March 1787 and the last 27 August. He then travelled to Dijon from where after a week he moved into the nearby country. His last letter is dated from Burgundy on 20 October.

SINCLAIR, Sir John (1754–1835) MP 1780–1812, mainly for Caithness where he had estates. A prolific writer; his best-known work is his *Statistical Account of Scotland* (21 vols, 1791–9). He made two visits to France before 1789: 1. In 1775 he accompanied a younger brother to Aix for the latter's health, travelling through Paris, Dijon and

Appendix A

Avignon. 2. At the end of 1785 and the beginning of 1786 he spent several weeks in Paris.

SMITH, Adam (1723–90). As tutor to the 3rd Duke of Buccleuch he was in France from February 1764 to October 1766. They spent only ten days in Paris before making their way south to Toulouse. From there they explored a considerable area of Southern France. They visited Geneva on their way back to Paris where they remained from December 1765 until their return to England.

SMITH, Sir James Edward (1759–1828), botanist. He was in France from 27 July to 16 December 1786. He spent three months in Paris where he met many naturalists and then travelled via Lyons, Montpellier and Marseilles to Antibes and into Italy. He returned via Strasbourg and Paris to Boulogne, spending the period 8 September–2 November 1787 in France.

SMOLLETT, Tobias George (1721–71). If the information supplied in *Travels through France and Italy* is to be accepted as correct, he arrived in Boulogne in June 1763 and proceeded by way of Paris, Lyons, Montpellier and Marseilles to Antibes, which he reached at the end of November or the beginning of December. After a long stay at Nice, interrupted by a journey to Rome, he returned between May and July 1765 via Marseilles, Avignon, Lyons and Paris to Boulogne.

SPENCER, Lady Henrietta Frances [Harriet] (1761–1821). In 1780 she married Viscount Duncannon who in 1793 succeeded as 3rd Earl of Bessborough. When she had just passed her eleventh birthday, she accompanied her parents and her elder sister on a tour which began at Calais on 1 August 1772. After a journey through the Austrian Netherlands they arrived in Paris on 28 October and then travelled via Orleans and Toulouse to Montpellier. They were back in Paris in May of the following year. The diary breaks off there on 6 June; shortly afterwards the Spencers were in Spa.

STANHOPE, Walter (1749–1822). Matriculated University College, Oxford, 1766. MP for various constituencies 1774–90, 1800–12. On a journey to Berne he landed at Calais on 7 June 1769 and spent some time in Paris. He was back in Paris from May to July 1770 on the return journey.

STERNE, Laurence (1713–68). He arrived in Paris in January 1762 and in July travelled via Lyons and Montpellier to Toulouse. He remained there for a year and then moved on to Montpellier. Apart from visits to Aix and Marseilles he remained there from the summer of 1763 until he returned to Paris in March 1764 and to England in May. In October 1765 he was back in Paris on his way to Pont-de-Beauvoisin and Italy. In May 1766 he returned home via Dijon.

SWINBURNE, Henry (1743–1803) and Martha (?–?). Apart from the years which Henry spent at school in France, he made numerous stays there: 1. In March 1774 he was in Paris and was presented at court. In June he set off for Bordeaux and seems to have remained there until the summer of 1775 when he was in Bagnères and Barèges. In September he began his tour of Spain which lasted until June 1776. 2. In the second half of that year he made the journey described in *Journey from Bayonne to Marseilles* before setting out on his travels in Italy. 3. In June 1779 he crossed France on his return from Italy via Lyons, Paris and Calais. 4. In February and March 1780 he crossed France into Italy via Ostend, Lille, Paris and Lyons. 5. He lived near or in Paris from September 1786 to June 1788. In 1796 he was sent to Paris to try to arrange an exchange of prisoners. (He is also said to have been in Paris in 1783.) Mrs Swinburne appears to have accompanied her husband on his travels in France, and when he went off to Spain, she remained with the children at Tarbes. In 1788 she stayed on in Paris until about mid-November.

THICKNESSE, Philip (1719–92), army officer and a well-known eccentric. His first stay in France seems to have lasted from May to October 1766 and to have been spent mainly in St Germain. He was apparently back there in January 1767, returning home via Calais in August. In 1775 he arrived at Calais on 20 June on his way across France to Spain. He travelled via Rheims, Lyons, Montpellier and Perpignan. He returned through Nîmes and Marseilles, which he left on 7 March 1776. After a month in Lyons he returned via Paris to Calais, having completed the journey 'rather within the revolution of one year', i.e. in June.

THRALE, Mrs. *See* Piozzi.

TOWNSEND, Rev. Joseph (1739–1816), geologist. BA Cambridge, 1762. Fellow of Clare. Studied medicine in Edinburgh. Rector of Pewsey, Wilts. On his way to Spain in 1786 he was in France from early February to the middle of May. He travelled to Paris via Calais and then moved on to Lyons, Montpellier and Perpignan into Spain.

VILLIERS, John Charles, 3rd Earl of Clarendon (1757–1838). MA Cambridge, 1776. Called to the Bar in 1779. MP with breaks from 1784 to 1824 for various constituencies. Succeeded his elder brother in 1824. The letters on his tour cover the period from 2 August to 3 September 1788. He landed at Dieppe and visited Cherbourg and Caen before arriving in Paris on 12 August, in time for Brienne's resignation and the riots which followed.

WALKER, Adam (1731?–1821), writer and inventor who made a career as a lecturer on science. His first visit to France lasted from 10 August to 7 September 1785; it took him from Dieppe and Rouen to Paris, the return journey being made by Lille and St Omer to Calais. In 1787 he landed at Calais on 22 August and passed via Dunkirk into the Austrian Netherlands and Germany. He called in at Strasbourg on his way south to Italy. He returned to France on 26 October by Pont-de-Beauvoisin and made his way to Paris via Lyons and Moulins. He left Calais on 9 November.

WALPOLE, Horatio (Horace), 4th Earl of Orford (1717–97). Apart from visiting France on his grand tour in 1739–41, he made five visits to Paris via Calais between 1765 and 1775: 1. 10 September 1765 to 21 April 1766. 2. 21 August to 11 October 1767. 3. 18 August to 10 October 1769. 4. 8 July to 5 September 1771. 5. 17 August to 15 October 1775.

WARNER, Rev. Dr John Warner (1736–1800), classical scholar. BA Cambridge, 1758. Rector of Stourton, Worcs. In 1790 chaplain to the British embassy in Paris. He was in Paris in the period 1778–9.

Appendix A

WHARTON, Rev. Robert (1751-1808). BA Cambridge, 1773. Rector of Sigglesthorne, Yorkshire. He arrived at Calais on 17 February 1775 and travelled via Lille to Paris. After a stay there and at Dijon he made an excursion to Geneva and then travelled via Lyons and Avignon to Marseilles on his way to Italy. He returned through France in June 1776.

WILKES, John (1725-97). During his period in exile, from 1763 to 1768, he spent a good deal of time in France. He landed at Calais in December 1763 and, after a year's stay in Paris, he left for Italy via Lyons at the end of 1764. In August 1765 he visited from Geneva Voltaire and the Grande Chartreuse. He was back in Paris in September of that year and was still there in March 1766.

WILLIAMS, George James ('Gilly') (1719-1805). A member of the Walpole and Selwyn circle. In 1774 he was appointed Receiver General of Excise. He was in Paris at a critical moment, December 1770.

WRAXALL, Sir Nathaniel William, Bart. (1751-1831), historical writer. MP from 1780 to 1794. Created a baronet in 1813. Travelled with the aim of 'visiting the unfrequented provinces of France'. In August 1775 he landed at Cherbourg and travelled via St Malo, Nantes, La Rochelle and Bordeaux to Bayonne. From there he went through Toulouse and Montpellier to Marseilles, where he stayed from January to April 1776. After going up the Rhône valley to Lyons, he made once again for less-frequented regions, passing through Auvergne to Clermont-Ferrand and then on to Bourges, Blois, Angers and Rouen, leaving Dieppe in June without visiting Paris.

YOUNG, Arthur (1741-1820). Apart from a three- or four-day trip to the Calais region in 1784, he made three visits to France: 1. From 15 May to 11 November 1787 with a break (10-21 July) for a trip into Spain. He landed at Calais and, after following the shortest route to Paris, he set out for Bagnères-de-Luchon via Orleans, Limoges, Souillac, Cahors and Toulouse. After visiting Spain he made a tour through Perpignan, Montpellier, Nîmes and Mirepoix back to Bagnères. He then travelled back to Paris via Lourdes, Pau, Bayonne, Bordeaux, Poitiers, Tours and Fontainebleau. From Paris he travelled to Calais via Soissons, Cambrai, Lille and Dunkirk. 2. From 4 August to 15 October 1788. He landed at Calais and travelled via St Omer, Amiens, Rouen, Le Havre, La Roche-Guyon and Rouen to Dieppe. 3. From 5 June 1789 to 24 January 1790 with a break (16 September-25 December) for a trip into Italy. He travelled from Calais via Abbeville to Paris where he spent three weeks. He then travelled to Antibes and Italy by a meandering route — Rheims, Metz, Nancy, Strasbourg, Belfort, Besançon, Dijon, Moulins, Clermont-Ferrand, Le Puy, Montélimar, Aix, Marseilles and Toulon. He returned from Italy at Pont-de-Beauvoisin and travelled back to Calais (?) via Lyons, Nevers and Paris.

Appendix B
Notes on Other Accounts of Travels in France

ANON. *A Tour of Spain and France* (West Suffolk Record Office, E2/33/6). Towards the end of this travel diary, which also takes in Portugal, there are 4½ pages of jottings on France, describing odd points on a journey from Bordeaux to Paris; no dates are given.

BECKFORD, William (1760–1844). *The Travel-Diaries*, ed. G. Chapman, London, 1928, 2 vols. Contains an account (vol. I, pp. 277–310) of a journey from Geneva to the Grande Chartreuse in 1788.

BOUSQUET, Mrs Mary, *Diary 1765*, ed. E. P. Tindall, Norwich, 1927. Describes a journey to Paris (2–23 August 1765), returning through the Austrian Netherlands back into France to sail from Calais (30 August–2 September).

CRAVEN, Lady Elizabeth, Margravine of Anspach (1750–1828), *A Journey through the Crimea to Constantinople*, London, 1789; *Memoirs*, London, 1826, 2 vols. She spent two months in Paris with her mother and sister in 1763. After her separation from her husband she went to Paris from where she travelled to Antibes in June–August 1785 on her way to Italy, Russia, Constantinople and Greece.

FREWEN, Mary (attr. to), *Journal* (West Sussex Record Office, Frewen MS. 779). Describes a journey from Boulogne to Paris via Calais, Lille and Cambrai, returning to Rye via Chantilly, Abbeville and Boulogne (18 July–19 August 1770).

JARDINE, George (1742–1827), Professor of Logic and Rhetoric, University of Glasgow. See *Selections from the Family Papers preserved at Caldwell*, Paisley, 1883–4, 3 vols (vol. II.2, pp. 273–323), which prints fourteen of his letters written from Paris between 15 Octber 1771 and 3 June 1773 while he was acting as tutor to the two sons of Baron Mure.

JONES, Rev. William (1726–1800). BA Oxford, 1749. FRS, 1775. From 1777 vicar of Nayland, Suffolk. *Observations in a Journey to Paris by way of Flanders, in the month of August 1776*, London, 1777, 2 vols. His journey took him through St Omer and Lille and back to Calais via Chantilly and Montreuil.

KNIGHT, Edward, *Journey to France with Mr. West* (Kidderminster

Appendix B

Library, Archive no. 293). The period covered is from 11 April to 30 May 1767. The route followed was unusual: Calais, Dieppe, Rouen, Caen, Le Mans, Angers, Tours, Poitiers, Angoulême, Bordeaux, Tonneins. At this point the journal suddenly breaks off.

PELHAM, Thomas, 3rd Earl of Chichester (1756–1826), *Travel Diary* (British Library, Add. MS. 33125). This describes a journey from Falmouth to Lisbon, through Portugal and Spain to Perpignan and from there via Montpellier, Nîmes and Lyons to Chambéry. He entered France on 12 January 1777. The journal breaks off shortly after his arrival at Chambéry.

PRATT, Samuel Jackson ('Courtney Melmoth') (1749–1814), *Travels for the Heart*, London, 1777, 2 vols. This is generally regarded as a weak imitation of Sterne's *Sentimental Journey*.

ROBSON, James (1733–1806), *Travel Diary* (British Library, Add. MS. 38837). This covers the period July to October 1787 and is mainly concerned with Italy and Switzerland. The opening part of the diary until the writer arrived at Dijon is practically illegible. He returned through France via Lyons and Paris to Boulogne.

RUSSELL, Francis, 5th Duke of Bedford (1765–1802), *A Descriptive Journey through the interesting parts of Germany and France, by a Young English Peer, of the Highest Rank*, London 1786. The journey seems to have been made in 1784–5. On his arrival in France at Strasbourg he made an excursion into Switzerland. On his return he went via Nancy and Épinay to Paris. After several weeks there he returned via Caen, Le Havre and Dieppe.

SELWYN, George Augustus (1719–91), MP. Although he was a frequent visitor to France, only two of his letters written there appear to have survived, reproduced in W. S. Roscoe and H. Clergue, *George Selwyn. His Letters and Life* (London, 1899, pp. 118–21). Both were written on 18 April 1779.

TEMPEST, John, *Travel Diary* (West Yorkshire Record Office, MS.5 f/11). The writer was in France from 21 March 1769 to 26 June 1770. He travelled via Calais and Paris to Toulouse, where he remained from April to October. From there he gradually made his way back to Paris via Marseilles, Lyons and Dijon, making some lengthy stays on the journey. He returned by Calais.

TURNER, John, *Travel Diary* (Northamptonshire Record Office, D (C.A.) 347). The writer arrived at Dieppe on 25 July 1774 and, after visiting Rouen, moved on to Paris. The diary breaks off after an account of Versailles, dated 15 August (only 10 folios).

Index

Note that sub-entries to be found under the main entries relating to the travellers, and the other individuals cited, have been ordered with regard to the structure of the text, rather than strict alphabetical sequence.

Abbeville 99–100, 114, 198
Adélaïde, Madame 237, 263, 297
Agoult 289
agriculture
  buckwheat 66
  droit de parcours 44
  enclosures 44
  irrigation 39
  livestock
    cattle 35, 37–8, 39, 41–2, 44, 46–7, 48
    horses 42
    pigs 42–3, 47
    sheep 37–8, 39, 41–2, 44, 46–7, 48
    see also peasants
  maize 32, 38–9
  olives 35, 36
  ownership of land 52
  poor farm equipment 41–3
  potatoes 36, 67
  rotation of crops 34–5, 40–8
  rye 44, 66
  vaine pâture 44
  vineyards 31–2, 35, 35–7, 41, 65
  waste land 39–40, 42, 45–6
aides 15, 16, 294
Aiguillon 55, 183
Aiguillon, Emmanuel Armand, Duc d' 183, 248–53, 257, 258
Aire 72, 109
Aix-en Provence 6, 11, 20, 90, 148
Alembert, Jean Lerond d' 270
Alsace 5, 16, 35–6, 53, 99, 306

American Independence, War of 1–4, 97, 107, 112, 262, 268, 270, 280
  influence in France 280–1, 285–6, 292, 294
Amiens 1, 2, 22, 114, 116, 121, 161
Andrews, John x, 309
  Salpêtrière 128
  Bicêtre 128–9
  merchants 136–8
  bourgeois defined 137, 178
  clergy's loss of influence 151
  bear garden 219–20
Angers 111
Anjou 45, 55
Anzin, Compagnie d' 111
Argentan 41
Argyll, James, 5th Duke of 87
Argyll, Elizabeth, Duchess of 87
aristocratic revolt 255–9, 282–99
Arkwright, Sir Richard 81, 103
Arles 7, 35
Armstrong, John x, 309
  game laws and galleys 61, 202
Arras 18
Artois 35, 48, 54
Artois, Comte d' 163, 223, 235, 240, 262, 264–7, 272–4, 277, 283, 297
Artois, Comtesse d' 223, 272
Asemblée des Notables 282, 299
atheism 150
Auch 21, 55, 156, 180
Auge, Pays d' 37, 52
Austrian Netherlands 32, 50, 82, 130
Auvergne 37, 55, 306

Index

Avigon 39, 68
Ayscough, George L. x, 309
  officers compelled to go to theatre 211
  Pierre-Encise 192–4

Babeuf, François Noël 209
Bagnères-de-Luchon 21, 66
balloons 224–7, 270
banned books 223
Barèges 6
Baretti, Giuseppe 78, 266
Bath 119
Bayonne 6, 16, 21
Béarn 11, 52–3, 64, 292
Beaucaire 20, 116–18
Beauce 54, 179
Beauvais 23, 99, 102, 114
Beauvau, Charles Juste, Prince de 258–9
Beauvau, Élisabeth Charlotte, Princesse de 256
Beckford, William 186, 318
Bédarieux 102, 143
Bedford, Francis Russell, 5th Duke of 319
beggars 50, 111–12, 149
Bennet, Rev. William x, 309
  Flemish agriculture 33–4
  Garonne valley 36
  Protestants 175
Bentley, Thomas x, 213, 309
  Sèvres porcelain 77
  Palais Royal 221
  St. Cloud 223
  Louis XVI and Marie Antoinette 267
Bernay 37, 43
Berry 55, 60, 100, 101
Berry, Charles, Duc de 272–3
Berry, Mary x, 309
  roads 20
  haggling in shops 77
  Lyons industries 85–6, 120
  Marseilles 87–8
  Nîmes 91–2
  dancing 224
Besançon 24–5, 147–8
Béthune 33, 42–3, 49, 72
Béziers 175

Bigorre 11
Biron, Louis Antoine, Maréchal de 288
Blagden, Francis William 17
Blaikie, Thomas x, 305, 310
  customs barriers 18
  poor agricultural methods 40–1
  potatoes 67
  relics 147
  entertained by monks 163
  executed criminals displayed 206
  royal family at breakfast 267–8
Blanchard, Jean Pierre 225
Bordeaux 3–4, 25, 36, 93–6, 113–14, 175, 182, 201, 220–1, 275–6, 306
Boswell, James x, 306, 310
  galleys 202–3
Bouchardon, Edme 243–4
Bouillon, Godefroi Charles Henri, Duc de 182
Boulogne 5, 42, 58, 59, 130, 180, 183, 197, 198, 300
Boulton, Matthew 80–1
Bourbonnais 44, 45, 55
Bourg-en-Bresse 224
Bousquet, Mrs Mary 318
bread, large place in diet 49, 64–6
Brest 23, 63
brewing 79
Brienne, Cardinal Étienne Charles Loménie de Brienne 4, 158–9
  in power 213, 273, 282–98
  unpopularity 284, 298–9, 300, 301
Brighton 82
Brittany 5, 19, 23, 39–40, 45–6, 55, 64, 67, 96–7, 178, 180, 259, 306
  clashes with monarchy 248–52, 290–3
Brive 51, 103–4
Buccleugh, Henry, 3rd Duke of 89
buckwheat 66

Index

Burgundy 11, 25, 42, 291
Burney, Charles x, 310
  customs barriers 18
  roads 20
  peasant poverty 50
  fortified towns 72–3
  Lille hospital 130–1, 133
Bute, John, 3rd Earl of 251

R.W.C. x, 310
  Occitan 7
  Garonne valley 36–7
  Toulouse 89–90
  religious processions 153
  entertained by monks 164–5
  noblemen drawn to court 180–1
  attends execution 208
  Louis XVI and Marie Antoinette 274
Caen 41, 67
Cage, — x, 310
  Protestants 175–6
Cahors 64
Caisse d'Escompte 296–7
Calais 1, 5, 17, 18, 19, 20, 22, 32, 33, 34, 42, 49, 50, 62, 72, 109, 122
Calas, Jean 170–1, 197
Calonne, Charles Alexandre de 283, 285
  in power 281–2
  low reputation 282, 285
  subsidies to industry 81, 104, 106, 281
Cambis, Gabrielle Françoise Charlotte, Vicomtesse de 2
Cambis, Jacques François Xavier, Vicomte de 4
Cambrai 18, 72
Canal du Midi 175
capitaineries 60–1, 69
capitation 10, 15, 56, 294
Carcassonne 21, 92–3, 102
Carentan 64
Carlisle, Isabella Byron, Countess of 2, 310
  Estates of Languedoc 9–10
  roads 20
  Beaucaire fair 116–17

Castelnaudary 36
Catholicism
  behaviour in church 148–50
  confréries 153–4
  clergy
    Assemblé du Clergé 290
    commendatory abbots 162
    curés 154–5
    don gratuit 170, 290
    higher clergy 155–9
    regular clergy (female) 168–9
    regular clergy (male) 159–68
    tax exemptions 56, 169–70, 281, 290
    wealth 52, 156, 161, 162–5
  hostility to 150–2
  religious orders 160–1
  non-observance of Sunday 149
  number of church festivals 170
  processions 151–4
  relics 126, 146–8, 152–3
  saints 146–8
Caussade 102
Caux, Pays de 43
Cayley, Cornelius x, 310
  peasant poverty 50
  maréchaussée 200
centralisation 8–11, 25–6
Chabot, Duc de 292
Chalon-sur-Saône 306
Champagne 53, 55, 62, 103
Chanteloup 182–3, 255, 256, 258
Chantilly 20, 50, 60–1, 180, 198, 256
Charente, River 182
Charité-sur-Loire, La 62
Charles, Jacques Alexandre César 224–6
Charost, Armand Joseph, Duc de 191–2
Chartres, Duc de *see* Orléans, Louis Philippe Joseph, Duc d'
Chateaubriand family 45
Châteauroux 101

Index

Château-Thierry 24
Chatham, William Pitt, 1st Earl of 251
Cherbourg 40, 41, 50, 111, 142
chestnuts 67
Chichester, Thomas Pelham, 3rd Earl of 319
Choiseul, Étienne François, Duc de 1, 182–3, 240, 247–8, 253, 255–6, 258, 259, 277–8
Choiseul, Louis Honorine, Duchesse de 240, 248, 275
Choisy-le-Roi 22, 267
Churchill, Charles 251
Cîteaux 163
Clermont 52
Clermont, Louis de Bourbon-Condé, Comte de 162
Clermont-Ferrand 37
Clermont-Tonnerre, Jules Louis Henri, Duc de 291
Clive, Robert, 1st Baron xii, 51, 168–9, 206
Clive, Lady Elizabeth 168–9
coal industry 106–7, 109–12
coke 106–7, 110
Coke, Lady Mary x, 305, 310
  customs barriers 18
  Flemish agriculture 33
  peasant women 62
  galleys 203–4
  Mme Du Barry 241–2
  1771 crisis 255
  unpopularity of Louis XV 260
Colbert, Jean Baptiste 92, 116, 157
Cole, Rev. William xi, 198, 310
  customs barriers 117–18, 119
  cattle 41
  fortified town 73
  Paris shops 76
  Salpêtrière 127–8
  hostility to religious orders 160
  commendatory abbots 162
  droit d'aubaine 188–9
  Bastille 191
  mountebanks 216

Louis, Dauphin 239, 247
  trouble ahead for monarchy 247
Combourg 45
Commutation Act 112–13
Compiègne 256
Comtat Venaissin 68–9
Condé 109
Condé, Louis Joseph, Prince de 11, 60–1, 181, 256–7
Coniac, — de 250
Conti, Louis François, Prince de 243
corvée 57–8, 278, 281
Cotentin 111
cotton industry 81, 82, 83, 92, 99, 102–4, 114–15
Cour des Aides 281, 282
Cour des Comptes 283
cour plénière 289–90, 295
Coutances 50
Coxe, William 272
Cradock, Mrs Anna Francesca xi, 105, 149–50, 163–4, 205, 210, 213, 217, 218, 219, 220–1, 224, 310–11
  Paris water works 79–80
  Marseilles 87
  Sèvres 104
  Hôtel-Dieu, Lyons 132
  La Charité, Lyons 132–3
  relics 148
  religious processions 154
  Protestants 175
  Foire St. Germain 215–16
  Foire St. Laurent 216
  St. Cloud 223
  ascent of balloons 225–7
  Marie Antoinette 270–1
Cradock, Joseph xi, 80, 87, 104, 154, 210, 215, 216, 223, 226, 271, 310–11
  newspapers, shortage of 25
  Indret, Ile d' 105
  relics 148
  behaviour in church 149–50
  entertained by monks 163–4
  Protestants 175
  galleys 205
  Carnival 217

mountebanks 218
water sports 219
Midsummer festival 220–1
ascent of balloons 225
meets Charles 225
Marie Antoinette 270
Craven, Lady Elizabeth 318
Creusot, Le 106–7
Cumberland, Henry Frederick, 4th Duke of 174, 224

Damiens, Robert 209, 235, 236
Dauphiné 109, 134, 291–2
Decrétot, Jean Baptiste 100
deism 151, 152
Derby, Lady Elizabeth 87
Diderot, Denis 150
Dieppe 82, 83, 217–18
Dijon 11, 25, 131–2, 135, 152–3, 161, 163
Dillon, Arthur Richard de 13–14, 156–8, 176, 282, 290
Dol 45
domestic industry 93, 100, 101–3
Dordogne, River 62, 182
Dorset, John Frederick, 3rd Duke of 245–6, 272
droit d'aubaine 188–90
droit de chasse 60–1, 69
droit de parcours 44
Dromgold, Jean 162
Du Barry, Jeanne, Comtesse 236–7, 239–42, 244–6, 253, 258, 262, 263, 277
Du Deffand, Marie Vichy Chamrond 1–2, 248
Dumont, Pierre Étienne Louis 129
Dunkirk 5, 16, 18, 50, 109, 111, 112–13
Duras, Emmanuel Céleste Augustin, Duc de 259

East Indies 89
École Militaire 295
economic liberalism 157–8
Écouen 22
Eden, William 113
Eden Treaty 113–16
Elbeuf 43, 100–1, 102
Élisabeth, Madame 267, 270, 271
Ellis, Henry xi, 311
 Necker's departure in 1781 280
enclosures 44
England
 agriculture 31–2, 35, 38, 41–5, 47, 48, 51, 54, 57–9, 63, 65–6, 68
 coal exports 110–12
 decentralisation 9
 footwear 61
 industry 83, 88
 noblemen's attitude to estates 181
 political model 157, 183, 231, 286, 294
 prices 66
 roads 26–9
 trade with France 112–16
 wages 68, 119–20
 weights and measures 8
English language less unfamiliar in France 306
Englishmen working in France 80–1, 83, 103–7
Épinal 169
Esprémesnil, Duval d' 288–9
Essex, James xi, 311
 peasant poverty 80
Esates General 281–2
 demand for it to be summoned 249, 282–3, 285–6, 287, 288, 290
 form 299
 summoned 213, 295
Étampes 206

fairs
 Beaucaire 20, 116–18
 Guibray 115, 116
 Paris 211, 216–17
Fersen, Hans Axel, Comte de 279
Fielding, Lord 272
finances 252, 255–9, 273, 275, 277, 278–97

Index

Fitzgerald, Lady Charlotte 90
Fizes, Antoine 7, 91
Flanders 18, 32–5, 42–3, 46, 48, 50, 53, 169
Flèche, La 40, 45
flour milling 97
Fontainebleau 23, 62, 234, 266
Forrester, Colonel 172, 186
France-Comté 19, 67, 291
Franklin, Benjamin 216
French language 4–5, 26
  other languages
    Basque 5–6
    Breton 5
    Catalan 6
    Flemish 5
    German 5
    Occitan 6–7
  travellers' command of 4, 306
Fréron, Élie Catherine 4
Frewer, Mary 318
Fumel, Comte de 3–4

gabelle 15, 16, 58, 140, 281, 294
Gardenstone, Francis Garden, Lord xi, 311
  Occitan 6
  vineyards 32
  poor farm equipment 43
  peasant poverty 57
  potatoes 67
  Marseilles industries 87
  Nîmes 92, 176
  curés 154
  Protestants 176
Garmston, Richard xi, 311
  Louis XVI and brothers at Mass 273
Garonne, River 35, 36–7, 53, 55, 68, 93, 97, 182
Garrick, David xi, 1, 311
  customs barriers 19
  peasant poverty 50
  reactions to executions 207
Gascony 6, 53
The Gentleman's Guide ix, 308
  Bordeaux 93
  expenditure on clothes 183
  galleys 204–5
  Montpellier 91
  peasant poverty 51, 65
  Toulouse 90
The Gentleman's Guide (1788) ix, 308
  Estates of Languedoc 12
  haggling in shops 76
  Hôtel-Dieu, Paris 124
  Paris boulevards 212
  Paris streets 74
  Rouen 82–3
Gibbon, Edward xi, 1, 4, 305, 306, 311
  English and French noblemen compared 181
  entertained by Neckers 279
Givors 111
glass industry 77–9, 81, 88, 104, 106–8, 111
Goislard de Monsabert 288–9
grain shortages 34, 64–6, 116, 293
Grande Chartreuse 165–8
Gravelines 50
Grégoire, Abbé Henri 5
Grenoble 63
Guerchy, Claude François Louis, Comte de 237, 248
Guibray 115, 116
Guinea 98
Guines, Adrien Louis, Duc de 4
Guingamp 5, 23
Gustavus III 270
Guyenne 46, 53, 55

Havre, Le 67, 97–8
Helvétius, Claude Adrien 150
Hénin, Charles Alexandre Marc, Prince d' 236
Henry IV 301
Herbert, Lord George xi, 311–12
  in France in wartime 2–4, 268
  customs barriers 19
  Garonne valley 36
  Bordeaux 95
  entertained by Duc de Chartres 177, 268
  Louis XVI, Marie Antoinette

325

and Comte de Provence 268
Hertford, Francis, Earl of 124, 219, 234
highwaymen 200-1
Hobhouse, Sir Benjamin xi, 312
  Occitan 7
Holbach, Paul Thiry, Baron d' 1, 150
Holker, John 83, 103
Holland, Lady Caroline 312
  welcomed at court 234, 237
hospitals
  medical 121, 122-6, 131-4
  prisons 126-30
  workhouses 126-31, 132
hours of work 85-6, 120
Huguenots *see* Protestantism
Hume, David xi, 305, 306, 312
  religion despised 150
  presented to Louis XV 234
  Louis, Dauphin, one of his admirers 238
  eulogised by royal children 238, 262
  presented to Mme de Pompadour 239-40
Hyères 87

illiteracy 5, 26
Indret, Ile d' 105-6, 107
industry
  backwardness 98-9
  brewing 79
  coal 106-7, 109-12
  cotton 81, 82, 83, 92, 99, 102-4, 114-15
  domestic 93, 100, 101-3
  flour milling 97
  glass 77-9, 81, 88, 104, 106-8, 111
  iron and steel 104-7, 111, 112
  linen 46, 82, 92, 97, 103
  porcelain 77, 88
  silk 35, 78, 85-6, 88, 91-2, 101, 103
  soap 88, 89
  steam engines 80-1, 105, 106

sugar refining 88, 110
tanning 104
woollen 47-8, 78-9, 82, 92-3, 99-103, 114-15, 158
inns 18, 21, 22, 23-4, 72-3
insurance, maritime 94
intendants 9-10, 25-6, 56, 69, 90, 249, 280
iron and steel industry 104-7, 111, 112
Isle-sur-la-Sorgue, L' 39
Italy 2, 39, 64, 84, 273, 305, 306

James II 146
Janninet, — 225
Jardine, Lt. Col. Alexander xi, 312
  centalisation 8-9
  Flemish agriculture 32-3
  criticizes French agriculture 41-2
  peasant poverty 49
  mirror factory 78-9
  urban poverty 118, 135
Jardine, George 318
Jaucourt, Marquis de 291
Jervis, John, 1st Earl of St. Vincent xi, 312
  peasant poverty 49, 50-1
  mirror factory 78
  Lyons 84
  Bordeaux 93-4
  urban poverty 120-1
  Enfants Trouvés, Paris 123
  merchants 137
  noblemen 178-9
Jesuits 150, 161-2, 173, 277
Johnson, Samuel xii, 216-17, 266, 312
  converses in Latin 4
  mirror factory 78
  brewing 79
  Enfants Trouvés, Paris 123
Jones, Rev. William Jones (of Nayland) 318
Joseph II 158-9, 268
A Journal of a Tour to Italy ix, 308
  expulsion of Jesuits 161

Index

justice
  civil laws 8, 26, 195
  criminal procedure 196
  crimes
    murder 199–201
    robbery 198, 200–1
    sacrilege 208–9
  injustices, cases of 197–8
  manorial courts 59–60,
    194–5, 201
  penal code 58
    breaking on the wheel 196,
      206–9
    galleys 61, 140, 201–5
    game laws 60–1, 69
    hanging 140, 205–9
    pillory 201–2
  state prisons 190–4
  torture 196–7

Knight, Edward 318–19
Knight, Ellis Cordelia xii, 312
  Estates of Languedoc 12–14,
    156–8
  Toulouse 89
  Montpellier 91
  Loménie de Brienne 158–9
  Protestants 174
  Louis XVI and Marie
    Antoinette 267
Knight, Lady Philippa xii, 89,
  90, 158, 267, 312
  Estates of Languedoc 9

La Barre, Jean François
  Lefebvre, Chevalier de
  197–8, 209
La Bellangerais, – de 249–50
La Chalotais, Anne Jacques
  Raoul de 249–52
La Chalotais, Louis René de
  249–52, 257
La Fayette, Marie Joseph,
  Marquis de 292
La Roche, Marquise de 249–50
La Rochefoucauld, Louis, Duc
  de 301
La Vrillière, Duc de 191–2,
  241, 250
Lally-Tollendal, Comte de 191

Lamballe 180
Lambert, Sir John 10
Lambesc 11
Lamoignon, Chrétien 289, 294,
  299
Languedoc 6–7, 9–10, 19, 21,
  29, 53, 56, 102, 157–8,
  258–9, 292
Latham, Mrs xii, 312
  peasant poverty 51
  visits convent 168–9
  executed criminals displayed
    206
Latin, oral use of 4
lawyers 135–6
Lekain, Henri Louis 244
Levant 88, 89, 92, 93, 158
Layrac 68
Liancourt 23, 51–2, 183
Liancourt, François Alexandre
  Frédéric, Duc de 51–2,
  183, 273
Libourne 284
Lille 2, 5, 18, 20, 33, 34, 72,
  82, 109, 112–13, 114–15,
  130–1, 133, 159–60, 211
Limagne 37
Limoges 55, 66, 67, 112
Limousin 38, 46, 55, 66
linen industry 46, 82, 92, 97,
  103
Lodève 143, 168–9
Loire, River 5, 6, 19, 42, 97,
  104, 111
London compared with
  Paris 21–3, 75–6, 80,
  95
Lorraine 53, 55, 60, 63, 67,
  154, 291, 306
Louis XIII 282, 284
Louis XIV 146, 157
Louis XV, 95, 158, 172, 182,
  183, 198, 209, 216, 233,
  263, 266
  character and appearance
    233–6, 241–6
  conflict with Parlements
    248–55
  final unpopularity 260
  Maupeou's reforms 254–9

mistresses 236, 239–42,
    244–6
  piety 235, 251
  weaknesses as ruler 247
Louis XVI 57, 79, 81, 189, 192,
    212, 236, 237, 238, 240
  character and appearance
    262–74
  final unpopularity 286, 288,
    300
  political role 175, 277–8,
    280–99, 301
Louis, Dauphin 234, 237–9,
    247, 260, 270
Louis Joseph Xavier François,
    Dauphin 269–70
Louise, Madame 237, 241
Lourdes 100, 190
Louviers 93
Luynes, Cardinal de 234
Lyonnais 103
Lyons 2, 18, 19, 20, 50, 63, 67,
    77, 83–6, 89, 110, 111,
    119–21, 132–4, 155, 169,
    192, 200, 202, 211, 268,
    306

Mâcon 38, 224
Maine 45, 55
maize 35, 36, 38–9, 66
Malesherbes, Chrétien
    Guillaume Lamoignon de
    191–2, 277–8, 301
Mallet du Pan, Jacques 129
Manchester 81, 83, 103
Mans, Le 45
Marche 38, 55, 120
Marche, Comte de la 241, 243
maréchaussée 200–1, 276
Maria Theresa 263
Marie Antoinette 81, 224, 279
  character and appearance
    263–74
  final unpopularity 284, 288,
    300
  political role 277, 291, 297
Marie Josèphe de Saxe,
    Dauphine 237, 238, 262
Marie Leczinska 234, 237, 238
Marmande 36

Marsan, Marie Louise
    Geneviève, Comtesse de
    277
Marseilles 3, 4, 6–7, 16–17,
    20, 24, 25, 61, 83, 86–9,
    90, 94–5, 110–12, 149–50,
    202–4, 217, 218–19, 280
Maupeou, René Nicolas de 242,
    252–60, 275, 278, 289
Mazarin, Cardinal 126, 127
merchants 95, 136–9, 306
Mercier, Louis Sébastien 129
Metz 16, 24, 47
middle classes 118
  dissatisfaction with place in
    society 246–7
  ownership of land 52, 134–41
  rise into nobility 137–9
milice 69
Miolan, Abbé 225
Mirabeau, Honoré Gabriel de
    Riquetti, Comte de 129
Mirepoix 21
monarchy, French attitude to
    231–3
Montagu, Mrs Elizabeth xii,
    278, 312–13
  Enfants Trouvés, Paris 123–4
  Paris shops 76
Montauban 12, 20, 64, 102, 171
Montcenis 106–7, 112
Montélimar 6, 177
Montesquieu, Charles de
    Secondat, Baron de 233
Montpellier 7, 9, 12–14, 20,
    87, 89–92, 117, 154, 156,
    171, 173, 206–7, 306
Montreuil 58, 73
Moore, John xii, 313
  Paris streets 74
  Lyons 84
  French attitude to monarchy
    231–3
  Louis XV 242
  1771 crisis 259
Morlaix 63
Moulins 25, 110
Mousseaux 177
Muirhead, Lockhart xii, 313
  Basque 6

328

Index

Occitan 6-7
customs barriers 19
roads 20
peasant women 63
  housing 64
  diet 67
  potatoes 67
Lyons 84
Carcassonne 93
wood shortage 108-9
coal 109-10
coke 110
Hôtel-Dieu, Lyons 133-4
La Charité, Lyons 133-4
aristocratic churchmen 155-6
peasants dancing 223-4

Nancy 223
Nantes 39, 46, 96-7, 105, 106, 111, 112, 115, 148, 292, 306
Napoleon I 8, 95, 302
Narbonne 21, 93, 156
Necker, Jacques 39, 278-81, 297-9, 301
Necker, Mme Suzanne 125, 278-9
Newcastle upon Tyne 110, 111
newspapers, shortage of 24-5
Nice 6, 87, 91
Nicolai, — 283
Nicolet, Jean Baptiste 214, 227
Nîmes 20, 91-2, 117, 118, 171, 172-6, 306
Nivernais 44, 45, 55, 179
Noailles, Comte de 275-6
nobility 306
  army career 179-80
  attitude to *roturiers* 75, 136, 137, 178, 184
  court nobles' estates neglected 181-3
  drawn to Paris and court 180-1
  droit de chasse 60-1, 69
  exemption from *taille* 56, 179, 281
  extravagance 183-4
  feudal dues 59, 179
  hold posts in Church 155-69

  large number of noblemen 177-8
  manorial courts 59-60, 179, 194-5, 201
  ownership of land 52
  provincial nobility 89, 179-80
  poverty frequent 179-80
  upbringing 178
Normandy 16, 35, 37-8, 42-4, 52, 54, 62, 83, 103, 104, 115
Northumberland, Elizabeth Percy, Duchess of xii, 313-14
Marseilles 87
Bordeaux 94-5
Pierre-Encise 192
pillory for theft 201-2
Paris boulevards 212-13
mountebanks 218-19
Louis XV and Mme Du Barry 236-7, 240-1
Louis XVI as Dauphin 262-3
Notes made in a Journey into France ix, 308
noblemen and bourgeois 136
sabots 62
Noyon 72

olives 35, 36
Orleans 22, 23, 34, 110, 206
Orléans, Louis Philippe, Duc d' 256-7
Orléans, Louis Philippe Joseph, Duc d' 60, 108, 119, 177, 221-3, 265, 273, 287
Orléans, Philippe, Duc d', Regent 221, 248

Paris *passim*
  ascent of balloons 224-7
  Bastille 184, 190-2, 209, 245, 249, 278, 280, 291, 292
  bear garden 219-20
  Bicêtre 126, 128-30
  boulevards 73, 211-14
  Carnival 217
  Enfants Trouvés 122-4
  Foire St. Germain 211, 214-16

Index

Foire St. Laurent 216
Foire St. Ovide 216–17
Hôpital Général 126
Hôpital Necker 125
Hôtel-Dieu 124–6
industries
  brewing 79
  cotton 81
  glass 77–9, 81
  Gobelins 77
  Sèvres porcelain 77
  water works 79–81
mountebanks 218–19
mur des fermiers généraux 73–4
Palais Bourbon 181
Palais Royal 221–2, 298
police 199, 287
Salpêtrière 126–8
shops 75–7
streets 74–5
theatres 211, 213, 215, 218, 268, 270
water sports 219
Parlements 135, 247–55, 256, 259, 275–6, 278, 280–3, 287–91, 293, 299
  Besançon 257, 258
  Bordeaux 258, 275–6, 287, 303
  Douai 258
  Grenoble 258, 291
  Paris 57–8, 146, 195–6, 209, 251–4, 259, 275, 278, 281–4, 287–90, 294–5, 299
  Pau 291
  Rennes 248–52, 290, 293
  Rouen 284, 293
  Toulouse 90, 138, 255, 259, 284
Parlement Maupeou 254, 259, 275–6
Parminter, Jane xii, 313
  Louis XVI and Marie Antoinette 271
Pau 52–3, 291
pays d'élections 10, 15, 26, 55–6
pays d'états 11–14, 26, 55–6
peasants 306
  corvée 57–8, 278, 281

  diet 64–7
  droit de chasse 60–1, 69
  feudal dues 59–60
  footwear 61–2
  gabelle 58
  hard toil of women 62–3
  housing 63–4
  ignorance 7
  manorial courts 59–60
  métayers 54–5
  milice 58, 69
  ownership of land 52
  poverty 32, 48–51, 68, 224
  smallholdings 52–4, 64, 68
  taxes 55–7
  tenant farmers 51–2
  tithes 58–9
  wages 67–8
Peckham, Harry xii, 313
  customs barriers 18–19
  roads 20
  poor farm equipment 43
  feudal dues 59
  sabots 62
  industrial backwardness 98–9
  beggars 121
  Lille hospital 130
  relics 147
  highwaymen 200
  Paris boulevards 213
  St. Cloud 222–3
  Louis XV hunting 243
  epigram 243–4
Pembroke, Henry, 10th Earl of 272, 302
Pennant, Thomas xii, 186, 313
  roads 20, 22
  peasant poverty 50
    housing 63
  glass factory 77–8
  Lyons industries 85
  beggars 121
  Enfants Trouvés, Paris 122
  Hôtel-Dieu, Paris 124
  Salpêtrière 126–7
  La Charité, Lyons 132
  Hôtel-Dieu, Lyons 132
  relics 124, 146
  curés 154
  received by archbishop 156

Index

expulsion of Jesuits 161–2
Massacre of St. Bartholomew 171
Bastille 191
enjoys executions 207–8
executed criminals displayed 208–9
Paris boulevards 211–12
Foire St. Germain 214
bear garden 219
visits Versailles 234–5, 236
Penningon, Rev. Thomas xii, 313
roads 22
haggling in shops 76
religious orders 159–60, 161
aristocratic convent 169
influence of American War 280–1
Périer, Auguste Charles 79–80
Périer, Jacques Constantin 79–80
Périgord, Comte de 13–14, 174
Péronne 18, 50, 82
Perpignan 6, 21
Pézenas 7
Philosophes 150, 238–9, 246–7, 270, 277
physicians 125, 134
Picardy 16, 54, 103
Pierre-Encise 192–4, 289
Piozzi, Mrs Hester Lynch xii–xiii, 213, 314
 Flemish 5
 roads 22
 cattle 42
 fortified towns 72
 Paris streets 75
 shops 75–6
 Lyons industries 86
 poverty 119
 Enfants Trouvés, Paris 123
 Lyons merchants 136–7
 behaviour in church 149
 noblemen drawn to Paris 180
 Foire St. Ovide 216–17
 Palais Royal 221–2
 ascent of balloon 226
 Marie Antoinette 265–7
Pitt, William 105, 112–13

Plombières 67
poissardes 150, 160, 266
Poitou 38, 46
Polignac, Yolande Martine Gabrielle, Duchesse de 272
Pompadour, Antoinette, Marquise de 239–40
Pont st. Esprit 19
Pont Ste. Maxence 20
Pont-à-Mousson 112, 223
Pont-Audemer 38
Pont-de-Beauvoisin 64
Pont du Gard 91, 117
Pont-l'Évêque 35
Pontoise 23
popular amusements
 ascent of balloons 224–7, 270
 bear garden 219–20
 boulevards 211–14
 Carnival 217–18
 dancing 223–4
 fairs 211, 214–17
 midsummer festival 220–1
 mountebanks 213–19
 Palais Royal 221–2
 St. Cloud 222–3
 water sports 219
population 65, 67, 68
porcelain 77, 88
potatoes 36, 67
poverty
 rural 32, 48–51, 68, 118, 224
 urban 118–35
Praslin, Renault César Louis, Duc de 291
Pratt, Samuel Jackson (Courtney Melmoth) 319
prices, rise in 68, 120
Priestley, Joseph xiii, 106, 313
 Flemish agriculture 33
 Alsace 35–6
 pigs 42–3
 fortified towns 72
 Lille 82
 wood burned 109
 Louis XVI 264, 275
 political situation in 1774 274–5
Protestantism
 conventicles 171–7

331

edict of 1787 158, 176-7
increasing toleration 158, 171-7
legal position 170, 171
pastors 170, 171, 173, 174, 175, 176
persecution 170-2, 246
Provence 6-7, 11, 39, 51, 55, 291
Provence, Comte de 238, 240, 262, 264, 266, 272-4, 277, 283, 297
Provence, Comtesse de 266, 272, 277
provincial estates 11-14, 26, 255
  Béarn 11
  Bigorre 11
  Brittany 12, 248-9, 290, 293
  Burgundy 11
  Languedoc 9-10, 12-14, 156-8
  Provence 11
Prussia 114
Pulteney, Daniel xiii, 314
  smuggling from France 112-13
  trade relations with France 112-13
Puy, Le 6, 25
Pyrenees 5-6, 11, 21, 22, 53, 306

Quercy 35, 53

Rabaut Saint-Étienne, Jean Paul 174
railway, horse drawn 106-7
Remiremont 63, 154
Remarks on the Character and Manners of the French ix, 308
  noble rank acquired by *roturiers* 138
Rennes 96, 293
Revolution of 1789 5, 8, 58, 79, 95, 116, 139, 159, 160, 199, 200, 209, 222, 301-2, 304, 305
Rheims 102
Rhône, River 2-3, 19, 67, 84, 91, 109, 117, 118, 306
Rigby, Edward xiii, 314
roads 20, 22
  Flemish agriculture 34
  peasant women 62, 63
  Lille 82
  Beaucaire fair 118
  Hôtel-Dieu, Paris 126
  Dijon hospital 131-2
  Hôtel-Dieu, Lyons 134
roads underused 20-4
Roanne 62, 111
Robert brothers 224, 226
Robson, James 319
Rochefort 202, 205, 211
Rochelle, La 25
Rochford, Lord 199
Roget, Mrs Catherine xiii, 314
  peasant houses 63-4
Romilly, Sir Samuel xiii, 63, 314
  Bicêtre 129-30
  Grande Chartreuse 166-7
  Louis XVI and Marie Antoinette 268-70
  1788 crisis 300-1
  French hopes for future 301-2
Rouen 4, 82-3, 97-8, 102-3, 108, 110-11, 115, 149, 178, 217, 293-4
Rousseau, Jean Jacques 151, 216
Roussillon 6, 55, 93, 100
Roye 20,
Russia 2, 248
rye 44, 66

sabots 33, 49, 61-2
St. Brieuc 5
St. Cast 291
St. Cloud 222-3
St. Denis 22, 146, 147, 260
St. Étienne 110
St. Florentin, Comte de *see* La Vrillière, Duc de
St. Girons 21
St. Gobain 107-8
Saint Huberty, Mme Anne Antoinette 97, 270

Index

St. John, James xiii, 314
   mur des fermiers généraux 73–4
   Paris streets 74
   Hôtel-Dieu, Paris 125–6
   lawyers 135–6
   hostility to catholicism 151
   civil courts 195
   criminal procedure 196
   torture 196–7
   attends execution 208
St. Malo 96, 97, 250
St. Omer 17, 20, 23, 49, 50, 72–3, 82, 146–7, 161–2, 211
St. Pol-de-Léon 45
Saint-Priest, François Emmanuel, Comte de 9–10, 13–14
St. Quentin 18, 107
St. Remy 224
Santerre, Antoine François 79
Saône, River 67, 84
Saumur 111
Saverne 5, 36
Seine, River 22, 97–8, 108
Selwyn, George xii, 1–2, 9–10, 319
Senlis 243
Sens 103
Seven Years War 1, 89, 94, 161
Sèvres 77, 104, 225
Shelburne, William Pettry, 2nd Earl of 33, 42–3
shopkeepers 75–7, 136
shops, haggling in 76–7
silk industry 35, 78, 85–6, 88, 91–2, 101, 103
Sinclair, Sir John xiii, 314–15
   meets Necker 278–9
Sketch of a Trip to Paris in 1788 ix, 308
   Eden Treaty 116
   illiteracy 5
   Louis XVI and brothers 273–4
   Paris streets 75
   roads 22
   1788 crisis 301
   wood shortage 108
Smith, Adam xiii, 234, 305, 315

taille 15, 55–6
gabelle 16
tobacco tax 16
aides 16
traites 16–17, 19
capitation 56
corvée 57
footwear 61
Toulouse 89
wages 119
trade despised 137
tax farmers 140
life annuities 140–1
Smith, Sir James Edward xiii, 315
   Paris streets 75
   nobleman's attitude to *roturiers* 75, 178
   Hôtel-Dieu, Lyons 133
   Louis XVI 272
   hostility to absolutism 286–7
Smollett, Tobias xiii, 306, 315
   Occitan 6–7
   customs barriers 18, 19
   inns 23–4
   maize 38
   sheep 42
   peasant poverty 51
   oppressed peasants 59
   importance of bread 64
   haggling in shops 76–7
   Marseilles 87
   Montpellier 91
   French industrial backwardness 98
   Sens 103
   Enfants Trouvés, Paris 122
   workhouse, Boulogne 130
   middle class hostility to nobility 139
   behaviour in church 148–9
   hostility to Catholicism 150, 246
   curés 154
   clergy's *don gratuit* 170
   number of church festivals 170
   Protestants 171
   noble rank 177–8
   provincial nobility 180

extravagance of nobility
183–4
droit d'aubaine 188, 189
a gross injustice 197
maréchaussée 200
trouble ahead for monarchy
246–7
Parlements 248
soap making 88, 89
Soissons 107
Sologne 44, 45, 55, 66
Sophie, Madame 237, 263
Soubise, Charles de Rohan,
Prince de 182, 241, 243
Souillac 51, 64
Spain 6, 39, 84, 89, 92, 128
Spencer, Lady Harriet xiii, 240,
305, 315
  Estates of Languedoc 12
  Protestants 173–4
  executed criminals displayed
  206
  an execution under one's
  windows 206–7
  Versailles 244
  Louveciennes 244–5
  Toulouse Parlement reformed
  255
  Louis XV and Marie
  Antoinette 263–4
Spencer, John, 1st Earl 12, 174,
206–7
Spencer, Lady Margaret
Georgiana 12, 174, 206–7,
244–5
Staël, Anna Louise Germaine,
Baronne de 278–9
Staël, Eric Magnus, Baron
278–9
Stainville, Jacques Philippe,
Comte de 193
stamp duty 281–4, 303
Stanhope, Walter xiii, 315
  relics 147–8
  Duc d'Aiguillon and
  Parlement 253
Stanislaus Leczinski, King of
Poland 252
steam engines 80–1, 105,
106

Sterne, Laurence xiii, 305, 306,
315
  visits France in wartime 1, 89
  Estates of Languedoc 12
  Toulouse 89, 90
  Montpellier 91
  Jesuits on trial 101
  droit d'aubaine 189
  Foire St. Germain 214
Strasbourg 2, 3, 24, 36
subvention territoriale 281–3, 294
Suffren, Pierre André de 273,
302
sugar refining 88, 110
superstitions 220–1
surgeons 125, 126, 133, 134
Swinburne, Henry xiii, 2, 305,
315–16
  Basque 6
  provincial estates 11–12
  Commat Venaissin 68–9
  Marseilles trade 88–9
  Carcassonne industries 92–3
  French coal 111
  Toulouse 138–9
  pénitents 153–4
  Narbonne 156
  Calas case 170–1
  noblemen's extravagance 184
  presented at court 245–6
  unpopularity of Louis XV 260
  Louis XVI and brothers 264
  Marie Antoinette 264
  recall of Bordeaux Parlement
  275–6
  1787 crisis 283–4, 287,
  288–90
  1788 crisis 290–1
Swinburne, Mrs Martha xiii,
315–16
  1788 crisis 291–2, 297–8
Switzerland 84, 97, 268, 279,
305

taille 10, 15, 55–7, 281
tanning 104
tapestry
  Beauvais 99
  Gobelins 77
Tarascon 117

Index

Tarbes 11
tax farmers 73–4, 139–41
taxes 68–9
  direct
    capitation 10, 15, 56, 194
    subvention territoriale 281–3, 294
    taille 10, 15, 55–7, 294
    vingtième 10, 15, 289, 294
  indirect
    aides 15, 16, 294
    gabelle 15, 16, 58, 140, 281, 294
    stamp duty 281–4, 303
    tobacco tax 15, 16, 140, 294
    traites 15, 16–19, 98, 281
Tempest, John 319
Terray, Joseph Marie 241, 255–9
theatres 95, 96–7, 211, 213, 215, 218, 265, 270
Thiard, Henri Charles, Comte de 290–1
Thicknesse, Philip xiv, 4, 248, 261, 316
  Catalan 6
  customs barriers 17
  peasant poverty 49
  Lyons 84
  Marseilles 87, 88
  coal 109, 110
  urban poverty 118
  beggars 121–2
  Hôtel-Dieu, Paris 124
  tax farmers 139–40
  hostility to Catholicism 150–1
  tithes 154
  curés 154–5
  Protestants 171–3
  droit d'aubaine 189–90
  La Barre 197–8
  policing of Paris 199
    highwaymen 200–1
  galleys 204
  executed criminals displayed 205–6
  breaking on the wheel 208
  Damiens 209, 236
  Marie Leczinska 237

  Louis XV's weaknesses as ruler 247
  admires Parlements' struggle for liberty 249
  l'affaire de Bretagne 249–50
Thrale, Henry 79, 266
Thrale, Mrs Hester Lynch *see* Piozzi
Thrale, Queeney 266
Tippoo Sahib 300
tithes 58–9, 154–5
tobacco tax 15, 16, 18, 140, 294
Toul 16
Toulon 202, 204–5
Toulouse 7, 21, 36, 64, 83, 89–90, 92, 93, 138–9, 153–4, 158–9, 170–1, 172, 175, 206, 208, 306
A Tour of Spain and France 318
A Tour, Sentimental and Descriptive ix, 308–9
  coal and steel 111
  cotton industry 81
  Eden Treaty 116
  fortified towns 72
  Havre, Le 97
Tours 101
towns, fortified 72–3
Townsend, Rev. Joseph xiv, 316
  Hôtel-Dieu, Paris 125
  Salpêtrière 128
  Carnival 217
trade
  foreign 32, 88–9, 92, 94–8
  internal 15, 16–19, 84, 88–9, 98
  relations with Britain 112–16
traites 15, 16–19, 98, 281
travel
  by canal 175
  river 2–3, 19
Travel Diary ix, 309
  Carnival 217–18
  domestic industry 102–3
  Louis XVI and Marie Antoinette 272
  Paris water works 80–1
  wood shortage 108
Travels into France and Italy ix, 309

Index

aristocratic convent 169
beggars 121
impoverished noblemen 179–80
Louis XV's goodness of heart 236
no uniform system of laws 8
nobleman's attitude to *roturiers* 178
peasant women 62–3
Protestants 173
Troyes 283, 284
Turbilly, Louis François Henri, Marquis de 40, 45
Turgot, Anne Robert Jacques 57–8, 274–5, 277–8, 280
Turkey 248
Turner, John 319

United Provinces 2, 50, 114–15, 157, 158, 284
Uzerche 51

vaine pâture 44
Valenciennes 18, 34, 109, 111, 112
Valogne 40
Van Robais factory 99–100
Vannes 64
Vatan 60
Vendôme 163–4
Verdun 16, 47
Vergennes, Charles Gravier, Comte de 2, 272
Vermond, Abbé Matthieu Jacques de 297, 303
Versailles *passim*
Vienne 19, 108
Villiers, John Charles, 3rd Earl of Clarendon xiv, 316
  poor agricultural methods 41
  capitaineries 60
  poor housing 118–19
  relics 147
  hostility to Catholicism 151–2
  Bastille 191
  Paris boulevards 213–14
  Palais Royal 222
  Louis XVI and Marie Antoinette 273
  1788 crisis 291, 293–300
Villers-Cotterêts 60, 256
vineyards 31–2, 35, 36–7, 41, 65
vingtième 10, 15, 289, 294
Vivarais 292
Voltaire, François Marie Arouet de 150, 151, 168, 216
Vosges 64, 67

wages 67–8, 85–6, 119–20
Walker, Adam xiv, 316
  sabots 62
  Paris
    industries 81
    streets 75
    water works 80
  Rouen 83
  Hôtel-Dieu, Paris 125
  Hôtel-Dieu, Lyons 133
  Louis XVI and Marie Antoinette 271
Walpole, Horace xiv, 177, 278, 305, 316
  crowds of British travellers 1
  corvée 57–8
  hostility to religion 150
    religious orders 160–1
  Bastille 191–2
  robbed 198
  presented at court 234
  inspects Mme Du Barry 236, 240
  arouses interest of Marie Leczinska 237
  Louis, Dauphin 238–9, 260
  Choiseul 248
  séance de flagellation 251–2
  1771 crisis 255–9
  Louis XVI as Dauphin 262–3
  Marie Antoinette 265
  political situation in 1755 276–8
Warner, Rev. John 2, 316
Watt, James 80
Wedgwood, Josiah 77, 100
weights and measures 7–8, 26
Wendel, Ignace de 106–7

Index

West Indies 51, 88, 89, 94, 97, 98
Wharton, Rev. Robert xiv, 317
  Estates of Burgundy 11
  religious processions 152–3
  entertained by monks 163
  galley slaves 202
  Foire St. Germain 214
  peasants dancing 224
  Louis XVI and Marie Antoinette 260–1
Wilkes, John xiv, 251, 317
  Grande Chartreuse 167–8
Wilkinson, John 105
Wilkinson, William 104–7
Williams, George James (Gilly) 317
  clash between Parlement and Crown 254
wine *see aides*, vineyards
women
  hard life 62–3
  peasant barefoot 61–2
  travellers 305
wood, shortage of 107–12
woollen industry 47–8, 78–9, 82, 92–3, 99–103, 114–15, 158
Wraxall, Sir Nathaniel William xiv, 305, 317
  Basque 6
  Occitan 6–7
  Auvergne 37
  peasant poverty 50
  Marseilles 87, 88
  Nantes 96
  archbishop of Auch 156
  galleys 203

Young, Arthur xiv, 31, 41, 304, 306, 317
  language problems 5–6
  weights and measures 7–8
  intendants 10–11
  capitation 10, 56–7
  taille 56–7
  vingtième 10
  roads underused 20–4
  inns 23–4
  newspapers, shortage of 24–5
  agriculture
    vineyards 32
    rotation of crops 34–5, 40, 43–5, 46–7
    maize 35, 38–9, 66
    olives 35
    cattle 35, 37–8, 39, 44, 46–7, 48
    sheep 37–8, 44, 45, 47–8
    irrigation 39
    waste land 39–40, 45–6
    rye 44, 46
    droit de parcours 44
    vaine pâture 44
    enclosures 44
    pigs 47
    poor farm equipment 48
    tenant farmers 51–2, 54
    wealthy graziers 52
    land ownership 52
    smallholdings 52–4, 64, 68
    métayers 54–5
  burdens on peasants
    taille 56–7
    corvée 58
    milice 58
    gabelle 58
    tithes 58–9, 154
    feudal dues 59–60
    manorial courts 59–60, 195–6
    capitaineries 60–1
  peasant women 64
    housing 64
  importance of bread 64–6
    buckwheat 66
    rye 66
    potatoes 67
  wages 67–8, 119–20
  industry
    coal 106–7
    cotton 82, 83, 92, 99–104, 114–15
    domestic 100, 101–3
    glass making 106–8, 112
    iron and steel 105–7, 112
    linen 46, 92, 103
    silk 86, 90, 92, 101, 103

Index

steam engines 105, 106
sugar refining 110
tanning 104
woollen 90, 92, 93, 99–105, 114–15
trade
  fairs 115, 116, 117–18
  foreign 95–8
  effects of Eden Treaty 113–16
hours of work 120
religion
  curés 155
  wealthy abbey 162

Protestants 177
noblemen
  attitude to *roturiers* 170
  provincial nobles 180
  court nobles neglect estates 181–3
privileged orders, tax exemptions 169–70
state prisons 190
Louis XVI and Marie Antoinette 272–3
1787 crisis 284–6
1788 crisis 292–3

For Product Safety Concerns and Information please contact our EU
representative GPSR@taylorandfrancis.com
Taylor & Francis Verlag GmbH, Kaufingerstraße 24, 80331 München, Germany

www.ingramcontent.com/pod-product-compliance
Lightning Source LLC
Chambersburg PA
CBHW070228230426
43664CB00014B/2240